CONTENTS

Acknowledgements

How to weigh and attribute key contributions by friends, acquaintances, even chance encounters? Pertinent critiques, a lunch delayed, a reunion foregone, a moment of impatience forgiven ("A moment," my Gordon will splutter!)—each a gift, each inestimable and deeply appreciated by the pen under pressure. My heartfelt and special thanks, in alphabetical order, to: Krista Bristow, Aggie Casselman, Geri Childs, Lori Ciaralli, Rod Haney, Veronika Hart, Penny Hayden–Hinsley, June and Derek Hester, Elizabeth Hogan, Sally Jorgensen, Geoff Knight, Isabel Marti, Katherine Monahan, Peter Morgan, Alphoncine Mtui–Kajubile, Alberto Palacios–Hardy, Anne Pearson, Allison Phillips, Jean Seeley, Anthony Shaw, Jane Touzel, Peter Voigt, Heather Wall, Lois Wraight, and, of course, the Foxes!

I am indebted to the Internet and Wikipedia as guides to pertinent source material, the Lonely Planet for jumpstarting my approach to the book, and Carleton University for prompting my original Master's research in Tanzania many years ago. It goes without saying that any mistakes are mine, although I have made every effort to remain true to source information—key among them Vicky's letters, the Fox NGO reports (often adapted, sometimes reattributed among Geoff Fox, Geoff Knight, Jenny Peck, and Vicky in the text), as well as interviews with both Geoff and Vicky, and my own first-hand experience of Tanzania.

Then there are Jane Karchmar, editor par excellence, as well as Tim Gordon, Magdalene Carson, and other dedicated professionals at General Store Publishing House. Not to mention my empathetic custodian of endless drafts, Jo–Anne Doherty.

Finally, my beloved SGGB, a.k.a. Gordon Breedyk . . .

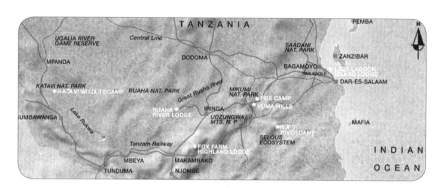

Map of Tanzania, formerly Tanganyika.

(Foxtreks, **http://www.tanzaniasafaris.com**)

PROLOGUE

Welcome to an unusual love story set in a tiny corner of East Africa, in an almost forgotten world of virgin forest, tea fields, and isolated villages; a world relatively untouched by the urban sprawl that now represents such Tanzanian cities as Dar es Salaam and Arusha. These are cities where supermarkets overflow with consumer goods, as they do anywhere else; cities where entrepreneurs thrive; cities where a person might live from cradle to grave without ever setting eyes on wildlife.

By contrast, Mufindi is isolated by unpaved roads (many impassable in the worst of the rainy season) and home to some of the poorest folk in Tanzania. That is where our family friends, Geoff and Vicky Fox, put down deep roots.

From the panoramic isolation of Mufindi, their story spreads into the vast hinterlands of Tanzania, home to the best and worst that humanity has to offer, from the rotting carcasses of poached elephants, with gaping holes where tusks should be, to open vistas throbbing with protected lion and zebra, giraffe, and kudu. It tells of Geoff and Vicky's part in preserving Tanzania's world wildlife heritage, a heritage that the rest of the world likes to enjoy; likes to view from the comfort of luxury camps; likes to protect for future generations . . . but does not like to pay for. Also of their fight to alleviate the calamitous impact of HIV/AIDS.

The Fox family has spent a lifetime trying to solve such dilemmas. Are they the only

Mufindi roads in rainy season.

ones? No, most certainly not. Indeed, Tanzania—one of the poorest nations (economically) and one of the wealthiest (in biodiversity)—has set aside more than a quarter of its own land for some level of nature protection.[1] Tanzanians of all races and all walks of life are playing a part. So why choose to write about the Foxes, expatriates of British descent (although Vicky has since taken on Tanzanian citizenship)?

When other expatriates were giving up on Tanzania, particularly in the toughest years (from the late 1970s to the late 1990s), the Foxes invested in it. Everyone said they were crazy. Everyone except for my parents, Helga and Werner Voigt—mainly because, like Geoff, Werner was a pioneer who followed his dreams; and, like Vicky, Helga boosted his lead.

Both families began their love affair with Tanzania in Mufindi: Geoff and Vicky as postwar British employees of an international enterprise, Werner and Helga as pre-war German settlers. Together, they represent the spectrum of expatriate influence on Mufindi.

But why focus on expatriates when there are so many amazing Tanzanian stories to tell? Because it is said that one should write about what one knows. And, being an expatriate raised in Mufindi myself, that is the story I know best. Yet how to distill someone's life when you haven't lived it? How to blend, rather than fuse; immerse rather than drown another's story? Herewith is a cautious attempt to do so and, in the telling, hopefully let our mutual love of Tanzania shine through.

So welcome now to Geoff and Vicky's living room. I have decided that theirs should be the predominant voices in this story; that this be a record of their recollections. The year is 2012. And they have finally agreed to be interviewed. Outside, a late rainy season storm rumbles and flashes me back to my own childhood, at the other end of Mufindi. There, torrential downpours pummelled into submission not only our ancient corrugated iron roof, but any attempt at normal conversation. Even as I miss that raucous roof, I revel in today's cushioned patter of rain on tiles, snuggle down, cozy and dry, on a reclining leather seat, and, as Geoff and Vicky start to talk, allow myself to drift backwards into their childhoods. Well, first, perhaps just a little further back . . .

---

1 For more on this, please refer to Natural Resources and Tourism statistics on forest protection, plus Tanzania Parks Authority statistics on wildlife reserves (*Eastern Arc Mountain Strategy, Coding Forest Reserves as Protected Areas*, 2006, **http://easternarc.or.tz/downloads/ Thematic-strategies/IUCN%20Coding%20of%20TZ%20FRs_final.pdf**, and TANAPA Serengeti Handout, **http://www.serengeti.org/fzs_ta.html**, respectively).

PART ONE

AFRICA AT LAST!
(1939–1972)

Two, maybe three of humankind's ancestors cautiously move through the vast East African plain. Under glowering skies, their calloused and hairy feet sink into soft dust. Hot! On they plod, anxiously scanning rock and horizon for danger.

At last, some rain. They raise their heads; luxuriate in moisture, cool and delicious against scorching skin. Suddenly, and much too soon, it stops — but not before volcanic ash, now mud, begins to suck at their feet and to slow them down.

Behind them, a long line of perfect prints forms in drying clay. Exposed. They try to hurry. The sky darkens. Strange. Hot, grey ash spews into the air, arcs, drifts back down to the ground, bakes their footprints . . . over time into rock. Wind and rain and heat and cold first bury, then finally release them again.

About 3.6 million years later, two young humans are helping a third one. She is archeologist Mary Leakey. Together, they hope to help unravel man's origin. Crossing the same East African plain, at a time now registered as 1978, they reach a place since named Laetoli, near Olduvai, in Tanzania.

One of the young humans playfully aims some dried elephant dung at his companion. Andrew Hill ducks, loses his footing, and — there they are: strange, dark marks in the rock. Leakey later identifies the footprints as those of our earliest ancestors, hominids she calls Australopithecines, whose remains have only ever been found in East Africa.

All of humankind linked by common footprints in the same sand, 3.6 million years apart.

WHITE RAJAHS

They were probably born in the same room, Vicky[2] a year later than Geoff, in 1939. They were certainly delivered in the same tiny nursing home in Tavistock, England, by the same doctor (who later even attended their wedding).

Vicky's first foray into "farming."

It was this beloved home, where we found kindness and goodness and dear hands which made our abandoned life shorter.

For all the nice hours and everything, you gave to us –

Dear Mrs. Shaw

and All of 'Edgemoor' we say our hearty thanks.

We shall always remember you in love and gratitude.

With the best wishes for the future we say:

'Good-bye!'

to all our dear friends at 'Edgemoor'.

Hans Meuco.
Helmut Maurice Briour Riedbing Charl Hallas
Wille Halle
Wolfgang Roop. – Alex Fihs – Bart Gandig.

—— 4th May 1948 ——

Copy of letter written to Micky by the German prisoners of war.

Vicky's early roots dig deep into Middlemoor, Dartmoor, Devon. There, she runs wild on rolling heaths, through a childhood of sheep and ponies, of craggy rocks under sullen winter skies and summer solstice suns, of purple heather, rusty bracken, and sweet, wild berries. There she is cradled in rippling piano music courtesy of her mother (an accomplished concert pianist) and the mellow viola of her great-uncle ("father of the viola" and virtuoso, Lionel Tertis) in the lean, rationed, bomb-shelter years of World War II. Also spoiled by German prisoners of war, who fashion wooden toys for her, and once, the most beautiful sewing cabinet, in moist-eyed gratitude for little kindnesses unexpectedly shown to them by her mother, Micky, after the war—Micky, who helps them out where she can with hampers at Christmas; warm, knitted scarves for frigid days;

---

2   Vicky is actually christened "Mary–Susan" but referred to as "Vicky" because at birth she resembled an ancient Queen Victoria. Her nickname will forever stick.

musical evenings; and gentle smiles. She receives a lovely farewell letter from them all, thanking her for looking after them; and from one, a lifelong friendship.

Meanwhile, little tow-headed Geoff goes with his parents to Poona, now Pune, in India. His father is in the Indian army, and will end up as a colonel in the 3rd 11th Sikhs, while Vicky's father, Fredrick Arthur Shaw (Josh), will retire as a brigadier from the Royal Army Service Corps.

Geoff in Pune, India.

Little Geoff stays in India for seven years, returning as the war ends in 1945. He will forever remember seeing all the celebrations and fireworks at Port Said but retain little else, apart from a house and garden in Poona; a naked little girlfriend looking for ant lions in the sand with him; and Juhu Beach, where he got into trouble for transferring all the rejected puffer fish that the fishermen gave him into the rainwater butt of the beach house they were living in (there being no alternative water supply), and how very upset he was when all the fish died.

During the First World War, Geoff's father, Ronald de Vere Fox, boards a ship as officer cadet to join his regiment in India. Fellow travellers include a number of families, wives and children. Torpedoed, his ship goes down in the Mediterranean. When Ronald manages to resurface, he finds two children, a girl of five and a boy of three, struggling to stay afloat near him. He grabs them and stays with them until, after a considerable period of time, a lifeboat appears. Although crowded, he persuades the crew to take on the two children. They also invite him on board, but he realizes that he would overload the lifeboat ("He was a big guy, taller than I right to the end," Geoff remembers in later years) and swims away, to be picked up much later by another vessel. For this, Ronald is awarded the Royal Humane

Society Medal, a civilian medal, which to the envy of his brother officers he is allowed to wear on his right chest (all military medals being worn only on the left).

The rescued children turn out to be those of the Third Rajah of Sarawak—or rather, of the Third Rajah of Sarawak's brother, Bertram, who alternated as Rajah whenever asked to stand in for his sibling, Charles Vyner Brooke.

As the years pass, Ronald's own son, Geoff, becomes increasingly fascinated by the notion of White Rajahs of Sarawak from England, especially since the little church his family attends in nearby Sheepstor village has a large wooden panel outlining their history. He learns that the church was in a bad state of repair when the First White Rajah established his UK base there at Burrator House, so he refurbished it, hence the dedication. Indeed, in that quiet English churchyard are all their graves: those of the First, Second, and Third White Rajahs. Running his hands over the cool, moss-covered headstones, Geoff tries to imagine himself back to 1839 when British-born James Brooke, later the First White Rajah, began his exotic career.

《•》《•》《•》《•》

As requested by the Sultan of Brunei, Brooke agreed to help quell a rebellion by local Malays. Duly accomplished, he claimed his reward: sovereignty over Sarawak—about 3,000 square miles of coastal lowlands. They were swampy, pirate-infested, and linked by the mighty Batang Rajang River to steaming jungles, seemingly impenetrable except by fierce, eternally warring and headhunting Dayaks, who routinely presented a new mother with an equally new human skull (acquired for the occasion to both honour and safeguard her child) and accompanied any self-respecting proposal of marriage with an offering to his future bride of—what else?—a freshly harvested skull.

Brooke eventually managed to all but stamp out head-hunting, quell piracy, and persuade the warring tribes to form a cohesive, united country. They invited him to be their first rajah. By popular demand, this honour was passed from one generation to the next.

By the time the Third Rajah held office, still with absolute power over his people and still administering his country with its best interests at heart, World War II had broken out. Charles Vyner Brooke was forced to escape to Australia, taking with him the entire Treasury, to the value of one million pounds. After the war, he decided that the task of administering a country was too great, asked Britain to take over, and handed them the million pounds for that purpose.

《·》《·》《·》《·》

"Ungratefully, they refused to allow the Third White Rajah ever to return to Sarawak," Geoff will comment, still fascinated decades later, "in case it might cause disruptions for some reason. His brother Bertram served in the British army during part of the First World War (possibly Mesopotamia [Iraq] where my father served, too—fighting Turks). History doesn't relate whether he was on the ship that was torpedoed in 1915. But probably their mum had grabbed two of her daughters and lost the other girl and her son when the ship went down.

"On my father's death in 1987, someone in the Ministry of Defence must have pressed a computer button, retrieved this information, and added it to my father's obituary in the *Telegraph*. Awaiting me in the UK, when I later went back on home leave from Tanzania, was a letter from the little boy (by then in his seventies). He offered his own condolences and those of his sister, who was also still alive. Sadly, I've lost this letter. Vicky and I recently visited their graves. Antoni (the three-year-old little boy in the water) was buried only last year (2011)—at ninety-nine!

"My father later received the Military Cross for bravery under fire, rescuing a colleague, and being shot through his kneecap. Meanwhile, my mother, I think, had a splendid time in India. While my father was away during the war, she served as an ambulance driver and, during the same period, became the All India Ladies' Golf Champion, quite a feat, given the number of contestants in those days. A popular socialite in demand with all the subalterns, she constantly played practical jokes and was just great fun. My father, who was sixteen years older than Gelly, probably became quite jealous. And, with the separations of war, they parted company in 1945. She returned to live again in Tavistock, Devon. My father stayed on in India, to retire near us, in Cornwall, at Independence, in 1947.

"Gelly was his second wife. His third was his landlady in Cornwall, whom I am sure he married in order to save paying rent. He took me aside one day and said, 'Geoff: I do hope you are more successful with your women than I have been with mine. My first wife was very flighty. My second wife was sixteen years younger; we separated. My third wife was my landlady—she could cook.'"

AFRICA BECKONS

The hominids of East Africa evolved into *Homo habilis* (Stone Age toolmakers) and then *Homo erectus* (upright and more adept with bones and axes). Each in turn marked their passage: Some in Stone Age sites at ancient lakes like Isimila (not far from Mufindi) and Olduvai Gorge (where it all began); others through rock paintings, like those in Kondoa, miraculously preserved in the dry heat of the Dodoma Region, with its arid expanses seemingly dead for miles and months until new rains carpet them with exquisite garlands of palest pink convolvulus.

Nilotic pastoralists moved in from what is now known as the Sudan, Cushitic herders of cattle from Ethiopia, and Bantu settlers from the west. Trade winds blew merchants in from the east (Near, Far, and Middle East). Religion and dominion drew strangers from across the globe and curiosity explorers from the north. Portuguese and Arabs in turn settled its coast, Muslim sultans in Zanzibar, and Chinese traders in Tanga. Swahili emerged as their early lingua franca of commerce in ivory and slaves, cloth and trinkets, cross and minaret, accompanied by English (after Germany and Britain spilled blood across their lands in local uprisings and two world wars).

So it was that migration after migration added and subtracted, each its own thread, ultimately to form the rich tapestry of 121 ethnic groups, collectively known today as Tanzania, whose national borders, colonially imposed, now demarcate its East African neighbours, Kenya and Uganda.

《•》《•》《•》《•》

All too soon after her return to England from India, Geoff's mother makes plans to leave for the tropics again, this time to join her second husband, "Jimmy" (James), in Uganda. Geoff will stay behind at school in England, as is customary for children of parents posted to the colonies. Geoff, who is not involved in the planning, never really understands what is happening. Very attached to "Mum," he thinks her Uganda absence is merely temporary — during which he is staying with his wonderful grandparents in Tavistock. Then, at some stage, he finds himself passed on to "Father" and never is told that "Father" has now been granted custody.

Taken away from one school and friends to attend another, and unhappy, mainly with his stepmother, and also because he hasn't seen his mother for so long, Geoff is delighted when finally passed back to his grandparents, his old school, and his friends in Tavistock.

Meanwhile, her face pressed against the window, and soon covered in dust from red-earth roads, Geoff's mother marvels as lush, green waterscapes around Lake Victoria give way to stunningly arid Karamoja, a district over which her husband is the legal and administrative guardian of British colonial administration.

Oh, my, thinks Gelly, as their car bumps endlessly along beside enormous chunks of granite, sometimes rounded like familiar Dartmoor tors, but more often jagged, and relentlessly piercing ever-receding, dry-season skies.

Her first morning in Moroto, a naked Karamajong, a denizen of Karamoja, walks into the house. He is there to talk business with her husband, the District Commissioner (DC). *Oh, my. Indeed.* Gelly's initial shock soon gives way to deep respect.

Accompanying her husband on official *safaris*, she witnesses first hand how brilliantly the Karamajong have pitted themselves against unforgiving, semi-desert conditions. "For thousands of years," her husband tells her. She watches how respectfully he interacts with their elders, wrapped in centuries of pastoralist tradition; sits with them under the counsel tree; tastes with them the issues of their people; calms with them their common fears, as etiquette demands, through debate and consensus.

The Karamajong, badly scarred by recruitment into the British army during World War II, from which their men return ashamed of their nakedness and with venereal and other deadly diseases, have since

Geoff's mother, Gelly, and stepfather, Jimmy.

rejected all foreign influence. They are particularly averse to sending their children to schools that they believe will steal their young by bringing them far from their ancestral way of knowing, far from the influence of their elders, far from their *manyatta* homesteads and their cows. They know that, in the end, it could be the pencil and not the gun that could destroy them from within.

Back in the official residence (a rather grand name for their whitewashed, brick bungalow), Gelly can still picture the clustered *manyattas* sheathed in mystery under African nights; cattle murmuring soothingly, stars streaming over savannah grasses, strange and haunting calls of night creatures, perhaps even a leopard or jackal treading softly on silent, moon-washed paws.

"How Geoff would love this," she exclaims to Jimmy one day, grabs a pen, and writes, "We'll be retiring soon, Geoff. So this may be your last chance to visit. You can even go on an official *safari* with Jimmy [by now the district commissioner for Ankole in Southern Uganda]." Geoff jumps at the chance and—at last!—lands at the tiny Entebbe airport on the shores of Lake Victoria.

Fresh from the tors of Dartmoor, he enthusiastically scrambles into his parents' Land Rover. They head past ungainly maribou storks and hippos, periodically catch sight of crocodiles sunning on the banks. Onward, through the lush, green banana groves and forests of Southern Uganda. Over wide, open plains, sometimes dark with buck and buffalo, and finally into Ankole—land of huge-horned cattle of the same name.

Twelve-year-old Geoff in Uganda.

In and around tiny homesteads, the inquisitive twelve-year-old forms his early respect for African survival skills; for their unsurpassed knowledge of nature. He gets an inkling of the safety offered by thorn-encrusted enclosures against predators lurking beyond. He explores unknown places, accessible only by foot. And he has his first taste of hunting, with his stepfather's 410 bore gauge shotgun. For what more could a boy ask? Above all, it is during his holiday, in that heartachingly beautiful land, that Geoff falls in love with East Africa, and vows to return as an adult.

"Ankole is SO beautiful," he enthuses on his return to England, "with its volcano crater lakes, larger lakes, forests, mountains nearby, and plenty of wildlife. I will forever have happy memories of quietly paddling around one of these crater lakes on my own in a dugout canoe and watching colobus monkeys overhead."

His parents retire in 1952 to a house a couple of moorland fields away from Vicky in Middlemoor. Geoff joins them and thoroughly enjoys Mount House Preparatory School. Another matter altogether is secondary school at Kelly College across the Tavy River. "Only my boxing, shooting, and rugby (as member of the first fifteen team) is saving me from ignominy," he laughs with friends, "compensating in some way for my academic disinterest and, to my surprise, even elevating me to school monitor."

SMITTEN

Meanwhile, Vicky excels academically. So much so that at sixteen she qualifies to be an exchange student at the prestigious *Schule Schloss Salem* / Salem Castle School in Germany, as had her highly talented brother, Anthony, before her. Anthony's scholarship to Cambridge preceded a lifetime of travel, learning (with varying fluency in seventeen languages), and music (including a stint as solo clarinetist in Mozart's Clarinet Concerto at Salem).

Salem was founded, with the help of Prince Maximilian von Baden, in 1920 by Dr. Kurt Hahn, a pioneer in experiential education. Dr. Hahn also set up the equally elite British Salem School of Gordenstoun, attended among others by Prince Charles and fellow royals.

Vicky loves Salem. Not that it is always comfortable in the drafty old castle, despite its beautiful location "over the hills and a bit of a bike ride away from Lake Constance a.k.a. Bodensee" as Anthony put it. May still brings snow this year, and the old *kachelofen* (tiled stove) for which they receive only a few sticks of firewood, barely heats their rooms. Food is also scarce in these postwar days of 1955.

"It's pretty Spartan" she writes to her good friend, Jan Reed, back home. "We have to get up at six every morning to go for a run, come hell or high water. The boys are allowed to get up at six-thirty. That always rankles with me. There are only a few of us girls and I think we are rather considered lesser beings—I don't know. After our run, we have to have a cold shower. Every now and then, Dr. Hahn invites us foreign students to tea, complete with cucumber sandwiches, in true English style. But I do love it here!"

And then again, later: "I chose German agriculture as my subject for our special project. Why agriculture? You know that I've always wanted to be a farmer. My friend chose wildflowers. For some reason, Dr. Hahn made us swap, so I was dispatched to the biology master. I duly collected flowers, pressed and titled them. Then, when the time came to submit my project, it had disappeared from the storage area. That seemed a bit lame, so I told Dr. Hahn that I thought mice must have eaten it. Luckily, he had a sense of humour."

With temperatures gradually warming up toward summer, they are allowed to swim in the Bodensee, only when accompanied by a certified lifeguard. Vicky has never actually received any training, but since she has watched the lifeguards at school, she decides to take Salem's test. She has also heard somewhere that if someone is in trouble, one should swim to them and drag them to shore—unless they struggle, in which case one should hold them under water and then drag them to safety. "My friend struggled," Vicky later writes home. "I held her under water and headed for shore. She nearly drowned."

Qualified as a lifeguard despite this little glitch, Vicky enjoys a glorious summer of swimming with her friend, whenever their stringent schedule allows, since Salem expects highest academic achievement while instilling in equal measure a spirit of community responsibility, respect for the individual, and appreciation of the key role played by the democratic process. She writes to Jan, "Each afternoon we played sports. Standards not being very high for girls, they decided that I could run fast enough to represent Germany in the Five Country Youth Competition.[3] We were duly bused to our respective sports meetings, I with strict instructions: 'Remember, Vicky. You are representing Germany. Please, do not speak English!' Needless to say, I didn't. In fact, I didn't speak at all.

"The royal wedding was amazing!"

Another day. Another letter to Jan. "The service itself took place in a part of Salem castle still being used by Prince George of Hannover, our headmaster (a very nice man). He and his family occupy one half of the castle. Like aristocrats all over Europe, certainly in Britain, they need to supplement their income. So they rent out the other half to the school.

"As part of the school choir, I sang for the bridal pair. Quite awe-inspiring, actually: all these kings, queens, princesses trooped into what was called the *Betsaal* (prayer hall), where two ex-pupils (who had attended Salem long before my time) were getting married. What a setting they had: with baroque pictures all over the walls, dripping chandeliers, and glittering royalty."

《•》《•》《•》《•》

---

3   Typical Vicky modesty.

1. Anthony (Vicky's brother) with her parents, Josh and Micky.

2. Vicky.

3. Schloss Salem.

A schoolgirl had left the UK; a young lady returns. Well, sort of. Reinforced are not just the seeds of community first instilled by Vicky's mother during the war, but also the imp in Vicky. She is still as comfortable holding a friend's hand as planning some reckless prank; still as eager to help a local farmer to deliver a calf as play the piano.

One day, Geoff's mother asks him to run an errand over to Vicky's mum, two fields away. Micky answers the door. Geoff hands her a package. "Gelly says you'll know what it's about."

"Thank you so much, Geoff."

As they are chatting, who should appear, but Vicky. "Hello, Geoff," she says. "Sorry to rush off like this, but I'm going to be late!" With that, she leaps onto her bike and cycles away, as she has done a hundred times before. Only this time, Geoff notices a particularly comely pair of red slacks. Actually, not just the red slacks, but also some rather enticing curves.

He returns home, bewildered. Where has the tomboy gone, the one attracted to adventure and all things dangerous? The one who climbed trees with the village boys and planned daring escapes from her cloistered school, just for the thrill of it?

From his room, he can see Vicky's house; finds himself waiting for a glimpse of the ever more intriguing, petite brunette next door; thinks of a thousand ways he could approach her but, somehow, cannot take the next step.

Unbeknownst to him, Vicky is also smitten — in her case, with her tall, blond neighbour.

"Why don't you just ask him out?" her best friend asks.

"Good girls don't do that!"

"Extreme situations call for extreme measures."

"Not my style."

"Are you just going to wait forever?"

"At seventeen, I hardly think I'm on the shelf!" They both giggle.

And then, what seemed a lifetime later: "Guess what! Geoff has asked me out. Actually, a friend of his has made up a party including both of us."

"Well, how was it?"

"Perfect! First we went to the golf club and then to see *Oklahoma*. Best of all: we're going out again! Just the two of us."

《・》《・》《・》《・》

And so it is that the two can be seen wandering together over the moors, young and increasingly in love. More often than not, they head to Sheepstor. Like other hilly tors scattered over Dartmoor, it is festooned with massive, granite boulders; here, there is a giant rock on which four others rest, ruggedly honed by millennia of erosion. A nearby cave boasts many legends. One has the fugitive future King Charles II take refuge there, hence the pennies on the ground left by visitors to sustain him.[4]

---

4 To quote Geoff: "As our good friend Rick Ghaui once said, the British are pretty good at pageants, funerals, and weddings. Our son Peter's wife, Sarah, went to the headquarters at Ruaha Park one day and there were all the rangers watching Princess Diana's funeral on television."

Vicky and Geoff.

Vicky and Geoff squeeze into that same cave on their last day before Geoff heads off for his two-year national service with the 42 Commando Royal Marines.

"Did you know that Charles also hid in a house in Plymouth, and supposedly slept in the same bed my mum later used?" Geoff asks Vicky.

"And did you know," says Vicky, not to be outdone, "that some of these pennies are meant to placate the pixies living here?" Their small talk falters. Time is flying too fast. And then time slows. Geoff has gone.

《•》《•》《•》《•》

"Guess what," Geoff says to Vicky on a weekend's furlough a few months later. "I won't have to stay away after all."

"Wonderful. But why ever not?"

"Turns out that they want me to teach others to shoot, since I came second at the Royal Marine Corps Championships. If I don't apply for a commission, I could serve most of my national service at the barracks close to Tavistock. That way I won't miss out on Mum's home cooking."

"And . . ." Vicky prompts him. Geoff looks blank. Vicky kicks him. They both know that, as well as the added benefit of commuting from home, this means he can stay close to Vicky. Already averse to anything resembling paperwork, he will also be free to enjoy an active life, not just as a crack shot, but also as light welterweight champion in boxing.

"I arrived back at the barracks to find 42 Commando had gone," Geoff later writes to Vicky. "We had suddenly, with no notice whatsoever, been required to embark for Lebanon, where there was some form of disorder. When I caught up with everyone, we boarded an aircraft carrier and headed for the Mediterranean. Later, we diverted to Tripoli in Libya for exercises in the desert, before going on to Malta. Quite enjoyable!

"I was surrounded by men with fiancées and wives," he later confides to his buddies after completing his national service, "and not willing to admit that my girlfriend was still in school."

《•》《•》《•》《•》

"The verdict is in, Vicky." They are, as usual, wandering around their favourite tors on Dartmoor–Sheepstor and now also Vixen Tor.

"They've accepted you?"

True to his dream of returning to Africa after that wonderful holiday in Uganda, Geoff has applied to Brooke Bond, a tea company in East Africa. "Yes, indeed!" He looks very excited. "I'm one of several trainees going to a coffee, or chicory, plant, or some such."

Vicky in teachers' training.

Despite mixed feelings, Vicky is pleased for him; indeed, quite jealous of his impending adventure, but does not look forward to their separation. Yet she herself still has two years to go at Roehampton Teachers Training College in London, plus another year of practical teaching before graduation. Despite qualifying for agricultural college, she got cold feet when she realized that farmers seldom hired females, and entered teachers' training college instead. "How soon will you leave?" she wants to know.

"Training and assessment will take about six weeks. And then, I imagine I'm off. The good news is: I'll be in Huntingdon, not far from you, and I'm going to buy a car so we can see each other often." True to his word, Geoff immediately buys his first car, an Austin 7, for £7.15 (just over $20). Not only do they have a lot of fun with it but, before leaving for Africa, he sells his car for £12 (about $36). "I was very pleased with my profit," he later tells friends, "only to find that the classic collecting market almost immediately pushed the price up close to £1,000 (over $3,000)!"

Vicky finally has to see Geoff off. With one last wave, he ducks into the VC 10. Next stop, Tanganyika, a country one day to be known as Tanzania.

AFRICA AT LAST

Tanganyika is also the birthplace of a child named Kambarage (the spirit that gives rain). He is born into the tiny Zanaki tribe on April 13, 1922. Like other children, he soon contributes to his family's welfare by herding their cattle—in his case, near the vast lake, named after a British queen: Victoria. Out he goes at dawn, with fellow herders, calling each cow by name, to a day of banter and responsibility until the evening sun invites them back home.

Then comes primary school, and, later, his father's instructions: of all the children in their family, he is the one chosen to attend secondary school.

Twelve-year-old Kambarage dutifully carries his pristine uniform and walks twenty-six miles to Tabora High School, run by Roman Catholic missionaries. How he misses the outdoors. Still, he knows his duty and, if truth be told, even begins to enjoy his studies. He converts to Catholicism and takes on a Christian name, Julius.

Before Julius knows it, school in Tanganyika gives way to Makerere University in Uganda. That students from Tanganyika should form a discussion group about issues affecting their country seems only logical to him and, without knowing it, Julius Kambarage Nyerere begins his earliest foray into politics as organizer of Tanganyika's first student group, followed by a stint as a teacher back home (where he gradually influences the African Association away from just protesting colonial policies to actively working for independence), and, finally, studies at the University of Edinburgh.

When he graduates in 1952, he is one of just two Tanganyikans to have earned degrees from universities outside Africa, in his case a Master's degree, and the foundation for a political philosophy that blends socialism and African "communalism" into what Nyerere will in later years refer to as being "communitary" rather than communistic. This philosophy he carries into his continuing work as a teacher back home. By 1954, Nyerere has managed to fuse all the nationalist factions into the fledgling Tanganyika African National Union (TANU), of which he becomes president, after Britain (at that point still stalling moves toward what they fear is impetuous independence) makes him choose between teaching and politics.

Although Nyerere opts for politics, he will always be known affectionately and with great respect simply as Mwalimu ("the teacher" in Swahili, and also an honorific title); as he puts it, a schoolmaster by choice and a politician by accident. Contrary to a more militant approach in Kenya, where an anti-colonial movement among some members of the Kikuyu tribe has escalated into violence, TANU's manifesto calls for non-violent, multi-ethnic politics and for the promotion of social and political harmony. The last British governor, Sir Richard Turnbull, after initial official hedging, backs Mwalimu.

On December 4, 1959, a DC3 sets down at Iringa Airport in Tanganyika. Geoff, who transferred in Nairobi, eagerly rushes to the door of the aircraft then stops for a moment to take in the baked-earth landing strip and tiny brick airport office with its corrugated iron roof. A small group of people is gathered to greet the plane, including his new manager and his wife. Little does he know it then, but June and Derrick Hester will remain lifelong friends. Being most efficient and helpful, June has already listed everything Geoff will need to set up house in Mufindi. He takes one glance at her mammoth list, offers his appreciation, and admits, "I can't possibly afford it."

"That's all right. In Tanganyika, you buy everything on credit," June says. At least that's how Geoff will always remember it, to June's inevitable denials: "As I was brought up always to live within my means, I doubt I ever said that!"

Every item on June's list is dutifully acquired at Iringa Stores, making Geoff the best-equipped bachelor in Mufindi. ("What with curtains and even a meat mincer," he will forever joke, "it took me three years to pay off Iringa Stores," to which a smiling June will invariably answer, "My excuse? I thought he was a rich young man who would want his home to be well equipped.")

At last, Geoff, his luggage, and his new acquisitions are piled into the Hesters' sturdy vehicle, redolent of seasonal fruit and vegetables garnered in the Iringa market. Then they all but slide to Mufindi over eighty miles of muddy road rendered almost impassable by the rainy season, except (barely) for vehicles equipped with four-wheel drive.

Sudden and torrential downpours alternate with brilliant sunshine. Under stunning indigo skies, exotic trees throb—yellow, purple, red—almost blinding after the muted shades of a UK winter. There are men dressed in traditional white togas and women draped in vivid cloth. He revels in it all.

TRANSPORTATION BEFITTING A PLANTATION MANAGER

The day after Geoff arrives in Mufindi, Derrick introduces him to the chairman of the Tanganyika Tea Company, owned by Brooke Bond. Dickinson, permanently sucking on his unlit pipe, fixes Geoff with an appraising eye and, after a fleeting welcome, says, "Of course, you are of no use to the company for at least six months, until you have learned to speak Swahili. Your transport will be a bicycle, until you qualify for a car grant scheme. And, there are two gentlemen on your

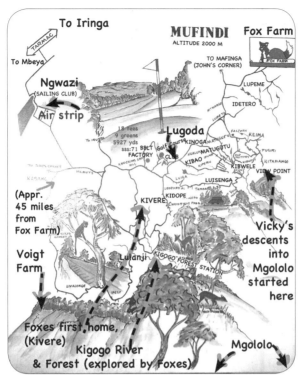

Mufindi Highlands map.
(Original watercolour by, and courtesy of, Jonathan Niblett, adapted by Evelyn)

estate who have been there longer than you will ever be."

One of them is Nallos Kihega. He has been tending tea since the Germans first planted it in Mufindi and, luckily for Geoff, proves himself a great mentor.

The bicycle Brooke Bond gives Geoff is old, has no brakes, and definitely does not contribute toward what Geoff considers his rightful image. His first visit to the Mufindi Club (a small, centrally located bungalow sporting a tiny kitchen and sizable bar, two clay tennis courts, and a rough, nine-hole golf course) allows Geoff to comment on this to a sympathetic company wife, Pat Somerville. She generously offers him the use of her horse. Geoff borrows Pat's horse, some tack, and rides ten miles home to Kinoga house. There, he cuts the doors of one room in half to make a stable.

"My long-suffering manager, Derrick," he writes to Vicky, "was tolerant of my vandalizing the company house in this manner and allowed me to ride around the estate with my head held high. Then,

Geoff and "tea teacher," Nallos Kihega, with whom Geoff will keep in touch until his death at nearly 100, still pensioned by BBLT.

after about ten days, Pat's horse escaped and ran all the way home to Ngwazi, so back to the bicycle I went, because in fact the horse was very much slower."

Geoff's bicycle eventually gives way to a Lambretta scooter, arriving courtesy of the nearby Sao Hill airstrip, a ribbon of packed earth graded into a field. East African Airways uses Sao Hill regularly as part of its internal East African circuit, linked to its external circuit from Nairobi and Dar es Salaam. Their very old DC3s, built in 1939, provide a very good East African service.

"Major Garlic,[5] who manages the Sao Hill terminal, drives to the airstrip every Friday," Geoff writes Vicky, "opens his office—the size of my sofa—looks very serious, and writes out tickets. I collected my Lambretta from his farm, and am now the proud owner of my first motorized transport in Africa."

REUNION

And then, in June 1960: "Extraordinary news, Vicky! Both Alex Boswell and Chris McIntyre are coming to Mufindi!" Geoff and Alex have been in regular touch since he and Vicky both met him in Huntington (where Geoff and Alex were being checked out at the chicory probationary posting before being sent abroad). So Alex's

---

5   Yes, that really was his name.

transfer to Mufindi is not that surprising. But Chris's? And on the same flight out?

"Now there's a total coincidence," Geoff tells Derrick. "The last time we met was at Kelly College secondary school, after completing Mount House primary together. In fact, I often used to visit Chris at his home in Cornwall on holiday. And most weekends away from both schools, he stayed with our family."

"Since you know them both, why not ask if you can meet their plane in Iringa?"

So it is that the three young friends end up driving back to Mufindi together. "This is the Great North Road I've read so much about?" Chris asks disbelievingly, "Just a dirt track all the way up from South Africa?"

"Wait until you experience our highway into Mufindi, let alone those on the tea estates. Speaking of Mufindi, here's John's Corner and the turnoff."

"Why 'John's Corner'? All I see is bush and more bush."

"See that house just ahead? The one with 'Hoteli' whitewashed on its walls?" Chris notices a traditionally built structure with a thatched roof and a neatly cleared, earthen courtyard. "That's John's place. He sells sodas, biscuits, and tea. If we carried on another thirty miles, we would reach 'James Corner.'"

"All right, let's have it. Who is James?"

"A Kikuyu imported from Kenya to teach people how to ox-plough; his claim to fame is being linked by marriage to the Mkwawa dynasty, famous for resisting the Germans."

"Mkwawa dynasty?"

MKWAWA—"BLACK NAPOLEON"

Imagine, if you will, a tall young man in about 1880 named Mkwawa, bowing his head in sorrow. Like the elders in flowing white togas around him, he is dwarfed by a canopy of trees, whose massive branches meet overhead to form a cathedral of leaves, through which diffused light illuminates seventeen graves in a place still called Kalenga—about fifty miles from here.

As with his predecessors, a giant elephant tusk marks his

father's grave. Praise names chanted by mourners tell of the late Chief Munyigumba's exploits. How he absorbed from the Ngoni their throwing knives, from the Masai their spears, and from the Sangu their shields. How in less than thirty years, not only through his fearlessness in battle, but also through his wisdom in victory, and sometimes ruthlessness, too, he united the people of the eastern highlands into a single nation, the mighty Wahehe (singular Mhehe, members of the Hehe people), a name derived from their dreaded war cry: "*Hee! Hee! Hee! Vatavangu twihoma ehee!*" ("Hee! Hee! Hee! We are fighting the enemy!")

As one, the Wahehe warriors ranged in formation around the burial site echo their blood-chilling call in guttural unison, "*Hee! Hee! Hee!*" pounding their spear shafts on the ground to punctuate each "*Hee!*" as they do before battle.

Young Mkwawa inherits not only lands of unprecedented proportions for those times, covering as they do the whole of what are now the Southern Highlands of Tanzania, but also power sufficient to keep at bay his arch-enemies to the south (the Wangoni) and tightly control incursions from the east, where slavers routinely herd humans on corpse-littered footpaths between the Kilombero and Ruaha rivers (including parts of the current main road from Dar es Salaam to Iringa).

Like his father before him, Mkwawa proves to be a charismatic strategist, with extraordinary leadership skills and some cruelty. He easily establishes his authority through councils of elders and an intricate network of local units headed by sub-chiefs. He seamlessly absorbs into his network a succession of other ethnic groups, some because they have been defeated in battle and now report to Mkwawa's trusted generals or relatives, and some because they choose to join him and retain their traditional leaders. He also forges the Wahehe into a tightly administered, hierarchical, fighting machine and masterminds brilliant military campaigns.

With time, his lands expand far beyond those of his father. Through a network of intelligence reports delivered by runners working in continuous relays of up to sixty miles per day, he knows at all times exactly what is going on in his 14,000-square-mile kingdom. From lakes Tanganyika and Nyassa in the west, Ifakara and Kilosa in the east, the Ruhinga–Kilombero rivers in the south, to the Central Caravan route in the north, Mkwawa charges anyone crossing his lands "*hongo*" (tolls). Anyone. German colonizers are furious—even more so when audacious Hehe raids strike within about 180 miles of Dar es Salaam, their new capital after Bagamoyo.

Yet precisely how to deal with Mkwawa eludes them. The governor would prefer a negotiated settlement to outright war. However, for reasons still disputed by historians, the hawks among his advisors win the day, and Germany prepares a punitive expedition under the command of Emil von Zelewski. Mkwawa's belated efforts at negotiation turn out to be too little and too late.

A young German officer, Tom Prince, accompanies General von Zelewski to the banks of the Rufiji River, noting in his diary that something about the dark African night at the lonely, ominously rumbling Rufiji River prompts him to ask his revered commander and father figure yet again if he doesn't want him and his Somali soldiers to accompany him after all.

"Not necessary, my dear Prince," von Zelewski answers. "We can take care of them . . . These fellows do not even have guns, just shields and spears."

Those are the last words spoken between the two friends. Weeks later, an exhausted runner reports the total annihilation of the Uhehe *Expeditionskorps*, except for one German medical officer and fourteen African soldiers.

Germany responds with a full-scale offensive. However, instead of the relatively quick victory they anticipate, seven years of guerrilla war are to pass before Tom (by then elevated to "von Prince") can dispatch to Germany a bloody head. It is punctured by two bullets, but apparently still identifiable as that of Mkwawa, or "Black Napoleon," as he is now called in Germany—although rumours persist to this day among some Wahehe that Mkwawa in fact escaped.

Twenty years later, the Treaty of Versailles will detail among Germany's conditions of surrender after World War I, that they must return Chief Mkwawa's skull to the Wahehe of East Africa. Germany agrees. But by then, no one can find his skull.

It isn't until 1949 that Sir Edward Twining (later Baron Twining), governor of Tanganyika, will take up the matter. Five years of personal leave will pass before Twining locates a skull exactly fitting the description of Mkwawa's head and injuries. At last, on June 9, 1954, the governor of Tanganyika ceremoniously presents Mkwawa's skull to his grandson, Chief Adam Sapi Mkwawa, at Kalenga.

A MOTLEY GROUP

"Here we are," Geoff tells Chris and Alex. The three young friends have turned off the highway and are now bumping along the loop road into Mufindi. "How about a picnic by this stream?"

The car has hardly stopped before Alex jumps out, his binoculars at the ready, and immediately starts "glassing" the vast bush around them looking for big game. Chris, who has arrived in a suit and with a furled umbrella, is only interested in Mufindi's social life.

"Girls?" he asks.

"No girls," Geoff answers.

"What? No girls? Roll on, three years!"

Brooke Bond insists not only on three-year contracts, but also that new recruits have to be bachelors. One reason is the cost of return flights from London to Dar es Salaam, £300 (about $1,000), compared to an assistant's annual salary of just £600 (about $1,800). Another reason, Geoff firmly believes, is that life in Mufindi is very much more attractive to men (Chris clearly excepted!), and Brooke Bond management fears that wives might persuade their husbands to go back to England early.

"This way, they at least got three years out of us," he later jokes. "Not only that, but I'm sure they targeted 'unemployable' people. Clever guys generally moved on. 'Unemployables' generally stayed on. And here I still am, more than fifty years later. In those days, the company chose public school boys with a sense of adventure but not necessarily academic achievement. That's how the British Empire was built: usually by 'misfits' and 'remittance men,' some because they didn't fit in the UK and others because they were an embarrassment to their family, or both. Great characters!

"Speaking of characters," he tells Chris and Alex, "I've just heard a fascinating anecdote about Latham Leslie–Moore, who used to have a farm very close to here—by the Sao Hill airstrip (later the National Service Camp).[6] Leslie–Moore retired soon after I arrived. He now lives in an old Arab fort on M'Simbati Island, some say peninsula, in southeast Tanganyika. His fort, like many others along the East African coast, was initially built to prevent relatives of captured slaves from trying to release them before their transport to Zanzibar.

"Anyway, having bought M'Simbati, Leslie–Moore announced that he had changed his religion. And now being Muslim, that he should henceforth be referred to as the Sultan of M'Simbati."

"Didn't BBC have a story on him? Is he the British man on this tiny island declaring independence and threatening to join the United Nations even before Tanganyika?"

"That's him. Apparently, one day a friend of his from Dar es Salaam asked a pilot flying a light aircraft to Mtwara to give a letter to anyone on the mainland who could deliver it to M'Simbati. As the pilot was flying over the island, he thought, 'Since I don't really know anyone on the mainland, why don't I just drop the letter directly onto M'Simbati from the plane?' All he had on him to weight the letter was his bagged lunch. Selflessly forfeiting a ham sandwich, the pilot duly bombed the Sultanate of M'Simbati with it.

"Soon after, the British governor, Turnbull, received an irate letter of protest claiming that the sovereign Muslim state of M'Simbati had been violated with a pork product. The governor of Tanganyika ultimately sent the Sultan of M'Simbati a bottle of whisky, upon which peace was restored."

(In a web posting, many years later, former resident of Tanganyika John Bottern will describe how Leslie–Moore once asked Mwalimu's government to recognize M'Simbati's independence. Although President Nyerere declined, he did promise [tongue in cheek] that no government official would set foot on M'Simbati without

---

6   There, his wife, still remembered to this day by Geoff's friend Emanuel Mdemu, runs a little dispensary for Tanzanians.

Leslie–Moore's prior permission, assuming the automatic granting of said permission. He further granted Leslie–Moore the right to hoist the M'Simbati flag, but only if flown under the Tanganyika flag, on the same flagpole.)[7]

"Leslie–Moore always used to mysteriously say, 'my ancestor of Agincourt wouldn't have done this,' or 'my ancestor of Agincourt would have done that,'" Geoff will add in later years, "but he never said anything more about this mysterious ancestor. After independence, the government of Tanganyika sent a gunboat across and removed him (some say because the government could no longer ensure his welfare). He went to Lamu, in Kenya, and eventually died in a nursing home in Nairobi. It was then revealed that he was the illegitimate son of Edward VII and a descendant of Henry V, who successfully led the English against the French at the battle of Agincourt—as described by William Shakespeare in his play *Henry V*. So Leslie–Moore probably was a remittance man. Like many others, a great character and fiercely independent."

《•》《•》《•》《•》

Unbeknownst to Geoff in 1959, he will one day fall into the same category. For now, he is a green young man eager to introduce Alex and Chris to his Mufindi, beginning with its magical forests. An occasional elephant passes through. Buffalo are often observed, even in Lugoda, the tea company headquarters. Red duiker, bushbuck, and bush pig are common, providing a healthy living for leopards. Not surprisingly, hunting is what bachelors and young people are excited about.

To his parents: "About an hour ago I shot my first buck. A red duiker. I had borrowed a shotgun and an Ssh cartridge off my manager . . . and sat under a tree on the edge of one of our tea fields. Within a few minutes, this duiker came along and promptly met its death with a shot right into its brain (I don't suppose that I was aiming there though!)." In fact, he probably was, given his numerous awards for marksmanship—and boxing—that his mother proudly displayed in their home.

---

7   John Bottern, 25 Nov 2005, **http://www.fotw.net/flags**.

"The forests also relieve the boredom of tea supervision," Geoff confides in them with humour. "But don't get me wrong. I love being a tea planter; the crop is so green and grown in such natural surroundings. Still, I have to admit that you don't have to be an expert agriculturalist to be a tea planter. Maybe that is why, perhaps, there's a policy of employing 'unemployable' people like me: to reduce the numbers who would otherwise move on."

Every weekend, the bachelors find something interesting to do. Often spearheaded by their irrepressible fellow assistant, Jonny Niblett, they explore, they hunt, they shoot and fish, or play golf, tennis, and rugby. Often at the Mufindi club, but sometimes hundreds of bumpy miles away at "neighbouring" clubs run by pockets of scattered expatriates.

One such rugby excursion is to Dodoma, where, before the game, a pride of lions has to be removed from the field. Both sides recruit American Peace Corps volunteers to make up numbers. At the bar that evening, a diminutive Chris looks up at two hulking Americans, declaring that he knows exactly what their last thoughts are when they go to bed at night: "How I wish I were British!" He then somehow squeezes through them, like an orange pip, to escape. Dodoma has a particularly strong team from the Geological Survey Department, which goes on to form East Africa's first touring team, the Scorpions.

《•》《•》《•》《•》

Thursdays and Saturdays are "club night." That's when all and sundry wander in from various isolated estates and outlying farms for a rare chance to socialize, often exchanging anecdotes about hijinks late into the night around the bar. For example, the one about young tea assistant Jonny, returning home with his eyesight perhaps slightly impaired by excesses at the club, when he sees a wild boar in the headlights. (Jonny always carries a gun in his very low-slung, bachelor van, the cheapest available vehicle.) He shoots the boar and somehow manages to stuff it into the back.

The next morning, his cook brings him early morning tea. Still somewhat the worse for wear, Jonny thankfully accepts the tray and says:

"Please remove the bush pig from my car." His cook returns a little while later.

"Sir, you had better look at this pig. It has got a ring in its nose."

Commander Harrison Wallace, who lives on the neighbouring estate (Idetero), has recently imported an expensive boar from Kenya. Although covered in mud, there should have been no case of mistaken identity. What to do?

No bachelor owns a refrigerator, least of all a freezer. In fact, there is not a single freezer in the whole of Mufindi, so Jonny quickly distributes his spoils in confidence, to prevent word from getting to the commander. It does.

Young Niblett is cordially invited to dinner, and over port after their meal, the commander raises the subject of his prize boar, declaring that, being of a sporting nature, he is prepared to toss double or quits. Jonny loses and has to pay out double the cost of the pig.

"Justice is served—I suppose," says Geoff, with a grin. Jonny begs to differ.

FOREST SECRETS

Throughout, Brooke Bond employees continue their love affair with the surrounding forests. The forests, in turn, will increasingly offer up their secrets, including endemic chameleons, birds, three varieties of bush baby (one as small as an apple), deep in the Kigogo forest. Many of the tea planters will develop amazing expertise in various fields.

Charlie Paget–Wilkes's vast collection of botanical specimens ends up in Kew Gardens. Liz (since Baker) and her husband Neil will go on to become the recognized top Tanzania bird experts, followed closely by Shanna Sheridan–Johnson and Liz de Lyser. Colin Congdon will go on to become one of the leading butterfly experts over an area including Tanzania, Malawi, North Mozambique, and Zambia, also touching Madagascar and the Comores. From Ivan Brampton he will learn how to identify the food plants of the various butterfly species. Together they will gain botanical expertise on anything linked to butterflies, collect all the known species of butterflies in Tanzania, and add many new ones to the list. Their ultimate project—to document the complete life cycle of individual species, twenty species per year—will lead the by then septuagenarians happily to announce that they have another eighty years' work ahead of them. Even Ivan's death in 2010 will fail to deter Colin, who at the ripe old age of seventy-nine will still be constantly on the move, up mountains, down valleys, in deep bush, brandishing his butterfly net.

GERMAN TREASURE

There are three tea companies in Mufindi when Geoff first arrives, the largest being his employer, the Tanganyika Tea Company (Brooke Bond), and the two smaller ones being the Mufindi Tea Company at Idetero, and Stone Valley Tea Company at the northern end of the Mufindi tea area.[8] Stone Valley Tea Company produces excellent quality tea, with probably the lowest yields in Mufindi (quantity and quality being inversely related: when one is up, the other is down).

The owner, Mr. Stone, has an attractive daughter called Cherry, much sought after by the many bachelors in Mufindi but well protected by her father. Rumour has it that a young tea assistant, Colin Congdon, tries his luck one day. He has just bought a new car. Driving it to Stone Valley, he proudly shows it off to the family. Father Stone invites him to get into his new car and switch it on so that he can hear its engine purr. Colin proudly obliges.

"That sounds very nice, young man," Mr. Stone says appreciatively. "Now, thank you for coming. Goodbye!"[9]

Signs of the pre-war German presence keep cropping up. Exploring his attic one day, Geoff notices a little hole in a bricked-up section, clearly opened up by someone before him. He scrambles through it and into a space above his bedroom and finds it full of old letters and photos. They belong to the original owner of his house, a German doctor named Meuschke,[10] who, as it turns out, delivered the first-born son of some older German settlers (Helga and Werner Voigt), whose isolated farm Geoff had recently come across.

"There were also a couple of German stick hand grenades," he writes to Vicky. "One of them had deteriorated. The other I brought

8   The Itona house, owned by Mufindi's first tea planter, Usher (for whom Jobst de Leyser worked) and built by Freddie Thomas (Bill Usher's cousin), was a lovely, two-storey structure overlooking a small lake in the forest. Unfortunately, it was built of sun-dried bricks and later had to be demolished. Freddie also built Idetero house, this time of stone. It still stands.

9   The Stones later sold out to a British, but India-based, tea company and went to live in South Africa, where he bred horses. The Mufindi Tea Company and Stone Valley Tea Company later merged under single ownership, with Mike West as general manager. Sadly, this meant that the two erstwhile managers, Laurence Napier–Ford and Pat Mathers, lost their jobs. Laurence, the force behind the Mufindi sailing club, always drove at high speed without too much imagination. He and his wife were incredibly generous and very kind to all the bachelors, particularly in Mufindi, always inviting them back to their house. They returned to England. Pat and Jane Mathers chose to stay as independent farmers and bought the Marenda tea farm from the Pattersons, from where Jane continued as Mufindi's hairdresser.

10   The pre-WW II German doctor in Mufindi and post-WW II owner of the Iringa Pharmacy.

down, together with sundry letters and photos undamaged by rats. The next morning, I got up early, gave my gardener the hand grenade, told him to pass it on to my manager and shot off to muster parade before Derrick arrived. The gardener later told me that the manager had ordered him to drop it down a nearby latrine pit, and I escaped being accused of trying to blow up my manager."

Looking for German "treasure" soon becomes a regular pastime, with little thought given to original ownership. "Funny, that," Geoff will muse many years later when chatting with his German settler friends, the Voigts. "After the war, people didn't regard it as belonging to anyone.

"While staying at Lulanji, previously owned by Herr Wolff, I bought a metal detector, carefully crisscrossed the lawn, and struck gold! Digging down, I excitedly unearthed . . . an empty corned beef tin. That was the only thing I ever found." Helga will giggle. Werner will smile. "Speaking of treasures," Geoff will continue, "how did you deal with yours?"

The Voigts will look at each other and this time both burst out laughing. "We waited until late at night to avoid prying eyes. And, since we didn't think that we would be gone long, we hid our family silver under 'the tall tree.' When we returned eight years later, all the trees were tall. But we did eventually find it."

"Von Oehnhausen's treasure is apparently still buried under his garage," Geoff will mutter, rubbing his hands in mock greed. "Unfortunately, his garage is on company property and therefore out of bounds."

"Did you know that he was the head Nazi in Mufindi?"

"I did hear something to that effect. When he left, there were still pictures of Hitler on his walls, one or two of which were of him accompanied by Hitler. He also had a wooden mantelpiece carved with a swastika, which, sadly, due to postwar bad feeling, was planed off by the subsequent tenant."

"Speaking of swastikas," Werner will offer, "Helga and I were almost allowed to stay on our farm during the war. However, when the British found a wooden relief among our assets (a small replica of a monument commissioned in 1919, carved by my father to honour German soldiers from his hometown who had fallen during World War I, and clearly inscribed '1914–1918'), they accused us of harbouring Nazi sympathies and sent us off to prison. This, even though Helga had had to flee from Germany because her mother was born Jewish; even though I had been warned by Von Oehnhausen not to marry Helga (on pain of exclusion from the German community, a serious punishment in that isolated environment); and, when I did marry Helga, both of us were shunned by extremists in the German community for years leading up to the war."

"Interestingly, Bad Oehnhausen, Von Oehnhausen's family seat, was the first place Vicky's brother and Vicky visited in Germany, because their father was stationed there after the war," Geoff will offer as an aside, before adding, "the Mufindi club walls were covered with German treasures when I first arrived, including some decorative hanging plates found under the garden at Kibwele, Werner Ocker's old house.

"One day there was a knock on the door. 'My name is Ocker,' a tall stranger said. 'Werner Ocker. I built this house.' He stayed the night, and to this day, I regret not quizzing him more closely about those early days of German tea development in Mufindi. What can you tell us about them, Werner?"[11]

"As far as I know, Geoff, the German tea story in Mufindi began with the arrival of an Englishman! It goes something like this . . .

TEA TAKES ROOT

In 1929, Bill Usher (son of whisky baron Sir Robert Usher) buys a lot near Hermann Hummel in Mufindi East. Like most German settlers, Hummel is growing coffee, because, late in the nineteenth century, a German agricultural officer published an article about wild coffee thriving in the Mufindi forest.

Not so, the settlers discover. Far from flourishing, their coffee regularly succumbs to coffee berry disease, exacerbated by excessive rains and low-lying clouds. Rumours soon persist that the so-called "wild" coffee (later referred to as *Coffea mufindiensis*) was actually abandoned by Mufindi's earliest German missionary, Mr. Bunk ("Bungu" to the Wahehe[12]).

---

11   Ocker later engaged Werner to work in Rwanda. See Werner Voigt, *60 Years in East Africa: The Life of a Settler* (Renfrew, ON: General Store Publishing House, 2004). **http://www.gsph.com**.

12   "Bungu also grew '*mfinzi*,'" ninety-year-old Lazaro Mbedule told Evelyn Voigt in 1976. When

The young English newcomer, Usher, decides to try his luck with tea. It thrives. Another Englishman, Cyril Mayer, soon follows suit. Hummel, their German neighbour, also switches. And, within a few years, Mufindi East is dotted with 290 acres of fledgling tea estates in various stages of development.

The East African Railway Association of Berlin agrees to finance the construction of a tea factory through a collective loan to the settlers. Repayment will be in green leaf ("green gold") delivered for processing. Dr. Weddige, a man alternately described as stubborn, bombastic, and ambitious by those who know him, becomes the first factory director. Construction begins in 1931, and on June 25, 1932, the Kibwele Tea Company Ltd. is officially registered.

The new factory, quite aside from benefiting the Germans, also has far-reaching effects on the Wahehe. Colonial demands for "hut and poll taxes" from Tanganyikans have remained constant. However, the Great Depression has reduced available jobs. Without work and unable to pay taxes, the Wahehe face severe tax evasion penalties, so the new tea factory attracts lots of labour.

The district commissioner reports in his annual report that year something to the effect that, "Native administrators, led by Paramount Chief Sapi Mkwawa (son of the famed Paramount Chief Mkwawa) walk hundreds of dusty or muddy miles, pending the season, to induce reluctant constituents to bear their share of the economic burden."[13]

None other than the British Governor of Tanganyika tours some of the Mufindi tea estates on August 22, 1932. He meets with the Mufindi Tea Planters Association and subsequently confirms Weddige's election as official advisor to the territory in "all questions relating to tea."[14]

---

she asked Lazaro what *mfinzi* looked like, he pointed at the fir trees planted by her grandfather. "Those trees," he says. "They gave Mufindi its name; because the *mfinzi* trees were so different from any other tree we knew, everybody started calling this 'the place where the *mfinzi* grow.' Just like Udumuka (literally 'to tear up') got its name because that's where our warriors once slaughtered enemies."

13   Courtesy of the Tanzanian National Archives, which allowed Evelyn Voigt access for her Master's research in 1976.

14   Translated from Kibwele Factory correspondence, in a German file found after the war and

By 1934, the year in which Tanganyika tea experts predict that Mufindi tea will clear the market of any other Tanganyika-grown tea, German tea planters find themselves firmly embroiled in tea politics. Their main concern is with East Africa's leading tea producer, Kenya. It graduated into the international export market during the Great Depression, just before world tea prices dropped drastically, causing international tea producers to scramble for new ways of reversing the trend. As a last resort, when a voluntary restriction on production failed, they initiated the 1933 International Tea Agreement, which not only prohibited the sale and lease of new land for tea, but also restricted tea exports for five years to the maximum volume of tea exported between 1929 and 1931.

Given Tanganyika's, particularly Mufindi's, late entry into the tea trade, these restrictions threaten to thwart any further tea expansion in 1934. However, Weddige manages to negotiate a compromise agreement with the Tanganyika government. "One must differentiate between official statements and unofficial action," he writes to Germany on August 22, 1934. "Officially right down to its correspondence with the tea associations, the government acts to appease the International Tea Committee . . . in order to merit its tea seed quota. But with private planters considered trustworthy by the director of Agriculture, it acts otherwise . . . and has no intention of letting a single acre revert back to . . . Kenya. Rather, whatever cannot be planted in Rungwa, will be planted in Mufindi."[15]

NAZIS

Also in 1934, an affluent urban teenager of eighteen, Helga Stein, flees Germany to marry a stranger, Werner Voigt. He has a farm somewhere in the African hinterland called Mufindi. Why does Helga have to flee? Because the Nazis have suddenly labelled her Jewish, even though she was raised as a Lutheran by her Lutheran parents, Dr. Otto Stein and his

consulted for Evelyn Voigt's Master's thesis; courtesy of Brooke Bond.

15   Ibid.

33

Jewish-born wife, Margot. Margot herself converted to Christianity in her late teens after being shunned by her Jewish community for marrying the Lutheran Otto.

Nazi sympathizers, covertly active in Mufindi since 1934, are increasingly aggressive. Baron van Oeynhausen becomes Mufindi's National Socialist cell leader. His wife supports him under the guise of the Women's Red Cross Association for Germans overseas. The Mufindi Women's League of the Colonial Association (*Frauenbund der Deutschen Kolonialgesellschaft*) thrives, and "appropriate literature for Germans" begins to find its way into the Mufindi library. Mufindi's German children are increasingly schooled in Lupembe, a school known to provide "appropriate" education for Germans born on foreign soil. Each page of *Das Hochland* (*The Highland*), a monthly magazine for East African Germans published in Mufindi, is emblazoned with slogans such as, "Germans! Buy German wares!" and "Give the German homeland work and bread!" One of Germany's largest tea firms offers to sell all Mufindi's tea in Germany under the slogan: "Germans! Help the German tea planter in formerly German East Africa!"

Defying the Nazis

Werner Voigt is warned not to marry Helga Stein, on pain of ostracism. He ignores the warning. By 1935, most of the Germans (especially the tea growers in Mufindi East) no longer associate with them. Then, out of the blue, the newlyweds are surprised by an invitation, carried to them on foot, asking them to a party deep in the forest at their friend Kletke's house.

"Thank you, Herr Kletke," they answer, or words to that effect. "But it's probably better if we stay away."

"Of course you must come," he insists. "Heaven's sakes! I can invite whomever I choose to my own home!" Kletke is well known for infuriating the Nazis by singing loud snatches of folk songs to drown out political speeches at social gatherings. Once it took several men to prevent a huge Nazi — Buettner — from breaking an empty bottle over his head.

So Helga and Werner risk it and walk through the bush to the party. The whole of Mufindi appears to be there—hardcore Nazis, non-committal camp followers, and anti-Nazis alike. After a while, their friend Kletke approaches. "I am sorry, Helga and Werner," he says quietly, clearly embarrassed. They understand, and leave.

The rainy season sets in. One sodden night, there's a knock on the door. A messenger hands Werner a note. It's from Buettner, the huge and aggressive Nazi referred to above. "Please hurry over. My wife has to get to hospital."

Reluctantly, Werner gets into his precious new car, one of the few in the area. He splashes and skids five miles to Old Kasanga, down a dangerous incline, over an equally treacherous causeway, and finally arrives at Buettner's place. His car threatens to leave the road several times, but he successfully delivers Mrs. Buettner to the mission hospital—just in time for her to give birth to twins.

A few weeks later, Werner sees Buettner walking along the road. He stops the car. "Come on, Buettner," he calls. "I'll give you a lift."

"I don't associate with the likes of you," comes the cold reply. "Very soon, this country will belong to Germany, and you will be the first to go."

"He wasn't a bad sort," Helga later recalls. "He was just a 200-percent devotee of a bad cause." In fact, Mufindi politics drive Helga and Werner to take their honeymoon in the form of a thousand-kilometre foot safari through the bush, some of it through blank spots on the map.

German Enemy Aliens

On the evening of September 3, 1939, young Schmidt (a German bachelor living in Mufindi East, not far from where the Foxes will one day own a farm) turns on his radio, eager for the latest news from Germany. The crackling finally gives way to an audible announcement, one which sends him racing to his motorcycle, stopping just long enough to grab his goggles. Britain, France, and Germany are at war. He must warn his fellow Germans in Mufindi, many of whom are without radios and will be caught unawares if the British decide to take immediate action in Tanganyika. By the time he reaches Mufindi West, he is exhausted; wonders whether he should include the Voigts.

The Brits probably won't do anything to them, given Helga's non-Aryan status, he thinks, trying to justify heading home. Then he remembers how close they all were before his Nazi conversion.

"We are at war," he says, in a rush, when they finally answer their door. "I'm sure you won't be harassed, given your politics, but you may want to hide your valuables and pack some things, just in case." With that, he prepares to take off again, but not before (as in the old days, prior to shunning them) he puts his hand on his heart in farewell to Helga and sings her a snatch of his favourite love song. Then off he rides into the night. (That is the last Werner and Helga ever see of him. He escapes into the bush and gradually makes his way to the front, where a bomb almost immediately tears off one of his legs. Rather than live with his injury, he unwraps his bandages and bleeds to death.)

The next morning, Helga and Werner wake to a farmhouse surrounded by armed soldiers.

《•》《•》《•》《•》

At gunpoint, the British arrest thirty-three-year old Werner; label him "Enemy Alien #235"; and "concentrate" him with all the other German males older than sixteen—first in tobacco barns near Iringa, then in the Salvation Army Camp in Dar es Salaam, pending either repatriation to Germany or internment in South Africa.

Meanwhile, twenty-three-year old Helga, dubbed "German Enemy Alien #514," is held under isolated farm arrest in Mufindi, with their two-year-old toddler, Werner Junior (#515).

"My dear little Helga!" reads a typical letter from Werner, dated December 6, 1939, under the heading: "Internee No. 235, Internment Camp, Dar es Salaam."

"Whatever you do, don't reproach yourself at all.[16] I am very proud of you and rejoice each day that we belong together and have such a beautiful boy. You don't have to worry at all. As long as the two of us stand by each other we will somehow overcome our fate. My deepest wish would be to move to a corner of the world where we need not hear or see anything to do with politics . . . So, may you both be well and greeted from the heart, by Dad. Section D30."

---

16   Presumably he is referring to her Jewish heritage.

《•》《•》《•》《•》

At year-end, the Iringa provincial commissioner notes somewhat smugly in his annual report how the province has
"weathered the storm of 1939 with remarkable buoyancy,"
despite the hole left by the imprisoned Germans, given that
they owned 90 percent of all plantations and farms in the province (employing approximately 8,000 natives); 25 percent of
alluvial diggings in gold fields (employing about 3,000 men
at the Lupa Gold Fields); 50 percent of the garages and hotels;
supplied 75 percent of the materials used on plantations and
farms; handled 90 percent of the produce, excluding pyre-
thrum; and financed the majority of the farms. Also, how 297
enemy aliens have been interned without incident, of whom
sixty-two are paroled (mainly missionaries); and how arrest-
ing parties were forced to travel extensively on foot to find
some of them, since the Germans were scattered over an area
of about 20,000 square miles.

The German monopoly on tea in Mufindi disintegrates
abruptly as the British set about organizing the profitable
maintenance of cash-crop agriculture. A Kenya-based British company (Brooke Bond) wins the contract to supervise
enemy-alien farms. In anticipation, Motor Mart, an auto
dealership in Dar es Salaam, sends mechanics and spare
parts, including car batteries, upcountry to fix all the German
vehicles (which were dismantled while the German women
were still under farm arrest). Brooke Bond takes its pick. The
remaining vehicles are auctioned off by Mr. Fernandes in
Iringa, with all proceeds officially earmarked for the accounts
of their enemy alien owners.

《•》《•》《•》《•》

Although the war ends in 1945, Werner and Helga are not released
until 1948. By then they have been imprisoned for eight years — Helga
under farm arrest for a year, before being sent to a women's internment camp in what is now Zimbabwe; Werner in South Africa for
four years, before being reunited with Helga in Norton Internment
Camp in 1944 (where their son Peter and daughter Evelyn are born,

as Enemy Subject numbers 868 and 1098, respectively[17]).

While most Germans are repatriated to Germany, the Voigts — to their delight — are allowed to return to their farm in Mufindi, partly on the strength of their anti-Nazi stand before and during the war. After days of travelling by boat, train, and bus — with three children and little food — they finally make it to Iringa, exhausted and almost broke. To quote Werner from his memoir, *Sixty Years in East Africa, The Life of a Settler, 1926 to 1986*:

> Before the war, we had quite a bit of money in the bank, as we had been saving to go on leave (we got our leave, all right — eight years at King George's expense) . . . So I went to see the British administrator.
>
> "Mr. Fooks," I said, "We have just arrived from our internment in Salisbury. I have very little money on me and would like to draw some cash from my account before we return to Mufindi."
>
> He looked at me. "You want what? Money? Do you think your internment did not cost anything? There is no money for you in the bank. What do you want here, you Nazi?"
>
> I was stunned. I had not anticipated this.
>
> "First, I want to state that I have never been a member of the Nazi party. Furthermore, we were told in the camp that our property would be returned to us and that we could reclaim our assets as soon as we arrived in Tanganyika."[18]

Mr. Fooks eventually does allow them to return to their farm, on a temporary basis, without their pre-war money, as "Tenants at Will" — in other words, they can be kicked off at any time.

《•》《•》《•》《•》

---

17   Hence one of Evelyn's favourite lines, "I was born in six countries." (Geographically, Norton was in Southern Rhodesia, which became Rhodesia, then Rhodesia–Zimbabwe, and eventually Zimbabwe. At the same time, the only reason we were geographically in Southern Rhodesia in the first place was because Tanganyika did not have enough prison space [some say female wardens] for all the enemy aliens, so the governor of Tanganyika rented facilities from Southern Rhodesia. Like high commissions and embassies, the rented prison grounds politically belonged to Tanganyika, which was later renamed Tanzania.)

18   Werner Voigt, *60 Years in East Africa: The Life of a Settler*, 177.

"That must have been devastating for you, Werner and Helga," Geoff says.

"Not as devastating as what happened to our fellow ex-internee, Mr. Schneider," Werner responds. Like all the other tea estates in Mufindi East, his farm had been handed over to the Tanganyika Tea Company in 1939. In 1940, the company asked for longer-term arrangements than those granted during the first nine months of its operations, declaring itself unwilling to invest money in further maintenance without sufficient time guarantees to allow for profit generation. The British government agreed to a security of tenure for new factories amounting to at least fifteen years' right to tea production in Mufindi.

"So, the Iringa District Commissioner rescinded Schneider's permit to return to his farm after the war, effectively rendering him homeless on the spot."

"What happened to him?"

"He moved in with us for the rest of his days (including, to Helga's chagrin, for those first months when she had no idea how to feed her own family, let alone anyone else—especially not a man whom imprisonment had scarred with such a fear of hunger that he obsessively hoarded anything edible. Luckily, our pre-war farm employees brought us gifts of eggs and corn to tide us over the worst stretch).

"In the meantime, the British administration allowed us to stay, but only if we repurchased the farm we had never sold—leading to decades of Land Bank debt. A few weeks later, Helga's ex-German neighbour walked over from her place two miles away. (Ex-German because she had escaped internment by marrying an Ally right after war was declared and was consequently living very comfortably when we returned.) With her was another recently dispossessed German, Mr. Sommerfeld.

"'You are already so many people here,' Mrs. Marowski said. 'I'm sure you won't even notice one more.' Despite Helga's attempts at protesting without embarrassing Mr. Sommerfeld, he, too, remained on our farm for the rest of his life. And that is at least some of the early history of German tea in Mufindi."

《•》《•》《•》《•》

"Imagine, Vicky," Geoff writes in 1959. "My introduction to tea includes looking after the first German tea field in Mufindi![19] Mr. Hummel's number-two headman, in charge of planting this field in 1933, was Nallos Kihega. After the sudden imprisonment of the German owners, Nallos persuaded Hummel's workers to complete the clearing and planting of tea fields on Matugutu Estate, with the assurance that sooner or later they would be paid. Indeed, they were. Such a kindly man is Nallos, my teacher of tea."

ELEPHANTS

Come the dry season, and his local leave, Geoff will inevitably head off on foot somewhere in the bush, accompanied only by trackers and porters, with the purpose of hunting elephants. Elephants abound and have to be controlled by the Game Department, so the idea of seeking out that big 100-pound tusker[20] doesn't seem as terrible as it will many years later. Quite aside from the adventure, selling ivory tusks helps to supplement Geoff's less-than-stellar wages. He is not, and never will be, a headhunter for trophies.

Geoff's safaris nearly always start at the top of the Mufindi escarpment, at a place called Lulanda. Someone drops him off there to arrange for porters and trackers, many of whom are to become lifelong friends and mentors.

The descent usually begins with early morning mists on the high plateau, lifting quickly under clear skies to reveal breathless views over the Mgololo plains, with distant mountain ranges fading in endless shades of blue toward the horizons below . . . at his feet, a profusion of dusty-rose protea, golden straw flowers, multicoloured ground orchids, and tiny star-like blossoms of burning violet and deepest fuchsia, all glistening with dew.

The first day, they head down the escarpment and then out, in one direction or another, guns at the ready, porters fully loaded with basic supplies: a pan or two, camp beds (no tents), and minimal produce, to be supplemented by game meat. Their loads get lighter and lighter, as

---

19   Hummel owned horses, which were ridden by Jobst De Leyser as a young boy (Jobst still lives in Iringa with his wife, Liz) and also by a children's nanny who later married Bill Usher. She originally lived on Kidope Estate, additionally owned Itona Estate and, together with others (among them Commander Harrison Wallace), also Idetero Estate.

20   Popular designation for an elephant with a 100-pound tusk on each side.

flour and oil, onions, rice, and vegetables are consumed (there being no markets along the way).

Experiencing the bush at such close quarters is heady . . . sights, smells, little things: insects, flowers, berries, birds. One day follows the next in a riot of grasses, now stunted, now swaying over their heads, cutting and rustling and home to a thousand creatures that crawl and fly and sing in endless variations of dizzying emeralds and indigos, rubies, and golds; of thorn-bearing bushes, isolated palm thickets, bush and more bush; of the ground underfoot sometimes swampy, sometimes baked to cement; of graceful umbrella trees and isolated doum palm thickets; lazy, meandering, sluggish rivers, babbling streams, and tall papyrus; of dripping sweat and blinding heat, of cool nights under mosquito nets, guns at the ready; of weaving head loads, now in swathes of silence, now ruptured by the raucous cacophony of water birds; of hippos bellowing into the night, branches cracking underfoot, elephants grazing on distant slopes; of scrambling up grassy hills, down rocky inclines, around and sometimes through dense *miombo* shrublands; of endless ticks clinging to arms and legs; sometimes leeches; of buffalo spoor at their feet, elephant droppings, impala, kudu, zebra, giraffe; of wild pigs, their forelegs folded like worshippers as they worry the earth with razor tusks.

A startled mother squeals off with her three piglets in single file behind her, their little bums bouncing on comical legs, tiny tails upright like miniature flagpoles. Eden itself!

The only thing missing is Vicky, but she is due to arrive on a visit soon. Geoff can't wait to share with her the sense of timelessness stored in streams spanned by trees or convenient stepping stones; released with campfires warming the night, in insects thrumming, cicadas chirruping, rivers chortling and gurgling; in exultant tracking, bagging, resting, camping; in long evenings of deep contentment, of wisdom and jokes exchanged with trackers and porters in the camaraderie of shared exertion, beneath a miracle of dazzling stars. Here, a hyena laughs. There, something snorts. A night bird calls.

All too soon, they are almost home again. Hot! Hot! Hot, as they begin their ascent back up the Mufindi escarpment; deliciously cool before they finally reach Lulanda at the top.

"On one occasion, I wanted to bag a buffalo not far out from the Mufindi escarpment," Geoff shares around the club bar. "I was climbing a hill on one side, while most of my porters carried on below on another side. The buffalo herd caught wind of them and thundered down the hill toward us. We didn't have time to move, so I fired at a buffalo, and the herd just literally parted on either side. We could almost touch them as they thundered past. I am sure that I will regret forever that I wounded a buffalo, which I followed through the grass but never found . . . Just as well, perhaps; a wounded buffalo tends to hide and catch you from behind."

BLOODSHED

Meanwhile, the British territory known as Tanganyika is inexorably moving toward so-called home rule. In other words, toward an African majority in LEGCO, the colonial legislature currently dominated by Europeans, with some Asian and African representation. Majority representation is a long way from the independence Mwalimu and his TANU party are seeking. But it is a step in the right direction.

《•》《•》《•》《•》

The Brooke Bond Tea Company bachelors care more about where to take their next local leave than about local politics. And, true to their word, Geoff's German settler friends Helga and Werner also have as little to do with politics as possible, isolated as they are geographically and by virtue of their status as Germans in a post-World War II British community. Around them, Africa teems with millennia of oral traditions. These are passed on to their children, Peter, Evelyn, and Veronika,[21] by little playmates. They offer glimpses into ingenious interdependence with nature, including the mysterious Great Rift Valley spreading below the escarpment, periodically visited by Peter on his lone hunting excursions . . . Peter, who as a child secretly slips out of his bedroom window to run naked through the night, who learns to wear the forest, armed with his gun and the knowledge gleaned from rare and privileged invitations to discussions with elders, who tries to absorb, simulate, practise their symbiotic relationship with the wilderness, even as the farmhouse sleeps in European isolation behind him.

---

21   Veronika was born in Tanzania after the war. Werner, their older son, is by now in boarding school.

Inside the farmhouse, without running water or power, telephone, or other industrial comforts, German customs reign supreme, complete with homemade gingerbread cookies (using the rich, dark African honey Chotimbau brings to them from combs harvested deep in the forest), Christmas trees (cypresses harvested from their farm), and Brothers Grimm at bedtime. Then come British-type boarding schools, geographically located in Africa, yet Dickensian in their rules, and focused on Oxford and Cambridge syllabi and sports, rendering the younger Voigt children oblivious of African politics raging around them — including the seemingly sudden and bloody eruption against decades of colonial subjugation in the neighbouring Belgian Congo.

《•》《•》《•》《•》

As whispered by the Semliki harpoon found near Katand, some 80,000 years before the land becomes known as the Congo, the most skilled of men provided for their people by harpooning giant catfish, despite the ever-present danger of crocodiles sunning on banks, or snakes hiding in tall papyrus reeds and among thorny balsa trees.

Over time, the mighty Congo, the most powerful river in Africa, washed past tiny but growing settlements nestled in natural clearings under giant rainforest trees, far from its source inland.

Another story, told much later by engravings on the Ishango bone tool, thought to be about 20,000 years old, points at the very least to Congolese familiarity with counting and, probably, with more sophisticated mathematical knowledge.

Above ground, men fished in the Semlinki, the Congo, and other waterways; discovered the power of the rubber trees thriving in their forests; hunted and gathered in the vast plains of savanna grasses. Meanwhile, beneath their feet, the earth continued to crystallize into gold and glitter — ultimately to prove as deadly an attraction to humans as the red seeds of the rambling alchornea bush are to the greediest of birds trapped by sticky latex smeared on nearby branches.

And so it was that the kingdoms of Kongo and Anziku thrived from the fourteenth to the eighteenth century, only to be coveted first by the Portuguese, and then by the Belgians; more to the point, by King Leopold II of Belgium, self-proclaimed chairman of the Association Internationale Africaine, sole "owner" of the Congo's vast terrain and all that it contained.

A subsequent influx of guns, disease, greed, and maladministration culminated in large-scale depopulation of the so-called Congo Free State (and by1908 in an international outcry when Leopold's cruel excesses, resulting from his haste to harvest rubber, were finally publicized to outraged Europeans and Americans). King Leopold II grudgingly handed the Congo "Free" State over for subsequent administration (very loosely defined) by the Belgian Parliament.

If Parliament offered the Congolese any education at all, it was mainly through missions with a focus on Christianity, at the expense of indigenous faiths and related traditions. And, although less ruthless than Leopold, its arrogant tone increasingly fostered overt resentment. On June 30, 1960, with minimal notice as responsible colonial handovers go (five months, to be precise), all Belgian colonial administrators leave the Congo, lock, stock and barrel.

Within weeks, decades of pent-up Congolese rage erupts, largely directed against foreign residents, but also against dissenting nationals untrained in countrywide government. Almost overnight, a tidal wave of 100,000 or so frantic Belgian refugees surges across national borders, often only with the clothes on their backs.

《•》《•》《•》《•》

"Who are they?" Geoff's friends, the Voigts, are on their annual shopping trip to the capital, when a group of whites stagger off the back of a truck on to Acacia Avenue, Dar es Salaam's main road. They are dusty, their children wide-eyed, their language foreign, some of their shirts torn and bloody.

"Refugees from the Congo," Helga and Werner answer their children, almost in unison.

"What happened to them?"

"Politics," Werner says. "Politics."

"Politics," Werner continues to mutter periodically under his breath, making for a subdued, 600-kilometre drive back to the Voigt farm, mostly on dirt roads.

Once home, the children overhear that their English neighbour's son, their only child, has enlisted with the British forces fighting in Kenya against the so-called Mau Mau. Then, that he has been found, chopped up, under a bush.

Only much later is it clear how protracted and frustrated have been the Kenyan attempts to negotiate self-government before impatient Kikuyu extremists (Mau Mau) brutally turn against the British colonialists (as well as against fellow Kikuyus who do not participate). And how colonial administrators, often at odds with their British government at home, retaliate by detaining almost 80,000 Kenyans in "rehabilitation" camps.

In the 1960s, the young man's death simply "proves" quixotic African volatility. The Voigt children try to block out the horror of his mutilated body, images of expatriates fleeing the Congo, and fears of what might happen to them when Tanganyika gains independence. Helga and Werner finally relent on the taboo subject of politics long enough to tell them not to worry. "There are no Mau Mau in Tanganyika."

"What's a Mau Mau?"

It turns out that Mau Mau stands for *Mzungu Arudi Ulaya* (white man go back to Europe) and *Mwafrika Apate Uhuru* (the African should regain freedom).

"Why aren't there Mau Mau here?"

"Relations between settlers and Africans are different, here. We can all get along. No need to worry."

INDEPENDENCE

In August 1960, Mwalimu's political party, TANU, wins majority status in Tanganyika's legislative assembly. Unlike its neighbours, it continues to promise non-violent, multi-ethnic politics in an independent Tanganyika, as well as promoting social and political harmony. Not quite full independence, but ever closer: Mwalimu is now head of government and leading internal self-rule in place of a British governor. "Independence will follow as surely as the tickbirds follow the rhino," Mwalimu promises.

《•》《•》《•》《•》

Still, very little of this registers with Geoff and his fellow tea assistants in those heady early days. They are, after all, young, exuberant, adventurous, and (under the protective umbrella of their multinational employer) enthusiastically bent on following their dreams of adventure in East Africa.

Independent settlers, like the Voigts, feel more vulnerable as they await self-government. Despite their parents' reassurances, the Voigt children periodically find them huddled over Australian offers of cheap land for immigrants to Papua New Guinea. Pamphlets spill over the coffee table in front of their fireplace, on whose facade the Germanic hero Siegfried still slays a dragon decades after Werner's artistic father immortalized his feat in wet cement. Their discussions, punctuated by the hissing of pressure lamps, inevitably falter and predictably stall on one familiar refrain:

Werner: "We'll have a farm, just like here."
Helga: "What kind of a farm?"
Werner: "How about dairy?"
Helga: "Who will milk the cows?"
Werner: "I'll be too busy running the farm."

Or,

Werner: "We could open a bed and breakfast."
Helga: "Who will do the cooking and cleaning?"
Werner: "I'll be too busy running the business."

VICKY VISITS GEOFF

While Geoff savours East Africa, Vicky's studies and practicum confirm her passion for teaching, although agriculture still comes a close second. "Libby," she screams one day. "I've done it! I've finally saved enough money."

For almost a year now, she has been squirrelling it away, shilling by meagre shilling scrimped from her tiny salary. The next day, they visit the travel agency together, Vicky nervously clutching £360 (just over $1000) for a return ticket out to Tanganyika by Christmas, when Geoff's parents have offered to chaperone her. "Isn't it the most exciting thing in the world to go to Africa!" Vicky beams. "All your friends are green with envy," her best friend, Libby, confirms.

At last Vicky steps off the plane into the heady blend of Dar es Salaam's warm coastal air, tinged with ocean, coconut oil, charcoal, and some tropical blossom she can't quite identify. "Probably frangipani," she later decides. Although Geoff's parents are also there, she has eyes only for him. Blond. Tanned. Gorgeous. And he for her: petite and perfect! They all pile into a second-hand Land Rover, which Geoff's parents have rented from Cooper Motors in Dar es Salaam.

"Right," Geoff says. "Off we go to the Tea Company beach house." The next morning, Vicky wakes to turquoise water and blinding beaches beyond stately palms. "Heaven," she says as they lazily swim in the Indian Ocean.

A week later, she scarcely notices how tightly the four of them are squeezed into the Rover for their trip upcountry, amid her luggage, sundry purchases of oil, tinned fish, and butter (luxurious by Mufindi standards). Instead, she soaks in the whitewashed colonial offices and residential bungalows of Dar es Salaam, ablaze in purples, crimsons, apricots, and creams of bougainvillea and other blossoms.

Beyond coastal palm groves, they head into the lush greens of rainy season Tanganyika, past spiky stretches of Greek sisal, through urban Morogoro, and onto the spreading plains of Mikumi (with its glimpses, despite rainy season foliage, of buffalo and elephant, ubiquitous, inquisitive giraffe, and dainty gazelle).

After Mikumi township (really, a petrol station and turnoff to the sugar fields of Kilombero), they start the slow ascent toward Mufindi's plateau, glad of their four-wheel drive on the muddy, narrow road. (*And they call this the main road!* Vicky thinks to herself. "The roads are appalling, and we felt like we were driving along on wooden wheels. It almost made our teeth rattle loose," Geoff's mother will later write home.)

The mighty Ruaha flows past them, almost red in its swollen, rainy season descent toward the Indian Ocean. Lianas compete with ferns and grasses. Baboons watch them from a safe distance. Older males squat, contemptuously vigilant. Babies gambol in universal games of childhood to predictable maternal discipline, while lovers groom each other—so human it makes them laugh. And then, without warning, the car stops. Dead in its tracks.

Silence. The silence of Africa. For a moment, everything seems to hold its breath. Then explodes once more in a raucous mélange of chirping crickets, crying birds, and winds rustling leaves through dense undergrowth.

How can I describe to folks at home the pulsing energy around us? thinks Vicky, as sounds and sights assault her. She imagines roots and tendrils communally sucking in rain, each drop infusing leaf and bird and doe-eyed buck; dripping and scurrying; rich, damp earth disgorging shoot and fern; sudden showers running in rivulets off giant leaves.

Time slows. Not a single vehicle passes. Geoff's mother remains stoically philosophical, Vicky beside herself with excitement, and Geoff, would-be knight in shining armour, increasingly deflated as, with his stepfather, he gradually concedes the futility of further encounters with the bowels of their unresponsive vehicle. All they can ultimately do is wait for another car to happen along.

"The four of us had to camp for more than twenty-four hours," Geoff later tells friends, "during which time only three vehicles went by toward Iringa."

"We spent the night on the side of the road," Vicky adds. "In the morning, I saw that a snake had sloughed its skin beside my head."

Geoff again: "The only vehicles to pass were a bus, a lorry, and a private car. We stopped the private car and gave a note to the manager of Riddoch Motors in Iringa, who sent us down a lorry, a bottle of whisky, and flask of coffee."

After returning the broken-down Land Rover (having had it towed to Mikumi, where it was put on the train to Dar es Salaam), Geoff's parents go to Iringa in the lorry. Vicky and Geoff take the only bus to pass by. It drops them in Iringa. Since Vicky wants to get to the New Year's party in Mufindi, because it is the best opportunity to meet all the far-flung folks in Mufindi, and because Geoff is proud to have and show off his girlfriend to the eighteen fellow bachelors in Mufindi, they take a taxi. ("Vicky looking very swell in her long evening dress," according to a letter home from Gelly.)

"Up here, it is only a little hotter than the hottest English summer and it is now the hottest time of the year." Another letter, this time from Vicky to her best friend Libby, in what is to become a lifelong correspondence. Unfortunately, only Vicky's letters have survived, so Libby will remain a silent partner in this book. "While we were staying in the Brooke Bond beach house at Kunduchi, Geoff's cousins came from Nairobi to Dar es Salaam, accompanied by a friend with his deep-freeze van—he brought meat, even half a smoked salmon! Mind you, he also put some beer into his van to cool. It froze and exploded. That was a fun time. We have been shooting, at last, although I haven't fired a shot yet."

Geoff's vivid recollections of their first shooting venture are fodder for many a bar anecdote. "Vicky and I scooted off, literally, on my Lambretta scooter, to collect a red duiker or two that were accustomed to come out of the forest and graze in the tea.[22] Near where I

Vicky's best friend and lifelong correspondent, Libby White.

shot my first duiker, Vicky and I first perched in a grevillea tree, planted for its shade, and waited. We heard movement in the forest, descended the tree, slowly crept around the tea boundary, and knelt down. In a little while, a large male bush pig emerged.

"'Big white hunter' Fox fired—and does not admit to missing it. (As the bush pig's head slopes forward, I think the buckshot must have deflected off its skull.) After staggering, the pig turned and fled back into the forest, closely followed by Vicky—with God knows what intention if she had caught up with it!"

《•》《•》《•》《•》

On December 9, 1961, thirty-nine year-old Nyerere becomes prime minister of Tanganyika. His people are jubilant. Mwalimu, meanwhile, braces himself for daunting challenges ahead. As he tells the *New York Times Magazine*, in an article

---

22   This would appall tea planters today, because now you have a cover of tea bushes so dense that not a weed is allowed to survive under it. Such also is the efficiency of weeding. In the early days, the tea was full of weeds, there being so many gaps between the tea bushes. "I even used to produce tantrums if I ever saw anyone pulling the magnificent Gloriosa lily out of a tea field. And glorious indeed is that lily, with its hand-shaped, crimson petals, lined in glowing yellow!" Geoff recalls many years later.

published on 27 March 1960:

"Having come into contact with a civilization which has over-emphasized the freedom of the individual, we are in fact faced with one of the big problems of Africa in the modern world. Our problem is just this: How to get the benefits of European society—benefits that have been brought about by an organization based upon the individual—and yet retain Africa's own structure of society in which the individual is a member of a kind of fellowship."

Although the British colonial administration has been more accommodating of self-government than its Belgian counterpart, they also leave behind empty national coffers, only two trained African lawyers, twelve African doctors, and 106 other African university graduates to help Mwalimu shoulder his stupendous task of nation building.

True to TANU's philosophy of evolution rather than revolution, Mwalimu compensates for this by retaining many ex-colonial British officers in their pre-home rule positions, as well as other foreign workers, on condition that they help to train Tanganyikan replacements.

"Africanization" Mwalimu calls this policy, a key component of his immediate focus on education and training. Next step, full independence.

"TRAPPED"

"Vicky's nearly due back, poor thing," Gelly writes home on January 10, 1961, after a heavenly month in Africa, including a second week at the Company beach house. "She's hoping she'll get pneumonia or something that will prevent her." Unfortunately, Vicky's strong constitution lets her down and she heads home to the UK for another two years of studies (including a probationary year of teaching after teachers' training college).

Although she and Geoff do not meet up throughout this time, they do get engaged. Geoff's preferred version of their engagement goes something like this: "Following Vicky's visit, suitably chaperoned by my parents, she presented me with a bill for an expensive engagement ring that she had got for herself. I have no recollection of having proposed to her, although she claims I did so, on the summit of the precipitous Vixen Tor on Dartmoor. However, I don't believe that because I suffer from vertigo and would surely have been speechless with fright."

Pending the day, he might add any one of the following anecdotes:

"The true reason why we had to get married is twofold: One, after you had done a bit of probation with Brooke Bond, you were allowed to join their company car grant scheme, in which you paid half the cost of your car, and the company paid the other half. I didn't have the money (witness his joking reference in a letter to his parents: "Incidentally, have I any rich aunts on the point of 'departure' who would like the odd letter from me!!?"). So Vicky lent me her life savings of £300 (about $1,000), bequeathed to her by her grandmother. This enabled me to pay for half of a second-hand VW Beetle, known as a poor man's Land Rover, with a Brooke Bond grant financing the other half.

"I went hunting in it all through southern and western Tanganyika." ("I saw my first African wild lion during one of my treks," he informs Gelly and Jimmy in one letter. "In fact, owing to the poor light and visibility in the dense woodland, I nearly stepped on a sleeping lioness with cubs. We were walking back to camp, rather weary after a long day's hike, when we were startled by the low growls of these lion cubs only ten yards away on the path! Mum was asleep near the carcass of a Roan antelope and never heard us. We discreetly changed direction to that from which we had just come! And made a detour.")

And another time: "Dear Gelly and Jimmy . . . All the photos were taken by Africans who had never touched a camera before. . . . The white stuff in the buffalo picture was a vulture line—they came in hundreds when I was away fetching an axe to cut off the head (which was 40 inches outside width incidentally). The open 'mbuga' (plain) on which I shot the buff is now two feet under water as it is every year during the rains."

"Those were fun, carefree days," he will reminisce in later years. "I travelled everywhere exploring Africa. Every time the VW bogged down in mud, we could lift it up and take it out. On some weekends we organized social duck shooting excursions, and I was always pleased to have what I considered the best gun dog in the country. Stroppy would watch a bird falling into the rice paddies and not move until commanded, whereupon she would retrieve my bird.

"I remember Mike Merett from Njombe (a neighbouring community ninety miles from Mufindi), who was standing some fifty metres away, asking me to send my dog to fetch the spur wing goose that he'd shot down. It had landed right in front of me. Stroppy obediently went off, fetched it, and took it to him. I may have been her master, but that was Mike's bird.

"Then there was the time after shooting my first two elephants in western Tanganyika, north of Lake Rukwa, when I joined a Mufindi duck-shooting weekend at Chimala on my way back. Everyone complained about a dreadful smell coming from my car (I had forgotten an elephant foot in it). They later told me that they couldn't sleep. I was upwind from them.

"The leg finally ended its days as a stool. First, it was hollowed out, then cleaned very well by rubbing salt and ash inside, and finally covered by a wooden lid to make a seat." (Vicky and Geoff will keep it for years until it becomes politically incorrect, with people saying, "Look at that poor elephant's foot over there.")

"The house of a retired German admiral, Boetke, was used as accommodation for tea estate assistants. In its time, it was a venue for many bachelor parties. One of them, Jonny Niblett, was an artist. He spent prolonged periods in the loo, leaving the wall covered in decorative murals." (History doesn't relate whether he was seated at the time.) "Another assistant, Charles Paget–Wilkes, built a sailing boat in his bedroom and then had to remove the window and most of the wall to get it out, before launching it at Ngwazi. Later, the company decided that the roof had to be replaced and when they removed it, all the walls fell outward, like a house of cards.

"I have to say, those three bachelor years were fun, filled with weekends of hunting, fishing, golf, tennis, rugby, exploring, and shooting. Speaking of shooting, some bachelors were quite wild. I remember, I think it was Trevor Walker spraying Charles Paget–Wilkes with birdshot in the duck shooting line. Even more guiltily, I was standing between Colin Congdon and Jonny Niblett as we were walking up a marsh near Chimala one time, when a flock of red-billed teal flew across. As quick as a flash I was onto them. As I swung round and squeezed the trigger, I heard a voice somewhere crying: 'Nnoooo!'

"Colin's hat was later to be seen floating on the surface of the water. He was under it . . . fortunately unharmed. That reminds me of my good friend Chris Harker, now in Vancouver, who later wanted to join me snipe shooting near Irundi. A snipe got up, flew across, and I shot it, with the wadding embedded in the little bird. A crack shot! Then a voice spoke up: 'A good thing that you hit that bird, because I was on the other side of it!' As I fired, he had gone down, too—into the reeds. Chris also survived.

"I took a marvelous photo of an elephant charging me on Sunday," Geoff writes home on one occasion. "I hope it comes out. This is the elephant that has been on Ngwazi (the lake where I lost my gun), for the last two years. When I first got up to it, it was in a hollow with its back to me. I was only fifteen paces away but well above it, and as it was in a bad position for a photo, I yelled to make it turn around. It immediately bolted into some trees. I could see it, followed, and got to within twenty paces when it dashed through the bushes at me. I took the photo and prepared to run along my escape route when it stopped and I tried to roll on the next film for another photo. It, however, decided to clear off before I could do so. The photo should be terrific with the elephant's trunk and tail up and with its ears out. Although a bull, it wasn't worth shooting. I must get a good camera next tour, as photographing game can be as exciting as shooting.

"What fun! Also expensive! Now, back to Vicky's loan for half of my car: After the first three years, I couldn't afford to repay Vicky. I also couldn't run fast enough. Vicky had, after all, represented Germany in a five nations' junior athletics meeting, in the 100 metres. So I was trapped!" As are more and more of the Mufindi bachelors. For example, "Jonathan Niblett is getting married and spending his honeymoon in the Kilombero Valley shooting elephants," Geoff writes home. "Frank Godwin is still disgusted and declares even more vehemently that he intends never to get himself into the same position as Jonathan and have a woman spoil his life!"

PRESIDENT NYERERE

On December 9, 1962, Mwalimu Julius Kambarage Nyerere takes office as the first president of the Republic of Tanganyika. Amid ongoing public euphoria, the earliest signs of reality are beginning to set in as people realize their lives are not going to improve dramatically or suddenly. They do know that their young leader is doing his best for them, although not the degree to which he must balance dreams and resources, as anticipated overseas support trickles rather than flows in.

STORMY START

It's Friday, the day Major Garlic leaves his farm every week to open his miniscule Sao Hill office, where with great pomp and circumstance he issues airline tickets — this time for Geoff to fly to Nairobi in an East African Airways DC3 (built in 1939) before transferring onto an onward flight to London for his first home leave.

"Thus, I returned to Tavistock," Geoff will later intone. "Within a week, on December 29th, 1962, we got married. Even though I had six months of leave ahead of me, they tied me up in that first week. As I've said before, there was no escaping . . . Actually," he will finally admit, "it was always just assumed that we were going to get married." To which Vicky will add, "Geoff wrote a letter to both my dad and the company to ask their permission to marry. Isn't that amazing?"

Vicky is wed in a tiara once owned by Gordon of Khartoum.

At the time of his death in 1885, General Gordon was the last British governor of the Sudan. His mandate was to evacuate about 1,500 people, mostly civilian, endangered by a major revolt at the hands of a self-proclaimed Mahdi (redeemer of the Muslim faith), Muhamad Ahmad. As impassioned about Christianity as Ahmad was about Islam, Gordon ignored his orders to leave, opting instead to challenge (and if at all possible convert) the Mahdi (who had the same intent in reverse).

A year later, by which time Gordon of Khartoum had become a household name in Britain (to the chagrin of the British government, which had tried to avoid being sucked into the Sudanese conflict), he and a small group of soldiers were trapped in the besieged capital, Khartoum. Public pressure finally forced the government to send in a relief force, but they were too late by two days. The Mahdi had beheaded Gordon of Khartoum.

(Vicky's paternal grandfather told her brother Anthony that he and his friend "Uncle" George were on that expedition as boy soldiers.)

Vicky borrows the tiara (something old) from her godmother, Marjory.[23] Marjory's first husband was General Gordon's nephew. He died early in their marriage, and Marjory, his widow, was, by the time of Vicky and Geoff's marriage, already widowed again by her second husband, Commander N.H. Beaver.

Her son David Gordon studied at Cambridge. The prime minister of the Sudan, descendant of the Mahdi who beheaded his great-uncle, also studied at Cambridge. When the prime minister later returned to his old university, David contacted him, introduced himself as a great-nephew of Gordon of Khartoum, the one beheaded by the prime minister's grandfather, and said, "How about our two families bury the hatchet?"

Invited to Khartoum, and at the ensuing formal banquet, David then formally presented all the medals earned by General Gordon to the Mahdi's grandson. The prime minister made a reciprocal gesture of a book on Khartoum plus a tour of the city and surrounding countryside. Sadly, within weeks of their reconciliation, he was deposed and imprisoned.

"For some reason, General Gordon's nephew inherited the tiara, later lent by his wife to Vicky for the wedding." Geoff and Vicky are chatting with friends after their honeymoon.

"Actually," says Vicky, "it was half of the tiara! They had sold the bottom, so I only got to wear the top."

"Problems started on our wedding day," Geoff continues. "I was sitting at the front of the church with my best man, Robin. On the dot, when Vicky was supposed to come in, Robin turned to me and said, 'You'd better give me the ring.'

"And you know that cold feeling when you're supposed to have a ring and you don't? I had left it behind in my suitcase at home! Attracting much attention in a fully packed church, we both raced round to Robin's mother (my aunt) and asked if we could borrow hers. She had

---

23   Vicky's godmother later left her farm to her second son, Martin. He was a Lloyds Insurance Company "name" ("to be a 'name,' you put up some surety, rather than putting in money"). When Lloyds ran into financial difficulties, he had to sell the farm, half of which was bought by us to protect the land between our two "family" houses from any possible construction development.

never taken it off in twenty-five years. Seated in a forward side pew where everyone could see, she started pulling and heaving. It finally yielded . . . and dropped to the floor and under the pews. About six of us fell to our knees, searching frantically. We finally retrieved it, next to a drain grate, a ring large enough to have fitted on Vicky's thumb (when eventually she arrived, she was warned at the church door what to expect).

"Vicky arrived half an hour late. (I have to make it clear from the beginning that I most certainly have lost one whole year of my life waiting for Vicky. It may be fifty years of life that we have shared since our wedding, but it is surely only forty-nine years of marriage. The rest of the time was lost waiting for her.) However, this is one time that I was pleased that she was late!

"She had got stuck in snow. It was December 29, 1962, the day of the worst blizzard in eighty years, a date still remembered to this day. The hired taxi got stuck. Ever ready to jump out and help, Vicky was firmly told: "This is one day you don't push." Middlemoor villagers rushed out from everywhere and forced them through deepening snow up the hill.

"In the meantime, I had surrendered my suitcase key to my best man's sisters in an attempt to retrieve the real ring in time for the reception. They eventually joined us with it. But unfortunately, they had also vandalized the suitcase, and it dribbled confetti wherever we went on our honeymoon. Everyone kept giving us knowing looks. Embarrassing.

"After church, we managed to get to our taxi and drove to the reception at Whitchurch House, owned and hosted by Vicky's godmother. The others were all late, having had to trudge through the now deep snow to get there. I was getting nervous about having to make a speech. So I filled the time by imbibing lots of 'Dutch courage'—champagne. In short, I got plastered. When it finally came to the actual speechmaking, Vicky had to quietly tell me to stop!

"After the reception, we got into the brand-new car that was coming to Mufindi with us and, crossing moorland, drove into a deep snowdrift in which, totally concealed, there already was another vehicle. The contact caused an electrical fault. Our car started filling with smoke.

By sheer luck, the last vehicle to get through the storm from Tavistock to Plymouth for three days was a little Morris Minor, driven by a Frenchman heading through the night blizzard to Plymouth. We flagged him down. Priorities. First we got the bottles of champagne into his car and then the bride. Finally, off we went . . . slowly. We could barely see the road for the snow."

"Then we just rented a little van and had a lovely, three-month honeymoon, bombing about in Europe," Vicky later wrote to her friend Libby.

"Not quite that idyllic," according to Geoff. "I had skied quite a lot before we got married. I used to go skiing almost every year in my late teens. We habitually frequented Wengen and Grindelwald, with the heights of Kleine Scheidegg in the middle. You can ski down to Wengen on one side and down to Grindelwald on the other.

"Taking the ski lift up the Lauberhorn one day with my uncle Peter, I launched myself down the top of the mountain with gusto and promptly dived into a snowdrift, out of control, only to emerge with a suspected broken leg. A message went down the ski lift to Scheidegg to call up "the blood wagon" (an elderly man with a ski stretcher), which showed up with the requisite bottle of brandy routinely sent along.

"'Right,' said my uncle Peter. 'This bottle of brandy is included in the cost of bringing you back down. We're not going anywhere until it's finished.'

"Between the two of us, we consumed the lot before budging. I don't have much recollection of the trip back other than being strapped down and steered by this old man on skis at great speed. No break, so we finished the holiday with a 'ski bicycle.'

"It was difficult to know what the dominant language was on the ski hill. In my first year at Wengen, I was part of a class lined up across the slope when there was a desperate call from higher up: 'Achtung! Achtung!' No reaction from the ski class. 'Attention! Attention!' Again, no movement. Finally, 'Get out of the bloody way!' And everyone scattered.

"Skiing back to the hotel from Grindelwald on one occasion, we had to pass through wire-fenced farmland. Idle teenager that I was, I didn't want to remove my skis to cross a barbed-wire fence. So, facing upwards and with great difficulty, I managed to get one leg over the barbed wire. Then, horrors, I started sliding backwards. The situation was extremely grave, and I was separated from permanent disaster by barely a centimetre as barbed wire ripped through my ski trousers at the crotch. Aunt Penny spent the evening doing a repair sewing job and, four sons later, obviously no damage. But now back to our honeymoon.

"In Obersdorf, there was a fantastic cable car going up the mountain but only one way down: on skis. Vicky had never skied in her life before. The trouble is the ski slope went through a long stretch of forest tracks with deep ruts. You put your ski in the rut. Then, off you go . . . and go . . . and go. Vicky arrived at the bottom — very bloody. No matter! On we went to the next ski resort.

"At the top of the mountain in Innsbruck," Vicky interjects, "I said, 'Geoff, I don't feel very well.'

"'Nonsense,' my chivalrous groom responded, 'it's only the altitude.' By the time I reached the bottom, there were spots on my arm. I showed them to Geoff. 'See. I don't feel very well!'"

"So Vicky was confined to the room, to avoid infecting Innsbruck with chickenpox. I went on out and had a wonderful time. In the evenings, I returned to tell Vicky about all these beautiful French girls I had seen — with no spots on their faces!

"At our next bed and breakfast in Kuehtai (Cow Valley), we were put up in a separate little summer house outside. Everyone except for the mother was a hunchback, so while we were lying in bed all these hunchbacks — father and sons — were coming in to stoke the fire. Surreal.

"We then joined up with my aunt and uncle in a village in Austria, just behind Switzerland, where tourism was scarcely beginning to catch on. They had only one ski lift, and no hotels. People offered tourists rooms in their houses. The cobbler and his family took us in. The long drop loo (outhouse) was on the veranda outside our room. The owners had their own long drop loo, too — on their balcony right above ours. It used the same drop and you could hear all the splashings and bangings overhead. I had never come across a double-decker long drop before. They all built their own houses there."

("No planning officer. No building regulations. No health and safety inspector . . ." he would have added later in life, by then thoroughly bruised by years of watching from the sidelines as visiting European health and safety inspectors, in his view, absurdly transplant European conditions into a context that demands African solutions.)

AFRICA TOGETHER

After six months of "home leave," the newlyweds board the SS *Uganda* of the British India Line—first class, no less, this still being cheaper than flying to Tanganyika. "We shared a table with two nice couples," Geoff later tells Mufindi friends. "The men were very competitive when it came to sporting events, so I challenged them to race my wife around the entire deck. Vicky was already pregnant at the time, although they didn't know that. She hitched up her long evening dress and off they went. The guys never stood a chance and were not happy—at all!" (This will become a frequent party piece on all sorts of occasions over the years, with Vicky—of Five-Country Salem running fame—never to be beaten.)

"Dear Libby," Vicky writes in her first letter home from Tanganyika, "it's very exciting. I don't mind living without electricity. All we have are Aladdin lamps with long glass chimneys (*fanusi*). Their mantels are quite difficult to cope with, since they tear quite easily. And ducking a bit is mandatory when going through doors, to avoid cracking the glass, which is expensive and difficult to replace. Unfortunately, whenever Foxey goes from room to room, the *fanusi* catches on doorframes and showers us with splinters.

"The fillet steak is chewable when beaten for half an hour and soaked in a marinade sauce overnight. Once a month we get boiling bacon from Kenya, which is a marvellous change . . ."

And later, "Our first-ever fridge runs on kerosene and is very uncooperative. Everything is tricky, really, but also quite romantic. Someone has to carry our water up the hill, since often there is no running water. And we only have one bedroom. (Our baby, when it comes, will just have to sleep in a basket cot in the bath!). If this sounds a bit dreary, it isn't. What it lacks in rooms, Lulanji (as our house is called) makes up for in character. Lulanji House was originally owned by a German planter, Herr Wolf, whose wife, Charlotte, is still buried in the forest behind our home."

Over toast, tinned butter, homemade marmalade, and freshly brewed Mufindi coffee at breakfast, Vicky and Geoff can watch Blue Sykes monkeys running across the lawn. Vicky admires their boldness, marvels at their similarity to humans; how they arrive, swinging from branch to branch, then sit and chatter at them, before disappearing back into the undergrowth. Crimson red-winged turaco and hornbills also visit.

Like Geoff before her, Vicky falls deeply in love with the Mufindi forests. "The walk down the Kigogo River is really beautiful," she enthuses in a letter home, "walking through bamboo and palm trees along the river bank. There are four waterfalls, graduating from small to huge. The final fall shoots down at an angle of forty-five degrees. Impressive!" Together they explore teeming, dank undergrowth beneath canopies of towering giants, their trunks now slick with rainy season mists, when everything seems to writhe and burst; now rattling with seed-pod thirst under parched, dry season skies.

《·》《·》《·》《·》

One day, soon after Vicky joins him, the estate's director, Richard Hartley, requests Geoff to select a new generation of potential "mother bushes" for company tea clones that will hopefully prove outstanding.

"No problem, sir," Geoff tells Hartley.

"Wife, follow me!" Geoff tells Vicky. And off they go into a tea field on Kivere Estate, where Geoff points out to Vicky the bush characteristics that she has to look for.

"With that, I went off in one direction," Geoff will say later in life, "staking about 200 carefully and very skillfully selected potential 'mother tea bushes.' Vicky went another way, stuck in ten sticks, got bored, and went home. Subsequent quality and yield testing eliminated every single one of mine, while one of Vicky's selections, V1 (for Vicky1) rose into the top three clones of Brooke Bond. It became the first-ever tea clone to be selected by, and named after, a woman, and still covers large areas of Mufindi and Njombe [a tea-growing community about ninety miles away]."

Mufindi rainforest.

New tea in front; in the distance, land about to be planted with V1 tea (Vicky's clone).

Soon after Vicky's arrival, Geoff and Vicky decide to build a large dam on Lulanji Estate, entirely out of their own pockets. The thought of asking for company permission doesn't occur to them. (Neither do they then know that Lulanji dam will one day be noted for the largest trophy trout caught in Mufindi [7.5 pounds] and prove indispensable for future tea irrigation.)

Ian Somerville, Geoff's manager at Lulanji, is very tolerant, but not quite the same stickler for time as his first manager, Derrick. "I had to be on muster parade at 7:00 a.m. sharp for Derrick," Geoff jokes. "To ensure this, Derrick drove to my house every day and pretended to be arranging assignments with the carpenter, whose workshop was just behind the kitchen!"

Club nights are on Thursdays and Saturdays, following golf and tennis. They are very busy, with a roster of wives supplying club meals on Saturdays. When it comes to Vicky's first-ever turn, the *kuni* (wood) stove won't heat up. She panics, bursts into tears, and sends Geoff into the club on his own with a few tins. Pat Somerville, a seasoned Mufindi wife, takes the tins and cooks up a splendid meal.

It isn't only the wives who cook. The bachelors also take their turn. "Everyone looks forward to these evenings," Vicky writes home to Libby, "because the bachelors always serve game meat. However, their behaviour often leaves much to be desired. One evening, Jonny Niblett shocked the assembled company by producing his own water, filled with worms, to add to his whisky, declaring that he didn't trust the bar water. Not to be outdone, Colin devoured with seeming relish an outsized, live sausage fly."

《•》《•》《•》《•》

Meanwhile, Mwalimu struggles to keep his Africanization policy afloat. Training and educating his people costs money. So does fixing roads, providing medical care, and even eliciting continued foreign support. Germany, Britain, and the United States are helping—although not as much as pre-independence discussions suggested they would. And with more strings attached. How to ensure that such assistance will bolster rather than dilute his dream of a sustainable African nation built on traditional values?

VICKY'S FIRST WALKING SAFARI

"I'm so excited," Vicky tells Geoff. "Finally, my first, real, long, walking safari!" They are surrounded by what seems like mountains of endless supplies. In fact, they are travelling relatively light, not even taking a tent along (they never will, except for one safari, much later, during the rains). Their beds (which double as chairs) fold away to nothing, as do their mosquito nets (included for privacy rather than as protection against mosquitoes, which are not a great issue in the dry season). By far the bulk of their luggage consists of sufficient basic food stocks for two or three weeks, there being no markets along the way.

"Right," Geoff says, with an affectionate pat on Vicky's bum. "Let's double check the rations, Mrs. Fox." Based on her trusted *Kenya Cookery Book*, as well as on advice from other spouses who have had more experience with catering for safaris (albeit in their case by vehicle rather than on foot), Vicky has spent weeks preparing. Now she checks off various baskets (covered in plastic for extra protection) against her list.

"Homemade peanut butter, Beefex [a meat extract], some bread for the first few days, and fixings for our cook, Alimoni, to make more en route [basically in holes in the ground filled with embers, which act as ovens, or so she has been told]."

Since they often won't have a lot of time for cooking, she includes a pan. This will be for quickly frying eggs, potatoes, and onions; or cooking meat and vegetables. Their neighbours (well, sort of neighbours—settlers and good friends living about thirty miles away, Phyl and Albert Ghaui) have provided enormous baskets of vegetables from their market garden, which will take another two porters to head-load. "The vegetables will last a long time," Vicky is told, "because even when outer leaves are completely rotten, the inner parts will remain fresh and hard."

There is also rice, as well as flatbreads and biscuits, baked a few days before. (Fried Ryvita with Beefex later becomes a favourite for breakfast.)

"Other than that, we lived off the land—off whatever was bagged," Vicky writes to Libby. "Geoff was a great hunter-gatherer. If he shot a bird, we would put it on a stick and roast it over the fire. And if it was an animal, we would do something different with it every day, starting with the offal—the liver or kidneys and so on. The following day we would fry up some of the remaining meat, at the same time as cooking the rest in a big casserole or stew, with carrots and so on from Phyl's cornucopia.

"To stop it from going off, the casserole was duly recooked day after day until Geoff shot something else, preferably not the same type of animal to give us a bit of a change."

"After eating warthog for a week," Geoff adds, "Vicky finally said to me, 'Geoff, shoot something, but not a warthog!' I walked all day and saw nothing. And then on my way back, just on the perimeter of the camp, I saw something and shot it—another warthog. We almost had a divorce, but the porters were very happy."

"And then, of course, there was always honey," Vicky continues, "with the beautiful green, red, and gold honeyguide flying through the bush to show us the way."

Found through huge swathes of Africa, this tiny bird has as its unlikely partner in crime the honey badger, a ferocious creature resembling a black, stocky weasel, covered in snow-white fur on top, black fur beneath—both thick enough to provide full protection against bees (except for its nose)—and long, sharp claws ideal for invading hives. The honeyguide (as the bird's name implies) instinctively leads the honey badger to the hive, where its sharp claws make short work of retrieving the comb. Once the badger has moved on, it's the honeyguide's turn to feast on leftover honey and grubs. Astoundingly, these tiny birds have also learned to hunt with humans.

Not a safari goes by without Geoff's being guided to a wild beehive by this diminutive creature. The bird whistles and flies a little way at a time, then waits for the trackers to catch up before continuing, with both parties whistling to each other, until it finally circles frantically over a gap in the rocks, or a hollow tree. That is the signal for the trackers to light a small fire under the hive and happily widen the opening to the hive, with angry bees buzzing all around them. In go their bare arms, and out come handfuls of combs dripping with honey and full of grubs.

Without exception, the grubs and some honey are put to one side as a reward for the honeyguide, still perched on a bough nearby. The failure to perform this essential ritual might lead the little bird to stop showing them the way to further hives (or, even worse, some believe, to bring them instead to a predator's den).

Despite all the bees, Geoff and Vicky's trackers are never stung. On one occasion, Geoff cine-films them on 8mm film. Years later, their son Christopher will try to do the same—only he will withdraw his arm totally covered in bee-stings. The bees will sting him, but never their equally unprotected trackers!

"How I love these safaris!" Vicky writes to Libby. "Cooking up what we can at the end of the day, and then sitting in the quiet of an evening, chatting around the campfires with trackers and porters; absorbing their stories and experiences."

All in all, Geoff and Vicky will complete some twelve annual walking safaris in their time, only one of three weeks; the rest of two weeks.

> open plains, and dusty
> cool at night
> with campfires burning
> and wise, wise legends
> rising with the smoke
> mellow and strange[24]

Since they have the companionship of very much the same head-load porters from Luanda village on every safari, they will get to know them very well over time.

"It's hugely exciting to be right in the bush, without a car between us and reality, isn't it, Geoff," Vicky exclaims time and again. "Every

---

24   All poems are by Evelyn Voigt.

experience seems more vivid, even though we don't usually spot as many animals as we would in a car, because of course cars can cover far more land at a time. But we see so much more — especially the small things in life: genet cats, butterflies, red hot poker flowers half hidden in *miombo* or *brachystegia* thickets, how the sun reflects off a branch, the line of lichen, the feel of grass, the look of an ant. Each and every detail admired, even that of the enormous, yellow-bellied spiders. Somehow you see things differently and absorb them. Infinite perfection."

"We also have wonderful views of animals," she writes to Libby, "who are quite unaware of us. Herds of elephants bathing in rivers, or browsing on the edge of forests — spraying water on themselves, blowing sand onto their bodies, and digging for salt. My favourite pastime is watching the little ones sinking below the surface and seeing their tiny trunks snorkeling up above the water to breathe.

"From our vantage point, we also get a real sense of how gargantuan some forest trees are by the way they dwarf elephants standing beneath them. Puku antelopes — about the size of an impala and also sandy brown — are so tame you can almost touch them.[25] Because it's the dry season, we see females in groups of about twenty, with their stag. In the rainy season, they will often merge into larger groups of up to fifty, for added safety in the confining undergrowth. Intoxicating is the only word to describe the privilege of such trust and proximity."

《•》《•》《•》《•》

there were times when we smiled
there were times when we frowned

there were times when we heard lions roar
a few feet from the edge of our bed,
while zebra, spooked by the moon,
thundered around us in herds
and elephants crashed through the thickets

---

25   This changes once the railway along the edge of the escarpment brings human contact and fear.

> there were times when the din of the crickets
> drowned out your gentlest of sighs
> there were times when the night bathed our love in white light,
> there were times when we sang out of tune
> and times when we cried

but my love, it was always with you

《•》《•》《•》《•》

"Vicky does have one affliction," Geoff later tells friends. "She doesn't seem to be able to walk and think at the same time; so, very quickly after setting off each day, she will be a good 100 metres behind, and remain at this distance, which I consider very unsociable."

"I do walk at a slightly slower pace," Vicky agrees, mock-punching Geoff. "Except when going up hills."

"She had to get that in, didn't she?" Geoff expertly evades her fists from obvious experience. "Actually, Vicky is right. She, who trails after us during our day marches, when we return to face the exhausting climb up the 2,000 foot escarpment at the end of our safaris, will always scamper up like a rabbit and be at the top a good half hour before I arrive, usually with the comment, 'What kept you?'"

"The longer I'm here, the more I like it here, and it seems to be the case with everyone else who lives in Mufindi," Geoff writes home. "Although elsewhere in Tanganyika, we hear of people still leaving."

BABY CHRISTOPHER— WAS IT SOMETHING YOU ATE?

"Would you rather have a boy or a girl?" Vicky wants to know.

"A boy would be good to carry on the name," Geoff answers. "But I also fancy a dutiful daughter, who will spoil her old man incredibly, bring him his slippers and drinks, and generally adore him."

Tough and optimistic as Geoff and Vicky are, they do have some misgivings, confided in a letter from Vicky to Libby. "The hospital is eighty-five miles away. What happens if it pops out too soon? Geoff dreamt he had to act as midwife in the car and, as people stopped, he nonchalantly cried out that all was under control, even the tummy button. One mother-to-be from Mufindi made it to the hospital with fifteen minutes to spare. At least we've got an estate car.

"How we shall feed and clothe the baby I can't imagine, as Iringa, the largest town for eighty-five miles, has absolutely nothing for babies and toddlers. After that, you go miles and miles to Dar es Salaam (400 miles) before you find anything as big as Tavistock. Still there are hundreds of experienced mums around, so it can be done."

Low-lying clouds of May and June, with what Vicky terms "moorland drizzle" gradually give way to the cold, dry season, perfect for weekend getaways. "Nick and Geoff and I are almost inseparable," she writes to Libby in August 1963, "partly because Nick is a close neighbour (by Mufindi standards) and also because he is such an all-round prince of a man."

September 1963, Vicky to Libby: "We now have lived two days through a terrible tragedy. Nick was drowned in a large lake near Mufindi whilst sailing with a friend at Ngwazi. He must have got cramp when he tried to swim ashore. It was an awful thing to happen to such a generous and nice person. I don't think he had a single enemy. He was given a wonderful funeral in our tiny stone church but what a waste, to die so young. His poor mother lost her husband only last year. It does seem so unfair. We miss him a great deal."

"We miss him very much," Geoff echoes in a letter to his parents, "as he was a very close friend of mine, and we were accustomed to him popping in to see us almost every day whilst he was living close by. Hundreds of Mufindi Africans expressed genuine sympathy for us in losing a friend, and there was a large number of them at his funeral. His mother was very touched to hear this."

Somehow it seems fitting to honour Nick by setting free the tiny suni antelope, even smaller than a dik-dik and equally shy, which had been found in a trap and nursed back to health.

"It all feels so sad and empty," Vicky says a few days later. Geoff is withdrawn. *Stiff upper lip grieving*, Vicky thinks to herself. "I wish there was something else we could do, Geoff. Why don't we go to the park as planned next long weekend?"

"Good idea," says Geoff. "How better to celebrate Nick's life than in the African bush he so loved." They decide to drive nearly 200 miles to camp on the banks of a river in the Rungwa Game Reserve.

"Vicky and I don't seem to have much spare time of our own these days," Geoff writes home. "But the pace is beginning to slow down as she gets fatter."

"We will spend Friday night and Saturday in the Rungwa Game Reserve," a heavily pregnant Vicky writes to Libby, "and then travel back on Sunday evening—400 miles of bumpy mud tracks. I hope poor cupid [baby] will survive the trip." He does.

"We spent a long weekend on the banks of the Great Ruaha River," Geoff reports home after the trip, "and saw and heard the 'lot': lion, elephant, leopard, giraffe, waterbuck, hyena, and so on. The lion and the leopard came to within thirty yards of our camp at night. Also impala and baboon were extremely numerous. We spent the w/e fishing for tiger fish in the river and lazing on the banks watching the game come down to drink. The weekend resulted in eighteen punctures."

Back home again, they slowly adjust to Mufindi without Nick. But after this stark reminder of how quickly things can change, absences from Geoff, however short, begin to weigh on Vicky.

"This is payday," she confides in Libby, "which I hate because Geoff leaves from seven a.m. to seven-eight at night." And then later that same evening, clearly comforted: "Geoff brought home two baby nightjars![26] I'm trying to feed them on hard-boiled eggs and insects, if I can catch them, but they're so ferocious I can't even put my hand in the box."

《•》《•》《•》《•》

"On January second, as all babies seem to," Vicky soon reports to Libby, "the baby starts to arrive at eleven o'clock at night; most inconvenient of him."

"Having babies is tough," Geoff adds. "I'm convinced it is a world-wide conspiracy that women deliberately wake up their hard-working husbands in the middle of the night with the command:

"'Time to go!'

"'Are you sure?'

"'Yes.'

"'Can't you wait till morning?'

---

26 Nocturnal birds that settle on sun-warmed earth after sunset, earth roads being a favourite. They are typically caught in car headlights at night, seemingly shooting up from right under the wheels at the last minute, only to settle back down and repeat the exercise over and over.

"'No.' And, as a last resort:

"'Perhaps it's something you ate?'

"We had almost a hundred-mile journey from Lulanji over the most ghastly road imaginable," Vicky continues. "Geoff was armed with scissors and string and almost had to use them."

"Just short of Iringa, Vicky decided to wait—for ages!" It's Geoff again. "She announced that it might have been a false alarm after all, and there we sat for an hour, in a nearby gravel pit."

"Was it a gravel pit? I didn't really notice! By the time we arrived in Iringa, the pains were two or three minutes apart. After all that, he didn't arrive till noon the next day. Apparently the membranes had ruptured or something, which made it slower.

"His name: Christopher Anthony, Born: 3rd January 1964; Time: 11:55 noon," Vicky jubilantly informs friends and family: "Weight: 6 pounds 8.5 ounces; description: gorgeous, tall, bald, and handsome. Christopher arrived early, just as I said he would, and is naturally the best baby in the world . . . None of the nurses speak English and they really are so sweet to us both. Everything is much less stiff and starchy than in England. I have a room of my own, but it's so hot I'm nearly passing out. There are no outside windows. Christopher Anthony doesn't seem to mind at all. He arrived with a yell and a sneeze, absolutely icy cold."

"When Christopher was born, I got into trouble," Geoff tells friends. "And that after slipping away to a hotel to have breakfast and, very thoughtfully, shopping for a box of chocolates for Vicky. On my return to the hospital, there, standing threateningly at the top of the stairs, arms folded, was the hospital's large Zulu matron.

"'Where were you?' she demanded. I nervously pointed to myself.

"'Me?'

"'Yes. You! Where was the father when your son was born?' with which she strode off and reappeared with Christopher.

"'There! That's yours!'

Vicky: "Interestingly, Hannah Meuschke [daughter of Dr. Meuschke, in whose Kinoga house Geoff lived during his first three years in Mufindi] was one of the midwives. She looked in and was shocked that my first meal was a bit of cheese, spread with jam. I found it delicious."

《•》《•》《•》《•》

"His dad absolutely adored him at once," Vicky's birth announcement continues, "and it's so funny to see Christopher's tiny little form in Geoff's vast hands."

On his way back to Mufindi, Geoff gives a lift to an English hitch-hiker who is forced to listen to the trials and tribulations of a proud father. "I didn't stop talking until John's Corner, where he got off," he tells anyone who will listen.

Having been told by Dr. Ian Clarke to collect Vicky the next day and take her away "before she catches something in hospital," Geoff rushes back as ordered. Unfortunately, he has to repair nineteen punctures between Mufindi and Iringa—nineteen! Very quickly he runs out of hot patches and resorts to sticky Elastoplast strips. Each repair involves pumping up the tire, then racing as far as he can before the tire deflates again. *If this had happened yesterday*, he thinks, *Christopher's arrival would have been much more interesting!*

Geoff, Vicky, and baby Christopher return to their new home in Kivere. Whereas Geoff remained on one estate, Matugutu, throughout his first three years in Tanganyika, he and Vicky will move house a total of thirteen times during their first three years together, with Geoff filling in as acting manager now here and now there. This will in no way dampen their enjoyment of life in Mufindi. Quite the contrary, each move will bring its own excitement and opportunities for exploring another corner of their new environment.

Kivere is an exquisite case in point, with its lovely forest estate and one-bedroom Lulanji House. Vicky, with Christopher snugly strapped to her back, and Geoff revel in long, exploratory treks down the Kigogo River.

March 21, 1964, Vicky to Gelly and Jimmy: "We have been quite active during the last few weeks. I strapped Christopher on my back African style and we went on a six-mile walk down the Kigogo River. It was quite eventful, as I fell into the river twice and once down a hole, landing with only my head above ground. Christopher opened one astonished eye on each occasion and promptly slept again without a murmur. Then Geoff and I were crossing a rickety bridge when the main log broke. Geoff landed flat on his back in the river and I managed somehow to straddle the rest of the bridge, only getting wet up to my knees. Lastly, to shelter C. from the rain, I was holding a raincoat over us both whilst we walked through the undergrowth, which reached my middle. This was no mean feat and I walked straight over the edge of the bank and into the river. We all arrived home exhausted and wet through."

By now, Vicky and Geoff can distinguish one indigenous tree from another in the various Mufindi forests: the chestnut look-alike, winged bersama (*Bersama Abyssinica*), with its white, candle-straight blossoms (later turning into holly-red berries); the vibrant mauve of blossoming *Milletia Oblata*; the distinctive quinine trees (*Rauvolvia caffra*) stretching up to thirty metres into the skies, with massive, rounded crowns and sweetly scented blossoms, from May to October morphing into clusters of fruit as green as limes in their prime and as round as golf balls. And, of course, there's the unfortunately labelled red stinkwood trees (or, more palatably, *Prunus Africana*).

("Look," Geoff says the first time. "Here's an old giant." Vicky runs her hands over desiccated sandpaper bark, crinkled with age into squares of browns on black, and peeling to reveal huge, red gashes beneath.

"No wonder it's called a 'red' tree," Vicky says. "But why 'stinkwood'?"

"Take a deep breath.")

But nothing can compare with the delicate *Albizia gummifera*, whose canopy arches intricately above slim, light stems, its blossoms a dazzling white in the late dry season, its young leaves burning red in

Vicky with Christopher at their Lulanji dam
(built out of their own pocket with just one wheelbarrow!).

71

spring. (No wonder both Geoff and son Christopher in years to come will choose the *Albizia* as their flagship tree—with Geoff transplanting it around his designated final resting place behind his "modest English manor house in Africa," and Christopher throughout his proposed retirement property a few miles farther into the Mufindi forest.)

OF BLOODSHED AND SOVEREIGNTY

Sightless eyes stare at her from what remains of her husband. Flies are just beginning to feast. Red seeps into his prayer cap. His *kanzu* robe spreads incongruously white against interlocking tiles of cobalt and ochre, now pooling with scarlet.

Outside, she can hear the sound of running feet. Shouts of panic. Screams. Uncertain, she holds her toddler ever closer; instinctively hides him under her black *bui-bui*, as though its diaphanous folds might protect him from the revolutionaries.

"They'll be back any minute. Flee! Flee!" she hears her neighbours shout and, undecided as she is, joins the flood of black-and-white-robed humanity pressing through narrow, cobblestone streets . . . old, young, crippled, some carried, some hobbling, some falling down in exhaustion. All of them Arab.

Once out there, her only choice is to try and stay on her feet as the terrified mob surges past the magnificently carved doors and lintels of historic Stone Town in Zanzibar, their inscriptions from the Holy Quran marking the Arab quarter.

"Allahu Akbar!" she intones, with each desperate breath clutching her child closer. At last, the crowd spills beyond the maze of buildings and onto the beach. Her momentary release from the pressure of too many bodies in narrow streets shatters. A wave threatens to break over her child's head. The same ocean, visited so often on clove-and-salt-scented family walks, now a deadly trap. Out of nowhere, large shadows. Screams. The glint from reflected gunfire on a massive blade. A final, anguished, "Allahu Akbar!" as she falls onto others butchered before her.

《·》《·》《·》《·》

Vicky and Geoff listen in disbelief to the latest BBC radio news bulle-tin. A clipped, disembodied voice dispassionately transmits in the Queen's English horrific images of beaches on the nearby island of Zanzibar drenched with the remains of Arab men, women, and chil-dren; of bullets and bush knives wielded by irate young revolutionaries spurred on by John Okello; of victims ranging in reported numbers from a few hundred to twenty thousand mowed down in cold blood. (Numbers ultimately settle at about 200 military-related deaths during the coup that overthrew the sultan on the night of January 12, 1964 — a national holiday thereafter celebrated in Zanzibar — and about 4,000 civilian deaths in the bloodbath that followed.)

At issue is pent-up resentment arising from two centuries of domination by the Arab minority through the sultan of Zanzibar, beginning when Zanzibar was still an Omani territory, continuing under British colonialism, fuelled by cold-war politics, and persisting post-independence even after the African-dominated political coali-tion won 54 percent of the 1963 election votes.

Like other residents of Tanganyika, Geoff and Vicky can barely grasp that such brutality would yet again engulf a close neighbour of theirs, Kenya having just recently emerged from its own Mau Mau atrocities (committed by both Africans and Europeans). Their only consolation is Mwalimu's consistent call for a bloodless path beyond independence. Little do they know it, but events are about to shake Tanganyika to its core.

《·》《·》《·》《·》

A week later, their German friend Helga drives to Dar es Salaam, with children Peter and Evelyn, to pick up youngest daughter Veronika from school friends and do an annual round of dentists and shopping.

That same night, unbeknownst to them, some African members of the Colito barracks mutiny. They belong to the King's African Rifles, a single regiment and Tanganyika's only army. At issue is the discrepancy between benefits enjoyed by British and African military personnel, as well as Britain's continuing military domination over independent Tanganyika.

Early the next morning, their hostess, who is linked into the polit-ical scene, says: "I can't tell you why, Helga, but you should get out of town right away. And, when you reach Mufindi, be sure to contact Brooke Bond immediately to ask for further guidance."

Desperate pleas for "just a short swim, Mum, pleeeaaase" fall on deaf ears and, leaving the tempting ocean behind, the Voigts drive the some 400 miles or so back to Mufindi. Brooke Bond Tea Company employees have been instructed to congregate at headquarters and await further word. Since they are not employees, the Voigts carry on to their farm. There, a crackling radio, their only link to the outside, spews ominous speculations on the fate of Tanganyika. Fortunately for them, the president of Tanganyika, while sympathetic to the mutineers' demands, won't tolerate mutiny. With help from Britain, he quells the uprising in short order before disbanding the King's African Rifles in favour of a new People's Defence Force. And, within a year, Tanganyika and Zanzibar (both buffeted by Cold War pressures from abroad) will merge to form the United Republic of Tanzania.

DYSENTERY

"Dear Libby, life is more hectic than usual," Vicky writes a few months after the foiled mutiny. This time, she is referring to personal rather than political upheavals—literally. "First I got dysentery. Then three weeks later, just when I'd recovered, baby Christopher caught it. He brought up everything. I washed twenty-four nappies a day, and fed him every one and half hours at first. Then more often. He simply lay there listlessly—too weak to even muster a smile. His face was almost transparent, it was so white, and his eyes were sunk deep into his head, with grey shadows around them."

Still not fully recovered from her own bout with dysentery, exhausted and weakened by fear for her son's life, Vicky has a relapse, "leaving poor Geoff to feed Christopher day and night for twenty-four hours AND change his nappies. We're still not out of the woods yet."

Finally, after almost a fortnight of terror, Christopher recovers—with a vengeance! "Christopher is now fighting fit again and crawls everywhere," Vicky reports jubilantly to Libby. "So nothing is safe—I just found the cat's milk overturned, stirred into the carpet with Geoff's keys, under a mound of sugar (removed from its polythene bag and cardboard container, which was positioned neatly upside down to cover the mess). Ugh. Geoff is convinced that HE has produced a genius. (I, of course, had nothing to do with it!!).ˮ

"Christopher is most adorable," Geoff concurs in a letter to his parents, "hardly ever cries and has almost a permanent smile. Everyone remarks on his strength and size. In fact his only disadvantage is that he still leaks!"

《·》《·》《·》《·》

March 13, 1964: Mwalimu makes it onto the cover of *Time* magazine—as a tribute to his leadership, his vision, and his growing international reputation. Also in 1964, Mwalimu demonstrates his prodigious powers of negotiation with the bloodless merger of Tanganyika and Zanzibar to form the United Republic of Tanzania.

《·》《·》《·》《·》

Life for the Foxes finally settles back into their now-familiar routine of work and baby, punctuated by long walks through bush and weekends away (these days, more often than not, to escape endless Mufindi scandals).

"A lot of wives are taking advantage of the bachelors," says Geoff.

"More the other way around," Vicky corrects him, "although the wives do seem quite happy to oblige!"

"Your honour," Geoff throws in smugly, "I refer you to the party at which one husband was reduced to saying, 'Wife. Put that man down!' Also to the government forest officer—"

"Which one?"

"The one who plays the accordion beautifully for Scottish dancing, at the same time drinking copious quantities of whisky, inevitably sliding slowly to the floor, where he continues playing without error. It turns out that his inebriated condition has enabled a young bachelor to climb through their bedroom window.

"Not to mention the bachelor caught in Nairobi with the doctor's wife, after requesting a weekend off. Imagine driving the better part of a thousand miles on unpaved roads for their naughty weekend in Nairobi. Too bad someone from Kericho [Brooke Bond's sister tea fields in Kenya] recognized him. That's rather shortened his career."

Scotty's Camp

Ruaha, which remains a favourite weekend getaway for Mufindi expatriates, becomes a fully-fledged Ruaha National Park in 1964. Its first park warden, "Steve" Stephenson, is followed by John Savidge in 1966. At his request, Geoff recommends his best trackers, Nati and Mastano, for the ranger force Savidge is setting up, with the condition that Geoff can use them whenever he and Vicky go on a safari—which Savidge will honour.[27]

《·》《·》《·》《·》

Both Savidge and Stephenson allow an old character named Scotty to live out his days on his small patch of land within park boundaries. As Geoff will recall in later years, "When Vicky was quite pregnant with Christopher, we stayed in one of Scotty's little *rondavels* (initially a Boer version of round African huts) built beside the Ruaha River, close to the new ferry. His wife, Muriel, who made a delicious fishcake meal out of the tiger fish we caught from the ferry pontoon, later 'escaped'—she hated being there—and was never to be seen again.

"Earlier, as a gold digger at the Lupa, Scotty decided there was more money to be made by providing game meat to feed other gold diggers. As with most prospectors, he always maintained that he knew where he could make himself rich—but this was never to be. Around the fire at night, he regaled us with fascinating stories.

"One was of Bert Lock, who, at the time, had extracted Lupa's largest gold nugget. Bert and his companions drove to Mbeya to celebrate and, at some stage, drunkenly engaged in a game of football around the Railway Hotel bar, using the precious nugget. Next morning, wondering where it had gone, someone remembered the kick through an open window; and there, in the flower bed, it still was! Bert later lived out his life on a smallholding near the Phillips's farm at Kabebe, Iringa.

"Together with a partner, Murray (I believe he was a teacher at St. Michael's and St. George's School in Iringa), Scotty later went into timber logging and sawing within the then Rungwa game reserve. They cut *mninga* logs from *miombo* woodlands and established a sawmill

---

27   John Savidge and his wife, Yvonne, were previously in Uganda (Murchisan Falls National Park). They now live in Devon, where they and the Foxes occasionally meet.

on the banks of the Ruaha River opposite Msembe. Scotty's partner returned to the UK and the sawmill closed down when Scotty decided to make a living at crocodile hunting (poaching, actually) in Ruaha. This became impossible after plans were being made to create a national park from part of Rungwa Reserve. So Scotty tried his luck with 'tourism'—building a number of small *rondavels* beside the river. John Savidge let him stay until the end of his days (when he shot himself during a long period of illness). He is buried in the Iringa cemetery, along with many historic others (including some German soldiers from Von Lettow Vorbeck's army and Tom von Prince's infant son)."

BREECH BABY PETER

"It's nearly your wedding day," Vicky writes to Libby in April 1965. "How I wish I were going to be there. I hope you're as happy as Geoff and I. We've had such a super married life, with no major worries," although she does then add one: "but we do always seem to be broke despite a very good salary. Actually, Geoff and I just had a lovely surprise. Yesterday we got an extra year's increment of £120 (just under $400) tacked onto our salary, because they decided that, as Geoff was the only married assistant, he ought to have a little extra. This means we can pay for our next baby (due late July). I plan to have four children, anyway. ("Did I write that?" Vicky giggles many years later. "How amazing. We didn't exactly plan them all.")

"We're selling our poor, bashed Anglia to buy a mini moke as a knock-around car," another letter informs Libby. "The company provides half the cash. The sale of our Anglia buys the rest." Then, later: "We may be going up to Nairobi in June, as the chairman has suggested that Geoff go up as the Mufindi representative to the main East African estates, at a place called Kericho. I'm planning to go, too. The snag is that the doctor might say no, so near to producing, but I shan't say anything to him unless asked."

And so the letters to Libby continue . . . "I've just had the nice news that this baby is in breech position (upside down). If it doesn't turn round by this time next month, they'll have to try and turn it. If they can't, I'll probably have to go to the Nairobi hospital to have the dear creature, which will cost about £100 (about $300), even if it's straightforward . . . All our plans are going awry now. We aren't allowed to get a mini moke vehicle. The company won't pay the grant for such a cheap car . . . I suppose we'll have to hang on to the Anglia until it falls apart at the seams."

On August 2, 1965, Geoff and Vicky's second son, Peter, is born. Peter, who will grow into an extraordinarily handsome and debonair young man, over whom girls will regularly swoon, has a less than auspicious start. "Number two finally made it a week late, on the second of August," Vicky writes home. "It is a boy and just as gorgeous as Christopher. Well, actually, he's a really ugly creature and Geoff says is just like a pig—but at least he's not red and wrinkled. He has lots of dark hair and long fingers. He weighed six pounds, fourteen ounces.

"We call him Peter James, known by Peter. Peter is so good and NEVER cries. I only fed him for the first time twenty hours after he was born and even then he wasn't crying. Not like Christopher, who wanted food from birth every three to five hours without fail. I feel very clever as I managed to produce him the day after Geoff's sailing race, which he won, and in time for Geoff to shoot an elephant to pay the hospital bill the following weekend!"

"Our first home leave to England starts on August 15, 1966, for six months. It's hard to imagine, but our first three-year tour is almost up. Still, before going to England, we may canoe down the River Ruaha, leaving both children with friends. In that way, we should see a great deal of the country unseen by most Europeans. Who knows—we may canoe into an elephant; or be eaten by crocs and hippos!!"

《•》《•》《•》《•》

As anyone can attest, multi-party elections are expensive. So expensive, according to Tanzania's leaders in 1965, that they opt for a "one-party democracy" under the Tanzanian African National Union. Up to now, TANU has enjoyed de facto single-party status because there were no other parties. Henceforth, it will officially be the only party, with voters choosing individual candidates.

Tanzania's first-ever elections come and go relatively smoothly, though somewhat marred by international aspersions cast on the validity of the concept—despite a range of sympathetic academic endorsement. (The second election, five years later, will, according to researcher Helge Kjekshus in 1972, result in a significant turnover of candidates [perceived to have underperformed in their first term], lending one-party democracy some credence—especially when even later compared, for example, with Milton Obote's puppet opposition in neighbouring Uganda's supposed multi-party democracy. Ultimately, however, Tanzania will opt for multi-partyism. But, back now to 1966 . . .)

《•》《•》《•》《•》

Two months after Peter is born, Geoff goes after elephant again, only this time it is for three weeks. A rather wistful Vicky stays behind. "I'm staying with friends, as Geoff is trying to make us solvent again," she writes. "But, seriously, I hope that he manages to shoot game during the three weeks he's there. Then I'll feel the separation is worthwhile. I hate it, even for such a short while."

Meanwhile, Colin Congdon has dropped Geoff off at Mfrika, his porters and their loads once more having preceded him by bus. The safari begins, as ever, with a descent down the escarpment, before cutting eastward for three days through bush to elephant country. They shoot their first elephant almost immediately after crossing the Ruhudji River by dugout canoe. The second, with tusks weighing sixty pounds, is downed farther east, near the Pitu River. Only then does Geoff realize that there aren't enough porters to carry his four tusks home.

Folks from a tiny village come to the rescue by telling him about a German geologist a day's march away, with a lorry, and near a track. Calling a halt, Geoff sends notes backwards and forwards to the geologist on a forked stick. ("I thought the old fashioned stick system, which was used before messengers had pockets, would appeal to him.") The geologist agrees to take the tusks home to Iringa. (His wife later furtively reveals the tusks to Vicky, carefully hidden under a bed, because they thought that Geoff had poached them!)

Meanwhile, having filled his quota of licenced elephants, Geoff heads back toward Mufindi over the Ruhudji River, again by dugout. He then cuts across, just following elephant tracks to the Mnyera River (which starts as the Kigogo River in Mufindi, becomes the

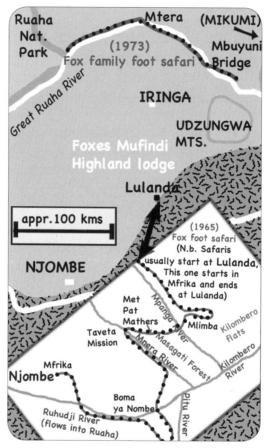

Map of Fox foot safaris highlighted in text.
(Evelyn, based on Geoff's information)

Ruaha River below the escarpment—where the paper mill now is—meanders farther to join the Ruhudji River at Mpanga, and flows on as the Kilombero River before meeting the Great Ruaha River).

"The Mnyera River was idyllic," Geoff later tells Vicky. "We followed it upstream, swam and fished in rocky pools, with riverine forests on either side; and on one occasion came across a big herd of elephants in the forest and on the river. It was a joy just to sit and watch them. Some were feeding under the trees, others bathing in the river or digging for minerals in the bank."

《•》《•》《•》《•》

I hear wood pigeons
blessing the silence of morning;
Mourning doves murmuring songs of wonder;
Cicada's taunting, seasoned song
from hidden lair, blending into warrior beat
and mountain air, into sun-dried heat, and glare
sun-scorched, sun-dipped, sun-baked plain
driving sheets of forest rain splattering,
mist-cloaked mountain range
elephant, insect, bird, gazelle—thudding, drumming,
whirring, running, distance-melting hoof, pug, humming
siren song

《•》《•》《•》《•》

Geoff eventually reaches Taveta Mission, in Lupembe, and, cross-ing over the Mnyera River, he travels through the Masagati forest to rendezvous with his friend from Mufindi, Pat Mathers, precisely as arranged. Quite amazing, given that they are in the middle of nowhere.

Pat and Geoff then carry on toward Kilombero, where they come across tracks of a huge elephant, which they sight briefly before follow-ing its trail deep into the floodplain. There they lose it and cannot get back to camp before nightfall. Instead, returning to Mlimba, a tiny village passed earlier in the day, they sleep in the headman's kitchen. Thereafter, back to Mufindi, ending up at Lulanda, where Vicky is waiting with a car.

"On another occasion," Geoff laughs, "when Vicky and I went on a shorter foot safari, Jonny Niblett met us. He saw us coming up the escarpment with sizeable, gleaming, ivory tusks only to find that Vicky had forgotten the money. 'Don't worry,' my head porter said. 'All women are like this. You can pay us later.'"

"Mission accomplished!" Vicky reports to Libby. "Three weeks of primeval bliss and solvency, just in time for our first home leave—with two babies to show off to doting grandparents, all four of whom still conveniently live all but next door to each other."

AFRICA UP CLOSE

Ian Smith, temporarily broken in body but not in spirit as a decorated flying ace in World War II, was born, bred, and lettered in Rhodesia. Returning to pursue farming and politics, he watched with increasing dismay as Britain granted independence to neighbouring countries. On November 11, 1965, his administration signs a Unilateral Declaration of Independence (UDI) from Britain, rather than accept black majority rule in "his" self-governing British colony.

Aftershocks buffet neighbouring countries, but particularly landlocked Zambia: newly independent, economically fragile, and used to transporting its key export, copper, by rail through Zimbabwe to ports in Mozambique. Despite Tanzania's own economic and political balancing of self-identity and survival in a world pummelled by Cold War interests, or perhaps because of them, Mwalimu steps into the breach.

Together, Mwalimu and President Kaunda of Zambia explore alternative routes and ultimately opt to link Zambia to Tanzania's harbour in Dar es Salaam by rail (pending overseas investment). Kaunda, who fears communism, approaches Britain. Nyerere, less concerned, talks with China as well as Britain and Germany.

To predictable criticism by the West, he counters that Tanzania does not have to be communist to appreciate what China has to offer in terms of development co-operation.

Mwalimu's and Kaunda's debates, fuelled by both Cold War camps, will ultimately coalesce into African Socialism and the Non-alignment Movement— an approach Mwalimu sees as being friends, rather than quarrelling with one-half of the world to curry security with the other half. To him, both democracy and socialism are mindsets, rather than rigid political edicts, long since integral to African society's way of caring for one another's welfare.

Within a year, Kaunda has a favourable aerial survey jointly undertaken by Britain and Canada (Canada's prime minister, Pierre Elliott Trudeau, being a great admirer of Nyerere's), and Mwalimu reports a serious Chinese indication of interest to fund the railway. Westerners bristle, but not enough to counteroffer.

《•》《•》《•》《•》

In the meantime, the Foxes return from home leave in England to their new home on Lugoda Estate and dramatically changed demographics—many married expatriate couples, with growing children. They ask Vicky to start a school.

Vicky's students range from three years to eight. At first only from Mufindi, they are later joined on Fridays by children from the Norwegian Saw Mill Project at Mafinga. ("For the best subjects," in Vicky's view: "English, riding, music, and nature lessons. They have fun and it's also broadening for our children to know children from another culture.") And so it is that life settles into a busy routine of work, children, school, club, and—of course—every year, for eleven or twelve years in succession, they use up most of their three weeks of local leave by going on wonderful walking *safaris*. Often, they cross deep rivers by dugout canoe from tiny, riverside settlements. Elsewhere, slung vine "ropes" prevent them from being washed downstream in raging torrents. Sometimes they simply wade.

"When paddled or poled by owners, usually standing, dugouts seemed stable enough." Geoff and Vicky are sharing safari stories with visiting relatives, after one such adventure. "I decided to demonstrate my prowess. Confidently, I pushed off from the Ruhudji River bank and promptly overturned. That was my last solo dugout excursion."

"Elephants, buffalo, everything is somehow more interesting, more exciting, on foot," he adds. "You see each in its own habitat, under its own conditions, and somehow see yourself become part of nature."

Vicky agrees. "You look down and there are the bushbucks in the valley, the plants, the foxgloves, lilies, birds, insects, all the little things that you don't see from moving vehicles—once even genet kittens in a hollow tree trunk—"

"Which Vicky picked up, cuddled, and put back again. We fish. We hunt. They are just good fun days."

"And, at the same time, we experience the companionship of our porters, whom we always engage from the same village and grow to know very well—their beliefs, their fears, their skills. Don't we, Foxey?"

"That we do. On foot safaris, you have the feeling that you are with friends, that you are all Tanzanians together. We never take tents, just mosquito nets. At night we sit together under the stars. Once, the guys with me pointed upward: 'See that star moving through the sky?' they asked. 'We will see that again twice in the night.' The 'star' was Sputnik. And on July 20, 1969, when we looked up from camp together, nobody believed us that an American was standing on the moon.

"We never knew what we might stumble on next. Once we camped close to the Ruaha River at Kidatu. The next morning before breakfast we climbed the hill above and there found either a World War I German observation or heliograph post (which sent messages using light on mirrors)."

Because Geoff and Vicky always use porters from the same village, their walking holidays invariably start with someone dropping them off at the top of the escarpment, followed by a steep, 600-metre clamber down to the Great Rift Valley below. From there, they wander out in different directions for as long as their leave permits ("Never long enough!" they both agree. "Although, of course, once the children come and are left in the care of kind friends, there would always be mixed feelings.")

"Vicky, as with everything she does, is a professional camper," Geoff tells friends on another occasion. "Meals are perfect, and any game shot expertly cooked or stored as *biltong*. One night, we strung up a 'clothesline' adorned with strips of vinegar- and brine-soaked *biltong*. Next morning, it had disappeared. A hyena evidently visited us during the night because not only the *biltong*, but even the line, was gone. That was a stupid error never to be repeated.

"Speaking of food, Vicky can now expertly gauge the right balance between having enough provisions to last us through huge tracts of bush without stores, and not weighing ourselves down unnecessarily.

"For a three-week safari, we need about twelve porters just to carry their own food, let alone others to carry ours," Vicky interjects. "We usually set off fully loaded. Then, as they eat into their supplies, head loads get mercifully lighter and lighter, until even the porters have nothing to carry."

"Then there are the trackers," Geoff continues. "Mastano, who still lives nearby at Lulanda, was our main tracker, but Nati joined us as well for many safaris. They were fearless, skilled, and enthusiastic, so we finally employed them at Lugoda."

Geoff hunted in a period when elephants were exceptionally numerous and needed to be culled by the Game Department to protect the villagers' staple food, maize. Never a "headhunter" (collecting trophies), he shot animals only for meat. His hope that "the big one" (an elephant with a 100-pound tusk on each side) might be over the next hill never materialized, but smaller tuskers enabled him to meet expenses.

《•》《•》《•》《•》

By now, Mwalimu's European allies are second-guessing him on many fronts: his ties with China; the tightrope he is walking between links with West Germany and East Germany regarding Zanzibar; the push and pull of his relationship as an independent country with erstwhile colonial Britain; and his struggle for recognition of African Socialism as a third party neutral between the Cold War superpowers.

Yet, like the vast majority of Tanzanians, they admire, in some cases revere, Mwalimu himself. (Evelyn Voigt remembers her own dyed-in-the-wool settler parents questioning some of Mwalimu's "newfangled" and "leftist" decisions, but never his integrity or his charisma. "He shook my hand," Helga will say reverently for the rest of her life. "There I was, just an expatriate farmer's wife on the periphery of an Independence celebration, and he shook my hand; made me feel a part of the country I loved.")

Such admiration does not shore up Tanzania's faltering economy, with its dual burden of growing foreign debt and decreasing commodity prices—a lethal combination for a country dependent on exporting a limited number of raw materials and importing virtually all its manufactured goods. Equally corrosive, from Mwalimu's perspective, is his countrymen's growing impatience with the slow pace of development and, even worse, signs of an emerging new class (the "Wabenzis"—those rich enough to own a Mercedes Benz), which threatens to undermine his vision of an Africa based on the traditional concept of *ujamaa*/familyhood (whereby the individual's sense of self and the welfare of the community are synonymous). For him, socialism is about fair returns for individual effort. Somewhat lost in this formula of redistribution is the need for capital generation.

University students test his mettle in 1966 by protesting two years of compulsory national service in rural areas. Mwalimu closes the university for five months. He also reduces all senior government salaries by 20 percent, starting with his own. Tanzania becomes for many years an example of relative integrity in the face of massive corruption elsewhere; sadly, no longer.

Geoff Renounces Hunting

On one safari, Geoff and Vicky cross the Mpanga River by dugout canoe, just below a bridge built many years earlier by Otto Frick at a place called Irangi. In the middle of the bush, their walking safari, including porters carrying a couple of elephant tusks, comes across a camp. No telling who is more surprised: the European sitting outside his tent, or the Foxes.

"Good afternoon," says Geoff. "Geoffrey Fox, and my wife, Vicky."

"Wonk Richards," he replies. "Would you like a cup of tea?"

"That would be lovely," Vicky answers. ("All very civilized, and very British," she giggles later.)

Wonk, it turns out, lives in Dabaga and has been engaged to survey a railway far down the Mpanga River. As he will remark to mutual friends, "I met an extraordinary couple the other day. They just came into my camp carrying gleaming ivory tusks, had a cup of tea, then simply walked on."

The next day, on top of a hill, before them an amazing sight: elephants, a herd of buffalo, even a sable antelope, peacefully grazing around a lovely small lake. "All this, without having to take another step," Vicky murmurs.

Geoff is keeping his eye on a lone bull buffalo, when — out of nowhere — rifle shots! The elephants scatter. Within seconds, their idyllic scene empties. Extremely annoyed, Vicky, their trackers (Nati and Mastano[28]), and Geoff race down the hill to the valley bottom ("where I fell flat on my face in mud," he later recalls). They then follow a side valley from where they heard the gunshots and emerge into an open clearing. Before them is an elephant. A couple of poachers are standing over it, with their muzzleloader.

Farther on, a second elephant is slowly dragging itself away. It is covered in suppurating wounds, about eight on each side, shot but not dispatched. "Poor thing," Vicky later tells friends. "Geoff was so angry, he did a sort of 'stick them up' in Swahili. The hunters stopped. Then they took off, racing up hill."

"I fired in front of the leader, which must have given him a big fright, since he fell flat on his face," Geoff adds, his expression grim. "His companion thought he'd been shot, and put his hands up, so we caught these two poachers and used them as porters for the rest of our safari. But I still had to put down the wounded elephant. It took a while.

"The sad carcass was in fact also riddled with muzzleloader wounds, some from the hunters we had captured, and some from previous hunters. In fact, our captives were just meat hunters from the villages, but we were so annoyed, we made them carry the loads to the top of the escarpment."

"This meant our guys had little to carry. They were very pleased, weren't they, Geoff?"

"They were, indeed. At the top, we just let the poachers go. We felt they'd had their punishment. It's not usually the man in the bush who's at fault but rather the man who wants the illegal tusks (in contrast to those who hunt legally, under licences issued in accordance with wildlife regulations)."

"Geoff was so upset by the whole scene, seeing the wounded animals and having the peace and tranquility of that idyllic African

---

28   Still living in Lulanda Village.

scene split apart by shots, that he said he would never want to shoot animals again. That was our last hunting safari."

ARUSHA DECLARATION

On February 5, 1967, Mwalimu's vision of *Ujamaa* finds national expression in the "Arusha Declaration."

"The policy of TANU is to build a socialist state," the radio broadcasts. From now on, it turns out, Tanzania is committed to socialist nation building, and, wherever possible, direct government participation in economic development with equal opportunity to all men and women irrespective of race, religion, or status, with effective control over the principal means of production and policies that facilitate collective ownership of national resources.

《•》《•》《•》《•》

The new policy's most prominent critic is Oscar Salathiel Kambona, arguably Tanzania's most popular minister after Mwalimu, and erstwhile staunch supporter. He particularly disagrees with Mwalimu's push to relocate Tanzanian farmers into *ujamaas* or communal villages within a socialist state.

Although he doesn't expect Mwalimu to abandon villagization altogether, he does want him to proceed cautiously, by way of model villages in a free-enterprise context. Mwalimu, for his part, worries that delayed villagization will lead to entrenched feudalism.

With that, he sets aside his fears about Tanzania's incipient civil service not being up to relocating huge segments of his population effectively, and proceeds. Those viewed as actively operating against Tanzania's best interests are threatened with detention. Kambona goes into self-imposed exile in London.

Following her uncle's sudden exile, Kambona's favourite niece, a teenager, moves into his house to settle his affairs and, almost immediately, is imprisoned (officially on suspicion of collusion, but she believes mainly to get back at her uncle). Amnesty International ultimately brings her to Canada by way of the United States. Understandably, she is among those described by Professor Cranford Pratt of Toronto as believing that Mwalimu deliberately turned a blind eye to brutal excesses—unlike his supporters, who, despite some errors in policy, still value Mwalimu's personal integrity and deep commitment to his people's welfare.

《•》《•》《•》《•》

Needless to say, the Arusha Declaration causes both jubilation and consternation in Mufindi. Huge numbers of enthusiastic Tanzanians take up the self-help challenge. Others, long past their physical prime, yet not daring to stay away, are regularly seen awkwardly trying to keep up with collective efforts to hoe, plant, and harvest communal plots, as well as to build or repair schools, clinics, and roads. Meanwhile, contingents of students regularly run in formation on fields near the Sao Hill Military Base as part of their compulsory national service. "*Uhuru na Umoja*" (Freedom and Unity) is back on everyone's lips, now interspersed with "*Uhuru na Kazi*" (Freedom and Work).

Werner and Helga notice subtle differences in attitude, for example, when they offer schoolchildren a ride home. In the past, their stationary vehicle (returning from delivering green tea to the factory) would be mobbed by giggling and squealing youngsters jostling for the best spots. Now, the children approach more hesitantly, some even muttering political slogans as they grudgingly accept a lift (still too precious to forego, political principles or not).

《•》《•》《•》《•》

Academics and development agencies, from both sides of the Cold War divide, embrace Tanzania's new direction. So much so, that the young nation soon leads all other sub-Saharan countries in overseas assistance. Most of it is administered through expensive foreign "experts" (many with little direct experience of the country, a plethora of demands born of customized reporting formats, varying fiscal cycles, and sundry development theories—often well-meaning but evolving in mutual contradiction). Only at some point in the future will "donor countries" begin to understand the burden this places (financially, administratively, and personally) on fragile social and economic infrastructures.

But for now, despite the pitfalls, Tanzanians are showing palpable signs of a growing national confidence and personal pride, particularly as Mwalimu gains international recognition following the Arusha Declaration.

BABY BRUCE, THREE COWS, AND A CALF

"Geoff. Why don't we buy some cows for fresh milk?"

"Cows?"

"Why not? If we find some real European milk cows, we need never be short of milk again—I could even sell the surplus." Vicky has been thinking about this for a while. However much she loves her children and teaching, she is itching to get back into her other passion, agriculture. And, besides, it's almost impossible to find reasonably priced milk these days.

"Think of it, Foxey. Homemade ice cream!"

"Definitely below the belt! Anyway, won't you have enough on your hands with our new baby?"

Vicky eyes her bulging stomach.

"All the more reason, Geoff. Everything is so scarce these days. I'll manage. No, more than manage; I want to do it. You know I've always wanted a farm. Here's my chance."

With that, they start searching high and low for quality milk cows and eventually locate some for sale at one of the Mufindi missions, Ikwega. Off they go at last to choose a few. Once there, Vicky extricates her bulk clumsily from the car, walks over to the cows, and reaches over to run her hands knowledgeably over one candidate. The next thing she knows, she is flying . . . and then falling back down—hard! (A fellow Brooke Bond employee, Paddy Finlay, later tells them of well-known Irish folklore about cows attacking pregnant women.)

"Ouch!"

Geoff rushes to her side. "Vicky! Are you all right?" He tries to help her up. Vicky puts her arms around him, as best she can with her bulging stomach but try as she might, she cannot move. Then it registers.

"Foxey," she says. "My legs—I can't move my legs!" Somehow,

Geoff manages to get her into the car, back home, and into bed. For three days, she is completely paralyzed from the waist down. The new company physician, young Dr. Gattenby–Davis, comes by. "Having never done a Caesarean," Geoff remembers, "he went into a spin at the thought of performing one."

Vicky: "Fortunately, after a few days, the feeling came back and I could walk again. A week later, we made our usual middle-of-the-night journey down the bumpy dirt road to Ilembula Mission, over eighty miles away, where Bruce put in his noisy appearance on August ninth, 1967."

Geoff: "Bruce's birth was the most boring, taking hours at Ilembula."

Vicky: "Boring for you, maybe. Bruce had a cord around his neck."

Geoff: "With only German magazines in the waiting room, it was boring. Actually, I have to say, Vicky never made a noise, so I never knew when he arrived."

In the end, Geoff and Vicky bring home not just Bruce but also three cows and a bull calf. They all thrive — Bruce in the madness of the growing Fox family; the cattle in their newly built byres, constructed from off-cuts and thatched in the traditional manner. Then Vicky comes down with a severe case of malaria, contracted in Iringa.

Geoff walks into the bedroom one day, finds Vicky nursing Bruce, even though she has a fever of 105 and is in the throes of a severe shaking attack from malaria. He can't help himself, has to ask: "Are you giving Bruce a milkshake?"

"No comment."

POLITICAL NEUTRALITY

On September 6, 1967, in a move that will galvanize Tanzania's European allies, Mwalimu and President Kaunda accept a thirty-year, interest-free loan from Mao Tse-tung. China will link them by rail — and none too soon, as overloaded trucks, hauling Zambian copper exports and oil imports, have reduced the Great North Road to the Hell Run or No Longer so Great North Road.

When confronted by nervous Western allies, Mwalimu rejects accusations of taking a Cold War position. Given that all the money in the world appears to be either red or blue, and being without green money of his own, he asks how else he is to build the railway.

《•》《•》《•》《•》

Meanwhile, about three miles from Helga and Werner's farm, a group of like-minded and independent subsistence farmers decide that it makes a lot of sense to live closer to each other and work together.

Their actual debates are lost to time. But, in the case of Lwanga, it likely began with the most senior of the elders addressing a group of men sitting under a shady tree. Some lived close by. Others would have walked for several miles to be there. "Today we are here to hear each other about Mwalimu's call for *ujamaa* villages," the leader might have said. In the case of Lwanga, it would have been Mzee Ruben Mpiluka, not the oldest of them, but respected as a man of his word, a man of integrity, a man to be trusted.

"Why would Mwalimu ask us to move, when we have followed the way of our ancestors so well for many years?" someone might have asked, as in turn they offered their perspectives.[29]

"Mwalimu believes that is the only way forward, the only way to have a better life. Think of how much more we can produce if we work together. Think of our children. He is asking us to trust him, to work with him, to give him time. And you know that he himself is working harder than all of us. Above all, you know that he has our welfare at heart."

"This is true," they likely murmured, "he works harder than all of us."

"If we lived closer together, we could help each other more easily with building new houses. We would spend less time having to carry seeds, fertilizer, and crops back and forth."

"And if we lived closer to a road, we wouldn't have to load it all on our backs."

---

29   N.B. In Swahili, one does not meet to "discuss" an issue, but rather to "hear one another" on the subject.

"Not only that, but with a school nearby, our children would no longer have to walk five miles to school each day. They could help more at home."

"My children walk ten miles there and ten miles back a day."

"Where would the school come from?"

"We would have to build it. But the government will help with supplies. And they will pay the teacher."

"We've all managed fine so far without *ujamaa*. Besides, my home is near the graves of my ancestors. Will I not be abandoning them?"

"What will I do with my current crop?"

"Each one will move after they have harvested and in time to prepare the collective ground for next year."

"Will I have no land of my own, then?"

"Of course, everyone will have their own land, but will also help with the communal land. That way we can afford to rent a tractor to plough a much larger field."

"We are wasting much time, here," some might say and go back to their own fields.

"It is a big decision. We have to be sure that we are all agreed. It can only work if we choose this. Nobody should be forced."

As custom demands, such exchanges would have continued until all had been heard. "Is it agreed that we will form our own Lwanga Ujamaa Village? That we will move closer to each other, pool our resources, work collectively to reap more than we can sow individually?"

"Eeeeh." There would have been a general nodding of heads. "It is agreed." Even as they congratulated each other, relieved to have made the decision, they would likely have wondered what they were committing to. (In fact, according to Tanzania's economic lingo, it is what Andrew Coulson, a political economist specialized in Tanzania will call a "self-initiated" *ujamaa* or collective village in 1982.) "Welcome to Lwanga Ujamaa," someone might have joked to widespread laughter, given that their *ujamaa* was but a concept.

BABY ON THE ROAD

The Foxes have no idea what will become of them, as Brooke Bond, clearly a capitalist enterprise, is now operating in an overtly socialist country. Unlike coffee plantations in Northern Tanzania, wheat farms around Hanang, and a vast array of other crops and businesses, Brooke Bond tea holdings have not, so far, been nationalized. However, Brooke Bond can no longer guarantee long-term employment. Instead, all employees are to continue on two-year contracts, renewable on a case-by-case basis, accompanied by Tanzanian grants of two-year residence permits.

"There's not much to be done about that right now," Geoff says to Vicky. "But what we *can* do is travel!"

"Great idea! Anything to get away from all of this for a while. Where to?"

"How about a driving holiday to Cape Town and back, camping on the way?"

"Camping? With a two-year-old, a three-year-old, and a six-month-old?"

"Why not? I don't think the kitty will run to much more."

"How on earth are we going to get everything into a small Toyota estate car?"

They pack. They repack. Until, at last, it works . . . barely . . . sort of. Christopher and Peter can fit in only if they lie down like sausages on top of the camping equipment under the roof. And baby Bruce if his basket is squeezed in right on top at the back.

With a triumphant flourish and farewell to their friends Kim and Johno Beakbane, Geoff and Vicky finally set off—whereupon the back door promptly opens and the baby falls out with the basket, "requiring," as Geoff puts it, "another restart."

This happens again in Malawi. Only there, they don't know, until a car overtakes them to point it out, that they have left a baby behind on the road. Back they go to scoop up Bruce. It seems the hatchback latch is acting up as a result of the heavily overloaded vehicle.

"Phew! That's finally over," Vicky says, referring to the roads rather than the baby. "Wasn't the driving awful between Mufindi and Tunduma [the Zambian border post]? At least the oil and copper lorries have been taken off the 'hell run' for now. What did they say the problem was?"

"A collapsed bridge near Dar es Salaam."

"No wonder, with all that weight."

"For some reason, that reminds me of all those lorries sloping at forty-five degrees in huge potholes when we drove to the rugby match in Mbeya."

"You mean when Mike Ghaui changed the wheel after our puncture?" Vicky laughs. Geoff joins in. "And us bumping along this same dreadful road when I noticed someone's wheel passing by and overtaking us. I remember asking you both, 'Where did that come from?'"

"The road was so chopped up, we didn't realize for some moments that it was one of our own rear wheels." By now they are almost in tears.

"Mike swears even to this day that he tightened those wheel nuts."

"How long did it take us to find the wheel?"

"An hour at least. Remember, it had crossed the road in front of the car and into the long grass on the other side."

"Spare wheels used to be slung underneath the rear wheel shaft of the car," Geoff explains many years later. "They would get covered in a thin film of dried mud, so when you tightened a nut, the film of dried mud was tightened between the wheel and the hub. All protestations to the contrary, we still accuse Mike of incompetence." (Mike Ghaui has since gone on to become an internationally celebrated wildlife artist and sculptor.[30])

When they finally arrive in Mbeya, Geoff and Vicky are told that there is absolutely no petrol to be found, as no petrol tankers are getting through. Fortunately, they are carrying seventeen extra gallons with them.

Zambia seems rather dull by comparison, except for the beautiful Kundilila waterfall on their third night; and, of course, the Victoria Falls. "Christopher still talks about them," Vicky writes Libby. "The huge Zambezi River falls thousands of feet into a gorge and the spray wets you as you watch from the top. Southern Rhodesia was terrifyingly arid in the wake of a fierce drought, with not a blade of grass to be seen all the way from the falls to Beit Bridge, the South African border post."

---

30   http://www.artnet.com/artists/michael-ghaui/

THE MIDNIGHT INTRUDER

"Three-year-old Christopher and two-year-old Peter were already proven pyromaniacs," Geoff remembers, "having lit a dangerous fire behind the house in Mufindi. So their daily job wherever we decided to camp was to collect firewood and light the campfire. Vicky looked after Bruce and prepared supper while I put up the tent, an old canvas type, full of holes, so we had to cover it with polythene sheeting. It also required us to cut two poles for it each day, which was no problem until we got into South Africa. There, the farther we went, the fewer available saplings could be found, until we had to furtively climb fences into people's private property. Actually, I got Vicky to do it, while I kept lookout."

After crossing the South African border at Beit Bridge, across the Limpopo River, they head for Tsaneen, a beautiful area, where they plan to find a motel with a much-needed bath. To beat the heat, they leave their windows open overnight.

Vicky wakes to see Geoff wandering around the room. "What are you doing, Geoff?" she asks. Then, realizing the figure is too small to be Geoff, shrieks. "There's someone in the room!" An intruder had climbed through the window and is now opening the door for his escape.

"The wretched man got away with my bag containing EVERY-THING," Vicky tells friends. "We were left with no passports, no health documents, no cash, no traveller's cheques, and no car documents. Horrors."

"However, Flash Fox was fast." Geoff takes over the narrative. "I raced through the now open door and gave pursuit (at three a.m.), shouting a mixture of English and Swahili abuse, and no doubt drawing attention to myself. After 100 metres or so, I realized I had gone to bed without pyjamas! There was no sign of the thief, so I returned to take stock with Vicky.

"We decided to rush to the police station, but since everywhere was pitch-black, the police could not do much till the next morning. They did bring out the dogs, which searched and sniffed but failed to find the trail. The police also went into the staff quarters and shone their torches on the staff to see if there was any mud on their feet.

"The next morning at breakfast, we told the manager we had no money and couldn't pay. He didn't seem at all sympathetic and replied that that was our problem. While Vicky was packing all the bags, I wandered down the same road that I had run along the night before, with my hands in my pockets (I now had trousers on), wondering what the hell we could do, when I saw a small disturbance in a garden.

"The owner of the house was being led by his staff to a small garden shed. There, somebody was holding Vicky's bag. With huge relief, I took ownership. Nothing was missing, except for our cash, about £50 (about $175), and one of our two American Express traveller's chequebooks. To have all the legal documents and passports back was enormous relief, given the rock-bottom relations between Tanzania and South Africa in 1967."

JOB OFFERS
AND FLYING TENTS

That night, the family stays with a friend near Pietermaritzburg. Celia Salmon is the wife of the famous Uganda elephant hunter, "Samaki" (Fish) Salmon. When Geoff sees a stuffed elephant foot beside her fireplace, he says, "That must have been one of Samaki's." Whereupon the diminutive lady answers: "No. That was my first."

"She offered us a job as farm manager on her idyllic estate," Geoff later recalls, "right at the edge of an escarpment overlooking the Valley of a Thousand Hills. We were indeed tempted, partly because it was so beautiful there, and partly because of our uncertain future in Tanzania at the time.

"We toured Celia's farm the next day before taking a room for the night in a Pietermaritzburg hotel, where Vicky and I dozed off in the late afternoon . . . and our two toddlers went walkabout. They simply disappeared. We searched high and low. Eventually, quite a long distance away down a busy street, we saw a policeman coming our way along the road, holding the hands of our little boys. I think it was probably their first ever experience of a real town.

"Our tent finally blew away off a cliff in a strong wind on the southernmost point of Africa. (Fortunately, we were not in it at the time.) Thereafter, it was guest houses and cheap hotels all the way. In Cape Town, we met up with our friend Celia again, who was also driving down for other reasons. She took us to her favourite restaurant.

Fox family on home leave, with Geoff's father at his house in Looe, Cornwall.

There, to my embarrassment, she kept rejecting the wine. After finally accepting the third bottle, she turned to me and said: 'I always feel sorry for the kitchen staff.' That was probably why all the waiters knew her and were buzzing around her.

"We tried to choose different routes on the way back. After an interview in Barberton near Nelspruit, in the eastern Transvaal, we were offered a job in tea. It was another beautiful place, very close to the Kruger National Park (which, incidentally, didn't impress us. It was all tarmac, just like a zoo!). Again, we declined and headed back to Mufindi, this time through the Eastern Highlands of Rhodesia (now Zimbabwe), into and up through Malawi, and then back home to Tanzania—still with baby Bruce!"

"We covered 9,000 miles on our safari!" Vicky writes to Libby after the trip. "It was all tremendous fun but pretty exhausting, as you could imagine. We saw so much in such a short time and with three lively boys were fully occupied. Actually, the children were very good. Their little suitcases full of toys and books kept them happy for hours.

"On our journey down, we managed to visit all kinds of game parks. The children saw almost every kind of animal there was to see. One of the nicest parks was Mkusi, just South of Swaziland. They have built two hides, in which you sit to watch the game come down to drink. But Bruce became thoroughly spoilt as he was with us every second of the day. He can now walk about holding on to the furniture and says 'Daddy.'"

"It was a fun safari," Geoff will say, looking back on the experience in later years. "But, even though Brooke Bond only guaranteed our future for two-year contracts at a time, after each renewal of our residence permit, and even though we were offered opportunities in South Africa, Tanzania was where we wanted to live."

Lwanga Ujamaa

Three years have passed since Mzee and his fellow volunteers decided to form Lwanga Ujamaa—not because they were forced to, but because they chose to in 1969. Like others, it now has a village council composed of twenty-five villagers, divided into five committees and supervised by an elected chairman. The committees look into matters of health, agriculture, security, commerce, and education.

Life is good. They are all still more or less enthusiastic about their venture, particularly since their communal maize field is thriving—this at a time when other villages are finding life more and more difficult. In fact, Lwanga can hardly keep up with the demand from all around them for maize meal during the "hungry months" (toward the end of stored corn from the last crop, and before the new harvest). Their *nyumba kumi kumi* (ten ten household) principle is working well, whereby every ten households elect a spokesman to represent them at monthly meetings or on the village council. In short, they are living proof that *Ujamaa* can work when members choose a collective lifestyle.

Although individuals may also grow vegetables on some private land, the main common crop is maize. Their day starts early, rising at dawn, about an hour after the second rooster crows, so they can have all their household chores finished before eight a.m. After that, everyone works in the fields until *the sun turns* at one p.m.—twice a week on the communal plot, and the rest of the time on individual plots. Then they help mend each other's mud and wattle homes, or replace them with brick buildings.

Grade-school leavers hold adult education classes three mornings a week from 7:00 to 8:00 a.m. Communal

Mzee Ruben Mpiluka, 2007 —
still hoeing his own fields to grow food.
(Gord Breedyk)

meetings often take place in the evenings, during the traditional storytelling time. Instead of walking up to ten miles to school every day, their children go to school next door and can help more at home.

But there is still much to be done. The pressure of leadership begins to weigh on Mzee, especially as agricultural inputs are increasingly hard to come by in the slowing economy. Luckily, Lwanga villagers have their own seeds. And they can still afford to replace their hand hoes every year. Others now often have to wait two years, which means twice as much work, because by the second year, the blade has been worn down to half its original depth.

ALEXANDER'S "EASY" BIRTH

Geoff to friends: "Alexander's birth in England on August 28, 1972, was very easy."

Vicky: "Was it?"

Geoff: "I was even allowed to complete my game of tennis."

Vicky: "I see what you mean . . ."

AFRICAN BEES ATTACK

"The bee story, Geoff. This would be a good time to tell it."

"Again?"

"Yes, Geoff, again."

"When the Ruaha National Park was formed, Mufindi folk were the only people who ever visited at weekends. We used to frequently go there, primarily for the tiger fishing that the great Ruaha River provided for the boys . . . the only accommodation being government *rondavels* made of tin, which were all right. Still, one had to bring one's own food and drink. So we would go down with a crate of beer, drink it warm, and have a lot of fun.

"One day, as we came in, to my horror we saw that a professional tented camp had been set up. Even worse, I could hear the hum of a generator, which meant one thing: ice-cold beer, with the condensation on the outside of the bottle. My feelings darkened by these intruders coming on to our "patch" (a whole ecosystem the size of Belgium), I muttered to Vicky that the next morning we would go somewhere far away from these dreadful tourists, up the Mdonya River and breakfast at the farthest end.

"At dawn, off we went, with Alexander, barely six weeks old, bumping along in a basket in the back of the Land Rover. He was covered with mosquito netting to keep off the tsetse flies. After driving for about an hour, we neared our destination, rounded a corner, and — horror of horrors! — two of the tourists were stumbling toward us along the road, a man and a girl, the man holding a toasting fork with a piece of toast still on the end.

"I uttered a curse, pushed forward the window, and said: 'Good morning.'

"'We have been attacked,' they replied.

"I could see no sign of danger, so, muttering that the toasting fork was perhaps an effective weapon, I was prepared to carry on. At that moment, an elderly, grey-haired lady emerged out of the bushes with her head surrounded by angry bees and, as it turned out later, with about a hundred bee stings.

"Vicky whipped off Alexander's mosquito net, covered the elderly lady, and together with the young couple, still holding the toasting fork, rushed her down the road to the safety of a nice, shady fig tree. There, Vicky established her bee sting 'clinic.' (Only a few days before, we had read a *Reader's Digest* article on the importance of picking out bee stings as quickly as possible without squeezing the venom into the skin. Under a magnifying glass, a bee's sting can be seen continuing to pump its venom.)

"Since there were quite a few members of the tourist party unaccounted for, off I went to rescue anyone I could find. Just up the road, I came across the tour leader, Don Turner, and the contracted owner of the camp, George Dove (who had actually started and owned Ndutu camp in the Serengeti, after a long stint as a professional hunter). Don and George had decided not to run from the bees. Instead, they had built a fire in the middle of the road, using sticks and dried elephant dung. This provided enough smoke for them to put their heads in and keep the bees away. They told me they were okay, but please, would I go and collect all the others.

"The party had, in fact, stopped by a massive baobab tree and lit a fire at its base to cook their breakfast. George Dove, with his experience, should have known better because baobabs are notorious for housing beehives in their hollow interiors.

"After a few trips backwards and forwards, I was turning around at the top end, seeing no one else to collect, when a movement in the bush about fifty yards away caught my eye. There was a woman, still standing, but with her head totally covered by bees, as if a swarm had settled there. I crashed through the bush with my Land Rover toward her, picked her up, and plonked her over the spare wheel on the bonnet of the car. (I couldn't put her and all the bees inside the vehicle, because our six-week-old baby was still in his cot in the back.)

"I then crashed back through the bush and down the road at speed, so the wind could blow off as many of the bees as possible, forgetting all about Don Turner and George Dove with their heads in smoke over the flames. I had to jam on my brakes and screech to a halt, just before their fire, at which point she rolled off the bonnet and into the flames where a bit of her clothing caught alight. This probably helped to dislodge more bees!

"The three of us (Don, George, and I) then scraped the bees off her face and head (just like scraping mud) leaving bee stings probably about a couple of millimetres apart all over her head. She must have had around a thousand bee stings. Her eyes were, of course, swollen shut, and she was bleeding out of both ears, so off we took her to Vicky's bee sting clinic. There, we mobilized everyone to pick off the stings as quickly as possible. She kept on saying that she had something in her ear. We didn't want to tell her that she was bleeding from both ears—whether from burst eardrums, or high blood pressure, no one knew.

"We had managed to recover one of the tourists' two vehicles and left the other one, full of bees, under the baobab tree. (When we collected it the next morning, there were three angry swarms hanging from the boughs of the baobab.) I sent Don off to the park headquarters to try to radio the Flying Doctor Service. We followed slowly with the rest of the party, including both the ladies who had been badly stung. Don arrived at park headquarters after us, having lost his way. But the radio was not working anyway, so no link to the Flying Doctor Service.

"I suggested they take the thousand-bee-sting lady to Mufindi (her eyes still swollen shut), where Dr. Ian Clarke was now working in the Brooke Bond hospital, and offered them our house near the hospital to stay in. With twenty-five years as a doctor in East Africa, Ian Clarke declared that he had never, ever in his life, seen a bee sting case like this survive. Pat Keeley, the nurse, grumbled that we hadn't taken out any bee stings, there were still so many left in her head and her hair. But survive she did and, when she blew her nose a week later, a bee came out. You can just imagine her discomfort during all this time.

"However, back in the Ruaha Park, the show had to go on. We were invited to dinner as guests of honour. And, what was on the table? Ice-cold beer with condensation outside the bottle!

"The white-haired granny with 'only' a hundred bee stings had been on antihistamines prior to the attack, and her face swelled only slightly, removing wrinkles. She was extremely happy, declaring that she now looked twenty years younger. Months later, I received a postcard from the thousand-sting lady, addressed to the 'man who saved her life.'

"I have to say that on our many walking safaris, we frequently encountered swarms of bees, often led to their hives by honeyguides. After the Ruaha experience, I gave them more respect than earlier, when often I would chuck a stick at a swarm and watch everyone scampering in different directions."

Bees also featured in the first significant battle between the Germans and the British in Tanganyika during World War I, when angry swarms temporarily routed British forces, before the Germans (outnumbered 8:1) ultimately prevailed. It was their first of many engagements successfully designed to draw as many British troops as possible away from the European front. To quote one British soldier after the Battle of the Bees: ". . . what with a bunch of Krauts firing into our backs and bees stinging our backsides, things got a bit 'ard."[31]

LWANGA'S MAIZE BLOWS AWAY

With one last look around his, the chairman's office, Mzee Mpiluka heads toward the ladder, past some wooden boxes (his only furniture) littered with papers, a guest book, and accounts. His eyes rest for a moment on Lwanga's certificate of registration, hanging on the wall. It is dated April 20, 1972, almost four months ago, and testifies that "Lwanga Ujamaa Cooperative Society Ltd. is this day registered under the provision of section 10 of the Cooperative Societies Act 1968."

People gathered in front of the huge Lwanga grain store at first see nothing but his feet on the ladder, as Mzee slowly climbs down from the office floor, it being a wooden platform suspended on stilts above this year's gargantuan harvest, piled in the godown (a name dating back to the British Raj in India, where workers were regularly asked to "go down" to fetch supplies from storerooms).

"We had a total of 600 bags of maize in the godown," Mzee will muse years later. "The children from Ihumasa School had come to help us. I joined them and all our villagers in sodas as a thank-you. After that, the children left, and we continued to celebrate.

"Suddenly, a huge wind tore the go-down apart. We had to run to escape the planks, thrown around like paper. And watch all our maize blow away. Then the skies opened, and everything was drowned in water.

"We were lucky that the children had just left, or there would have been many deaths." Some of the maize and wheat could be rescued and stored in neighbouring *ujamaas*, and Lwanga would have been all right had not a driver, dismissed for drunkenness, removed a vital part from the tractor they had rented in the ploughing season.

"As you know," Mzee says, "it can take months to replace any auto part." So the ploughing had to be done manually.

---

31   Byron Farwell, *The Great War in Africa*, **http://www.rhodesia.nl/farwell.htm**.

Family photo around the time of the last foot safari:
Alexander, Geoff, Vicky, Christopher, Peter, and Bruce.

This delayed the planting, and Lwanga missed the optimal growing cycle for maize. We also still owed money for renting the tractor. This reduced our harvest, affected our credibility, and—instead of receiving fertilizer on credit as in the past—we had to pay cash. So, of course, we could only afford to buy less. We just managed to scrape through that year and would have managed, but there was more bad luck to come."

LAST WALKING SAFARI

In 1973, Geoff and Vicky go on their last walking safari. Exceptionally, they include their three oldest children. Alexander, who is just one year old, ends up at their neighbours', where the Keeley daughters are happy to play with him, dressing and undressing him like a doll.

"To make it more fun," Geoff says, "we decided to follow the Great Ruaha River, starting at Mbuyuni Bridge on the Iringa/Mikumi road."

《•》《•》《•》《•》

As I write,
I remember, remember, remember
sweeping stardust in the night
falling stars, shooting stars—a panoply of African stars
impossibly bright against the deep dark shadow of the bulbous
baobab

Ruaha, Udzungwa, Mikumi
How we seemed to fall downwards through space
cutting through life's edges.
We drank it in then, and now, in memory
I drink it in again:
African sun, warm against my skin,
African breeze, warm against my face,
African laughter, warm against my heart.
Drink it in,
store it in my core, in my being.

《·》《·》《·》《·》

Twenty-three porters go down ahead of the Foxes by bus, more than half of them to carry their own food. A company driver then drops the Foxes off. On the way, they stop, as ever, to say hello to the Ghauis at Kisolanza. Phyl has again packed two gargantuan baskets of vegetables for them, which means engaging two more porters. The driver leaves them at the Ruaha Bridge and then returns to Mufindi.

For the first twelve days, in the heat, they follow the Ruaha River at 2,000 feet above sea level, averaging, according to their detailed maps, sixteen miles a day.

Little Bruce celebrates his sixth birthday en route on August 9, 1973. Peter is only eight, and Christopher nine. They enjoy themselves immensely, but seventeen-year-old Andi Gordon (great-great-nephew of General Gordon of Khartoum), who has joined them on the safari, later admits he hated every minute of it, but was glad he went — afterwards.

Each morning, they all set off together but gradually spread out as time wears on, some of them ending up way behind. Vicky, as usual, takes up the rear, unless they are going uphill. Then the rest of the Fox family brace themselves for her inevitable greeting when they finally stagger up: "What kept you?"

"Six-year-old Bruce was tough," Dad brags many years later. "He kept up with everybody, usually near the front, without complaint and managing to cover the daily sixteen-mile pace, which is amazing. His own stubbornness never allowed him to admit to being tired. Even after his terrible accident later in life, he has never felt sorry for himself.

But Vicky always knew when he was tired on that safari because then his question about how much longer they had to go before camping was usually accompanied by dried elephant dung hurled at her!"

Every day, they walk from daybreak until about eleven a.m., rest up until midday, eating nuts and raisins, then carry on until evening. Around five p.m., they make camp. Their first priority, once they have agreed on the site, is to open the folding camp beds, flop down on them, and enthuse about how lovely it feels. Yet, within five minutes, the boys, having recharged their batteries, jump up again and set about playing, collecting firewood, fishing, or shooting guinea fowl for supper, which will be turned over hot embers on a little battery-operated spit. ("Extraordinary how young kids can rebound so quickly," Dad mumbles and closes his eyes.)

The boys' job is to fish and hunt the evening meal, Vicky's to help cook it, and Geoff's to set up camp. Then they all enjoy the evening together. "We had torches, but mainly we sat around the firelight in the evening," Vicky reminisces. "Carrying kerosene with us would have been too difficult. We were never late to bed, having talked until perhaps nine-thirty p.m. And then up we'd get again the next morning, often in the dark, and start walking at first light, having had a cup of tea and a snack."

Geoff soon learns always to have their sharp-eyed trackers in the front, because they walk for a long time through a riverine forest area marked out to warn of traps with poisoned arrows set by poachers and hunters. Warnings take the form of a pole with grass wrapped around it. The traps themselves involve tripwires that, when stumbled on by animals, set off arrows tipped with a black tar-like substance sold by the Wakamba of Kenya and lethal enough to kill an elephant in seven minutes.

The traps are almost impossible for the Foxes to see, but the trackers find them easily, and show the Foxes the arrows and tripwires. They also come across some poachers and traditional hunters with their bows and poisoned arrows, sometimes with an impala over their shoulders.

The Foxes finally reach the border of the Ruaha National Park. ("I've never met any six-year-old who could have walked that distance," Geoff says, still shaking his head proudly many decades later.) They find a spot just outside the park boundary and stay there for the rest of their leave, near the Kisigo River of James Frederick Elton fame, dating back to the nineteenth century.

《•》《•》《•》《•》

The year is 1873. Britain has persuaded the Sultan of Zanzibar to stop supporting the slave trade. But in 1877, there are reports of slave activity continuing in the Usangu area, north of present-day Mbeya. Elton, posted to Zanzibar to assist the British representative, Sir John Kirk, offers to investigate. Because "hostile elements" are supposedly operating along the direct route inland from Bagamoyo, Elton elects to approach Usangu from the south. With two European companions plus a small support team recruited in Zanzibar, they sail down the coast to the mouth of the Zambezi River and then onward, by boat, into Lake Nyasa toward present-day Malawi.

The expedition stalls for three months at the northern tip of Lake Nyasa, when the chief of the Wanakyusa in Tukuyu refuses to give Elton porters — allegedly because of inter-tribal fighting over the plateau and in the Usangu plains, but actually because of an uprising by the relatives of captured slaves. He eventually relents, and Elton climbs up to the plateau above Chimala, which has only in recent years been renamed from Elton's Plateau to Kitulo National Park in protection of its astonishing carpets of iris and ground orchids.

He continues down into the Usangu plain on the other side of Mbeya, to enter the village of Chief Merere of the Wasangu at Utengule — also stockaded against people trying to free their captured relatives. Merere is accompanied by a slaver called Suleiman. And Elton and his party are compelled to shelter with them in the stockade. Three months later, the men manage to leave, with (at her request) the daughter of Chief Merere. Heading back to Zanzibar, they follow the Mzombi River, which forms the northwestern boundary of the Ruaha National Park, toward the Kisigo. There Elton's diary entries stop abruptly.

《·》《·》《·》《·》

"And here we are, all camping by the Kisigo," Geoff beams at the Hesters. As prearranged, they have brought the Foxes' Land Rover.[32] "Elton apparently died just after crossing the Kisigo River. His grave is marked on the earlier maps of Tanganyika. Alex, hunting in the area, once came upon it in an area frequented mainly by elephants. The rest of Elton's party continued on, ending up in Bagamoyo, before crossing to Zanzibar."

Derrick is the proud owner of an old-style camp bed, which he has just recently bought from Mother Pretorious, complete with a heavy, folding, wooden frame. When he launches himself into it that night, the whole thing collapses, forcing him to sleep in the car.

"Were you ever afraid on your safaris, Vicky?" a friend asks years later.

"We didn't have much imagination then, I think," she will answer. "I believed that Geoff could save me from anything. Later, before we had the lodge, and used to camp beside the Ruaha River with four small boys, hearing the grunts of an approaching lion certainly kept me awake—especially as it got nearer, and nearer, and nearer. And then stopped. That's when you don't know where it is. It leaves you tingling. We just had camp beds and mosquito nets. June once said she felt safe knowing that Geoff was nearby with a gun. Geoff didn't exactly comfort her with his answer: 'By the time it gets to me, it won't be hungry!'"

Soon after their return to Mufindi, the Foxes are regaling friends with snippets of their safari. Just after Geoff mentions the poisoned arrows, one of the guests points at the lawn and exclaims, "Geoff, are those the same arrows your boys are playing with?"

"By George, they are!" With that, Geoff leaps out of his chair, opens the window, and yells, 'Boys! Those arrows are lethal. Mind the chickens!'"

《·》《·》《·》《·》

As though Tanzania is not facing enough challenges, in October 1973, the Organization of Arab Petroleum Exporting

---

32   The Hesters later tell Evelyn Voigt that when Geoff heard that their son Malcolm had two teenage friends staying in Mufindi for the holidays, "with typical Fox kindness," he invited the Hester family and guests to join them for a few days' camping. "He took the boys shooting near the camp, and it was a really exciting time for them."

Countries initiates an oil embargo because of U.S. support to the Israeli military during the Yom Kippur war. Aftershocks from the 350 percent increase in the cost of oil will shake even the most stable of economies, let alone those of young nations, predominantly reliant on a few commodities for foreign exchange earnings. In Tanzania's case, these include sisal, coffee, tea, and cotton—all of which are subject to wild fluctuations on the world market totally beyond Tanzania's control. And yet, Tanzania now needs to export a greater percentage of its raw materials to pay for the same amount of oil. The cost of repaying its development loans increases accordingly.

《•》《•》《•》《•》

The Foxes' new Land Rover gives them amazing freedom of travel, albeit with challenges of its own. Vicky remembers having to build twenty-one bridges to cross many streams and swamps, on one safari from Mufindi to the Rungwe River, fording the Ruaha River before following outside the southern boundary of the Ruaha National Park and across the Chunya/Itigi road.

"We used to chop down the vegetation beside the track, lay it across the swampy ground, and when we finally had enough of a layer over the swampy bit, we'd drive across at speed with the trailer bumping around until its drawbar eventually broke apart. This was rather a problem. To solve it, we cut some strong branches and lashed them with rope onto the chassis of the trailer at one end, fixed the other end onto the Land Rover, and set off once again all the way home.

"But I always preferred walking. Of course, you could reach much more distant places with the Land Rover, and we would always walk when we got there; but on foot, you felt an enormous freedom because you didn't always have to stay with the road. You could go where you wanted to."

"Also, as Peter constantly reminds me," Geoff adds, "I suppose I am a bit rough on cars, which tends to become expensive. Shoes are cheaper; so, after reading the book by the famous 'snake man,' Ionides, who invariably preferred to walk everywhere in 'gym' (tennis) shoes, I decided to follow suit on our next walking safari. Stupidly I took along no other spare shoes for this two-week excursion. On the first night, having waded through streams, we dried my shoes on the

All part of the fun …

ends of sticks over the fire. One stick burned, and the shoe fell in the fire! Oops! Two weeks to go with just one shoe! Someone scratched his head and found a sewing needle that he had kept in his hair, another spun some sisal string strands into a fine thread, and there and then, in the glow of the campfire, a shoe was rebuilt out of the unburnt remains! This comfortably lasted for the rest of the safari."

Drastic Measures

By November 1973, Mwalimu's patience has run its course. Relatively few Tanzanians are heeding the Arusha Declaration's call for voluntary relocation into villages. Even worse, Tanzania's urban elite continues to mushroom. Forced villagization seems to be his only option. The pros and cons of such a drastic move keep him awake at night. He fears that any more delays will move his people too far from African familyhood to give villagization a chance.

On the other hand, he, like others, is acutely aware of the risks. How can Tanzania's fledgling civil service be expected to manage the smooth relocation of large numbers of individual homesteaders into *ujamaa* villages in a way that guarantees them timely delivery of seeds and fertilizer, not to mention improved health services and education?

And which of the rural population should be relocating? Clearly not the well-established, small-, medium-, and large-scale holders of perennial crops, especially not those who already live closely enough together to receive electricity, health services, education, and other public services — the coffee and banana planters around Mount Kilimanjaro, for example. Coffee in particular takes time to yield and cannot be relocated at will. Urbanites and peri-urbanites would equally be allowed to remain where they are; again, because their numbers and concentration already allow for delivery of cost-effective services.

Conversely, rural farmers in provinces like Iringa, he muses, could surely benefit greatly from collective maize, bean, and potato cultivation, among other annual crops. And aren't some rural folks in isolated areas already used to moving every few years, once the rains destroy their mud-and-wattle houses? Once exhausted lands yield less? Once disease-bearing rodents and insects take over? They may not find building a new house overly traumatic.

Of course, proximity to the graves of ancestors will be an issue if they are forced away from traditional homesteads. And what about those who have well-established brick homes? Then there are production considerations. Overly hasty relocation might be to infertile soils and insufficient water sources, and out of synch with the agricultural cycle. Then again, Mwalimu muses, subsistence farmers are among the most efficient farmers in the world. They have to be. Without their crops, their families die. They are also resilient, largely due to their close communal links with extended family and clan members.

Still, many isolated farmers are used to living in far-flung homesteads, where even a husband's wives are often no closer than a day's walk of each other. Strong and independent, these women are used to being responsible for their own children and individual plots of land. How will they react, if suddenly thrust into close proximity, not only with each other, but also with strangers, some friendly, some not?

Fundamentally, the optimist in him concludes, a country as poor as his has no choice other than to lift itself out of poverty by working together, and traditional communality will win the day—especially when folks start benefiting from new economies of scale. But at what cost to his most vulnerable people, the naysayer in him counters? Aren't they already living on the edge?

The optimist wins out, and Mwalimu signs into effect the forced Villagization Policy.

CROCODILES

Weekends away from Mufindi are still the norm in the 1970s, usually camping on the banks of the Great Ruaha, mainly at Lunda, where the Ilusi (Tungamalenga) River joins the Ruaha. Geoff and Vicky's companions on one particular trip are Ian and Pat Summerville, Johno Beakbane, Tim Dale, and an American Peace Corps friend, Ardis (who is a conscripted member of the Mufindi rugby team). Awakening on the first morning, Johno takes his shovel and wanders into the bush behind the camp. Almost immediately, he re-emerges at great speed with his trousers down by his knees. A buffalo had just poked its head around the same bush.

Tim and Johno compete with smart repartee, exchanging puns. After a five-mile walk upriver in the heat, Johno suggests that they log it instead of legging it back to camp. So everyone finds logs and floats down the river, including Vicky, who is about six months pregnant, so five miles of floating provides her with a restful return, crocodiles or no. ("We all lacked imagination," Geoff will remark to friends in later years, looking back on youthful hijinks. "Of all the things you might have lacked, imagination was not one of them," one of them will reply.)

Meanwhile, the older Fox boys are back from England for their school holidays, courtesy as ever of Brooke Bond. On family tiger-fishing weekends in Ruaha, Geoff spends most of his time tying on new hooks and bait for his sons, the tiger fish being a very aggressive species with sharp teeth, requiring wire trace on the hooks to prevent them from cutting through the nylon line.

Geoff's help means a lot to the boys because when they are at boarding school in England, Geoff and Vicky can only afford to give them very little pocket money, and almost all of it is spent at their favourite shop on the necessary lures and other tackle for tiger fishing in Ruaha. Inevitably, whenever their hook is caught on a log or rock in the river, it just *has* to be retrieved.

Geoff and Vicky don't know it at the time, but Christopher later tells them that when, at nineteen years of age, he used to drive his younger brothers down for weekends, they repeatedly had to recover their precious pocket money gear by diving into the hippo pool, which teemed with crocodiles. On any given day, they are literally draped by the dozen along the shore. (Then fellow Mufindi resident Liz Baker claims she once counted about 100 crocodiles, while standing on one spot.)

"Holidays are too short. The boys only arrived the other day," Geoff writes home to Gelly and Jimmy. "As usual, everything is left to the last minute, and we are supposed to go to Dar es Salaam today to put them on a plane—packing not done, food not ready, clothes can't be found, haircutting required, letters to be written . . ."

Meanwhile, Vicky's own school is growing, and her pupils perform very well when graduating to British schools. By the mid-1970s, she has thirty students of all ages, and some temporary help from another teacher. While home for the holidays one year, son Christopher donates for the school's "nature table" a baby crocodile! Tiny, extremely aggressive, it snaps at everyone and everything. After a while, Vicky worries that some mother's little child will be bitten and duly exiles Croc to the duck pond. It disappears.

Three years later, the Lugoda factory staff request Foxey to remove from the factory dam a dangerous crocodile that is threatening their children. Indeed, they find Croc sunning himself on a rock in the middle of the water. Crocodiles in the wild travel considerable distances overnight. Tiny little Croc must have found its way to the dam, over half a mile away, fed on black bass, and grown to its current length of five feet. Christopher has to shoot it. Otherwise, sooner or later, he could be held accountable for some accident. The Ellis family at nearby Idetero then throws a barbecue, with crocodile tail as the day's "special."

FORCED VILLAGIZATION

The day Mwalimu announces his forced villagization program over the radio, the following scene likely plays itself out across the young country. Those who have already moved to villages, as in Lwanga, would routinely cluster around the communal radio, with newcomers jostling their way into the growing crowd, and settling on to the ground as a spot opens up.

"Did you hear that? Loh!"

"What's going on?" they might ask.

"It's Mwalimu," neighbours might start to explain. "He says he can no longer wait for people to move voluntarily to villages. Now people will be forced to move."

"Everybody?"

"No, not everybody. Not those who are already living close to each other and growing crops that take a long time to mature, like coffee and banana farmers around Mount Kilimanjaro. But those who live far apart and grow maize, potatoes, onions—"

"Friends, friends, please." In Lwanga, it would be the chairman talking. Despite his quiet tone, everyone would listen. "Friends, we will have time to hear each other out after the broadcast. For now, let's just listen."

What they hear is Mwalimu's plea for co-operation with a policy he believes is the only way Tanzania can pull itself out of poverty.

After the broadcast ends, the chairman or group leader might quietly invite people to hear each other. And their conversations likely include at least some of the following points, in this case focused on Lwanga.

"Why would Mwalimu force people to move?" someone might ask.

"For the same reasons we decided ourselves to move into Lwanga."

"But not everybody wanted to move. And we would not have worked so well together if those who didn't want to work together had been forced to join us."

"Remember how hard it was for us in the beginning, even though we chose this path for ourselves? Imagine trying to do that with people who don't want to be there in the first place."

"But if people don't move, how can Mwalimu bring them clinics and schools near home, like in our village now? And what about seeds and fertilizer?"

"Others have managed quite well without forced villagization before."

"Yes, that is true. As long as they have the strength to carry everything home on their backs for miles. At least we can now afford a road right to our village. What a difference that has made. The government can deliver seeds, and we can deliver our harvests, without breaking our backs."

"And don't forget our children. They no longer have to walk five, even ten miles to school."

"First we had to build the school."

"True, it took a lot of work. But at least we lived close enough together to be able to do so."

"And where will everyone go?"

"And what about those who resist? Will they be forced with guns? Will there be fighting?"

"We'll have to wait and see. But how lucky we are in Lwanga that we moved when we did. Now everything is going well with us."

"Certainly better. We still haven't recovered from what that thief did around the tractor. Still, at least we know that Mwalimu is right. When you work together you can achieve great things. Remember our 1972 harvest? Six hundred bags of maize! Truly, to quote Mwalimu again, *ujamaas* can be the engine of economic growth."

Some might not be able to stop talking. Others might sit silently, their thoughts too deep for words. Thinking perhaps of the highest price of all demanded in the move, easy access to the graves of their ancestors. As is the custom, all voices are drawn out before the hearing concludes.

Yet others might point to Mwalimu's growing disappointment as some people cling too tightly to their old way of doing things. "Also, especially in the cities, there are those who no longer remember their African roots," someone would likely point out to justify why Mwalimu believes this to be the only effective way forward; the only path to a better life. "He is asking us to trust him, to work with him, to give him time. And you know that he himself is working harder than all of us," they might say. "Above all, we know that he has our welfare at heart."

"Thank goodness that we voluntarily gave up our former homes and moved to Lwanga when we did," Mzee Mpiluka of Lwanga muses. "Now we can rest easier at this time of national turmoil." Little does he know how deeply the forced villagization policy will affect them all.

EMANUEL MDEMU — BEE WHISPERER

Tanzania's economic conditions worsen. Public service incomes stall. Many government officials seek employment with private companies. Emanuel Mdemu, Tanzania's number one bee expert, who travelled the world while working with the Bee Division of the Forestry Department, has chosen to join Brooke Bond Tea Company. He wants to work closer to home — namely, Ifwagi Village. Geoff is tasked with introducing Emanuel to tea production in preparation for his eventual assignment as personnel manager at head office.

"Bees!" Geoff announces one day.

"What about bees?"

"I think we should put Emanuel's considerable experience to good use and start keeping bees. Everyone wants honey."

"Okay," sighs Vicky distractedly. "Bees it is!" (With a school and a dairy farm, Vicky understandably feels she already has enough on her plate. But little does she know what lies ahead!)

Geoff somehow manages to find an imported Modified Datant Bee Hive and contracts carpenters to copy it with modifications advised by Emanuel; for example, reducing the spacing between comb frames, as the African bee is smaller than the "Italian" bee (the bee generally used in commercial honey beekeeping throughout Europe and the Americas). Around 1,000 hives are made, baited with honey at the entrance and in the grooves of the frames, and distributed throughout the surrounding Lugoda forests in more than twenty apiaries.

"Guess how many wild swarms we've caught, Vicky?" Geoff is brimming over with excitement. "Some 550! We're in business."

In anticipation of huge quantities of honey, the tea company buys centrifuges and special honey filters and barrels, as well as a considerable number of honey jars. Then they wait, and wait — only to discover major setbacks: (1) Other people also like their honey (which forces

Geoff to put on twenty-four-hour guards to cover all apiaries) and (2) that the African bee builds three times as many combs for brood cells as for honey storage cells—there being no need to store honey for the winter, since bees can forage all year round and need only enough honey in storage to feed emerging pupae. As a result, their hives produce an average of no more than eleven pounds, compared to twenty-four pounds from the Italian bee on commercial farms in Europe.

"Our mistake," Geoff will explain many years later, "was to have returned the combs back into the hives to be refilled, rather than valuing the wax itself, from which we could have made value-added candles of various designs. Bruce, who was very keen on bees for a while, made his own beekeeping equipment, and acquired an assortment of wax candle moulds, one of which was a complete candle chess set. But, eventually proving commercially uneconomical, our bee scheme was abandoned. In retrospect, we should have simply 'plundered' the hives [in the traditional African way] and extracted all the wax, too.

"People now come out to Tanzania with the greatest ideas on beekeeping, but few want our advice. Regardless, here it is—based on our (unsuccessful) experience with 550 hives on a commercial scale.

"Pivotally, we concluded that commercial beekeeping should mimic what happens in nature. The African bee has survived the plundering of its hives (courtesy of honey badgers, man, and others) by reproducing itself prodigiously. In other words, indigenous methods of beekeeping using log and bark hives are probably the only solution. By opening the hive, extracting all the honey and the wax, before leaving the plundered hive available for the bees to return to, they do indeed respond to the bees' natural behaviour in the wild. (Incidentally, one only needs to wax bait the hive a single time, initially, because the smell remains strong enough to draw the bees back.)

"Emanuel's knowledge of the indigenous rainforest of Mufindi, of Hehe history (he was related to Chief Mkwawa), and the Hehe language was unsurpassed. I persuaded him to translate the complete *Teach Yourself Kiswahili* book into a *Teach Yourself Kihehe* text—the only one of its kind. For this he will be remembered.[33]

"Emanuel, when he retired, went on to keep a number of hives

---

33   The manuscript, which was lost for ten years but is still the only one of its kind, is currently in preparation for publication.

containing the tiny, 'stingless' bees, known by us as 'sweat bees.' They are attracted by moisture and always went for our eyes when we were hunting in the bush. Their honey is extremely sweet and sought after.

"Unfortunately, after a stroke, Emanuel's eyesight deteriorated considerably and I was anxious that he should write his own story. Although his eyes were tested, there was no prospect of obtaining glasses of that strength in Tanzania.

"So I talked to Specsavers in England, who kindly donated an outdoor and a reading pair. This delighted Emanuel, who said that he could see buildings on a hill opposite his house that he never knew existed. Sadly, he died soon after. I always hoped he would write a history of the Hehe."

EXPERIMENTING

While on leave in the UK, the Foxes also decide to rear pheasants in Mufindi. Apart from needing special containers, the Foxes are warned that pheasants must be medicated regularly and are unlikely to survive in Africa. Undaunted, they bring back the eggs of seven pheasant varieties: golden, ring-necked, melanistic mutant, and so on. Little do they know it at the time, but all seven varieties will hatch. Not only that but, defying expert opinion, they will breed profusely.

"Foolishly," as Geoff will later recall, "I released some for sporting purposes, which you don't do, of course. Where you have natural flora and fauna, you shouldn't introduce foreign species. Luckily, they didn't survive the predators—the buzzards and eagles—of Mufindi.

"Our 'wild man' also hastened their end," Geoff will continue. "He was a mentally challenged guy, whom the police detained one day but stupidly allowed to escape with a pistol that was left lying around. As far as I know, he never used the pistol, but he did build himself a simple little hut near us in the forest on Lugoda Estate, and then moved around frequently, building little shacks wherever he could. "He fed on our pheasants and on our next-door neighbours' [the Keeleys] vegetables, stealing them under cover of darkness. His brother from Nzivi village finally killed him and dumped his weighted corpse into the lake. His crime: stealing and selling his brother's cow. It was probably inevitable, since there was no accessible institution, the closest being the mental asylum in Dodoma."

《•》《•》《•》《•》

The international oil shock waves of 1974 and 1975 send the world into global recession, further gutting Tanzania's export earnings.

Vicky to Geoff's parents: "Food here is terribly difficult to get at the moment. No butter, no margarine, no Kimbo oil or cooking fat. A shortage of eggs, no bacon, and the maize is likely to run out early next year. What a carry on. Or, as Jimmy would say, "How about that, then?" We make our own butter and bacon with Lupeme pork. We have killed two poor little calves for veal since we got back, and the whole lot was gone in two days.

"I've been detailed to cut up a deep frozen pig, as all the men are too busy. I don't think I can saw through it, but everyone is frightened of defrosting it then refreezing it. Ah well, no doubt I'll manage. (It took two and a half hours to accomplish that little mission.) P.S. There is also no layers mash in the whole of Tanzania and hasn't been since April, so I have made a special Fox diet and never have the hens had it so good, at a quarter of the price. There must be a snag, I fear."

None of this deters the Foxes from envisaging a long-term future there for their sons, who desperately want to stay in Africa.

"How about trying to find *Centella Asiatica*?" an old friend of Vicky's asks over tea in Middlemoor one day. The Foxes are once more on home leave, this time brainstorming alternative moneymaking ventures with Mary de Portalès (née Fortescue), who married the general manager of a French pharmaceutical company.

"What is *Centella*?" asks Vicky.

"It's a very small herb used by only one company in the world: Laroche Navarone, owned by Madame Laroche and situated in France."

"Isn't that the company you manage, Charles?"

"Yes, indeed," Mary's husband says. "The problem is, we can only get *Centella* from a single supplier in Madagascar, and it's proving more and more difficult."

"Madagascar?"

"Yes. Madagascar. Which is why the active ingredient is called Madacassol. We use it for healing lesions."

"Can't you grow it yourselves?"

"We've tried, but when we grow it under glass, the active ingredient weakens. It would be a gold mine if you could find some out there. And there's no reason why it shouldn't grow in Tanzania."

Back in Mufindi, Vicky and Geoff search high and low, to no avail. So, with their boys' possible future in Tanzania in mind, they decide to try coffee growing instead. Again they are in their element, with Vicky digging through agricultural textbooks, Geoff offering his practical experience, and both of them exploring coffee farms in the region. Together they work out that the climate 2,000 feet lower at the foot of the Mufindi escarpment, in the Mgololo area of the Great Rift Valley, is likely to be the most suitable. Down they go together to inspect one possible site.

"Look! Look!"

They are both pointing at the same time and laughing out loud. A carpet of *Centella Asiatica* almost hides their feet.

"It's growing like a weed right on our land!"

"What do you mean 'like a weed'? It *is* a weed!"

"Not anymore!"

All around them are carpets of it, spreading wildly in every direction. They pick a few samples and head back up the 2,000-foot escarpment. As usual, Vicky soon disappears. When Geoff finally catches up with her, sitting at the top, "Spare me," he pants.

"You mean, 'what kept you so long'?" Vicky asks innocently and runs off, just in case he still has the energy to kick her.

Now the question is how to get the samples safely to France. Sending anything abroad from Tanzania is all but impossible these days. "I have an idea," says Geoff. Vicky cringes. Geoff is always full of ideas, and most of them involve something for her to do.

"Why don't you put on your best party dress, paint your face, and meet with the French ambassador?" he continues.

"Oh no, Foxey. And what would I say?"

"Ask him for permission to send the *Centella* samples through their diplomatic bag, given how desperate a French company is for the product, and how difficult it is to send things abroad from Tanzania right now."

To their delight, the ambassador initially promises to help but later backs out, saying, "I realize that it is wrong to have to risk the loss of the *Centella* through the regular mail, but it is also wrong to use the diplomatic bag this way, and two wrong procedures don't make a correct procedure."

Off go the samples by commercial mail—a tea chest full. Time passes. The Foxes lose hope and focus on other things, but the sample does indeed finally reach Paris. Laroche Navarone's response is ecstatic. Enthusiastic telegrams declare the quality "perfect" and ask for more . . . lots more.

"The boys will be taking some plants back for Charles de Pour-tale. It appears that we have found what he wants. The samples we previously sent him proved "excellent" (from his telegram), the price appears to be good, but we're being frustrated over obtaining enough land to grow it."

Charles confirms that Laroche Navarone want very much to do business with the Foxes and invites Geoff and Vicky to their factories in Paris and the Pyrenees, for a demonstration of their processes and products, used, among others, as medication for lesions caused by skin conditions such as leprosy, plastic surgery, and ulcers.

On their next leave, Geoff and Vicky head to Paris, all expenses paid. "As we approached Orly Airport in Paris, there was this official flypast in our honour," Geoff will later joke with friends. "Only it turned out to be the Paris Air Show."

They revel in lavish accommodation (all the more stunning after the deteriorating conditions in Tanzania) and enjoy enthusiastic meetings with the company in Paris before being flown—as guests of honour—down to Pau, close to the Spanish border, near the Pyrenees. To their surprise, it is a very English town, with pubs sporting pictures of English foxes, horses, and hounds.

"At a lecture on the origins of *Centella*, one of Laroche Navarone's experts announces that 'in Africa, lions and tigers were noticed to have healed themselves,' and similar rot (there is no African tiger), about which we had to correct him," Geoff later tells Tanzanian colleagues. At the time, he notices that Laroche boil the *Centella* leaves in vats to extract the active ingredient. Being a tea planter, Geoff suggests they do it the tea factory way and chop the leaves up first. Whereupon there is an embarrassed hush, followed by an admission that this is what they have decided to do in future.

The Foxes agree to a commercial partnership with them, and return from leave convinced that their future fortunes are now assured—especially after they gain the support of all the local villagers and the minister of agriculture to use their preferred plot, 2,000 feet below Mufindi, not just for *Centella*, but for coffee as well.

Both crops thrive. "Actually," Vicky remembers many years later, "the coffee grew much better down there than Geoff's coffee for Brooke Bond did at Ngwazi."

"Vicky has been energetically dashing up and down the escarpment visiting trial plots and a coffee nursery we have established at the bottom," Geoff writes to Gelly and Jimmy, "given my full-time employment with Brooke Bond." Indeed, once a week Vicky and her gardener, Julius Mdegella, drive on company tea estate roads to the end of the tea field closest to the forest near a track leading to the Kigogo River.

Then, because the road ends there, they have to walk on a tiny footpath through the forest. "Just over two miles," Vicky will later tell her family, while on home leave in England. "The good thing is that the forest trail to the edge of the escarpment is spectacular. In fact, so spectacular that Geoff is building a forest road.[34] So next time you visit we can take you there. Equally breathtaking but in a completely different way is the 2,000-foot descent down the steepest part of the Mufindi escarpment into the Great Rift Valley below. It's like being in another country down there. The first thing to hit us at the bottom is always the heat."

"They then walk for about forty-five minutes along the valley floor through razor-sharp elephant grass to the Kigogo River," Geoff adds. "And in the afternoon, they have to hike all the way back up. That's more than five hours of walking in total. I claim that no European has been up and down the Mufindi escarpment more often than Vicky." He beams.

Vicky shakes her head. "Any time that thought goes through my mind," she says, "I look at the Tanzanian women from down in Mgololo, whom I meet on the way, and feel ashamed. They routinely do the same. Only they have gargantuan loads on their heads and more often than not babies on their backs as well. That is how bananas make their way up to the highlands. And precious consumer goods [including heavy loads of oil, salt, and cloth] make their way back down to the valley."

《•》《•》《•》《•》

---

34   Used to this day by Unilever Tea Company to show VIPs the spectacular vista.

The *Centella* (and the coffee) thrive. The Foxes anticipate great things. Geoff completes the forest road between the tea and the escarpment edge. Then from Laroche Navarone: silence. It finally transpires that Mme. Laroche has sold the company to Americans. The Foxes write to the new owners and, receiving no reply, assume they are no longer interested . . .

MIRACLE RAILWAY

"They eat snakes!" Vicky learns from horrified Tanzanians ("They" being the Chinese working on the TAZARA railway, which by then has reached the Rift Valley below the Fox farm on its 1,160-mile journey from Tanzania to Zambia). Farm gossip is rife with tales of Chinese exploits that filter up the escarpment as men and women trade bananas and raffia from down in Mgololo for precious salt and oil from the Mufindi highlands.

The Chinese complete the TAZARA Railway two years ahead of schedule in 1975, widely recognized as a superb feat of engineering.

About one-third of its tunnels and bridges are concentrated in a ten-mile stretch up from the Rift Valley, through the escarpment to Makambako. Just as mango trees still mark the slave-trading routes (the seeds from mangos purchased on the coast being discarded inland along the route), so paw-paw and banana trees, as well as vestiges of vegetable gardens, now mark where the Chinese had put up their mobile construction camps.

Two years ahead of schedule or not, TAZARA cannot prevent Tanzania's continuing slide into critical shortages of anything requiring foreign exchange. However, it does take some pressure off the manic and often deadly traffic of delivering copper from, and fuel to, Zambia on the now paved but often potholed Great North Road. Meanwhile, agricultural production has fallen dramatically as Tanzania's relocated population gamely tries to implement collective farming in new environments.

"RATHER AMATEURISH, I THOUGHT"

Expatriate employees of the tea company remain relatively unscathed, thanks to regular paycheques and habitual improvisation. They continue to pool their private resources to create and maintain: a sailing club (with several men building their own boats to use on the substantial, manmade Lake Ngwazi); a rod and gun club for the fishing, hunting, and shooting fraternity (spearheaded by Jonny Niblett), including a tiny chalet on the banks of the lovely Luisenga Dam; and, of course, the Mufindi Club for social gatherings.

Then there's the beautiful little stone Anglican church (inspired by Dick and Dorothy Dickenson, with stained-glass windows donated by the mother of one of Geoff's best friends, Nick Ginner, who drowned at Ngwazi), and a squash court Geoff built for just 11,000 shillings (about £550 or $1,800 at the time), complete with a balcony for spectators (still in regular use in 2013, when Geoff reminisces, "In those days, a pioneering spirit encouraged tea planters to develop their own recreational facilities, whereas later on, new staff merely expected everything to be provided for them.")

Vicky continues to play the organ, harmonium, and later a piano (when the harmonium breaks down) at church services presided over by visiting ministers. Initially, she plays on a harmonium that needed to be pedalled. The sound is splendid but it eventually threatens to fall apart while she plays. Toward the end of its life, she has two of her sons, one on either side, physically holding it together as she vigorously pumps the pedals.

Vicky after playing the organ at St. John's Church in Mufindi.

When it dies at last, Vicky and Geoff cart their heavy piano to the church, to be used until the Sheridan–Johnsons provide their electric piano, which can be reset to organ music. Because the church is located on Lugoda, the estate that Geoff has managed for many years, it is his job to look after the grounds.

"One day, the wife of a planter died," Geoff recalls. "Shortly before that, we had buried an old settler, Mr. Muirhead. So I took the same gravediggers who had dug the grave for the old boy, located a spot, and told them, 'This is where we will put her. We will need to dig six feet, as we did before.' I should have returned to check the site before the funeral.

"The service began with Vicky playing the harmonium as people filed in. Then we waited for the visiting vicar. He was to come by bus to Kibao, a few miles away, where David MacDonald would pick him up and drive him to the church. After we had all waited for a while, and Vicky had played the same music over and over again several times, David MacDonald suddenly slapped his temple and rushed out of the door to fetch the vicar—he had forgotten that he had promised to collect him.

"It was gently drizzling. I was one of the four coffin bearers, followed by the mourners, protected under umbrellas, with Vicky playing, and some singing, 'The Lord Is My Shepherd.' As we approached the grave, to my horror, I saw that it was indeed six-feet—wide! It was also six-feet deep, sort of wedge-shaped. I had arranged for two ropes to be placed across the front so that we could easily pick the coffin up and lower our friend into her grave. However, to avoid being dragged into the grave ourselves, we had to be at least two feet away from the mud-slicked edge, which meant that the coffin bearers were now ten feet apart.

"As the coffin with occupant was heavy, this resulted in a desperate tug of war between the rope holders, each trying to avoid being dragged in by the other. Mournful faces were difficult to maintain . . . and the sounds of 'The Lord Is My Shepherd' faltered.

"When we had got our friend about halfway along the top of the grave, the worst happened; the ropes were wet from the rain, and she slid gracefully, feet first, into the grave. There the coffin stood—vertical. Shocked silence. Jonny Niblett, one of the pallbearers, jumped in, followed by myself and then the other two. We finally got our friend horizontal at the bottom of the grave and then tried to get out – bearing in mind that the side slope was some forty degrees; it was raining; the grave was pure wet, muddy, red clay, and extremely slippery.

"Out of respect for our friend, we couldn't jump on the coffin, so we had to try to manoeuvre ourselves out any other way. Finally, we emerged over the top of the grave in our best suits and ties, plastered in red mud!

"The imported English padre from Njombe, ninety miles away, had only a single comment afterwards: 'Rather amateurish, I'd say.' Anyway, it seems I lost my job that day, as I haven't been asked to bury anyone since.

"The same might, I suppose, be said about spreading ashes. Much later, David and Caroline Gordon, Vicky, and I were spreading the ashes of our good friend Baz Townsend at Pew Tor on Dartmoor in Devon—as he had willed. A bottle of champagne was opened, glasses were filled, and I was given the honour of casting forth the urn, where it shattered against a granite rock, spreading the ashes into the wind. Awkwardly, the wind changed direction, and Baz flew into our champagne—which we drank anyway!

"As for my own funeral, I have planned to leave a lasting memory for my boys by selecting a burial spot above our farmhouse that is so rocky they will have a hell of a job digging the hole, and will, no doubt, say: 'The old man gave us a hard time right to the end!'

"My friend Julius and long-term headman (who will also be buried there) and I have already planted the area with albizia (*mitanga* in Swahili), a lovely, indigenous umbrella-shaped tree that stands out in the forest in all seasons and appears to have no commercial value, so it will not likely be chopped down."

VICKY'S EXPANDING FARM

One day, Vicky hears about a freezer for sale at a nearby road construction project, along with other surplus equipment. A freezer would make such a difference to her little dairy farm.

"Life without a fridge is very similar to spending time on safari, isn't it?" Vicky sighs. Her friend Helga agrees. "I've tried so many ways of conserving other foods. A freezer would make all the difference." Quietly, they agree to buy it together. Quietly, because Helga knows that Werner would disapprove of her spending all this money. Since the Voigts also have no electricity on their farm, the freezer finds its home at the Foxes'.

"I think Helga and I became such good friends," Vicky will tell her daughter, Evelyn, years later "because we shared some of the same heritage. My great-grandfather was a Jewish German—paediatric consultant to Kaiser Wilhelm at one time, actually. He, too, had to leave behind a privileged existence, in what is now Beloruss for refuge in Germany in the 1800s.

"How we loved our rather dilapidated freezer! Whenever Helga delivered tea to the factory, she visited me, ostensibly to have tea, but also to drop off produce for freezing and to retrieve precious items for serving back home." (Home being a red burnt-brick house embraced by emerald tea fields and olive-coloured coffee trees, silvered grevillea, dark green firs, and a rainbow of fruit trees, each planted by Helga and Werner. These produced a cornucopia of limes, lemons, peaches, mulberries, pineapples, mountain papayas, oyster nuts, and passion fruit in season. Also sweet, small strawberries, apples, pears, blackberries, wineberries, gooseberries, bananas, quinces, loquats, grenadillas, and oodles of plums [bruised and swollen in times of overflow, with sun birds slumped on branches, their iridescent blue-green wings outspread for balance, eyes half closed, and long, curved beaks stuck deep in the fermenting fruit—as drunk as lords]).

"We are building masses of new rabbit hutches and are enlarging our garden to grow kale to feed them on," Vicky writes to Libby in May 1975. "We've decided that sheep are the next project. Werner and I have also decided on a joint venture to produce our own salami, a very precious commodity when nothing like that is available in the shops." And in December of the same year: "We're buying some sheep and starting a small sheep scheme."

The sheep in question are from a vast New Zealand sheep-rearing project on the elevated Kitulo (erstwhile Elton) Plateau. Vicky and Geoff have made several excursions to the plateau in the past, timing their visits around February, when carpets of ground orchids run riot in purples, reds, and pinks, between startlingly exquisite mountain streams. (So abundant is the selection that people start digging up bulbs for export to Zambia as food. Luckily, the endangered orchids will ultimately be protected by the renamed Kitulo National Park.) At the same altitude as the orchid fields, pedigree New Zealand sheep once thrived on the grounds of a New Zealand-sponsored project, peaking in numbers at 20,000 pedigree Corriedale sheep. (Since the expatriates returned home, the sheep have gradually been sold off.)

"With the beef, rabbit, and mutton," Vicky's letter continues, "we'll never have to buy meat. Our salami project has at last started. The first disaster involved trying to find suitable salami skins, after those in the initial batch from England weren't breathable, and the salami couldn't dry out. "Werner finally found some in Germany, and we later also discovered some English ones that worked. It was more difficult to get them in England, because salami is seldom made there. The second disaster was Werner's decision to try cypress wood for smoking. It turned out that soft wood taints the salamis. One of my smoking books suggested using wet corncobs. We tried those and—presto!—delicious salami, ideally bound for the company shop.

"My job was to produce the recipe (beef, pork, fat, spices, and saltpeter), Werner's to smoke them on his farm, Kifyulilo. We minced the ingredients at our place because by then we had electricity, which was also why we kept Helga's and my freezer in our house.

"Mum sent out the skins by airmail from England, and we made forty-two large salamis, which we hope to start selling. They now look fantastic hanging in the smoker. We are a bit worried that the skins may not be quite right but we're praying they are, as we now have 500 of them and they cost ten pence (thirty cents) each. Anyway, the insides tasted very good before we put them in. It was quite a long, hard job I must say to take the bone gristle and beef fat off before we could mince it all. Fortunately, the company has a huge electric mincer, which mashes it all up just as fast as you can feed it in.

"We now have nearly two acres of vegetable garden. The rabbits, second generation, are at last breeding, so we should begin to make money from them. I found a marvellous recipe for salt meat and I made salt beef the other day; so once we get our own pigs, I shan't even have to buy bacon and ham.

"All sorts of rumours abound that all the British companies will be taken over within two years. I don't know if it's true. But it would be in accordance with the government's policy. We are beginning to think very hard about where to go and what to do.

"Our boys all arrive in a fortnight's time for their Christmas holidays. I can't believe it's so soon. It doesn't feel like Christmas at all, without shops and town decorations to remind you."

《•》《•》《•》《•》

Vicky and Helga manage to keep the freezer deception up for three years before Werner finds out.

HIGHS AND LOWS OF UJAMAA

"In 1974–75, people were forced out of their villages to new settlements, where the houses often weren't ready yet (in the rains, so they missed a crop)," Dr. Rob Bosma[35] will later remember from his years at the Iringa regional hospital and surrounding villages. "We had a massive influx of pneumonia and malnutrition in the hospital with many deaths. I also witnessed the remains of village houses, burnt down to prevent people from returning, occasionally with burned bodies inside. The following year Prime Minister Kawawa's scheduled visit to Iringa was cancelled for security reasons. And Nyerere was unpopular there for years, although the *Daily News* suggested that he knew nothing about it. Mind you, Gerdine and I were and still are great supporters of Nyerere, one of the reasons we went to Tanzania."

The forced relocation of smallholder farmers into villages, particularly in the Iringa province, has led to massive disruptions, not only to people's personal lives, but also to national agriculture (Tanzania's domestic mainstay) and to cash crops (its only source of foreign exchange, already dwindling in the wake of the oil shock). This is strangling both the government's good intentions as well as Tanzania's economy. The cash-strapped government cannot pay farmers enough for their crops, and the national liberation slogan of "*Uhuru na Umoja*" (Freedom and Unity) has almost totally given way to "*Uhuru na Kazi*" (Freedom and Work). As the theory and practice of *Ujamaa* increasingly part ways, more and more people begin to opt out of communal work, especially in the forced villagization areas, concentrating instead on their own little patches of land.

Even so, progress elsewhere still bolsters confidence: more children in school, more adults in literacy classes, and more

---

35   Dr. Bosma, referred to in the Poor Marrick incident, later practiced in Mufindi.

clinics in villages (albeit running out of medication due to the foreign exchange crisis). But, arguably, Mwalimu's greatest achievement is how, in relatively short order and without armed conflict, he melded a disparate, clan-based society into a peaceful country with a growing national identity.

A lurching bus ride from Mufindi to Iringa just over a decade past Independence graphically demonstrates this. Eyeing the lone white person among them (Evelyn Voigt), fellow passengers launch into the relative merits of development aid to Tanzania from China, the United States, and England. Their discussion in Swahili is lively. Above all, they clearly and confidently define themselves as Tanzanians. Chinese assistance wins hands-down—another sideward glance at the *mzungu*, foreigner. Very impressive to think that isolated, rural Mufindi residents have moved from clan to nation in such a short time, particularly considering the huge personal sacrifices many have had to make along the way.

《•》《•》《•》《•》

In Derrick Hester, Geoff's first boss and now company director, Brooke Bond Liebig has a man of ideal skills for walking the tightrope between capitalism and socialism. Like Mwalimu, and like Mzee Mpiluka, he is a leader of integrity; reserved and principled, yet quietly tinged with steel when necessary.

Derrick wears several hats. Besides being director of Brooke Bond Liebig, he is also on the management committee of the Tanzania Tea Distributors Organization, as well as on the Tea Authority Board. He has been with the company in Mufindi since the fifties and has accompanied it through its evolution from a subsidiary of Brooke Bond Kenya to an independent company. He has seen it merge with Liebig and finally, in 1974, he helped to negotiate a 60:40 percent shareholding agreement for Tanganyika Tea Blenders in favour of the Tanzania Tea Authority.

"We are of course a capitalist company operating in a socialist country," he tells Evelyn in 1977. "We are very conscious of it, but we do, as far as possible, co-operate in every way. For example, there are the development projects. The minister of agriculture called the tea producers together (through the Tanzania Tea Growers Association) in May 1977. He said the private sector should consider developing the industry and not leave everything to the government. We have since organized a three-year project to add 200 hectares of tea, 100 of coffee and cinchona [a tree whose bark yields anti-malarial quinine, of which there is a huge shortage following the Vietnam war], as well as construction of a new factory.

"One of the largest capital investments since 1970 was the introduction of overhead irrigation on many of the estates, including new dams and costly pumps and equipment from Austria. This development followed the brilliant research into the hydrology of tea carried out by Dr. Mike Carr[36] at Ngwazi, which doubled company tea production within ten years. Eighty percent of this crop was exported, earning Tanzania valuable foreign exchange at a time of critical shortfall. Thus we agree to capital outlay in a country where capitalistic returns are questioned."

Then there is "self-help." "Because of the increasing food shortages," he continues, "we had to import everything, including maize, the staple food for estate workers. That proved to be a great strain on foreign resources. To counteract this, we started to grow our own maize and in two years have become totally self-supporting in milled maize flour. Not only the estate workers, but also their dependents (between 12,000 and 15,000 people) benefit from this."

《•》《•》《•》《•》

Among the beneficiaries is Christina Mvinge, born in a little Mufindi village named Luhunga. When her mother goes to work in the Brooke Bond tea fields, baby Christina is on her back, lulled by the motion of the long walks there and back. Or rocked when her mother bends, her fingers flying, as she plucks only the youngest shoots, ideally two chartreuse leaves and a bud delicately uncurling from olive old growth. Then, later, like other preschoolers, Christina plays in the grass at the edge of the tea fields in the sun, or under cover of giant trees when it rains. Her ready laughter is a constant beacon to her working mother, except for one day, as she will tell Geoff years later. She remembers his coming to the plantation and how she ran for her life to crouch silently behind protective bushes, because everyone knew that the only reason white people visited villages was to kidnap their children.

---

36   Dr. Carr's most recent publication is *Advances in Irrigation Agronomy: Plantation Crops* (Carr, M.K.V.), Cambridge University Press, 2013.

《•》《•》《•》《•》

As well as managing Lugoda and Kidope tea estates, Geoff now has the responsibility to cultivate up to 1,000 acres of company maize in Ngwazi. "This was the time of *Ujamaa's* villagization days when private cultivation by villagers was limited," Geoff reminisces years later, "and Tanzania suffered subsequent famine. However, private companies were allowed to grow maize, and this was my task at Ngwazi.

"I stored maize year round for issue to all estates on a controlled basis, according to workforce figures. The maize was sold at a fair and affordable price, which meant that during these 'famine years,' we never had any problem recruiting workers; they simply flocked in, knowing they would be fed.

"This provided me with the excuse to visit sunny Ngwazi on wet and misty days in Lugoda and Kidope! So, to this day, whenever I meet old estate workers, they always say: 'I remember you grew maize.' It's not the tea they recall, for which I was mainly employed."

Planting such an extensive area of maize requires mechanized seeders, which have to be used just before the start of the rains. After that, the mud takes over. "Dry seeding," as this is called, means that the seed has to be available on time, because every planting day's delay after the start of the rains reduces the yield by about one bag per hectare per day. So two weeks' delay can drop yields from between sixty and seventy bags to as low as fifty bags per hectare. However, if the rain is late, the seed in the ground is vulnerable to deterioration or being eaten by birds and insects.

Taking everything into account, Geoff selects November 25 as his optimum starting date for seeding, in anticipation of the rains arriving on December 1. ("In those days, the beginning and end of the rains was very reliable," he will explain in later years, "unlike nowadays, when every year seems to be an 'unusual' year.") The problem in 1977 is that Tanseed (a Tanzanian parastatal company and the only supplier of seeds in Tanzania at the time) can't guarantee prompt delivery. What to do?

"Brain wave!" Geoff shouts out jubilantly one evening. Vicky jumps. "I know how I'm going to get the maize seed on time!"

"How?"

"I'll ask Tanseed if I can grow the hybrid maize seed for them on contract, as long as they supply me with their parent stock. This way I could extract my own seed requirements before delivering the rest to them."

"Brilliant, Foxey," says Vicky. "Fingers crossed."

Tanseed agrees. Then comes another major hurdle: how to attract enough labour to weed the maize at a time when people are busy with their own crops.

"Brain wave!" Geoff says again. "*Ulanzi!* [bamboo wine] I'll plant it around the fields and issue free bottles to those who complete their tasks." Geoff does indeed surround the maize fields with *ulanzi* and issues free bottles after work to all who help to weed, thus getting folks from as far as Makombako, fifty miles away, to sign up!

《•》《•》《•》《•》

On a glorious Mufindi day in August 1977, Evelyn Voigt (back home from Canada to visit her parents, the Foxes' German settler friends) heads off to see long-time family friend Mzee Mpiluka, chairman of Lwanga Village. Everyone has been singing his praises, especially for his integrity and how—against all odds—he keeps bringing Lwanga back from the brink.

An electric-blue sky, periodically clashing with yellow cassia, reflects painfully off the whitewashed walls around Lwanga's co-operative store. A few people are milling about. Some have brought brightly coloured shirts into the sunlight for closer inspection. They are rubbing the cotton expertly between their thumbs and forefingers to test its quality. One woman, having just bought a little oil (for a change the shop does have some), asks the shopkeeper to pour it into a tiny bottle for her. This she balances on her head as she leaves, keeping one hand free to guide her toddler, the other to wave goodbye.

The shopkeeper continues joking with her, increasingly raising his voice as she moves off, even as he tends to his other, still laughing customers. He can usually offer them sugar, maize meal, tea, oil, salt, and soap (the blue-and-white metre-long bars he cuts into tiny squares); and a few hardware items such as torches, mugs, and knives, as well as two or three cloths and a handful of shirts.

His store stands in a cluster of brown mud-and-wattle huts with thatched roofs. A few boast brick walls or tin roofs—signs of status. Some older men are sitting around on homemade wooden chairs. Women gracefully saunter past, children on their backs, earthenware pots balanced on rings of leaves on their heads. Behind them, the wind blows in layers of sound through recently harvested maize fields. Broken stems, already dehydrating, rustle. A toddler chews on one, hoping for sweet sap.

Evelyn passes the two-room school. It is one of the few red brick houses in the village, set conspicuously beyond a driveway lined in whitewashed stones. Everything is swept and neat—probably because there are no cars to churn up the dust. Lwanga school has one teacher and 100 pupils. Besides arithmetic, reading and writing, he teaches civics (collective village administration), and—to keep the children in touch with their rural roots—he makes them practise what they learn about agriculture by cultivating maize.

For most of the children, graduation after seven years of basic schooling means the end of their formal education (unless they attend adult education classes with literate volunteer teachers, who are paid the equivalent of about £1 or $4.50 per month by the Tanzanian government as part of a nationwide campaign to raise adult literacy). Almost half of the adults in Mufindi can neither read nor write. While two-thirds of them are officially registered in adult *Ujamaa* education classes, they attend only sporadically when subsistence livelihoods permit. What they don't grow, they don't eat, so their energies go first to tilling, seeding, planting, and harvesting.

Mzee Ruben Mpiluka greets Evelyn. "*Kamwene*," he says. She curtsies, Kihehe style. "*Kamwene*." He seems quite happy to discuss his role as elected village chair, probably because he has known her since she returned with Helga and Werner from internment as a toddler of two.

"How is Lwanga faring, Mzee?" she asks, after the extended courtesies.

"*Haba na haba hujaza kibaba* [grain by grain to fill the vessel]," he says. "These days much more slowly." Then, shaking his head, he adds: "Some of it very good. Some of it very sad."

"I haven't seen you since 1974. How did forced villagization affect Lwanga?"

(For the most part, Mufindi people moved into the assigned

135

Ujamaa villages without incident, although trucks did arrive at night where trouble was expected. Once families had packed up their belongings, and still under guarded supervision, they would have to knock out any window frames and doors, fill the truck, get on themselves and wait to be transported to their allocated village sites.)

"We were lucky that we chose to move earlier. But, because the government thought we were so well organized, we had to accept 250 more members," Mzee responds. It transpires that Lwanga's new status as a hybrid between the relatively successful "self-initiated *ujamaa*," as political economist Andrew Coulson defines it, and the relatively unproductive "development village" resulting from forced resettlement has spawned predictable problems.

"The situation now is very difficult," Mzee continues. "There are lazy people who spoil the efforts of those who want to work together. We are discussing at the village meetings how to deal with the problem; how to force, or encourage, or punish the lazy ones. There are always those who spoil it for the others.

"We have petitioned the government to allow us who want to work together to do so and to let the others go their own ways. If one forces people, one spends one's time arguing and the work is left undone.

"There are also too many people for the village water supply now. It is no longer clean, except for the first users. The others have to do with muddy water. Also, people are still waiting for the compensation they were promised when they had to abandon brick houses and move into the mud houses in Lwanga.

"I'm getting old, these days, and tired. It is time for me to hand over to someone else, but they won't let me go."

And still the lines outside the shops in Tanzania grow longer, store shelves emptier. Unfortunately, the gains of Mwalimu's policies are not as visible, or Tanzania could display their increased adult literacy, a growing national health infrastructure that now covers the whole country, and the higher number of children in school. Instead, glaringly empty shelves speak only to the dearth of consumer goods.

《•》《•》《•》《•》

Like everyone else, the Mufindi expatriates make the best of it. They grow their own vegetables. They make their own wine, not to mention their own bread, or jam, or pickles, or mustard—in fact, most consumables. The order of the day: grow it, barter it, or do without. When even the tea company shop runs out of yeast, the Mufindi expatriates get recipes from the Norwegians on how to make flat breads. On the day yeast reappears, everyone gathers at the club for a spontaneous "thanksgiving" party.

"Imagine that! Real toast for breakfast!"

"I can't wait."

Finally, Brooke Bond organizes an annual container of food supplies to be shipped out, against mail-order catalogue purchases. "There were so many lovely people in Mufindi in those days," Geoff will later say, "but no one kinder than June Hester.[37] During those times of desperate shortages and annual containers, June, by then the company chairman's wife, made sure that this was divided fairly to match the size of the managers' families. In addition to the imported goods, June allocated local items in short supply—sugar, oil, etcetera—according to the number of workers on each estate. I do remember, when Derrick was chairman, they made sure that they lived in a very simply furnished house, no better than anyone else. That's the kind of people they are."

RABIES AND OTHER ALEXANDER ADVENTURES

For nineteen of his twenty years as manager of Lugoda Estate, Geoff is also the groundskeeper of the golf course. "This greatly relieves the boredom of tea and gives me an opportunity to inspect my greens every day on a *piki piki* [motorbike—that's how some of the Swahili words are made, by mimicking sounds, in this case of the motorbike: pikipikipiki]."

By 1977, the Mufindi course is perhaps the most attractive in the whole country. Although it has only nine holes, Mufindi Club will host the Tanganyika Open Amateur Championships (for only the second time, the first being in the mid-fifties), with Geoff elected chairman of the Tanganyika Golfing Association.

---

37   Pat Somerville, now Pat Dale, is Christopher Fox's godmother; and June Hester is Bruce Fox's godmother.

"Being the honorary groundsman, and preferring the golf course to tea, the greens are immaculate," Geoff says when congratulated. His smile fades as the discussion turns to a woman from Moshi, in northern Tanzania, who has applied to enter the tournament.

"It will make us an international laughing stock if we allow her to play," someone offers.

"Hear. Hear."

"What does the Tanzania Golf Union rulebook say?"

"Nothing."

"Anyway, it's a matter of tradition!"

"Hear. Hear." The lady herself neatly resolves the issue—by pulling a muscle in practice and having to withdraw.

On the opening day of the tournament, with the first tee area decoratively roped off, a very nervous visiting golfer had to be the first competitor to strike the ball off the first tee. His hand shaking, he manages to balance the ball on the tee, steps back and takes a practice swing. The silence from the crowd above is broken by a tiny voice, four-year old Alexander's, saying "missed!" The ball was still on the peg. Everyone collapses, relieving the tension for the golfer.

《•》《•》《•》《•》

Alexander, the Foxes' youngest son, now goes to the little kindergarten near Geoff's office, just over a mile from their house. Each morning, off he pads with his friends, barefoot, to school, the only white boy. *Uji* (maize meal porridge with milk and sugar) is the main attraction. One day, he shocks his mother by saying that he doesn't want to go to school.

"Why not, Alexander?"

"Because there is no sugar for the *uji*."

So Vicky gives him some sugar, enough for the school, and off he goes again quite happily. Another time, when his pregnant kindergarten teacher pats her tummy and announces that there is a baby inside, Alexander looks horrified. "Why did you eat it?"

《•》《•》《•》《•》

Just before the Foxes go on leave, a puppy bites four-year-old Alexander, drawing blood. Rob Bosma, the doctor in Mufindi (who has been asked to keep an eye on the puppy for any signs of illness) sends a telegram to the Foxes' UK address to say the puppy has died of rabies.

"However, we were spending a pleasant week in Munich with friends and didn't return to Tavistock in Devon for a while," Geoff tells Rob later. "When we eventually saw the telegram, our local doctor referred us to Plymouth hospital for rabies injections. At the hospital, they wanted to put Alexander into an isolation room, so he could not infect others — such was their lack of knowledge. The rabies vaccine was sent down on the night train from London, and they began treating Alexander. We eventually persuaded the hospital that our local doctor in Tavistock could complete the course of injections, which, because of the delay, had to be administered at double dosage in the lumbar or stomach regions.

"That would have been the end of the matter, if it weren't for the fact that newspaper reporters hang around hospitals for stories. It seemed like all the national newspapers in England phoned for a story. But I declined to give any interviews, until a pretty, young, *Tavistock Times* reporter appeared at our front door. I relented and gave her both the story plus a beguiling photograph of Alexander at three years of age. Within no time at all, Alexander was emblazoned on the front page of the Tavistock Times, with the headline: 'Boy, three, only an 80 percent chance!' (Apparently someone had commented that that was the efficacy of the vaccine).

"A couple of months later, Alexander had to visit the dentist and, much to the anguish of the dentist, bit him when he put his hand in his mouth. Alexander didn't return for about four years. When we took him back, Alexander asked us if we thought the dentist might remember being bitten by him. We of course said, 'No. That was long ago.' However, the moment he went into the surgery, the dentist announced: 'Last time you were here, you bit me.'"

Photo of Alexander used by *Tavistock Times* for the rabies article — Alexander learned to escape through the window early.

《•》《•》《•》《•》

Before returning to Tanzania from the UK, the Foxes load up as usual. "You wouldn't believe what we are taking with us," Vicky writes to Libby; "a huge tent and smoker, to name just a couple of things. Oh, yes, and all my school supplies as usual! We'll keep extra bits and pieces in the airport 'left luggage' lockers during check-in and retrieve them just in time to board our flights."

Back in Mufindi, Vicky resumes teaching. She is now also running Mufindi's little guest house (to accommodate people coming up for Mufindi's golf and highland air, often as a welcome respite from coastal heat), not to mention still managing her own expanding farm. "There isn't much time left over," she writes to Libby. "Oh, and by the way, Alexander really embarrassed me the other day when he told me to f-off in front of an eighty-two-year-old great-uncle. I didn't know where to look. The whole of Mufindi is recruited to teach Alexander naughty words that he must NEVER repeat, such as "district nurse" and "Huckleberry Finn"—dreadful swear words! It worked, when, shortly after he hammered his thumb, out came his new expletive 'district nurse!' (to which everyone feigned shock)."

《•》《•》《•》《•》

Alexander loves catapults. He goes to bed with his "cats" around his neck, generally two of them. His parents eventually forbid him to shoot the glorious, iridescent sunbirds on their lawn. Alexander also knows that he can only shoot what he can eat. One day, Geoff sees him stalking sunbirds, in their rose bushes on the lawn, which are definitely out of bounds for catapults. Opening the window, he roars, "Alexander!" Whereupon this infant tells him that the catapult is new and he is only "sighting it in"!

Alexander does indeed always eat what he catches with his little group of Tanzanian friends, using a white ant embedded in grunge (chewed *Loranthus*, "mistletoe" berries) on the end of a long stick. Birds go for the ant and get stuck in the grunge. The day's catch is then roasted over a fire. At other times, Alexander impatiently pushes aside fleshy forest leaves, lush and bursting with wet season juices, and fragrant ferns dripping with dew, as he rushes beyond the manicured lawn to find his friends.

"Alexander, once he was a little bigger, was always the guinea pig to test out everything his older brothers did," says Geoff. "Such as driving down our steep driveway in their go-cart, where he had to survive a stone wall at the bottom; or being launched from our high-up tree house down the 'death slide,' which contained a simple rope toggle. His only instruction: 'Don't let go!'"

LION-MAN

"*Simba yuko karibu!* [The lion is near!]," an estate worker tells the Foxes.

"He probably came up the escarpment somewhere in the region of Livalonge Estate, possibly passing through Kifyulilo [Helga and Werner's farm]," Geoff surmises. "Finding nothing to eat there, he likely proceeded out past Igowole onto the grassland, where, by day, smallholder farmers graze their precious Zebu (hardy little highland cattle, which thrive on elevated grasslands) and, by night, safeguard them in rudimentary pens. Like a fox in a chicken house, a lion jumping into a tight pen will kill every cow that moves in the confined space before choosing one to feed on. This is creating heartbreaking losses for small-scale cattle owners in the Mufindi area."

Slowly, the lion has worked his way toward Lugoda, where Vicky farms her fine and growing dairy herd of Ayrshires, providing milk to everyone who wants it. Then comes the chilling news: "*Simba amefika Lugoda.*" The lion is now on the Foxes' estate. Someone sights him taking refuge in a nearby gum plantation, full of undergrowth, below the Brooke Bond chairman's house.

"Time for a lion hunt!" says Geoff. He organizes about 100 beaters, who line up at the top of the hill, while three guns (Niblett, Boswell, and Fox) wait on the contour road at the bottom of the plantation. They can't see each other, so thick is the undergrowth.

To their amazement, they hear the 100 beaters instinctively chanting, "Hee! Hee! Hee!" just as Hehe warriors had done before battle under their legendary paramount chiefs Munyigumba and Mkwawa. That same, full-throated chant now accompanies their lion drive.

"We waited," Geoff remembers. "Then, suddenly, around the corner from me, a huge, red-maned head sticking out of the bushes confronts Niblett. He freezes momentarily, giving the lion just enough time to leap almost over his shoulder, just slightly to one side, cross the track in one bound and disappear. When Jonny recovers, he fires his rifle into the air, signalling to the hard-working beaters that the drive has not been for naught."

Nothing more is heard or seen from this lion for a few days, although everyone is clearly on the lookout for him, particularly Geoff and Vicky because of her vulnerable dairy herd. Soon after, Vicky is standing on the lawn talking with their neighbours (the Keeleys), and Alexander tries to attract her attention.

"Mummy!"

Alexander has just returned from running free and wild around the tea estates with his Tanzanian playmates. When cold, they warm themselves the African way: by putting burning charcoal into metal baskets, which they swing around to keep the embers red hot. All went well today, until the metal wire handle broke, sending the basket into the air and onto the roof of the cattle byre. Within seconds, its thatched roof caught fire. Panic! The entire building was erupting in flames.

"Mummy!"

"Just a minute, Alexander."

"But, Mummy!"

"Not now."

"But, Mummy, there's a fire!"

"The adjacent cowshed was vacated very fast," Geoff observes drily, many years later.

"Everyone in the vicinity rushed to save the cows and to try to put out the fire," Vicky adds. "Of course, our limited supply of water chose that particular time to run out, soon leaving us powerless to do anything but watch as the building and the hay barn burned to the ground."

This is a major disaster, as Vicky relies totally on the hay to see her through the coming six months of dry season.

"Alexander took one look at my face and disappeared for the rest of the day, to his friend's house," she writes Libby. "We were also still nervous about the lion, convinced that he would be attracted by the sounds of my cattle.

"Now for the final drama. Geoff is sitting on top of the cow-milking parlour awaiting the lion. For the past week, it has been doing the rounds of all the cowherds in Mufindi. It really is incredibly destructive, and the Africans are terrified of it. Just to give you some idea of the damage it has done, it killed five cows the night before last and a calf yesterday, two cows the day before, and two the day before that. Last night, we had three watchmen on our cows, and the lion passed through the Keeleys' garden and up the club road. We're certain it's after our cows.

"It is a huge, red-maned male, very cunning, and seems to have covered the whole area in the thickest bush. I keep thinking of Aunty Marjorie sitting up in her tree waiting for the man-eating leopard in Ceylon, and it quite puts me off offering to take a shift. It would be bound to come when I was there and whatever would one do if one missed. I hope the creature will go back down the escarpment again soon. It doesn't seem to be very lion-like, as it never comes back to its kill to have a second meal and when it gets into a cow *boma*, it kills as many cows as it can. The poor chap that lost five cows lost every one he possessed. It really is a shame."

Geoff and their neighbour Malcolm are indeed sitting on the cowshed roof overnight "with our loaded guns at the ready," as Geoff, raconteur par excellence, will later tell friends. "Into the silence and darkness came the blood-curdling sounds of an animal in distress beneath us. The bellowing convinced us that the lion was probably down there, under us, eating one of the cows in the shed. The source of the noise indeed turned out later to have been a cow—only this cow was bellowing in pain as it gave birth to twins, with associated groans." And then as an afterthought, "just like Vicky, I imagine."

"Wait a minute!" says Vicky, with a swift jab at Geoff. "Groans?"

"Actually," says Geoff, expertly ducking her fists again. Clearly this is not the first time. "Vicky was always totally silent giving birth. Still, do all women choose an ungodly time like two a.m. to decide they need to go to the hospital? With her, it was always at the wrong time. Again, and again, she woke me for our usual ritual: 'Was it something you ate?' etcetera. So, off we would trot. Three times in Tanzania—twice to Iringa (eighty-four miles away on a bumpy, potholed, murram road) and the third time to Ilembula (the same distance away, only this time toward Mbeya).

"To me, Ilembula was the worst. Vicky took soooo long to give birth. And the waiting room only had boring magazines. Anyway, enough about babies and back to the lion!

"Early the next morning, we followed lion tracks on the road up from the factory dam below Head Office. It had crossed the valley from our side. So perhaps it had been watching us that night! A scantily clad Pat (Malcolm's wife) appeared at her bedroom window. 'What are you doing?' she asked suspiciously. 'Following a lion across your flower beds,' I replied. It was true!

"Lion tracks had now been seen crossing the road at Kilimatembo village, heading north, and into the trees below. So, off we hunters went once more, this time following the lion into a dense forest at Calderara on Lupeme Estate. I had a rifle, but, owing to the thick bush, elected to use a shotgun with large buckshot for close quarters. Grass and vegetation, gently pressed down by the lion, led us on, but progress was slow. On hands and knees, we gradually crawled forward through the undergrowth, I ahead with the shotgun, my rifle being carried behind me. I wasn't quite sure what made me more nervous: the thought of the lion in the gloom ahead, or the risk of being shot in my backside by my gun bearer carrying my rifle.

"Suddenly, there was the most deafening, chilling roar, and our quarry crashed off through the bushes, causing the ground to tremble from the roots beneath them. I was so glad he was heading the other way. We must have given him a fright, but he certainly gave me a bigger fright, because at one time we were surely only inches apart."

Later, there was a report of the lion entering a hut, without hurting the person sleeping inside; and, finally, news of sightings back down the escarpment in the region of Lulanda village.

"In those days," Geoff concludes, "there was still a lingering belief in the powers of witchcraft and lion-men. Accordingly, villagers in the area duly declared that this was no ordinary lion but in fact a lion-man; furthermore, that this particular lion-man must have been a white lion-man because 'Fokisi' [Fox] had failed to kill it."

《•》《•》《•》《•》

As overseas development projects spring up around Mufindi, the club absorbs new members into its social circle. Now, there are international evenings: Norwegian (courtesy of the nearby Norwegian sawmill project); German (courtesy of the Voigts); and, of course, African. The men love that one. When Betty Sakaya hosts the first African evening, she announces dinner, and all the ladies head for the table. "Ladies, Ladies, please!" she says. "In Africa, the men eat first."

There are also family talent evenings. Vicky plays the piano; the doctor's mother—a former ballerina—dances some ballet, with her son, Bruce (the current company doctor), taking on the male part. Madhu and Naseem sing Indian songs. Unfortunately, because of the hard economic times, British Airways may no longer be flying in courtesy haggises at New Year's (usually enough for every household, as well as for the party) or the kilted piper to pipe it in.

The Mufindi rugby team, which for a short period has beaten all the other teams in the country, is still active, although age is beginning to take its toll. One-third of the team now has to ask the captain's wife, Mary Robley, to hold their false teeth for them during the match. When Dar es Salaam comes up to play against Mufindi one weekend and begins humiliating them in the first half, subterfuge is called for. Kimbo (married to Johno Beakbane) comes onto the field at half time with oranges and water for Mufindi and oranges and beer for their visitors. That, plus the altitude, fixes them.

After every rugby match, visiting teams are challenged to the boat race in the Mufindi club. This requires eight men and a female cox sitting in a line behind each other, holding a pint of beer. At the word "go!" the first man tries to down the beer with his next teammate only able to follow when the beer mug is empty and upside down on the head of the man in front.

"We will never lose," they crow at the bar, "for one reason: Vicky! She has an amazing ability to drink a pint of beer seemingly without swallowing. We could be three men behind the other team but will always win when it comes to the female cox.

"Remember Brooke Bond chairman Peter Knight? Himself a heavy beer drinker, getting on his hands and knees in the fishing lodge so he could carefully watch Vicky to see whether she was swallowing?"

SPOILS OF WAR

President Idi Amin, the infamous butcher of thousands in Uganda, is perceived internationally as cruel, irrational, and therefore dangerous. For his part, President Amin does not trust Mwalimu, who has granted asylum to his predecessor (the ousted President Milton Obote) and thousands of his supporters.

On November 1, 1978, President Amin, aided by Libya, invades Tanzanian territory near Kagera. Within four months, the Tanzanian army drives him into exile. But the cost of the invasion will be incalculable. None of the international voices earlier calling for an intervention against Amin help to defray the cost of war, which (coupled with the first oil shock) leaves Tanzania seriously exposed. Even more sinister and potentially devastating is the invisible pandemic being carried home by unsuspecting Tanzanian soldiers. In a few years, for no apparent reason, healthy young men and women will start to lose weight, develop lesions, and die from a mysterious ailment, then known only as "slim disease."

Suffering an Education

Meanwhile, Geoff and Vicky's children are suffering an excellent education in Britain, partially financed by Brooke Bond, including two flights back to Tanzania for holidays after each term. That this is an opportunity no parent can forego fails to impress each of the four Fox boys in turn. Having run free (if not sometimes wild) in Mufindi, they are concussed by the strict discipline of English boarding schools. Postcards such as this one: "We had a lovely safari in the Ruaha Park and swam every day in the river despite the crocodiles. We saw one enormous one. Love Mum" hardly help.

Eventually, the youngest, Alexander, arrives with a letter of apology to the headmaster of Mount House Prep School for being "totally uneducated but, if it is any consolation, also the last of the Fox boys."

They teach him to wear shoes and to stop digging out his own jiggers (parasitic sand fleas, the females of which lay their eggs in flesh. In Africa, they are routinely removed with needles, which have been sterilized by holding them briefly in a flame. The key is to remove them whole, since residuals can cause infection). This generates a lot of excitement for the school matron, who sends him to the doctor.

However, only two weeks after Alexander arrives at Mount House for the first time, his grandfather (the Brigadier) hears a movement in the attic. He pulls down the hatch ladder, climbs up, and finds Alexander and a friend playing there.

"What are you doing here?" demands the Brigadier.

"We have run away from school, Grandpa," replies a small boy who has habitually escaped his mother's home-school classroom, returning at lunch time, still in pyjamas, with a smile and a little plea: "You're not going to beat me, are you, Mum?"

Vicky's father sits down next to them, and together they work out an exciting plan whereby he will smuggle them back into school in his Land Rover without anyone noticing. Accordingly, he drives them back, slows at a prearranged corner, where they leap out of the back door and race away.

While he is turning the car around, the headmaster, who was looking through his study window, comes out and informs the Brigadier, "Yes, the two boys have been missed." Caught, Josh, as the family calls Grandpa, is very embarrassed.

Peter and Christopher soon become unpopular with head and housemasters at Kelly, their secondary school. The housemaster particularly dislikes Peter after catching him kissing his daughter in the cupboard; and for pulling up the floorboards of the junior study to crawl along and eavesdrop under the housemaster's living room floor.

Indignantly, Geoff says: "Peter! School is for education and not for playing around."

"Dad," Peter responds quietly, "when I shone my torch up, I saw your initials on the beam."

"Damn." Both boys are suspended from school. ("For unnecessary reasons, really," Dad Fox later says, clearly approving of the hijinks. "For example, Christopher led an enterprising night commando raid into all the dormitories at nearby School House, where they blackened the faces of sleeping boys with indelible spray ink. It could not be removed before chapel or classroom the following day.")

While on home leave, Vicky arranges an appointment with the headmasters of both the primary prep school and secondary public schools attended by the boys. Her father drives Vicky down to the first school, Mount House, which has turned out to be a fabulous and happy school for all four boys. She tells her father not to bother about waiting for her in order to drive her on to Kelly College, just across the Tavy River, because she plans to wade over, but please to pick her up after her meeting with the Kelly College headmaster.

After a good meeting at Mount House, Vicky walks down to the river some way off, only to find it in full spate. Undaunted, off come the tights, up goes the skirt, and she wades across the torrent and into a stormy meeting with the headmaster—stormy because he has mistakenly accused and suspended Peter for two weeks because of a misdemeanour carried out by another boy.

The boys in Peter's house write to Grandfather Josh assuring him that his grandson is in no way implicated and eventually force the culprit to own up. Peter is then allowed back (without apology from the school).

After an angry exchange (and Vicky hardly ever gets angry), the headmaster explodes when she tells him he really ought to apologize to Peter. He reluctantly escorts her out to the car, but the car is not there. Grandpa is late.

"How did you get here?" he asks.

"I waded across the river."

Sometime later, at an old boys' reunion in King's Canterbury, where Vicky's best friend Libby's husband, Gurney, studied, Libby meets the headmaster, also an old boy of this school. When she hears that he has come from Kelly College, she asks: "Oh, you must know the Fox boys?"

"Yes," he replies coldly. "But what could you expect with a mother like that?" He then turns his back on her, whereupon the headmaster of Mount House, who also happens to be part of the exchange, clearly embarrassed, continues their friendly conversation.

Because the name of Fox is not conducive for Bruce and Alexander to go there too, they are sent to Blundell's near Exeter instead. All the boys then go on to study for the necessary qualifications to allow them to work in Tanzania.

SECOND OIL SHOCK

The second oil shock hits in 1979. This time oil prices rise 130 percent after Iranian production falters in the tense transition between the Shah of Iran's departure and the Ayatollah Khomeini's arrival. "Developing" countries must now export an even greater percentage of goods to buy the same amount of oil. The cost of repaying development loans increases dramatically. And Tanzania's already faltering economy goes into a tailspin.

PART TWO

BIRTH OF AN ENTERPRISE

(1974–1988)

RUAHA DREAMS—FOXTREKS

"At least we still have our Ruaha getaway," Geoff says.

"I'll drink to that," Vicky answers lazily, gratefully sipping her tepid beer. It's a long weekend. And, as usual, they are camping.

"Guess what's haunting me?"

"It's too hot, Foxey. I give up."

"Visions of condensation running down the outside of an ice-cold beer bottle." Vicky laughs and continues watching a handful of zebra and a dozen gazelles sheltering under a shady tree.

"I know what, Vicky!" Geoff suddenly sits up straight. "We must build a tented camp that can hold a fridge."

"There's the small matter of permission," says Vicky.

"We'll apply to build a camp for tourists."

"What tourists?"

Vicky is right. There really are no tourists to speak of in Tanzania these days.

"But imagine how much more comfortable our life would be on weekends down here, if we had a fridge!" They both laugh at the idea and toast each other again, with their even warmer beer.

A little while later: "Seriously. Why not?"

"Why not what?"

"A tourist camp—there are local residents who would use it."

"Come off it, Foxey! Actually, on second thoughts, wouldn't the boys be delighted. They're absolutely desperate to live in Tanzania."

149

"And there it was, the germ of an idea," Geoff later recalls. "The boys, having been brought up in Tanzania, naturally all wanted to return and spend their careers here, but immigration policies only allowed companies to hire employees on two-year work permits, without any guarantee of automatic renewal. What to do? We could either accept our precarious existence or take matters into our own hands."

By 1981, at a time when no enterprise will touch Tanzania, favouring more predictable investments overseas, the Foxes are seriously considering creating a family enterprise to give their boys a future in their country of choice. Ruaha has always been their favourite patch, and, somehow, the possibility of building a tourist camp continues to crystallize. The only problem: ever fewer tourists! Still, the idea won't go away.

"It's too risky."

"Nothing ventured, nothing gained."

"Even the aid agencies are giving up. And the World Bank is threatening something called 'structural adjustment.' Whatever that is." (In fact, the World Bank is trying to influence Mwalimu to accept reforms that would allow more free enterprise in Tanzania, including foreign investment, to try to jump-start its failing economy. Predictably, this does not sit well with Mwalimu, who fears the demise of Tanzania as a socialist country built on traditional values.)

"Geoff, the economy of Tanzania is on its knees—everything is stagnant or bankrupt. There is no investment and no tourism at all. In fact, tourists are even unwelcome. And most businesses are shutting down."

"That's the best time to invest. Remember what that successful farmer said on BBC radio the other day when asked how he had done so well?"

"What did he say?"

"'The answer is simple. When they goes out, I goes in. And when they goes in, I goes out.' Anyway, the boys are desperate to stay here."

"This would be the only way."

"You know we could lose everything."

"We'll start small and see where it goes."

And then, finally: "Let's do it!"

"Agreed?"

"Agreed!"

"You realize, Vicky, that you will have to take care of getting all the approvals and so on. My contract with Brooke Bond strictly precludes me from any other commercial interest."

"I've already run the farm and guest house. To prove how serious I am, I'll take out Tanzanian citizenship and set this up in my name, on behalf of the boys."

The following day, Vicky applies to Tanzanian National Parks (TANAPA) for permission to build a small, six-tented camp on an island in the Ruaha River.

The Foxes also still love duck-shooting weekends — essentially social occasions for the companionship of camping and the early morning and evening flights of hundreds of wildfowl. A good retriever is essential. "I always claimed that my dog was the best," Geoff boasts, "but on dropping a spur-winged goose that fell the other side of a wide channel, I couldn't get my dog to cross. It didn't see the bird go down and wouldn't budge. So my backup retriever, Vicky, very obediently stripped off to bra and pants and swam across to the bird. This was recorded on cine film by some Norwegians who were accompanying us. Everyone was most impressed. I was proud."

"And I was thinking of dinner," says Vicky.

"Standing on the dykes, looking toward Chimala, the hills behind, listening to the honks of the crested crane and the cry of the fish eagle was rewarding in itself," Geoff recalls. "So restful; I remember firing a shot, and suddenly a small herd of buffalo splashed away through the swamp. Now, sadly, this immense wetland has been drained by massive rice cultivation. The Masai are always blamed because of their cattle. In reality, they are scapegoats who cannot protect themselves."

"Great news!" Vicky writes to Libby, months later — months of paperwork and laborious trips to Dar es Salaam, months of negotiating for loans from the bank (for a venture everyone labels "crazy," except for the Voigts).

"We have our permission to have a camp in the Ruaha Park and will open the camp next year. Christopher will come and run it after his Higher National Diploma course in business studies and tourism. It could be tremendous fun for all of us. Pretty hard work, too.

"There were apparently others after the same thing, so we are very pleased that they chose us, especially as two of them were large Dar es

Salaam hotels. Now we have to order all the equipment and design the tents. I just hope we can get them made in Dar es Salaam.

"We live from day to day. Imagine, I had to swap some of my beautiful cows to hire a lorry so we could bring supplies down to Ruaha."

"Supplies?" Geoff will laugh years later. "It was a load of rubbish. It really was! I remember that first 'supply' lorry, a hired truck, loaded with our friend John Gray's little water pump, some bent piping, and other junk. The lorry got stuck on the way down, and remained there for three months. And we thought we were going to build a tourist camp with that!"

Vicky is still teaching school, running the guest house, managing her farm—and now she is also flitting in and out of official meetings. Well, hardly flitting. Business flows like molasses. There are the hours of driving hundreds of miles to Mafinga, Iringa, Dar es Salaam, only to find the underpaid civil servants away from their desks, probably out in a field somewhere desperately growing food to feed their families.

"There's no canvas in the country, Geoff!"

"We'll just have to import some."

"We're not allowed to import canvas."

"Why not?"

"Government restrictions on imports because they are running out of foreign exchange."

Others might have given up, but if there is a knotty situation, Geoff, by self-admission, tends to sweep it under the carpet and concentrate on how something CAN happen; or wait it out and hope it goes away. But the problems around their Ruaha enterprise don't go away.

"The island in the river is submerged. We can't build tents on it," Vicky informs Geoff one weekend, back in Mufindi.

"How about cabins?"

"You're joking."

"Yes, I am."

"Well, don't. I'm not in the mood."

"We'll find another spot on the bank."

Anthony (Ant) Waterkeyne, a young civil engineer, has joined the conversation. Ant is between jobs, having just finished a contract in

Morogoro. His wife, Juliet, is an artist. Perfect credentials. Because they have just had a baby, they want to spend some quality time in Tanzania before looking for other work. Perfect timing. In exchange for camping equipment and food, they agree to spend three months jump-starting the business.

"I think I know a place that would be perfect," Ant says.

"I bet I know, too. That beautiful *kopje*[38] overlooking the island in the river," Geoff replies.

"That's it. And we'll put cabins on it."

"Not tin ones like the ones at Park headquarters," Vicky asks.

"Lord, no. We'll keep it all as natural as possible."

In the end, they settle for stone-built cabins, on higher ground, using Ruaha rocks as natural walls and blending as much as possible into the *kopje*.

The next weekend has them all scrambling up the slope between huge rocks in Ruaha to finalize camp designs. Estimated to be 450–600 million years old, the rocks are remnants of the buckling upheaval that created Tanzania's mountains, and a splinter of the Great Rift Valley, through which the Ruaha River now flows.

"We'll definitely need a viewpoint up here," Geoff says, standing on the top of the *kopje* and pointing past a massive baobab to the panoramic vista beyond. Directly below them, the Ruaha River follows its shrunken, dry-season journey, barely nourishing parched fauna and flora as it passes. In one pool, hippos snort and soak. Elsewhere, elephants meander down to drink, followed by several giraffe. To the left, a gaggle of mongooses; to the right, herds of doe-eyed impala; and peering out of a crevice in the nearby boulder, a family of rock rabbits — tiny and unlikely cousins to the mammoth elephant.[39]

A solitary giraffe now meanders slowly from acacia tree to acacia tree in the distance. Adult baboons idly contemplate life while youngsters chase each other. One baby rides on its mother, bareback and upright, like a miniature candidate for some Western stampede. It will warn mum of danger best seen from this vantage point. Another, much smaller one hangs on from below, curled into mum's belly, its fur-less skin too delicate for direct sun. All are heading to the scarce

38 A small, isolated hill.

39 Both are members of the Afrotheria grouping of mammals.

water source that will, with the rains, once more swell into its name, the Great Ruaha River.

They stand there, quietly absorbing and being absorbed by the idyllic scene below them.

"Why not make this a lookout bar?" says Anthony.

"Fantastic!"

"Imagine sitting here comfortably, beer in hand . . ." Geoff offers.

"Ice cold," the other three say in unison, "with condensation running down the outside of the glass."

"Predictable, aren't I?" Geoff laughs. "Jokes aside, let's finalize the rough designs." One idea follows another, until at last they all agree: "That's perfect."

"This way, the rooms fit into the natural rocks and become almost invisible."

"So tourists will have comfortable rooms, without blemishing our beloved Ruaha."

"Right," says Geoff in parting. "By next weekend, we expect to see detailed sketches. This isn't just a holiday, you know." With a wave and a smile, he and Vicky are off, back to Mufindi.

"I wonder how they will make out with the baby," Vicky says. "It's one thing to camp for a few weeks, but a few months?"

"They're young. They'll love it."

And they do. In no time at all, the Waterkeynes have their tents up, Phyl's vegetables safely stored in the Land Rover. ("Or they won't last a day, given all the competition we have. Look at those monkeys already watching us. I bet they would steal them in a jiffy.") Mosquito netting over the baby's carrycot effectively prevents close encounters with creepy crawlies, barring one scare when a scorpion ventures too close for parental comfort.

Each week, Vicky brings them another big basket of vegetables from Phyl, as well as meat and dairy products from her farm, and some fruit and incidentals from Iringa Store's dwindling supplies. Geoff joins them when he can, inevitably losing himself, with Anthony, in the world of water pressure and plumbing, weight-bearing walls, and other minutiae. Together, they work, they play . . . they take in an elephant sizing them up, having first nudged her little one to safety; the elegance of a nearby giraffe, perfectly still but for rotating ears. Otherworldly.

Magic stillness of the midday hour,
nor sound, nor movement,
save softly blows the wind,
teasing sleepy leaves;
a drowsy lion purrs;
In golden brilliance
rippling suns draw succour
from steaming watering holes;
blind the eyes of vultures
crowding stunted trees

"Thank God for support and encouragement from Werner and Helga," Geoff says. "I suppose they can see their own entrepreneurial ambitions reflected by us."

Vicky agrees. "Werner very kindly sold us his old truck," she tells Ant. "Because vehicles are so valuable in these days of desperate shortages, even a fourteen-year-old, one-ton Ford Transit is a lifeline."

"We'll use it to carry all the stones and sand for construction." Construction in Ruaha continues non-stop until the rainy season sets in, and begins again as soon as the early dry season permits.

"How long can it stand up to such wear and tear?" In fact, all the rocks in the early year or two will be carried in this one-ton vehicle, always three tons at a time, until there are no springs left. And still it will survive and keep them going.

Geoff devotes his 1981 local leave to Ruaha, coinciding with the boys' holidays. "These holidays have gone by so quickly with not enough time to do everything with the kids," he writes to Gelly and Jimmy. "Every day has been a mad rush, with Vicky doing most of the rushing—bus to Dar, hitchhiking back, up to Arusha, off to Iringa (several times) camping in the bush, hunting, duck shooting, and, of course, the Ruaha Park.

"I think the boys enjoyed it all and Christopher and Peter certainly seem keen on the Ruaha Camp project. We finally started construction on August 29th with Christopher and Alexander camping down there on their own for the first week. Christopher, in fact, went down in the hired truck with all the men and equipment, and the lorry then got stuck crossing a ford in the Ruaha River. He slept on the lorry roof. We used Werner Voigt's old Transit for moving building materials on-site, so Christie used this for transport while he and Alexander were on their own.

"Our biggest problem at the moment is a reliable vehicle, and we have had to temporarily hire a Land Rover at great cost for a very nice European couple. Ant's a civil engineer who will be supervising the building for us. They have just finished a contract in Morogoro and want to have two or three months in the bush before their next job, and in return for their service we are providing them with food, drink and transport. This takes the pressure off me, because the company (including London) is strictly against my involvement in any commercial enterprise.

"We look forward to hearing more UK news. Your letters are an excellent substitute to UK newspapers that no longer arrive!"

EMPIRE-BUILDING ON A SHOESTRING

A series of excerpts from Fox letters attest to ongoing financial challenges—and hand-to-mouth solutions.

"We're relieved to hear the Tarbridge tenants are carrying on. Our bank loan for the Camp will be dependent on the rent coming in . . ."

"Thank you very much for being so helpful with all our UK expenses. I just don't know what we would have done without you . . ."

"Bruce has been doing very well with his bees and now owns eight hives. He paid for five new ones this holiday by selling a large quantity of beeswax candles . . ."

"Could you look at my account to see if it's solvent, as we have lost touch with the situation . . . I have written cheques, but they hopefully will be covered by the amount that Vicky is borrowing from her dad. At least we have stopped work on the camp for the duration of the rains . . ."

"We're madly bartering Vicky's farm animals and produce for transport and labour. Speaking of bartering, a very nice fellow and great mechanic from DANIDA often spends his weekends in Ruaha for free, in return for mending broken vehicles . . ."

"We may well find ourselves without a job soon, mainly because the company is broke. For the first time ever, we shall be operating at a loss due to poor world tea prices, high wages and costs here, and the ridiculously strong Tanzanian shilling against pounds sterling . . . So we're keeping our fingers crossed and hope that we shan't have to move into our Ruaha camp permanently . . ."

《•》《•》《•》《•》

"We had a marvellous time thinking out the new buildings and seeing them grow up before our eyes," Vicky writes to Libby. "Geoff really got the place going during his local leave, as he has a much more artistic eye than I. Unfortunately, I had to spend a week in Dar es Salaam to sort out the business side of things, especially getting a letter of support from the Principal Secretaries of the Ministries of Trade and Tourism, as well as trying to get our loan finalized quickly and a legal agreement signed with the park." She sighs then adds, "Everything here takes time."

Finally, the kitchen and two cabins are ready. As planned, they are almost invisible, their thatched roofs and stone walls blending seamlessly into Ruaha's natural rock formations. But Geoff's and Vicky's excitement is tinged with sadness: the Waterkeynes are moving on. Vicky will now have to spend more time in Ruaha herself supervising construction.

"They're not used to female construction bosses," she worries. "And, Foxey, what if I can't answer their questions? I can hardly drive to Mufindi each time." (The Foxes do not own one of just seven telephones available in the whole of Mufindi.)

"You'll do just fine, Vicky. We'll go over the week's work before you drive down on Mondays, and you can bring questions home with you on Thursdays or Fridays."

"And what about the schoolchildren? I can't just abandon them."

VICKY'S BOARDING SCHOOL

"Do you think their parents would allow them to go to Ruaha with you?"

"That's an idea. We do have the two rondavels up and finished. One could be a dormitory and the other one a classroom, both very basic but functional. What a rich learning environment. Imagine all the things they could observe first-hand." The more she thinks about it, the more excited Vicky gets.

And so it is that each Monday Vicky continues to pack her few remaining schoolchildren (none of them her own, the four Fox boys now all studying in England) into a short wheelbase Land Rover, crammed like sausages, and drives them to Ruaha. This allows Vicky to both supervise the building team and teach. As for the kids, they love what becomes known as "Vicky's Boarding School."

They learn to observe everything, note everything. The most interesting cloud formation; gnarled branches, lichen-covered, grey and powdery, around emerald tea fields; the brilliant daub of blood-red erythrina[40] against a glaring turquoise sky passing Mafinga; leaves of all descriptions, single, feathered, fleshy, tapered. They are taught to observe them closely, to watch for unusual interaction, see how the liana bends and swings from ancient virgin giants as they leave Mufindi, how it provides the resting point, fleetingly, for some forest bird. At the Iringa market, they explore standard tropical fruit and common garden vegetables, baobab seeds, woven baskets, and beautifully decorated calabashes.

Then they are finally off to Ruaha. Beginning under the purple blossoms of the beautiful jacaranda trees, they drive slowly through shantytowns sprawling down the mountainsides in a jumble of *bati* (corrugated iron) roofs and brick walls. The road is unbelievably bad. The children don't care. They giggle with every bump.

Unfolding before them is an African panorama of bleached plains, tall elephant grass, and bulbous baobabs, their root-like branches reaching for cloudless skies. Flat-topped acacia trees grace the scrub, periodically punctured by bursts of cassia yellow.

---

40   Sadly, according to Geoff, this beautiful tree is disappearing. Its wood does not split and makes hardy wooden wheels for homemade carts.

Some tall and stately giraffes suddenly block the road. They never fail to amaze Vicky, time and again, with their gentle grace. Young faces remain glued to the window in anticipation of further game sighting, as the colours around them gradually change to those more typical of Ruaha in the dry season: a hazy, sultry canvas of mauves and purples, of tawny grass and huge, rounded granite boulders scattered in Henry Moore style over plains and riverbeds.

At last, they cross the Ruaha River into the park (courtesy of a hand-pulled ferry). Rocks immersed in the water are almost indistinguishable from hippos with distended bellies and accompanying tickbirds.

"It was a hippo!"

"No, it wasn't. It was a rock. Wasn't it, Mrs. Fox?"

"Look, a croc!"

"That's a log, silly. Oops. It moved. I suppose it was a croc after all."

And when they arrive, they hear the call of the ring-necked pigeons. In the evening, before a setting sun, the giraffe and their young are silhouetted, perfectly posed. They stare at the vehicle. Even the impala are craning their necks for a better look. Great skulking male baboons catch their attention, and playful tots, grooming and running and ducking and leaping onto mum's back to ride, bareback, over the rocks to the water. At this time of evening, everything is either heading to the water or returning, thirst slaked, into the cool evening air.

"We stay there Monday, Tuesday and Wednesday," she writes to Libby, "returning to Mufindi on Thursday afternoon, just in time for me to sort out the Mufindi guest house and our farm, as well as host/teach the Norwegian schoolchildren on Friday. Mufindi is quite full these days with a lot of Norwegians and streams of experts on just about everything you can think of, staying in the guest house and investigating the feasibility of the Pulp Scheme below the escarpment. Thank goodness it's nearly the end of term. Our children come out on the fifteenth to help a bit."

"Weekends in Mufindi, after time in Ruaha, felt like excursions into a previous life," Vicky remembers years later.

. . . Tendrils of soft green memories;
Fern under mossy branch, lichen draped;
Tree orchids, white against gnarled bark;
Emerald tea fields, azure skies, virgin growth.

Baked earth. Scorched.
Steaming from a sudden downpour,
and already the cicada makes its presence known.
A myriad brilliant insects sing and glisten
mirrored in refracted raindrop.

Smiles. Those wonderful smiles of Africa;
"*Hujambo, Dada?*" "*Sijambo.*"

Dusty flies drone.
A herd of zebra, tails flicking,
nostrils flaring, pawing nervously;
Waterbuck by the river's edge.
Elephants, trunks undulating
in search of apple ring acacia;
A tiny, perfect blade of grass,
dry, dusty, parched, at home.

Parched, that's me.
Too far from home.

《•》《•》《•》《•》

MADAM CEO OF FOXTREKS

"When I come up against knotty problems during the week in Ruaha," Vicky tells her friends, "I hurry back to Mufindi to ask Geoff's advice; for example, how to build the newest roof, or how to construct oddly shaped *bandas* [cabins]. I don't know very much, so Geoff draws little pictures for me, and I return to Ruaha pretending I have known all the time, thereby earning great respect from our builders, even though I am 'just a woman.'"

"Speaking of respect, nothing could have been more successful than Evelyn's and Vicky's deception of rock carrying," Geoff adds.

"Rocks were delivered to the car park at the bottom of the *kopje*, but the masons were building at the top of the hill. Every rock had to be carried up by hand. Not surprisingly, the guys tasked with lugging the rocks to the masons tended to spend time looking for the lightest ones, then slowly ascended the hill to deposit them. There they took a break to straighten their backs, before sauntering back down for more stones.

"'I'll show you how it's done,' says the Voigts' daughter, Evelyn, to the guys at the top. 'Stay here!' Meanwhile, Vicky—having said exactly the same thing to those at the bottom—selects the biggest rock that she can possibly carry, staggers halfway up the hill to where Evelyn is waiting, hidden behind a rock. There she passes the stone to Evelyn, who is very unhappy with the size. 'I can't carry that,' she moans but then duly staggers up to the folks waiting at the top and coolly deposits it. Vicky, meanwhile, has returned to the bottom of the hill for a second rock. And so it goes on for a short while—a demonstration that soon stimulates the rock carriers to prove that two slender *wazungu* (foreign) ladies can't outdo them."

《·》《·》《·》《·》

"Here I am sitting on an island in the middle of the Ruaha River at the start of the rains," Vicky writes to Libby on December 5, 1981. "I can't tell you the transformation of the park. Everything has turned green in the last week. We have been so incredibly busy that I haven't even started writing my Christmas cards or letters yet. Our friends are still staying in the park, thank heavens, and at last it is all beginning to take shape. The roofs are going on the kitchen; stores and two accommodation *bandas* are ready. Then the bar roof gets installed, probably next week. The bar is very difficult to describe, as it is built completely on the rocks. One has the most fantastic views for miles around and 100 feet above the river.

"The actual bar is built right into the rock surface with a stone alcove fronted by a wall as a bar. The water tank rises about the top as a natural rounded stone edifice. It's spectacular. Everywhere you look there are natural stone walls made into seating areas fitting into the natural rocks, from where people can watch the animals coming down to drink. Everything is rounded. No square corners. The *bandas* are part *in situ* rock and in part built from natural stone. The roof is treated wood of a rather attractive pale green. A thin layer of thatch will cover the wood to protect it from the sun. As I sit here, I can see hills all around, and the river slowly filling up. In a few months' time, when the river is in full spate, the scene will be dramatic. The small, rather tatty bushes that look quite dead in the dry weather have burst into an apple-like blossom all over the hillsides. I have to go to see the Parks director this week, to sort out a proper legal agreement."

"Together with her close friend Evelyn, they charmed the director of wildlife into not only giving his full approval but also suggesting an expansion," Geoff later tells friends.

"Slight exaggeration, Geoff!"

Actually, Vicky, the CEO of Foxtreks (as their company is now called), and Evelyn, her trusty secretary, always two steps behind, carrying her portable, manual typewriter and paper (including carbon paper for copies), do go to Dar together. Thwarted by red tape left, right, and centre, they become increasingly assertive, finally find out where the director of wildlife is staying, and decide to ambush him at breakfast. Although charming, he is understandably less than forthcoming, but politely agrees to give them a short audience the following day.

They stand before him the next morning, expecting a polite (Tanzanians are always polite) but slightly frosty reception. Instead, he greets them enthusiastically.

"Good morning, Mrs. Fox and Miss Voigt. Our government is looking for projects inland. Would it be possible for me to visit your initiative in Ruaha so I can see the developments there for myself? When would be convenient?" Vicky and Evelyn look at each other, stunned.

"Any time, sir. We would be honoured," says Vicky, recovering. "When were you thinking?"

"What are your plans in the next few days? If you are available, I could meet you in Mikumi tomorrow afternoon, and we could then drive up together the next day."

It turns out that following the breakfast ambush, the director had gone to a major party meeting. When the need for more assistance to Tanzania's neglected hinterlands was agreed to, he offered up the Ruaha initiative as a possible candidate.

And so it is that Vicky and Evelyn drive straight on to Mikumi National Park, straddling the main road to Iringa from Dar es Salaam. On the horizon, seemingly floating above the plains, are the ever-present mountain ranges, fading into blue and turquoise before vanishing into the heavens. Near them, some tall elephant grass. Farther back, busy little warthogs scrabble on bended forelegs for tender shoots emerging out of the charcoal residues of a runaway end-of-dry-season fire. Impala and zebra graze side by side, dappled in alternating sun and shade. Among them is the tiniest little baby zebra they have ever seen, skinny, its hide faintly orange, beside a sleek mother.

"Pinch me," says Vicky. "Are we really meeting up with Tanzania's director of wildlife here tomorrow?"

"Yes, indeed, Madam CEO."

Neither has the money for a night in the park lodge, so they decide to overnight in the car. Only the car is filling up with mosquitoes.

"I can't stand it any longer, I'm sleeping outside. At least the breeze will keep them away."

"Good idea."

"By the way, speaking of the car, it doesn't quite match your title, Madam CEO of Foxtreks." They make an exaggerated inspection tour of the Foxes' first sedan—an ancient Peugeot 404, very rusted, not to mention covered in a patchwork quilt of welding—and dissolve in giggles.

By now Africa's glorious night is blazing above with stars so bright, they crowd. Vicky and Evelyn make themselves as comfortable as they can, given that they have no camping gear whatsoever. Helga's homemade wine helps.

With their heads on the ground, they can now feel rather than see the wildlife. Hooves drumming what seems to be just inches from their heads could belong to anything from zebra to buffalo. They wonder what might be chasing them. More wine. More giggles. And then it is morning. The next few days unfold as

Vicky Fox, CEO of Foxtreks, in Ruaha.

in a dream, with the director inviting them to stay the second night in the park's VIP guest house, complete with comfortable beds (aaahhh!) and great food. The following morning, they set off in their respective vehicles, agreeing to rendezvous at the Ruaha Park headquarters. Vicky and Evelyn race up to Ruaha like bats out of hell to inspect the Foxtreks camp. All is well until they reach the lookout bar area. Enthusiastic workers who by now are all very proud of their role in creating the camp have carved their initials into the old baobab tree around which the bar extends, permanently wounding the bark with their knives.

So, while Vicky scrapes up a few precious bottles of Fanta and Coke to offer the director, Evelyn frantically tries to hide the initials under layers of mud and dust.

"Cheers!" The day is over. Vicky and Evelyn down the last remnants of Helga's homemade wine.

"Cheers! Unbelievable! Wow!"

"Imagine. He didn't just give us permission to build, he has asked us to expand. Wait until I tell Foxey!"

"And you thought you were busy before, Madam CEO!"

《·》《·》《·》《·》

"Dear Libby . . . now for some family news: Dear Peter has been suspended again for drinking in a pub, but I had a charming (don't laugh) letter from the headmaster to say there was no 'serious harm' in Peter, but he had no option but to stick to the rules!! Peter went off with Granny to a hero's sendoff, much to both his and Granny's embarrassment. I wrote a very *kali* (severe) letter to Peter to stop causing such problems to his house and headmaster. I don't expect he'll take any notice. Bruce writes very serious but happy letters from Blundells."

《·》《·》《·》《·》

Nineteen eighty-two flies by—fuelled by Vicky's "Mobile" School, the Mufindi Guest House, Vicky's farm, Geoff's work, and construction in Ruaha. "The new additions to the camp are six more stone accommodation *bandas*, each unique; each with a view of the river and hills," Vicky tells Libby. "I made Geoff put in so many windows that he worried the support walls wouldn't be long enough. They are.

All these houses should be finished by the end of the month.

"We have also completed the outside hilltop 'dining' patio. It is split-level, with a built-in barbecue, offering a panoramic view by day and meals under the stars by night. There are seven areas for sitting with folding, canvas safari chairs at tables on stone surfaces at different levels. Geoff has designed a beautiful dining room, also split level, taking full advantage of the hill that it's built on, to give everyone a lovely view upriver. A two-foot stone retaining wall now curves around the outside, and we are just starting the wood and thatch roof to cover it all."

Behind each achievement are countless barriers. Foreign exchange is so scarce that the government is forced to restrict even the most basic imports. Every widget needs a permit, including building materials such as "U" bends for sinks; basins; shower units; cement; even nails. Not to mention flour, sugar, margarine, rice, and cooking oil—salad oil is like gold. To get the permits, Vicky must drive to Dar es Salaam and back (400 miles each way) every month. The Ministry of Trade and Industries then needs a week to process permits. And, even with a permit, there is often nothing available in the shops.

"What little the country can afford these days," Geoff explains, "is imported by the State Trading Corporation, allocated through the Regional Trading Corporation, and then sent on to the Village Co-operative Shops, bypassing private traders.

"Especially in the Indian community, who really struggle."

Foxes' Ruaha River Lodge.

"Shopkeepers are opening a packet of matchboxes, and covering their shelves with individual matchboxes, just so they don't look completely empty."

"Too bad they can't display their increased literacy, health infrastructure, primary school attendees. That would at least show a more balanced picture of what is going on in Tanzania."

"True. But consumer goods are really lacking. I just saw packets of homemade potato crisps along otherwise empty shelves."

"They taste dreadful, don't they? Cooked in cottonseed oil — cooking oil being another luxury."

"And yet, ironically, there are tinned potatoes from China. Part of the TAZARA Railway Project deal; Tanzania has to import Chinese goods. Thank goodness this includes smoked mussels. Delicious."

"I have to say," Vicky tells friends, "in all this time the Ministry has never, ever turned me down for a permit. But it is all so time-consuming."

"Vicky's right," Geoff joins in. "The Ministry is always as helpful as they can be. They really are. We are probably among the very few expatriates at all interested in investing in Tanzania. I remember the words of the Iringa regional commissioner when we were about to start in Ruaha. He came down on an official visit to the park and, in a speech, urged the authorities to give all the help they could to the Foxes, declaring that we were showing confidence and investing in Tanzania at a time when no one else was."

"The expatriates all consider us crazy."

"True. Except for Werner and Helga. They understand."

《•》《•》《•》《•》

Another day. Another trip back from Dar es Salaam on a Great North Road increasingly churning and buckling under ever more gigantic trucks, overloaded with oil and copper, frenetically racing against Zambia's decline. Between potholes and careening tankers, Vicky still manages to enjoy the rolling scenery, cloudless skies, and distant mountain ranges, ever fading in blues toward distant horizons.

The Udzungwa slopes are covered in forests of baobab. Vicky recollects various fables about why their branches resemble roots, each involving an enraged deity who ripped them out of the ground and shoved them back in again upside-down (because the baobabs refused to come to a meeting, because the baobabs grew too tall, etc.).

A shocking-pink desert rose periodically punctures the grey of baobabs. One nestles right into an ancient tree, like a baby nuzzling its mother. Great mounds of onions and tomatoes, set out by roadside *Ujamaa* villagers, join the precious Dar es Salaam purchases in the back of Vicky's vehicle. They are cheaper here than in Mufindi.

As she winds her way along the Ruaha River and up the Kitonga Gorge, behind a long convoy of behemoths, Vicky wonders what this trip must have been like at the turn of the century, when Magdalene von Prince and her husband walked toward these same, brooding Udzungwa mountains and the elusive Hehe Chief, Mkwawa. Or when the Voigts and their friends manoeuvred a twenty-six-foot, self-crafted cabin cruiser perched on a trailer behind their five-ton truck around these narrow, hairpin bends, long before the Kitonga Gorge roads were widened or paved.

There is Iringa at last, its granite-strewn hills and massive boulders displayed in tumbled grandeur. Dry scrub. A few blood-red erythrina blossoms. Spectacular euphorbia, candelabra trees with flaming orange petals. The bamboo copses, dusty green and yellow promising *ulanzi* (bamboo wine, delicious fresh; lethal fermented). All so familiar, and yet, even after all this time, still exotic.

She turns off the paved highway at last, grateful to be away from the madness of TANZAM traffic. Pines line the sides of the bumpy, packed earth road. The air is sweet. She breathes in huge lungfuls of cool, highland goodness. Slowly, slowly, the tension peels away.

Almost home again, she thinks, as she begins the drive through Mufindi, past Lake Ngwazi, past the first tea fields, and up the driveway. *Almost home!*

INVISIBLE KILLER

Invisible. Deadly. Half a country away, toward the Uganda border, people are mysteriously dying. Unlike other diseases, which take the vulnerable, "slim disease" is beginning to fell the strong. Fathers and mothers in their prime fade away to nothing, leaving hapless rural grandparents to care for orphaned grandchildren—this in an environment where adult children are the only social safety net for the aged, and food is often only available when they themselves can coax it out of the ground, usually through hours of backbreaking work with hand hoes. Instead, here they are, their children gone, their grandchildren depending on their worn and used-up bodies for food, shelter, school uniforms. Where slim disease comes from or how it spreads, no one knows.

FOX COFFEE BUBBLE BURSTS

Dreams of an official title for their coffee farm way down in the Rift Valley falter and ultimately stall. "After initially being very confident of being able to get land for a farm, we have recently encountered opposition from the equivalent of the local district commissioner," Geoff writes to his parents. "He says the area is required for other development projects, even though we previously had got the support of all the local villagers and the minister of agriculture. So the farm is still in the balance. We should know within a month." Permission is rescinded.

The Foxes now have no option but to abandon yet another initiative, even though their coffee seedlings are thriving. Heartbroken, they look for buyers. "It's confirmed," Vicky informs Geoff at last. "The Tanzania Coffee Board wants to buy our coffee plants for Ludewa District.[41] The good news is that they are going to send their Land Rovers to pick up the plants."

"The bad news," Geoff beats her to it, "is that they can only drive as far as 'the viewpoint'!" (Geoff's forest road, now known as Fox's Forest Road, leads to the escarpment edge above their plot 2,000 feet below.) "More bad news, of course, is that I can't help you carry the 2,000 plants up the escarpment because of my employment contract with the tea company." (Which, as mentioned earlier, forbids employees to have any outside commercial interests.)

So Vicky heads down to the coffee nurseries with Julius and a large team of porters in tow. As loads are being allocated, Vicky and Julius soon realize that they are too heavy for a single trip back up the steep incline. Vicky's heart sinks. One such haul is a lot to ask of the porters, two almost unthinkable. But she has a fixed deadline to meet. The

---

41   Situated beyond Njombe, via Uwemba, toward Lake Malawi.

Agricultural Department definitely won't come back a second time to transport seedlings, given the desperate fuel and spare parts shortages in Tanzania. And Vicky and Geoff need the money. Even with the sale of their house in England, and proceeds from whatever they can sell or barter of Vicky's farm produce, they are teetering on the edge.

Now what? She dares not discourage the porters, so she waits until they all reach the top with their first load, before advising them of the need for a second one.

"*Hapana, Mama, hawezikani,*" they say, not unkindly but definitively. "No, Mama. It cannot be done." They refuse to budge. Vicky cannot force them, so she turns around, saying, "Okay. I will have to do it myself," and sets off back down the escarpment. Julius follows. Embarrassed to be shown up by a woman, the porters relent. By dusk, all the Land Rovers waiting at the top are loaded, and the seedlings are finally gone. "That," says Geoff, grinning wryly, "pays for what the farm down there cost us."

Years later, Geoff's knowledge of coffee in Tanzania will earn him undeserved kudos when he and Vicky visit the parents of well-known wildlife author, artist, and consultant, Jonathan Kingdon. They first met the Kingdons on their coffee farm in Mbeya, to which the ex-provincial commissioner and his wife had retired. Heading upstairs in the Kingdon's second retirement home, this time in Exmouth, Devon, many years later, Geoff will notice that Mr. Kingdon's conservatory houses a coffee bush. Taking a chance, he will confidently announce, "N39, I see," to a visibly shaken Mr. Kingdon (as no one can really identify such an arabica coffee variety—let alone in England).

"All I knew," Geoff will own up, "is that, around the time you were leaving Mbeya, N39 was the 'wonder variety' being planted by everyone, so I gambled that anyone taking a plant to the UK would choose this one."

MORE CLOSE CALLS

Meanwhile, the Fox boys are growing up. Christopher, the eldest, now helps to manage the Ruaha Camp during his holidays from college. "Poor Christopher has to do all the work at the camp," Vicky writes to Libby, "just when we had a week fully booked. Anyway, it's good practice for him. I just got a message to say that he is working a twelve-hour day with his friend who has come out from England.

We get reports the whole time from visitors telling us how good he is."

Christopher often brings his younger brothers down to Ruaha on weekends. "Dear Granny," he reports: "One day we went game viewing and got lost, ending up about twenty-five miles downriver from the Mwagusi Sand River, without any petrol. Then, by some miracle, we spotted an old house on a river. We saw some rangers, who were surveying there, for just one week. They lent us two gallons of petrol. On our way back, we were stampeded by a herd of buffalo. Peter, who was driving, stalled. The buffalo luckily filtered to both sides but one was left struggling to get up, on top of its calf. We thought its back was broken so I got out and from seven feet away I took a photograph, and then walked closer to take another. Whereupon, it got up and charged: I did a two-second mile back to the car, which was already pulling away. Anyway we got back safely."

Vicky has her own challenges. On the seventh of November 1982, she goes for a walk in the bush with Geoff and her friend Helga, when they come upon a ten-foot bridge ("if that's what one can call a few dicey-looking planks thrown over a stream," Vicky comments).

Geoff, as the heaviest of the three, offers to test the bridge. Nothing happens, so Vicky and Helga start to cross. With an almighty crack, the feeble structure collapses. Both of them end up in the water.

"Helga floated like a balloon with her skirt billowing around her, and both legs in the air, very embarrassed that she couldn't get them down," says Geoff. "A section of the broken bridge fell on Vicky, scraping her to the bone down one leg."

Vicky's description to Libby: "Unfortunately, my leg was pinned under a huge timber, which did rather a lot of damage." The company doctor tells Vicky to keep her leg up for two weeks. "All would have been well," Vicky's letter to Libby continues, "except I had to go and fetch the brand-new Land Rover we were allocated, and couldn't miss the chance of getting it, with the help of a bank loan. State Motor Corporation informed us that some new cars had arrived in Tanzania, and that they had to be picked up immediately, since they were being allocated on a first-come, first-served basis."

This involved the 640-kilometre road trip from the cool highlands to tropical and humid Dar es Salaam and, once there, the requisite footslogging between companies and ministries to finalize arrangements.

"Of course, the heat and walking around really didn't do my injury any good. On the way back, there was an awful smell in the car. My friend, Liz, and I decided that a rat must have died in the radiator. We searched for it in vain. The smell became almost unbearable.

"'You know what?' I finally said, 'I think it's my leg!' I smelled my leg and, sure enough, it was starting to rot. Our Mufindi doctor was furious. He had to burn the gangrenous flesh off with lime. Luckily, dead flesh doesn't hurt. I only felt it when the lime reached healthy tissue. Now I really have to rest it awhile." By one of fate's ironic twists, the medical cream prescribed for Vicky was manufactured by Laroche Navarone, using *Centella*.

"It worked brilliantly," says Geoff.

"But I'm not going to win any 'lovely legs' competitions," adds Vicky.

"Of course, I had to rebuild the footbridge that Helga and Vicky broke!" Geoff grumbles.

Vicky fixes him with a stare. Geoff quickly changes the subject.

"Slim" Disease Now Has a Medical Name

Slim disease now has a medical name: "Human immuno-deficiency virus infection / Acquired immunodeficiency syndrome (HIV/AIDS)" or "*Ukimwi*" in Kiswahili.

Ruaha Thrives

After the Foxes' Ruaha River Camp opens officially in January 1982, Vicky still has to travel to Dar es Salaam frequently for official permits to buy anything from a bag of flour, a tin of cooking oil, some rice, and even tinned margarine—each an item of extreme value in impoverished Tanzania with its empty store shelves.

Self-sufficiency is the order of the day, especially to make sure that there is a constant supply of food and money for the Ruaha River Camp. As Vicky writes home, "The disease that has swept through our dairy herd has now abated—I hope. We lost seven animals—it was a very rare disease normally associated only with sheep. Fewer animals to barter." In another letter, "Our construction moves forward only as fast as money coming in from visitors to the Ruaha. As in, 'Whoops! We've got some more money, Geoff. We can build another *banda!'* What a way to run a business!"

On top of keeping pigs, cattle, and sheep, the Foxes now produce as many consumables as possible, otherwise unavailable for sale in Tanzania. They freeze milk and butter, make cottage cheese, and produce bacon, sausages, hams, and other pork products, including liver pâté. Beef is smoked, ice cream churned, and various sorbets frozen. These are supplemented by Brussels sprouts, fennel, parsnips, broad beans, runner beans, and unusual types of lettuce that add colour to salads, such as lollo rosso and oak lettuce, red salad bowl, little gem, and red little gem.

All are dispatched regularly from Mufindi to the Ruaha National Park, first by car and then by Land Rover laden to the rooftop, a journey beginning on rough farm tracks for an hour to the highway, followed by another hour on tarmac to Iringa, and after that two to three hours (eighty miles or so) to the park on rugged roads of bone-jarring corrugation in the dry season, and almost impassible muddy sections when it rains.

As there is so little available in the way of consumer goods, and the Foxes are by now increasingly self-sufficient, Ruaha River Camp's reputation for fine cuisine is firmly established, under Head Chef Gideon, originally Geoff's golf caddy, whom Vicky trained to cook. He is brilliant. When a temporarily disabling stroke puts him out of commission, Geoff and Vicky bring him home to Mufindi, but he insists on returning to Ruaha.

Just as the Foxes start to relax a bit around finances, because of the camp's popularity, Tanzania virtually runs out of fuel. Few people are now able to travel for pleasure. By the time the shortages ease, and clients start to reappear, impending rains threaten an early end to the Ruaha tourist season.

MONTY THE PYTHON

"Dear Libby . . . We had a very exhausting Christmas holiday, but it was great fun. We enjoyed having all the naturalists here, I must say. They were so good with the boys, teaching them about all kinds of different creatures, particularly Kim Howell, a reptile expert at the University of Dar es Salaam. He now has Christopher catching snakes for him. Quite terrifying to my mind, but then snakes were never my favourite creature."

Christopher collects many snakes on Lugoda to be preserved and sent to Kim. Helga is most helpful and produces horned vipers from her farm. But perhaps the most unusual find of Christopher's is a sand boa, pinkish in colour, which he collects in the Ruaha area. This variety has previously only been known in the dry, arid area of northern Kenya and has not been observed in Tanzania before or since.

Christopher also collects another python and names him Monty (Python). He is fed on rats and seems comfortable curled around the neck of Christopher's first-ever girlfriend, a seventeen-year-old Norwegian named Wenka.

"I imagine having a python wrapped around your neck served a useful purpose in making space at the Mufindi club bar," his father jokes at the club.

Then the sad day comes when Wenka has to return to Norway for further studies, and Christopher still has to complete his first year as an employee, managing and expanding the Ruaha River Camp. Still, he is determined to visit Wenka on his way to England for his first leave.

"What do girls like as presents?" he wonders when the time comes.

"With no sisters and a mum who is the 'head boy' of the family (she really is!)," his father is joking with friends again, "he wasn't sure about flowers or chocolate. Instead, he decided on Monty Python, who was duly stuffed into a zipped cabin luggage bag, to be kept at Christopher's feet during an SAS flight to Oslo.

Monty the Python with Mary Ellis, close family friend and key Foxtreks supporter.

It sounds incredible, but is nevertheless true: at some stage during the flight, at 30,000 feet, Christopher looked down and saw Monty oozing out of the bag through the slightly opened zip and disappearing under the seat behind. The person sitting next to him wasn't looking.

"Monty was swiftly stuffed back into the bag, and eventually this gift of love and endearment was presented to Wenka when she and her brother came to meet him in Oslo.

"Wenka had to sleep with the snake for some six months in the winter, to maintain a suitable temperature for him. She fed Monty on Siberian dancing mice from the pet shop. They must have been quite expensive. Can you imagine what the pet shop owner would have thought if he had known where the mice were going?

"Perhaps in deciding to present Monty to Wenka, Christopher thought that a snake in her bed would deter other suitors. Sadly, when he arrived he found out that Wenka already had another boyfriend, so he spent all his time in Norway hanging out with her brother."

《•》《•》《•》《•》

"January 22, 1983. Dear Libby . . . Bruce is very interested in biology and we were very pleased (and rather shattered) to read in his headmaster's report that he is expected to do scholarship-level biology."

STRANGE REUNION IN THE BUSH

Because of his familiarity with Mgololo, Geoff is invited in 1983 to lead an expedition down the escarpment for a World Bank team from Washington tasked with investigating the proposed site of a pulp and paper mill. He and Vicky have already, with the help of their friend, Jack (the company engineer), been down the escarpment earlier to measure the nearby river. "We waded about in the river, measuring widths and depths and speed of flow, and so on," as Vicky wrote to Libby.

Now Geoff will show four World Bank representatives, led by a German economist, and several Tanzanian forestry officers the site. Vicky joins them. She is the only woman. Down the steep, 2,000-foot incline they walk. Their upper thigh muscles quiver. There are grumbles and groans.

"We should have brought something to drink."

"Don't worry," Geoff assures them. "It's all organized." On they walk through the bush. The World Bank folks are surprised that there are no roads. Further out, there are more grumbles.

"We should have brought some lunch."

"Don't worry," Geoff again, "it's all organized."

When he finally calls a halt for lunch, Vicky takes off her rucksack (she is the only person carrying anything), and out come all the drinks and food for twelve people.

"They were amazed at her strength," Geoff later laughs. "So, while we were munching the sandwiches, I told them the same story about Vicky representing Germany when she was schooling at Salem. The German economist started choking on his sandwich.

"'I represented Germany in the 100 metres boys' event at the same race! I remember you, Vicky, especially because you were so quiet.'

"'That's because I couldn't speak German well at the time, and as a German representative I was told not to speak English.'

"Such a coincidence, way out in the African bush!"

FIRST OFFICIAL CASE OF HIV/AIDS

In 1983, Tanzania officially reports the first cases of HIV/ AIDS in the Kagera region, bordering Uganda.

RUAHA MAYHEM

By 1984, Vicky and Geoff are still financing the Ruaha Camp on a wing and a prayer. The economy is on its knees—stagnant and bankrupt. No one is investing. So what do the Foxes do? With no indication that there will be international tourists to justify this crazy risk, they keep their fingers crossed that there will be enough income from resident tourists to tide them over until their bank loan is approved, and improvise.

They grow their own vegetables, produce their own meat and dairy products, and barter goods. But they also need money to pay for transportation, wages, construction, maintenance . . . the list of expenses seems endless. Meanwhile, their loan application disappears in mushrooming red tape, with first priority given to distributing scarce commodities among the faltering *Ujamaa* villages. Harassed and underpaid civil servants are spending fewer hours attending to official business, in favour of growing corn, potatoes, and other scarce staples. Official transactions pile up in empty offices.

"After four months," Vicky reports to Libby, "the loan was finally passed, but the money still hasn't come through [one month later]. We live from day to day, swapping cows for lorry transport. Geoff really got the place going, on weekends and local leave, as he has a more artistic eye than I.

"Now I'm on my own again, and it's quite nerve-racking sometimes, especially with a 1968 Ford Transit pickup and an eight-year-old Land Rover. You can just imagine what a good mechanic I am. I don't know one end of the vehicle from the other. The other day, the gear lever on the Transit snapped in two places, and we had to take it seventy miles to have it welded. We are so dependent on it for collecting stone and sand."

Luckily, domestic tourists are indeed flocking to the Ruaha camp. As Christmas approaches, Vicky braces herself for insanity. It looks like the camp will be full, but the cabins are not all ready. And there could be extra guests, too. Communications are so poor that advance bookings are very difficult to make, so people generally just tend to show up.

Two visitors arrive unexpectedly early that first Christmas, one an architect and the other a psychiatrist.

"Thank goodness," Vicky says after they've introduced themselves. "I am in dire need of both your services. One to advise me on how to fill the holes in the walls of the cabins [he suggested cotton wool, he really did] and the other to heal me because, when I have time, I'm going to have a nervous breakdown."

However, Christmas goes well, even though the kerosene freezers are impossible to manage. "Thank heaven for Gideon, our Tanzanian cook," Vicky beams. "He's brilliant with them. They never smoke around him. Of course, we do pay him well for his services."

"POOR MARRICK!"

"Marrick was our first horse," Geoff tells visitors one day. "We bought him jointly with the Boswells and Bosmas from the New Zealand-financed sheep project on the Kitulo (formerly Elton's) Plateau. He was a placid enough ride, except for one occasion when, still tethered to the fence, Alex mounted and sat on Marrick's back. Nothing moved. Until suddenly the horse bucked and almost in slow motion, Alex did a complete somersault over Marrick's head, over the fence and onto our lawn. It was most extraordinary. One moment he was just sitting there, the next he was doing a full somersault, and then he simply landed on his feet.

"Another time, fortified by gin, he tried his hand at bareback riding, was thrown again and has suffered a knee injury ever since. You do silly things with gin. However, back to Marrick: There was an experienced vet at a Swiss-backed cattle project in Mufindi, and Rob Bosma decided that Marrick had to be castrated.

"The Boswells and we shrugged and agreed. But later, in fact on the day that the dirty deed was scheduled to take place, we changed our minds. Again, our about-turn took place during the weekly Saturday ritual, when gin and tonics were imbibed on the lawn to celebrate the end of a week's worth of work. This perhaps also influenced the casual communication to Rob.

"Alex and I had to help organize a large sailing club barbecue at Ngwazi that evening, so we simply left a note on a stick in the middle of the lawn, with the instruction to Rob: "Save Marrick's balls." On our return from Ngwazi, the note was still there, under which was placed a tin . . . poor Marrick.

"Determined to get our own back on Rob, we took the tin and its contents to Ngwazi, planning to barbecue and serve them to Rob in the darkness. But unfortunately, he had to operate on an emergency case at the hospital that night and failed to attend."

FRIENDS OF RUAHA SOCIETY

"Things are getting really desperate in Ruaha, especially for the game rangers." Geoff and Vicky are now chatting with friends Shanna and Peter Sheridan–Johnson.

"Have you seen them recently? They are barefoot and boot-less—not to mention using antiquated firearms."

"No wonder they're not keen on challenging poachers, with the sophisticated arms they carry."

"And I've just heard that their wages are three months in arrears."

"I guess that's why some of them have taken down the odd impala for food."

"Surely there's something we can do."

"What would we focus on?"

"Good question. They need just about everything."

"How about starting some volunteer organization to raise funds for them?"

"Great idea."

And so is born the Friends of Ruaha Society (FORS) to assist and encourage those whose job it is to protect wildlife in Ruaha—more specifically, "through its comprehensive Environmental Education Program, FORS aims to conserve the Ruaha ecosystem by increasing environmental awareness in the communities that border Ruaha National Park, thereby ensuring that local people understand the balance between themselves, wildlife, and the environment."[42]

In its earliest days, the Friends of Ruaha provides boots and radios for the rangers, as well as graders, spare parts and blades, and equipment to rebuild the ferry and new ranger posts. They also create an incentive scheme for rangers to be rewarded for catching poachers. Particularly poignant, at their first annual "payday" (the day bonuses are awarded to rangers), they share the few berets available to them before marching forward, saluting, and receiving their awards.

"Imagine the scene," says Geoff, speaking at fundraisers. "These people, ill-equipped with uniforms, but proud enough to take the hat from the one person who has one and put it on before marching forward."

UJAMAA UNRAVELLING

As Tanzanians increasingly feel the economic pinch, more and more of Mwalimu's colleagues begin bailing out. His critics want to try a more capitalist approach, saying that his socialist agenda has failed.

Whether such failure lies primarily with socialism or elsewhere is hotly debated. Some blame Tanzania for focusing too much on wealth distribution and not enough on wealth creation. Some point to the effects of two global oil-shocks and subsequent rises in oil prices, which were reflected in the

---

42   http://www.friendsofruaha.org/home.html.

cost of imports to Tanzania, but not in exports from Tanzania (raw commodities, for which prices were set on the international market, many argue, riddled with unfair terms of trade that still favour rich countries).

The price for tea, for example, is still set in London, not overseas where tea is produced, and definitely not according to production costs. Coffee, sisal, you name it, are bought at rock-bottom prices (set overseas) and come back from overseas in the form of tractors and other goods at steep prices (set overseas with healthy profit margins included for the overseas producers). It is still cheaper to phone London, across the Indian Ocean, from Dar es Salaam than to phone Nairobi in neighbouring Kenya—a hangover from the colonial phone system, set up for efficient central administration from the UK. This means a phone call from Tanzania to neighbouring Kenya first has to bounce to London and back, with associated long-distance charges![43]

Despite all this, Mwalimu's supporters argue, he is achieving huge successes under *ujamaa*:

◆ Functional literacy among the highest in Africa, up from 30 percent at independence to about 65 percent[44] (his adult education program has been pure genius, they say, engaging as it did our rural children to teach adults in villages)

◆ Brilliant nation-building (who could have imagined that in so short a time Mwalimu would form a country out of more than a hundred tribes, let alone many hundred clans? And this, unlike surrounding countries, without violent conflict)

◆ The bloodless merger in 1964 of Tanganyika and Zanzibar, for example, to form the United Republic of Tanzania, and the fusion in 1977 of the Tanzanian ruling party (TANU) with the Afro-Shirazi Party (ASP) of Zanzibar to form the Chama cha Mapinduzi—CCM Revolutionary Party

◆ His East African, pan-African, and international influence. Not only has Mwalimu put Tanzania on the map, but, in

---

43   Since remedied.

44   http://education.stateuniversity.com/pages/1521/Tanzania-NONFORMAL-EDUCATION.html.

many ways, he is now the conscience of Africa, a champion of Africanism and an example for leadership ethics.

- An African official language (Swahili) in place of English
- Life expectancy up from thirty-five to over fifty years[45] because of improved health services in the villages (before Mwalimu, most of the health budget went into a few hospitals in urban areas; now, a nation-wide network of health centres and dispensaries reaches into each village level)

Ujamaa critics are quick to jump in here, pointing out that health centres can no longer afford medicine, let alone staff; that people's health is suffering because food production no longer keeps pace with population growth; and that the huge socialist infrastructure is bankrupting Tanzanians. "Everything is so expensive here, that even the rich tourists prefer to spend their foreign exchange in Kenya," they say. "And, because we borrowed so much money from 'donor' countries, half our national budget goes toward paying them back."

"You can't blame everything on Tanzania's socialism," *ujamaa* supporters counter. "What about the severe effects of drought, of cholera, of cross-border smuggling, and, of course, of corruption? What about the cost of war with Uganda, not to mention some international donors chasing now this development theory, now that one? Well-intentioned or not, that's about as helpful as trying to change a tanker's direction every half hour.

Their latest cure-all, so-called "structural adjustment," *ujamaa* supporters argue, sounds good in theory— if you really believe that the private sector will help the poorest folk more than communalism has—but what does it actually mean in practice? And who will suffer most in the process? Does Tanzania really want a Kenya-type "man-eat-man," capitalist society? ("At least we have something to eat," President Moi apparently once quipped to Mwalimu.) How extensively and how fast would the reforms be implemented, and at what cost to whom?

---

45   http://www.quandl.com/WORLDBANK-World-Bank/
     TZA_SP_DYN_LE00_IN-Tanzania-Life-expectancy-at-birth-total-years.

The bottom line, whatever the reason, wherever the blame, is that Tanzanians who were forcibly relocated, and even those who moved voluntarily, have grown tired of labouring so hard without proportional benefit. Already many have now given up working on communal lands, in favour of farming their family plots. With heavy heart, Mwalimu sees his dream unravelling.

FULL OF IDEAS

"I'm cut off by the river in Ruaha," Vicky writes to Libby in 1985. "We made a mistake and managed to get one vehicle bogged down this side of the river. Of course the river went up in the night, preventing the ferry from operating, and we've been stuck here for five days so far.

Old Ruaha ferry into the national park, when it works ... and when it doesn't.

"It really is beautiful at the moment. All the birds are breeding. We have red-cheeked cordon bleus, very aptly making a nest outside the kitchen, and a colony of golden-backed weavers in the reeds by the river. They are so intriguing, with the male building the nest and then trying to entice a female into it. There's a red-headed weaver nesting just behind the kitchen. It is a stunning bird. Then there's a striped swallow all the way from Europe with its nest under the eaves of one of the *bandas*. I wish we had some film to capture all the action.

"We are leaving Dar on the twelfth of April and taking advantage of Geoff's golf prize of two years ago: three days in a Swiss hotel at Lucerne, all paid for by Swiss Air. Isn't that lovely? We will then have four and a half weeks in England, starting with a mad rush down to Devon to catch the last of the children's Easter holiday—the usual chaos. I feel guiltier these days with both grandfathers well over eighty, although they're still in marvellous health, and both ride the horses when they're here. We're full of ideas about all the things we're going to do next.

"The boys will have a life's work keeping pace with it all: We are planning log cabins in Mufindi, plus a farm, beach *bandas* in Dar es Salaam, two tented camping areas in Ruaha, a farm guest house base in Arusha, and safaris up the Rufiji River in the Selous. Goodness knows where it will end. I do hope the boys get some hardworking wives to help with the catering!"

MWALIMU RESIGNS

"Mwalimu has resigned!" The news reverberates around Tanzania, from the capital into the farthest rural corners of the country. One imagines them gathering before communal radios and debating.

"It's very sad," many might agree. "He has done so much for his country. In fact, we would not even be a country without him."

Others might disagree: "What did he do? Aren't we suffering like we never did before?"

And so it might continue . . .

"It's not Mwalimu's fault. The colonialists made us poor. They set everything up to benefit themselves."

"Didn't they also give Tanzania more aid than any other country?"

"Yes, but how did they go about it? They gave us machines that we cannot maintain. They brought all their expensive experts and paid them more in one day than we can earn in a year."

"And doesn't Mwalimu's idea of educating our children more practically make greater sense than what they used to teach in school before?"

"What do you mean?"

"Don't you remember? The schools only used book learning before. Now they are also teaching children how to raise crops and animals. That will be useful in real life after school. It is education for self-reliance."

"Eh, but is it not also good to know how to read and count? Even I, in my old age, can now read. Imagine that. All my life I could not even write my own name. And now because of Mwalimu's adult education, I can read. I wonder whether they will continue these classes. I hope so."

"Mwalimu also brought us clinics right in the village."

"But where has all the medicine gone?"

"The *wazungu* foreigners must be using it all."

"Most of the *wazungu* are gone."

"The Vokisis [Voigts] are still in Kifyulilo in their big house."

"Have they not also helped us? They employ us. And just last week he brought more timber for the school and godown roofs."

"And Mama Vokisi [Voigt] gives us medicine and fruit."

"She took me to hospital. I would have died."

"Then where has everything gone?"

"The Wabenzi, maybe? I hear all the big shots driving the Mercedes Benzes are on their way back."

"Mwalimu tried to stop them. What can you do?"

"Now that *Ujamaa* is dead, will you stay in the village?"

"You mean we could go back to our old land? Near the ancestors?"

"I would definitely do so."

"Here, your children are close to school."

"There, I work my own field. Then at least I know who to blame when things go wrong."

"I still believe in *Uhuru na Umoja* [Freedom and Unity] and, of course, *Kazi* [Work]. I'm staying."

"Me, too. Maybe if enough of us who want to work together stay, we can be productive again, like in the early years."

"For sure, we will ask Mzee Mpiluka to guide us."

"He says he is tired and ready now to leave the leadership to someone younger."

"He will have to stay."

"Me, I am very sad that Mwalimu has resigned. He is a good man. He cares for us. He believes in us and our traditional ways."

"Eeeehh. That he does."

Support his policies or not, support his vision or not, support his priorities or not, the vast majority of Tanzanians continue to have huge respect for the man himself. His resignation leaves them holding their breath and wondering, what next?

《•》《•》《•》《•》

Geoff to Gelly and Jimmy, February 1985: "In a minute or two I am off to hear our local MP. He has come up from Iringa to explain to the African community the reason for the resignation of President Nyerere as prime minister. All the Africans here seem rather bewildered and don't know what to think or say about it . . . There is uncertainty for Brooke Bond employees, too, about what will happen . . .

"P.S. Yes, quite better from tick typhus, thanks. I was given some ghastly pills that worked like magic."

HELGA'S ACCIDENT

"October 13, 1985. Dear Libby . . . Helga Voigt, who is now seventy, fell through her ceiling and almost killed herself. She has five broken ribs, a collapsed lung, as well as a broken hip and has had to be flown out to Nairobi by the Flying Doctor Service."

The Voigts' wonderful cook, Oresto, found Helga lying on the cement floor (where she had landed hard, after bouncing off a wooden Bombay chair). He immediately fetched Werner.

Werner finally got Helga to the company hospital, twenty miles away on rough roads. Dr. Rob was on leave, so storm-proof Nurse Shanna had to care for her . . . calm and contained, unflappable and competent, always with a twinkle in her warm, blue eyes.[46]

Amongst others, Shanna organized a relay of Mufindi spouses to keep Helga awake and talking, for fear that she might otherwise not wake up again. Meanwhile, Colin Congdon tried to alert the Flying Doctor Service by radio—which Brooke Bond had installed after the phone service virtually died. When that didn't work, he was just about to get into his car and drive the eighty miles to Iringa, but decided on a whim to try the phone. It worked—for the only time in many months.

The Flying Doctor Service agreed to medically evacuate Helga to Kenya. Usually, no relatives are allowed onto the tiny craft, but somehow Werner managed to talk his way on anyway. "Good news, Helga. I understand Werner is allowed to come on the plane with you," Shanna told Helga, not even sure she could hear.

"I think I have problems enough," Helga mumbled, with the first faint twinkle in her eye. Shanna heaved a huge sigh of relief. *Helga may just make it.*

《•》《•》《•》《•》

The morning after Helga's accident dawns with a typical layer of low-lying clouds shrouding Mufindi. Radio calls summon all those with a vehicle to congregate at the airstrip as Helga's broken body is driven at a snail's pace toward Ngwazi. There, the other vehicles are already lined up facing the packed earth runway. When they hear the sound of the Flying Doctor plane, they all switch on their headlights. And, miraculously, the clouds part—literally just long enough for the little aircraft to land, load, and take off again.

"Helga was known as the 'Tough Old Bird from Tanzania' in the hospital," Vicky's letter to Libby continues. "She flew back to Mufindi and was just walking with crutches but rather unsteadily, when two

---

46   Personal note from Evelyn to Shanna: Thank you always, for saving my mother, Helga's, life those many years ago. Also for the other time, when you and Dr. Klaas de Jong helped make her comfortable that first evening back in Mufindi from Canada, more than a decade later, when the combination of cracked ribs and Larium induced a potent blend of pain and psychosis. Between the two of you, her quality of life was restored.

horrible characters from a nearby road-making crew held her and her husband Werner up at gunpoint. Helga couldn't put her hand up, so they shot her at point blank range. Fortunately, they hadn't packed the gun properly, and Helga only got gunpowder in her eye, whilst Werner got the wadding in his, and the huge ball bearings rolled away, useless. They both arrived at the hospital, one with a black eye and one with a red one."

《•》《•》《•》《•》

On August 15, 1985, Mwalimu declares Ali Hassan Mwinyi his successor and sole CCM candidate for president in the forthcoming October elections. Cold War adversaries predictably line up for or against the merits of multi-party politics and the validity of Tanzania's "one-party democracy."

Imprisonment

"This week, Geoff had to attend the judgment of a court case." Vicky is still so shaken, she can hardly write. "He ran into someone ages ago. At the time, he immediately stopped, picked the chap up, and took him to hospital, where they treated him for a broken leg. Geoff then reported the incident to the police. The victim admitted at once that it was his fault. Apparently, he is stone deaf, hadn't heard the car, and ran across the road without looking.

"After months of hearings, the day of judgment dawned on Thursday. We did not think we needed a lawyer, given the victim's admission of guilt in his statement to the police. The prosecution called only one witness in the case, the victim. When he finally understood the judge's question, he repeated that he hadn't heard the car because he was totally deaf.

"At no time did he confer any blame onto Geoff. Instead, he clearly stated that it was his own fault. So when Geoff was asked whether he wanted to question him, he declined, assuming that there was no need to do so under such cut-and-dried circumstances.

"The judge pronounced Geoff guilty of dangerous driving. He completely misquoted everything Geoff said, and sentenced him to one year's imprisonment and three years' disqualification from driving."

Vicky pauses, remembers Geoff's incredulity after the verdict—

how he kept trying to make sense of it. "Why would he rule me guilty?" And then, "Perhaps he thought I was admitting guilt because I did not question the witness." And then, "It makes you realize how the innocent, law-abiding citizen can be put at risk."

Slowly, she goes back to her letter.

"We couldn't believe our ears, Libby. But there was nothing we could do. I made one attempt to cheer him up by saying I'd bake him a cake with a file in it. And yet, it simply wasn't any laughing matter.

"The police took him off with all the common criminals in the back of their Land Rover and I rushed to Lugoda, into a directors' board meeting, and burst into tears. Finally, I was able to tell them what had happened. For the next three days, everyone was chasing all over the countryside, lodging an appeal.

"In the police station, they put Geoff in a cell, took his sweater, shoes, and socks and made him sit all day on the cement floor. Other prisoners just peed against the wall, as there wasn't a loo, so you can imagine the stench. Then he was moved to the prison and for the next two days he was in a cell transported into medieval days."

"I spent two nights in prison," Geoff later tells friends. "What struck me first was the stench of human feces that pervaded the air and remained on your clothing. Appalling, the stench!

"I suppose I was privileged, as I was locked up with just two fellow inmates in a tiny cell, whereas others elsewhere in the prison were squashed in with 100 to a cell, when they weren't in working parties, labouring under guard. There was a tin of water to wash with. And a communal tin to squat over."

"A tin in full view of others; and no loo paper—just water from the other tin," Vicky adds.

"Hence the stench of feces," Geoff continues. "I determined not to eat in order not to have to go to the loo. They did try to take care of me. I was *mzungu* [a white person], and, as per regulations at that time, you were supposed to be fed what you were normally accustomed to. So they gave me slices of papaya that I passed around to my companions.

"One of my two cellmates was a Njombe District prison governor, who had allowed some trusted prisoners out to pursue an escaped convict, whom they promptly caught and killed. The governor was a nice chap. I remember he was very concerned about his pension. My second cell companion turned out to be an elephant poacher, who had been caught as the result of my information about his elephant poaching in Ruaha. He held no grudge, and was also good company. He merited the special cell because of his advancing age.

"Of course, the prison was crawling with large rats. They peered down at us through the barbed- and-chicken-wire ceiling, aiming their droppings into our small bucket of drinking water. [Vicky to Libby: "They were enormous, as big as cats, and ran all over the prisoners all night, up the walls, along the ceiling."]

"Decisive action was called for! Vicky had secretly passed me a tiny torch. This we used for a major, combined operation. I held the torch. One of my companions beat the rats off the walls with a stick, and the other posted them through the peephole of the cell door. Next morning there was a mountain of dead rats outside to greet the warder.

"Our cell was apparently designed for prisoners that needed restraining, judging by a ring embedded into the cement floor, but we were allowed to exercise and only confined at night. The prison governor was a qualified veterinary doctor. We spent hours socially conversing—in his office. Everyone was civil, prisoners and warders alike. It was just the unbearable stench—an experience not to be repeated!

"Although I'm treating it lightly," Geoff says more seriously, "this can be a salutary example of what could happen to people who decline to respond to the threats and intimidation of those in power of some form or another, such as police. There were inmates who had been confined in this prison for years—awaiting their cases to be tried.

"When I got back on bail, the first thing was to bathe and wash out everything from my hair. But the stench stays in one's clothes."

"It was all a complete nightmare, Libby. The story Geoff told when he came back was horrifying. Geoff didn't eat anything at all and lost four kilos, most of it through dehydration, as he couldn't drink the rat-fouled water. For two days, I stayed with Geoff every minute, driving him everywhere. Afterwards, it transpired that the magistrate had asked for a bribe from Brooke Bond's African personnel manager, Albert Mwanjessa, three times, and had of course been refused. That was why he had found Geoff guilty.

"Anyway, the appeal should come up within a fortnight, so keep your fingers crossed. I don't think he could survive twelve months in one of those jails—worse than concentration camp."

Run over by a Buffalo

A few weeks later, Vicky is sitting on the veranda of her parents' *banda* in the hilltop camp at Ruaha. They are visiting from England.

"So lovely," says Vicky's mum.

"Indeed," the Brigadier confirms.

"We'll get up early tomorrow morning and go for a game drive," Vicky tells them. "I'll fetch you from your *banda*."

The next morning, instead of waiting for Vicky, the Brigadier and Micky decide to walk down to the main camp. On their way, they hear a scuffle. There, behind them, are three bull buffalo. Vicky's father, having nothing but a walking stick, commands his wife to stand still.

"Probably for the first time, she obeyed him," Geoff later jokes. "One of the buffaloes had a lion bite out of its bum. And it was mean."

The eighty-three-year-old Brigadier points his stick at him and his last words are: "Bugger off!"

By the time Vicky arrives, she finds her mother with a bleeding nose and future black eyes, standing over the Brigadier, prodding his prostrate body with her toe, and saying, "Get up, before the buffalos come back."

He is lying there, unconscious, gored on his inner thighs. Luckily Mary Ellis, the Foxes' good friend and a nurse, is in the camp. She takes the Brigadier to the park dispensary, where a new employee sews him up. Then, with eight broken ribs, they bump back to Mufindi on ungraded rough roads.

The Brigadier's first words to Geoff are, "I got run over by a buffalo." Broken ribs notwithstanding, the two-week visit to Vicky's brother in Cairo proceeds as scheduled only eight days later. And, within months, the Brigadier is back up his ladder in England painting the outside of his house.

Left for Dead

"November 1985. Dear Libby . . . Mufindi has had quite a year in 1985. A couple of days ago, our German friends, the Voigts, who have lived in Tanzania for almost sixty years (fifty-eight of them without violent incident) were attacked for the second time. Poor Helga was in the loo when they broke down the door, hit her on the head with the blunt side of a machete, and knocked her out. When she came to, she heard the robbers say:

"*Amekufa?* [She's dead?]

"*Amekufa.*' [She is dead.] On cue, Helga played dead, even though she was in agony from the blow to her hand, which she had flung up instinctively to protect her head, not to mention that she had fallen onto her broken hip. Even worse, she could hear Werner calling out to her in distress, but she did not want to alert the thieves. Tough old bird, indeed.

"They had tied Werner to the bed after hitting him with an axe. Fortunately not much damage. Then they completely cleared the place out, including their Land Rover.

"It turned out later that the blunt side of the machete had broken several bones in Helga's hand. 'Better that than the skull,' she used to joke. This left her still awaiting her hip replacement (to be done in Germany), but now having to somehow manoeuvre her crutches with broken fingers.

"Again, Mufindi folk showed their kindness. Dear Lucy Finch,[47] originally from Malawi and now married to the Sao Hill forestry officer, Tony, went as far as to move in with them—ostensibly to help Helga with the considerable chores of an African farm, but really to be there in case something else happened."

HIV/AIDS PANDEMIC

The world is now bracing itself for an AIDS pandemic. For reasons not yet clarified, it is the poorest countries in the world that seem the hardest hit; and there, as elsewhere, it is the strongest members of the community, the economically productive, who succumb. Tanzania, unlike some other seriously affected countries, decides to tackle the problem head-on. With international support, it sets up a National AIDS Control Programme (NACP) to coordinate its response. AIDS coordinators are to be located in each district. But their underfunded attempts at influencing communities to reduce transmission and find ways of caring for and

---

47   Evelyn to Lucy: Never to be forgotten, Lucy! Thank you so much again.

otherwise helping the sick fall on deaf ears. Knowing there is no cure, only stigma to be gained by coming forward, the sick are hiding and being hidden.

To be diagnosed with AIDS is like a double death sentence. The first death is social, as patients and their families are increasingly shunned for fear of transmission, and in some cases for perceived promiscuity. A code of silence grows. The second is physical, leaving behind a growing number of often impoverished grandparents to care for orphaned children. This presents another key challenge. In a country as cash poor as Tanzania, there are no resources to support the destitute. Their only recourse is to try to keep growing their own food, even as the strong ones die.

Gradually, HIV/AIDS specialists (newly minted) recognize a strong link between poverty, related malnutrition, and the rate at which some patients move from HIV to full-blown AIDS.

VERDICT

"Dear Libby," writes Vicky, "With only a month to go before the end of 1985, still no news of Foxey's appeal case . . . The rest of the news is good. A large crop of calves brings the herd to seventy-five. We now have a sweet new foal, upping the total of horses to seven. If our new project comes off, three will go to the Kigogo to start pony trekking through the natural Mufindi forest. Christopher is getting into the swing of organizing the Ruaha Camp, and I am busy collecting recipes for the African cooks with a translation into English on the adjoining page—hilarious, as we have to try out the failures as well as the successes!"

"Dear Gelly and Jimmy," this time it is Geoff writing early in 1986. "The appeal date still isn't fixed, and I continue to remain a convict! We had hoped to get it all over and done with well before Christmas, but the appeals registrar and advocate (from Iringa) are showing little interest and no activity. We chivvy them the whole time. Not being able to drive at all is a damned nuisance."

At last, in April 1986, six months after the accident, they nervously drive to the courthouse for the verdict, this time with a lawyer. The state prosecutor and judge both agree that they can find no reason at all for the conviction; so, without Geoff's lawyer having to say a word, the case is dismissed.

Two Bars of Soap and a Truck

Meanwhile, investment concerns about the impending effects of Structural Adjustment are threatening to destroy Tanzania's already teetering economy. Naysayers despair. Proponents say things will have to get worse before they can get better, much better. The country runs out of foreign exchange. Diesel trucks grind to a halt on the Tanzam Highway, formerly the Great North Road, even as residents of Dar es Salaam look out onto diesel-bearing tankers waiting in line on the horizon until Tanzania's Port Authority can rustle up enough foreign exchange to pay for demurrage charges, let alone for the diesel. If available at all, everything is now rationed: cooking oil, salt, torch batteries, you name it.

On one of her many 1,200-kilometre return trips to Dar es Salaam, Vicky sees a long queue of Tanzanians outside a shop, so, without knowing what is inside, she joins it. An hour later, she is thrilled to be allowed to buy two bars of soap! And all this just as the Foxes are desperate for new transportation.

"Dear Libby . . . The old Transit has served us very well, but eventually we had to get a Land Rover as well. To do so, we needed a permit from State Motor Corporation (again, because of Tanzania's dire foreign exchange shortages), but State Motor Corporation refused to grant us a permit for the Land Rover. Every month, we used to go down to Dar es Salaam, include State Motor Corporation in our rounds, and apply for this permit.

"Every month, they turned us down, until we were so desperate for a car that I decided that I would go to State House, the president's official residence, to ask them if they could get State Motor Corporation to grant us a permit. The person I wanted to see wasn't there, so I went back and told the State Motor Corporation that I had been to State House to ask them to support me in my request for the permit. (I failed to mention that I hadn't actually seen anybody there.) This seemed to prompt some action and the next month, the permit was granted.

"P.S. Just in time. Continuous overloading has taken its final toll on the old Transit. It died. We now need a larger lorry. The same runaround begins."

"P.P.S. What excitement and drama. Christopher and I have been rushing all over town trying to get a permit for a lorry. One can't just go out and buy one. Oh dear, no! I have collected three letters from our region, four from the Ministry of Tourism, one from the prime minister's office, and one from State House itself. Anyway, the price of lorries has just gone up from one million shillings to three million shillings, and is expected to rise to four million shillings by the end of the year.

"Everyone tried to tell me that no lorries were available. My first contact at State Motor Corporation also insisted that all the lorries were already allocated. Fortunately, I made a point of meeting with the general manager of Scania Tanzania Ltd. He told me there were ten lorries in stock, two still unallocated. I was so pleased and rushed to get a photocopy of the list of lorries. You should have seen the chap's face when I came back with it.

"We picked one, because it was still at the old price, knowing full well we'd be lucky to get it. On paper, our lorry has shrunk from ten tons to nine tons, but I don't think we'll worry too much about that as long as the final chap gives it to us. We'll know tomorrow, I hope, if not on Monday. But what an effort! My nerves are shot. More of a runaround, so I have finally decided that I will go to State House again, as I did about the Land Rover."

The State House gatekeeper responds to Vicky's request with a friendly, "Yes, Mrs. Fox. Please proceed." There before Vicky is a gracious driveway leading to the heart of Tanzania's government. State House is a gracious building originally erected by the Germans in the 1890s, almost destroyed by the British and later rebuilt by them in 1914 to its former splendour, plus scalloped arches and crenellated tower railings. Vicky hesitates, looks back at her car, then straightens her shoulders and starts walking up the long, formal driveway.

"I thought, 'No. No, I don't want to do that,'" her letter to Libby continues. "It was absolutely terrifying contemplating an interview with the principal secretary to the president. And you know how you get the sinkers? I had to walk up what seemed like a mile of driveway. As I forced myself to trudge along that endless driveway, I kept mumbling, 'What am I doing at State House?'

"When I finally reached the stairs leading to the entrance, there was a red carpet. It stretched out of the State House doors down the steps and out into the driveway. On either side toward the top was a full military band, just about to blare forth. I was so frightened of dirtying the carpet, I trotted alongside it, and finally into State House. There I was told to see Mr. Rupia, the president's personal private secretary. His office was not actually in State House but rather around the corner. To reach it, I had to go back down the main stairs.

"'Blow this,' I thought. 'This time I'm going on the red carpet.' With every step I took past each band member, they individually said "Jambo, Mama," [Good day, Madam] "Jambo, Mama," "Jambo, Mama" all the way down the line, until I finally reached the end of the carpet and thankfully ducked into Mr. Rupia's office. There I sat down and waited. At last I was introduced to him, and put in my request for a lorry. He was absolutely charming.

"'Mrs. Fox,' he said, 'I understand how valuable the lorry would be for generating foreign exchange through tourism. Regrettably, there are no unallocated lorries available for sale at this time.'

"'Mr. Rupia,' I answered, 'I was just at Scania to ask if there were any. They said there were, but that I would never get one from the State Motor Corporation and would probably have to come to State House to get a permit for it.'

"He was cross, to say the least, and asked his office to write a letter of support for my permit. He then rang State Motor Corporation demanding why he had not been told that there were two available lorries, and instructed them to give me one. What a star.

"I rushed over to the State Motor Corporation, precious letter in hand, to meet with the final authority on whether we could have the lorry, the chair of the Vehicle Allocation Committee. He was not there; he had been summoned to State House by Mr. Rupia. For half an hour I waited for him, nervously wondering what he was going to say to me. He didn't say a word. He just handed me the permit. Anyway, it all goes down to experience; but a few more days of this, and I'll be a nervous wreck.

"I can't remember if I told you the best of the year's news," Vicky's letter to Libby continues. "Bruce is accepted next year at Reading University, to do a degree in agriculture. Such a relief!"

In the meantime, he will spend a year in Tanzania learning about tea planting, mostly, but also wattle for tannin, sisal for mats and string, cinchona for quinine, pines for pulp and sawmilling, not to mention helping out with Foxtreks.

On September 22, 1986, Bruce finally arrives in Tanzania for his gap year and accompanies Vicky to "a very grand Arusha conference on tourism with over 200 delegates from all over the world. The conference hall was like a theatre, complete with earphones and interpreters in their little boxes, whom you could hear speak in four different languages. Not to mention grand dinners in the evening with very good food and Italian wine! Unheard-of luxuries in these lean times."

A few weeks later, the Foxes make new friends with the Schaeffers, a diplomatic family who visit Mufindi. Unaware that Wolfgang is a trained viticulturist and expert winemaker, Geoff and Vicky serve them the less than stellar Dodoma wine, Tanzania's only wine at the time. Sometimes they fortify it with local brandy in a vain attempt at improvement. Only later, when they visit Wolfgang and Mary Schaeffer in Dodoma, do they experience Wolfgang's magnificent, homegrown wine cellar. This prompts Geoff and Vicky to try their luck in Mufindi.

"Our latest project is winemaking . . . What doesn't work will be made into vinegar, as it is impossible to get any vinegar at all now," Vicky writes home.

They get hold of the requisite wooden barrel and, with peaches being the only fruit on their trees at the time, dutifully follow all the rules for making peach wine.

When it is finally mature and bottled, they organize a white wine tasting occasion. It starts off brilliantly. The bottle is clear, very alcoholic, ". . . and," says Geoff, sipping, pausing, "it tastes of . . . dog shit! So here we are," he laughs, "with our first-ever homemade wine, nearly 200 litres of it . . . and it tastes of dog shit."

Desperate times call for desperate measures. The whole lot goes to Ruaha for use by the chefs. To their amazement, with "dog shit" wine in use for cooking, the Fox River Camp gains the reputation for the best cuisine in Tanzania during these days of country-wide deprivation.

RESTRICTIONS LIFTED

In mid-1980, Tanzania opts to liberalize its entire economy, strongly advised to do so by the international donor community, which sees this as the key to increasing agricultural yields, productivity, and consequently incomes.

But the rationality of Five Year National Development Plans does not fully dispel residual fears that in some sense, the heart of what is uniquely and most essentially Tanzanian is at risk: "communality."

Even sympathizers with Tanzania's new efforts to reverse its economic free fall debate the merits of gutting Tanzania's civil service (bloated though it be) as precipitously as is called for by Structural Adjustment programs — not just in terms of its impact on those who will lose their income, but also in terms of what they contribute to their far-flung communities. "And what," supporters of the principle of *ujamaa* worry, "will happen to all the successes with education, all the progress in health infrastructure? The so-called 'Trickle Down' theory of development has long since been disproved, with most of the benefits from economic growth invariably sticking to the top. And surely selling off national assets at rock-bottom prices cannot be in Tanzania's best, long-term interest — or can it?"

FOXTREKS TAKES OFF

Foxtreks, meanwhile, is taking off. Economic liberalization and maturing sons, not to mention an inheritance, are spurring the Foxes to ever greater investments. "Dear Libby . . . At the moment, we are trying to get a plot of land just outside of Dar es Salaam for beach *bandas* and half a farm about twenty-two miles from here. It has 2,000 acres of flat grassland but is not arable. We would have beef cattle and a few pigs and dairy cows and a small guest house to catch the visitors travelling from Zambia to Dar es Salaam. We don't know yet if we will get either, but we're absolutely desperate to get a farm, as we're bursting at the seams. With seven horses and eighty cows to feed, extra land for grazing is a must.

"By the way, we have now hit the high technological age and are bristling with radios, one in each car and one in the house, for instant communications. We reached South Africa today with our little CB radio. I had a long conversation with someone in Port Elizabeth. Peter spent his entire holiday setting up the whole radio system, mending all our cars, repairing and installing brake linings, engine mountings, steering relays, clutch plates, etcetera, as well as a computer system with printer. I'm not sure I'm up to it all yet.

"Peter is finishing his tourism course this term and then he is doing a computer course, as he seems to be getting "A" grades for all his work with computers. He has that sort of brain, but not from me . . . We are thinking of starting a business to train horses and sell them to rich diplomats and Aid people for foreign exchange. They would only have to be trained for basic riding, as nobody show jumps or hunts here.

"Bruce is busy ploughing, harrowing, and planting maize, getting lots of practical experience. We are still trying to get a farm . . . I have bought six more horses. Although I really enjoy teaching, it is too much, now. That's why the Norwegian children only come here once a week for natural history, music, and horse riding lessons."

BROOKE BOND/UNILEVER FAREWELL —AND (QUOTH ANTHONY) THE RAKE'S PROGRESS—OR NOT?

"Is it true? Geoff, Vicky, is it true? You're leaving?" Mufindi is a-buzz.

"What made you decide to go?"

"A generous retirement scheme, the Brooke Bond (now Unilever's) policy to Africanize, and it's time to retire." (Not mentioned is a certain collegial jealousy that precipitated their move.)

"How long has it been?"

"Twenty-eight years of tea planting with Brooke Bond and Unilever." By now, he has either managed or worked on nine out of the ten company sections in Mufindi. Partly because Lugoda is central and convenient for the Brooke Bond children attending Vicky's school, Geoff ultimately manages Lugoda Estate for decades, at the same time as Kidope and Ngwazi Estates. No expatriate will ever stay on a single tea estate longer.

His only experience with Livalonge, the tenth estate, is when he goes there to demonstrate his "splayed bamboo flicking-rake." At issue: an obnoxious plant with a lovely blue flower, Commelina, which is extremely difficult to weed. And, having just introduced herbicidal weeding, the company does not look kindly on resistant weeds. ("Fox to the rescue," he jokes. Adding rather sheepishly, "The rake is a silly little thing, but effective.")

"Any plans yet?"

"Nothing specific, except buying land. That's top of the list. We need to move Vicky's farm."

"What? You're thinking of staying on in Tanzania?"

"Of course. This is where our boys want to be."

"And now, at last, Geoff can help with Foxtreks!" So it goes on, deep into the night at the club, liberally doused with homemade (but no longer "dog shit") wine and some precious Tusker beers.

《·》《·》《·》《·》

"Dear Libby . . . I'm sitting here in one of our new tents in the Ruaha River Camp admiring a group of elephants spraying themselves in the river. Heaven. We have had a nerve-wracking few months, what with not knowing about a job and having absolutely no house to live in or land to move our cattle onto once we leave the tea company.

"Now Geoff has suddenly been offered two jobs in the same week. One as general manager of a tea estate, very rundown, in Luponde, at an altitude of 7,300 feet; the other at sea level, to do with tourism, 10,000 head of Boran beef cattle, cattle rustling and poacher control, among other challenges. The latter is totally cut off, very hot, but with a beautiful beach—and not a soul on it. Actually, the place is called Mkwaja Ranch and is quite a long way out of Tanga. You reach it by ferry, which doesn't always operate!"

"Luponde is very remote, Vicky," Geoff says.

"It is, isn't it? But then we're used to that. Aren't we, Geoff?"

"And at least I know something about tea."

"On the other hand, Mkwaja Ranch will mean working with Peter Schachenmann."

"Isn't he working for Amboni? I'm confused. What has Amboni got to do with Mkwaja?"

"Apparently, Mkwaja Ranch was set up by Amboni in 1954 to keep their sisal cutters in meat. As far as I know, Amboni is the world's biggest sisal estate."

"That sounds impressive. A far cry from when he was a vet here in Mufindi! He's such a nice fellow. It would be wonderful to see him again."

"He sounds really desperate. I wouldn't want to let a friend down. On the other hand, the job offer is just for two years; and what do I know about managing a gigantic ranch, with 10,000 head of cattle?"

"Guess what, Libby?" writes Vicky. "We can't make up our minds. I think we may go for Mkwaja Ranch, but it's very far from Ruaha. If we do go there, the boys and Peter's girlfriend, Sarah, will just have to manage. Sarah is a positive gem, very efficient, and a marvellous cook. Geoff's salary goes toward building houses on our farm and a rather nice chalet hotel in Mufindi; so, for a few years, we will earn what we can to build up the tourist business. The plan is for the boys to start tours next year. I'll probably spend the high season months helping, and the rest of the time in Tanga."

"So, Libby, I have a choice," Geoff adds; "tea, which I know a lot about, or cows, where I really only know the front end from the back end. Contrary to her letter, Vicky is insisting that we have to do cows for a change, so She Who Must Be Obeyed has prevailed. And off we will go.

"P.S. A crocodile has violently broken the peace splashing around trying to catch a fish. A couple of days ago, everyone at breakfast in the dining *banda* was able to witness an enormous crocodile catching and killing a waterbuck. The croc reared up vertically out of the water during the struggle. Last night a large leopard walked around our tent; a couple of nights ago, a lion passed through the camp, joining the great numbers of other animals (elephant, buffalo, and down the food chain) that apparently find the camp a secure place to frequent. Perhaps that's why the lion and leopard are so interested, too."

《•》《•》《•》《•》

BY 1987, AIDS CASES ARE OFFICIALLY REGISTERED IN EVERY REGION OF TANZANIA!

《•》《•》《•》《•》

Hollywood Royalty Visits Ruaha

Despite impending upheavals, Vicky has no choice but to help out in Ruaha. "Speaking of high season, Libby," Vicky writes from the River Camp, "we are having one hell of a one. There were sixty-eight guests this last weekend. At one stage, we all wondered whether we would survive the season. The little Toyota land rover was shooting up and down to the park three times a week pulling its new trailer, trying to keep pace with the food requirements—a cow a week plus chickens, pork, and veal. Horrific. Last Saturday, we had ninety-one people! Sarah and I took turns making nearly two hundred profiteroles in my convection oven.

"James (Jimmy) Stewart, the famous film star, plus wife and friends, arrived on Sunday to stay a few days. Quite exciting. Their friend, Tom Jones, owns a huge aviation company in America and they flew out in a private jet aircraft with a crew of six awaiting him in Dar es Salaam. Over supper, he suddenly stood up and proposed a toast to Geoff and me. We nearly fainted. It was quite a strain but well worth it. We were invited to their own private dinner party, set alongside the river.

"Our chaps were wonderful and Sarah and I split ourselves to make a nice dinner. Geoff and I sat on either side of Jimmy Stewart. He was the most charming man you could meet, even insisted on pulling out my chair before I sat down. He's rather deaf, but we managed to have a very interesting conversation. He took lots of photos of us and we took a few of him, discreetly. I hope they come out again. He's a very intelligent man, with a degree in architecture. They all live in Beverly Hills. This morning we took them to the plane in a terrible, noisy, bone-shattering Nissan. They took more photos of the car than of the animals. Then they all kissed us goodbye and flew off to Nairobi for their wives to get their hair done!

"The funniest incident involved their friend, Tom. He borrowed a rod from Steve, our building mason, and, with vocal encouragement and coaching from Geoff, Tom hooked a tiger fish. He had almost landed it when the reel fell apart in his hand. It was hilarious, with Geoff desperately trying to screw the reel back together again, and the line winding ever tighter around Tom, from head to toe. Thank heavens they didn't lose the fish, as it made his day. To top it all off, on the way back to camp, we saw wild dogs hunting in a pack by the road."

UPROOTED
(LOO WITH A VIEW)

"It's perfect!"

"Well, not quite perfect, but what a welcome!"

Vicky and Geoff are discussing land in Mufindi offered to them by community leaders who have known them for years and recognize their huge potential for generating employment—not to be scoffed at in these days of shortages and insecurity, especially in an area as isolated as Igoda.

"We are still struggling to get the land approved for our farm," Vicky writes to Libby. "Signs are fairly hopeful, because the village, which would like us to start our business in their jurisdiction, has finally had its fifth meeting with the District Land Allocation Committee.

"They met last Friday, but we don't yet know their answer. It just can't be negative, as we haven't enough time to get permission to move anywhere else, even if somewhere else could be found.

"Right now, it's a piece of barren land, and friends in Mufindi think that we are mad to try and farm it, but we will persevere. We think it could be attractive in the end, but we know that we will need time and lots of money; hence Geoff's job is rather a necessity."

《•》《•》《•》《•》

July 30, 1987, Geoff to Gelly and Jimmy: "Bruce is working so hard right up to the end. He is currently spending twelve hours a day supervising sixty labourers on developing our farm so that we can transfer our livestock by the end of this month. No permanent go-ahead yet—just a temporary provision to cultivate and herd cattle, pending the completion of our application. But already the villagers are seeing the benefit of their offer to let us farm on their land."

September 6, 1987, Vicky to Libby: "Goodness, what chaos! Everything is half-packed and in turmoil. Geoff is busy trying to close his bank account and leave one company to join another. Alexander is back to school today, and Bruce is still very busy, as we have a temporary permit to move onto our farm for now. We are still waiting for the final district meeting.

"Already Bruce has half-built a dam, dug hundreds of holes for fence posts, prepared a vegetable garden, aligned a furrow, built a road by hand, and lined out cowsheds—all in two weeks, with, of course, an army of villagers hired to help him. If the district says no, we don't know what we'll do. We have to move the cows in three weeks and haven't started the dip[48] yet.

"Two of our dogs escaped with a troupe of males and are very obviously going to produce twenty puppies the day before we move house. The cat just produced five or six kittens. Oh, God.

"We think we will be able to rent two little houses on the old Touzet (road construction) Compound. It sounds awful, but they are cut off from the others, with a lovely view, and a paddock in front. The compound, which has a fence around it to keep out intruders, will be a good temporary base, albeit in 'suburbia.'

"On January 1, Geoff and I go to Tanga—actually, about 100 miles away from Tanga, toward Dar es Salaam. It's totally isolated. We aren't quite sure we made the right decision but without really letting down our friend, Peter Schachenmann, we couldn't do anything else. Also, their terms were better and the job more exciting, but such miles from Mufindi and Ruaha.

"Peter is going to America to get his commercial pilot licence next year (in case we get a plane—that'll be the day, as we first have to find a tractor, bulldozer, and grader to build an airstrip!).

"Just picture us all in three weeks' time, trekking our 100 cows, twelve horses, three sheep, four dogs, twenty puppies, cat and six kittens for twenty miles. It should be interesting to watch. I wish we had a video [camera]!"

《•》《•》《•》《•》

"Dear Libby . . . Here we are on a fleeting visit to the UK, as Geoff's dad died, and we rushed here to sort out all his affairs. I'm writing at the airport, on our way back to Tanzania with a mountain of luggage—100 kilograms. God knows where we'll hide it all. (The Foxes have become master excess-luggage charge avoiders, with last-minute retrievals of impossibly bulky hand luggage.)

《•》《•》《•》《•》

---

48   Cattle dips are pits (about four feet wide, five feet deep, and twenty-five feet long) filled with treated water, in which immersed cattle shed disease-bearing insects, primarily ticks.

Loo with a view.

"Dear Libby . . . Relocating our farm from the tea estate was a chapter of its own. Some of the animals walked. Others, too little to walk, were taken by lorry. One cow calved en route. The procession, including the pregnant cow, had nearly reached the farm when Sarah and Peter were told that it was delivering. They didn't know what to do.

"We told Sarah, who was just recently out from the UK, how—and disappeared, leaving her to pull the calf out. Meanwhile, we carried on by car with the cat, her kittens, two dogs, their puppies, and a parting gift thrust in through the window by one of our former workers: a rooster.

"All went well for a short while, until the cat went for the rooster. The rooster flew squawking around the car, disturbing all the cats, dogs, puppies, and kittens. Pandemonium!

Starting on the farm, the Foxes made their own bricks (built as a kiln for burning).

"Finally, all the animals reached our newly acquired land on which was . . . nothing. Thank God for the temporary rental of the two little burnt-brick houses on the Paper Mill campus at Sawala—one for the freezers (to preserve meat and other supplies for Ruaha) and one for the family to live in for a few months whilst we were starting up the farm. We lived there before going to Mkwaja Ranch, and the kids stayed on there a very short while. How grateful we were.

"Peter and Sarah then relocated to the farm. They started their married life in a tent on a windswept field. For a year and half that was their home. Mufindi winters can be pretty cold. Yet all Sarah had was a makeshift shower, using a *pipa* (drum) of cold water. And the only solid building was the loo, an outdoor long drop built with off-cut timber.

"Peter tried to make the loo a bit more interesting, by having the door constructed stable-style, with the top half opening to allow for a splendid view (probably copied from Jonny Niblett's fine loo-with-a-view at Luisinga Fishing Lodge). Unfortunately, because it was the only solid building on the farm at the beginning, the staff thought that it had to be the office and came to ask their questions at the door!"

PART THREE

OF CATTLE, CONSERVATION, AND CATASTROPHE

(1988–1998)

MKWAJA RANCH AT LAST

"January 19, 1988. Dear Libby . . . Here we are at the ranch at last, all the trauma of packing and farewells behind us. We had a wonderful welcome to the new company, both in Switzerland and Tanga. People are all very friendly and helpful, especially our friend Peter Schachenmann, the general manager (and vet) at Amboni.

"It's quite amazing to be here, in the middle of nowhere, with a totally new job in a completely different line, but we both love it. We are one kilometre from the sea and an unbelievable, palm-lined beach stretching for literally miles, without a soul swimming in the sea — just a few fishermen's houses dotted about.

"There are 10,000 head of cattle with all their attendant problems, including the loss of 1,680 animals last year to lions, thieves, disease, and, we reckon, gross negligence of the outgoing ranch manager. Peter has asked Geoff to focus on two problems in particular: the cattle rustling (at around 500 head a year!), and a virulent, tick-borne disease (*anaplamosis marginale*) that is killing the cows.

"We have only had one week so far but can already see many ways of putting things right. Nobody checks the animals properly; half the time, the herdsmen leave the cows in the middle of the bush and disappear.

"Each of the nineteen sections has 400–500 cows, some more, but nobody ever counts them in properly. I don't think they know how many cows come back each night. The whole place has an air of lethargy and disintegration.

"The first day, we decided to walk down to one of the nearby sections and have a look at the herds as they came back. There, we found the herdsmen busy tying up the calves, one by one by the neck to the fence, so that they could steal their mum's milk in the morning.

"We also saw cows with ropes on their legs come back to their night *bomas* [enclosures]. Somebody had clearly, unsuccessfully, tried to steal them. Geoff found that one section simply omitted to dip their whole herd one day. People wander around all day doing nothing.

"After Brooke Bond, we find it shattering. Geoff isn't able to do anything about it until he formally takes over in April. Day after day, the animals are grazing the same land instead of going to new areas, even when there is no longer any grass.

"The 'special dairy' herd (fifty cows with calves) are all beef animals, and the ranch staff only gets thirty litres of milk, all told — with fifty calves often going without."

《·》《·》《·》《·》

"February 12, 1988. Dear Libby . . . We were branding all last week, more than 600 animals. The days start at three a.m. All the branding irons have to be heated up by first light. This includes cattle sections many miles away. Huge, long, narrow fires are lit, and all the five-foot-long irons are put in, with wooden handles at the end to hold on to.

"Then the fun starts: catching and throwing the calves. It's hilarious. The animals to be branded are all eight months old and quite large. As yet, there are no handling yards, so they have to be put into a paddock with their mothers. The aim is to catch them by the back leg with a loop of rope twisted around a stick. Disabling the cow before it takes you three times round the paddock is a precision job. I declined the invitation to try my luck. Geoff is marvellous at it."

Again, Geoff adds his two cents' worth. "Libby. This is Geoff setting the record straight again. Did Vicky write that I am marvellous at it? That's news to me. Vicky has by now taught me which end of the cow is the front and which is the back. The first thing you have to do when branding is to go around with a stick and a noose and somehow whip it and catch the rear leg of the calf. Which I did, but what I didn't cater for was the strength of the animal, which promptly took off, pulled me over, and dragged me headlong all around in front of my Mkwaja Ranch herdsmen.

"There, if you can imagine, Libby, was the new manager being dragged around in circles in a small pen full of cow shit. My image was at stake. As the manager, I should be able to do this standing and not being dragged around on my stomach.

"We have only been on the ranch for a very short while, and I'm reminded of when I was first pruning tea in Mufindi. I stepped out in front of the workers and said, 'This is how you do it.' Unfortunately, I held the branch incorrectly and promptly cut my arm." (Or, as Geoff wrote to his parents on June 18, 1962: "The pruning season has now begun and I started it off by deftly pruning my arm! I've just had the stitches out—five of them.") "I still have the scar," Geoff's letter to Libby continues, "the one that all really 'experienced' tea planters have! I remember Ian Summerville showing me his."

Vicky takes the letter back from Geoff and adds. "Hi, Libby. Vicky here again. Where was I? Oh, yes, should the calf fall onto the wrong side, an intricate bit of manipulation is called for. You have to pull the rope and tail at the right moment, just as it is getting up, and throw it onto its other side, then twist the head, and sit on it.

"The first time I saw that bit, I thought it would break the animal's neck, but it doesn't seem to hurt the creature. It only disables it for a minute while you hold the branding iron on the animal for a couple of seconds—till it sizzles. Each animal is branded on the right side with an 'M' and an 'R' for Mkwaja Ranch. If it's not a meat animal, a

Vicky branding cows at Mkwaja Ranch.

number and an 'A' are added to capture the year. I did the last two bits and am quite proud of that. Geoff is an absolute expert now."

《•》《•》《•》《•》

"The branding, which Vicky took part in very successfully," Geoff tells friends later, "was also accompanied by castrating. That Vicky took such relish in castration was rather a matter of concern for me."

"He made me do it," Vicky retorts. "I hated it. The branding was okay. It took only three seconds."

"February 19, 1988. Dear Libby . . . We are amazingly happy here. It's all totally new for us. The job is a wonderful challenge and just up Geoff's street.

"He is in charge of a vast area (50,000 hectares, about 125,000 acres) of the coastland, and given total freedom of action by Amboni to protect, not only the wildlife but also the forests, where large trees are being felled and sent to Zanzibar for dugout canoes, as are mangroves for roofing.

Amboni has given Geoff a large bulldozer. He is like a child with a new toy, levelling everything from farm roads and game-viewing roads to sites for new catchment dams. (We need them all over the ranch so we have enough water to spread the cows around. At the same time, this means more water for the wildlife.)

"Cattle ranching has to be seen to be believed. We learn something new every day. Geoff is just dying to have full management. Only one and a half more months to go. We were really pretty worried about whether he would manage the job, but he's marvellous at it already.

"To get a firm handle on the numbers, each animal now has to be counted out every morning and in again at dusk. Even though the news is not always pleasant, it's a joy in the evenings to go around to each of the estates, counting the cows, and seeing what has happened during the day."

"What?" Geoff is reading over Vicky's shoulder. "Hand me that pen, Vicky."

"Hi, Libby. This is Geoff. A joy? Every evening I come back home to relax over a cup of tea. Before I've even had my first sip, I am told: 'Drink up, Foxey, we're going out.' Then she drags me off to see the cows, in one or another of the nineteen sections. I often think if I'd been a cow she would have treated me better."

《·》《·》《·》《·》

"Dear Libby . . . This week it's weaning. Horrid! All the calves mooing for their mothers from the thorn *bomas* that Geoff has just had built for them. There is no fencing left, and no money to build more. However, Caterpillar D7s and graders are all over the place, busily doing up dams and roads, as Geoff has to finish them all before the rains so that the dams can fill up."

LIONS STAMPEDE CATTLE

"It's heartbreaking to see so many cattle disappearing, Geoff." Vicky and he are on a daily cow inspection. "Any word yet on what is happening to them?"

"And why is it always five at a time," they wonder as each evening the herdsmen say: "Sorry. The lion stampeded the cattle and twenty-two went missing. I could only find seventeen"; or, "fifteen went missing and I could only find ten." At last someone tells them that the cattle are being stolen and sent to the predominantly Muslim population in Zanzibar, where they must arrive alive, as only meat from animals slaughtered according to Islamic tradition before witnesses can be eaten.

"But why five?" Geoff and Vicky want to know.

"Because only five trussed-up cattle can fit into a *mashua* (the sailing boats traditionally used for trading along the coast)." It turns out that Zanzibari rustlers are in cahoots with coastal villagers around Mkwaja, who, in turn, hire Mkwaja herdsmen to steal the cattle.

"That apparently takes care of about 90 percent of the missing cows," Geoff tells Vicky.

"And the other 10 percent?"

"They are disappearing to the Masai camping on our western boundary."

"That's a bit tricky, isn't it, since the Masai think they own every cow?" says Vicky. (Cattle are seen by the Masai as a gift from Enkai [the one who mediates between God/Ngai and man]. To the hunters and gatherers [the Dorrobo], Enkai gave honey and wild animals; to the cultivators [the Kikuyu], Enkai bequeathed seed and grain; and to the Masai, Enkai sent all the cattle. Just as the eating of communion bread and drinking of communion wine symbolizes for Christians

Geoff with his Mkwaja Ranch rangers and a government game officer.

their spiritual union with Jesus, the eating of cattle and drinking of milk symbolizes for the Masai their spiritual union with Enkai.)

"True," Geoff answers Vicky. "How does one deal with what is perceived as a God-given right?"[49] In the end, the solution to the Masai problem at Mkwaja is simple, and implemented quite by accident.

As Geoff later informs his manager, Peter Schachenmann: "A really nice, plum herd of cattle disappeared the other day.

"We located it in the Masai camp. 'Now what should we do?' the staff asked me. I exploded. 'Put the Masai on our predator list, to be shot on sight, together with the lions and hyenas!' Because we were so new to Mkwaja, and the staff didn't know me well enough to recognize a joke—tasteless as it was—they told the Masai what I was planning to do. And . . . the Masai decamped, never to be seen there again."

"Well done—if a bit unorthodox," says Peter. "That takes care of the 10 percent of thefts. Now, how do you think you can solve the other 90 percent—the Zanzibar problem?"

"Good question. The first thing we can do is to expand young Nevil Slade's branding on the body project. At the moment, every cow has an ear tag, and we are told that the thieves simply cut off the cows' ears before reaching Zanzibar. I am also forming a team of game rangers, to try and help to stop both the rustling and get a handle on

---

49 The same God-given right Vicky will run into on their Highland farm decades later when she asks her trusted Masai watchmen if they would supervise the milking to stop milk being stolen. "Please don't ask us to do that, Mama," they will answer. "We would have to take the milk ourselves."

the poaching we keep hearing about. Vicky and I are raring to go, just as soon as we can formally take charge of Mkwaja Ranch."

"Not long now."

FLYING SNAKES AND GREEN TURTLES

"June 16, 1988. Dear Libby . . . At last! At last! At last we are in charge of Mkwaja Ranch! Our house is now totally renovated and actually looks wonderful. It was designed years ago by a Swiss architect/builder who has gone on to become a millionaire. It's very light and airy with beautiful natural wood everywhere.

"The insects are having a heyday with all the fruit trees I planted: avocado, citrus, banana, cloves, peppers, guava, pineapples, and mango. I hope I can save most of them. The bananas are already four feet tall. The growth rate is fantastic.

"We hope to collect horses from Mufindi soon. Fingers crossed that they survive here. It's all a bit hazardous with the disease aspect."

《·》《·》《·》《·》

"Good morning, Dr. Mmbando," Geoff greets the Mkwaja Ranch vet one morning.

"Good morning, Mr. Fox. How are you settling in?"

"Loving every minute," Geoff laughs. "Any words of advice for me?" Although Dr. Samuel Mmbando has only been there a month longer than Geoff, he's already given him invaluable tips.

"Take care. There are lots of very dangerous flying snakes."

"Don't give me that, Dr. Mmbando. You know perfectly well that snakes don't fly."

Dr. Mmbando looks at Geoff, genuinely shocked. "Mr. Fox," he says. "You've been in Tanzania for twenty-eight years and have never heard of the flying snake—the snake that aims for your head and makes the sound of a cock crowing as it flies through the air? The one you can only protect yourself against by putting a bowl of *uji* [milky, maize meal porridge] on your head?"

"That's ridiculous!" Geoff scoffs.

About three days later, while visiting a ranger post, Geoff makes a passing remark to one of the rangers about someone telling him of a snake that flies.

"Yes, sir," the ranger replies. "We also have them in Songea and Dodoma. They make the sound of a cock crowing and you have to carry a bowl of *uji* on your head to protect yourself."

Geoff concludes inwardly that Dr. Mmbando has been there before him and primed the rangers to keep up the joke.

Two weeks later, he visits a distant cattle section, separated from Mkwaja by about thirty miles. There, he asks the same question and gets the same answer from the section headman, only in his case, he adds that the snake can also be found in the Usambara mountains.

That evening, Geoff searches the Mkwaja Ranch library and eventually finds a very old Rhodesian book called *Snakes in the Bundu*. At the back is a section on local beliefs. Among others, it describes the black mamba (probably the most aggressive and lethal of all snakes), which, when shedding its skin, retains a piece of its sloughed skin attached to the head for some time. So strong is this snake, the book continues, that it can propel itself on only one third of its length, positioning the other two thirds off the ground and, yes indeed, while it is flying through the air it makes a sound not dissimilar to a cock crowing. A local belief in Zimbabwe, it concludes, is that the best way to protect yourself is to carry a bowl of water on your head.

Shortly after, Geoff is driving along in his Land Rover when a huge black mamba slithers out onto the road and he just has time to push shut the sliding window of the Land Rover before the mamba hits the glass. Such is its aggression that the height at which it hit the window is level with Geoff's head.

《•》《•》《•》《•》

"The area fascinates us both, not only geologically, but also in terms of the game and different types of forest," Vicky's first letter to Libby from Mkwaja continues. "I love the feeling that the bush and the animals are meeting up with the sea, which is unusual. I can't think of another place in Tanzania where this happens."

("It was really strange, at first," Vicky tells her sons. "One might see a baobab tree, just as in Ruaha, only now it is silhouetted against the ocean. Then again, one might find a forest area that looked just like Mufindi, only with hippos in the river and dhoum palms among the shrubs on the bank; or even sable antelope, buffalo, and reedbuck [which one associated with inland savannas] grazing almost down to the beach.")

"There is a beautiful, twenty-kilometre length of pristine beach, including a five-kilometre stretch in which the green turtle (so called because that's the colour of its fat) lays its eggs. It's also the biggest hard-shelled sea turtle there is.

"The shore is lined with coconut palm, the main crop grown here, because the soil is totally unsuitable for maize, and can only sustain a little cassava. Most amazing of all, you can get into the car and drive on the beach.

"At one spot, Madete, we can still see the ruins of an enclosure once used by slave traders to prevent slaves from escaping, just like many others up and down the coast of East Africa. Some nearby graves have headstones decorated with genuine Chinese plates, indicating trade with China at some point in the area's history.

"We also have the small South Saadani Game Reserve bordering the ranch to the south, with hartebeest, waterbuck, bohor reedbuck, giraffe, several duiker species, warthogs, lions, and an interesting sable antelope. Geoff is more and more convinced that it has been wrongly classified and should be acknowledged as one of the rarest of antelope subspecies, the "Kenyan" sable antelope called *roosevelti*."

(Tanzania's 1999 *Wildlife Discussion Paper No. 25* will conclude that the Eastern Tanzanian Sable Antelope is indeed *roosevelti* and credit Geoff, among others, for questioning the earlier official recognition of the antelopes as being *H.n.kirkii*.)

ARM-DEEP IN DUNG

"September 23, 1988. Dear Libby . . . Since I last wrote, Bruce and I took a quick trip to Mufindi. Peter and Sarah are definitely living the rough life. And working so hard to keep Ruaha in meat and dairy products, not to mention vegetables! All this while they are camping, because, other than the brick loo, there are only two tents, one to house Peter and Sarah, the other to serve as an office. And was it ever cold!

"That sweatshirt you sent me came at just the right time. One sweater wasn't enough in Mufindi. Bruce and I ended up sleeping on the veranda of the office tent. We managed to last five days. Twice we woke to frost on the ground. It was so cold that we both got chapped lips, and were finally driven into the office to take refuge under the table. Bliss. The view made up for everything. It's just like Dartmoor, all granite rocks and rolling hills. We think we have finally got the farm officially, as the district has granted permission and the region meets this month.

"Now we're back on Mkwaja and doing quite a few experiments for Bruce. Holy smoke! He has his mother standing, arm deep in dung, trying to feel where the ovaries of a cow are, and whether or not it's pregnant. I can't believe it. And measuring nine-inch-long aborted fetuses (just like little toy cows), not to mention cow's innards—what a carry on! I never wanted to set up as an expert in artificial insemination but shall definitely request a degree at the end of all this.

"The latest mad idea is to put our terraced Tavistock house up as security for a half-share in an airplane, which is to be auctioned tomorrow.

"By the way, if Geoff can get away, we plan to be in the UK on leave in December, which would mean our first Christmas in the UK in twenty-one years.

"Jack [Libby's son] sounds as if he suffered like Bruce on his twenty-first birthday. (Bruce celebrated his in Mufindi. After three beer mugs of brandy, vodka, and gin, he started rushing around, bellowing like a bull, and later woke up outside the tent with the watchman!)"

《•》《•》《•》《•》

"October 31, 1988. Dear Libby . . . We went for a fantastic working week to Kenya. It was so enjoyable; it seemed like a holiday. We met up with some Kenya-born friends and went round to all the old farms and ranches looking for Boran bulls to use here. They are medium-sized beef animals, very fertile, nurturing, and docile, but—most important—they originated in northern Kenya, which means they are amazingly well adapted to harsh conditions and relatively resistant to ticks.

"At the same time, we had fantastic insights into a different corner of Kenya and the life of many old settlers. All the people we stayed with were either farmers, or played polo, or both. One beautiful farm overlooked Mt. Kenya, at an altitude of 8,000 to 10,000 feet. There was no sign at all of Mt. Kenya when we arrived, as it was pouring with rain, but the next day the sun was out, and the sky clear blue. We drove to the top of the highest hill. There, stretched before us, was its breathtaking, snow-capped peak."

IVORY POACHERS

"November 22, 1988. Dear Libby . . . I think you'll probably think the sun and isolation have completely sent me mad, but I'm writing to tell you a few facts just in case anything should happen to us.

"I think we have stumbled on a very large ivory poaching ring with our special beach as a centre of the drama. The action takes place about twelve miles away from the ranch itself. One night, our friends, the de Jongs, were camping on the beach. They noticed a light flashing out to sea and flashed back with their torches. This continued until a boat, which turned out to be from Mombasa, landed. The crew was there to pick up ivory from the poachers. They took one embarrassed look at the Dutch doctor and his wife and pushed off for the night.

"Unfortunately, the rangers weren't there at the time. Another person came to the beach in the morning. The boatman called him over to the boat, and later 5,000 Kenya shillings (about £40 or $90) were found in his possession.

"Next, a wealthy nearby villager came to Geoff on unrelated business. Geoff took him to task about the poaching problem, inferring that he might well be involved. He was so taken aback that he immediately told Geoff all about a ring of ivory poachers.

"Because there are no police anywhere nearer than thirty miles away in Pangani (and they don't go anywhere), the ivory poachers evidently freely and frequently pass through Mkwaja Ranch, transporting tusks in broad daylight to their hiding place for the ivory in a sandbank somewhere between Mkwaja village and the Saadani Game Reserve (a government reserve) on our southern boundary. Boats from Mombasa then come at night to collect it and take it to Kenya before shipping overseas. We think the Game Division is involved. A ring of Tanga-based Arabs is apparently using Mkwaja and the beach to smuggle out most of the ivory poached in Tanzania. Since the police, other authorities, and the law has never stretched that far, they load their booty onto boats with impunity. From there, they send it to Mombasa for transshipment to Dubai or wherever.

"Not much later, our vet was giving a lift to a policeman, near Pangani away to the north of us, when he was suddenly asked to pursue a car that passed them going in the opposite direction. The police had been tipped off that Arabs might have been transporting more ivory to our area.

"Anyway, typical Foxey, he immediately publicized all the information he had gathered to the Tanzania news agency, *Shihata*, who sent a reporter to investigate. He also contacted the regional game officer, the district officer, and eventually the director of wildlife.

"A few days later, some sleuths arrived to spy out our land. Yesterday, a district game officer and a few others attacked our retired 'People's Defence Force' man attached to the rangers. He obviously knew that our ranch rangers are armed only with shotgun cartridges because, before knocking our ranger down, he said to his friend, 'Those bullets don't work.'

"They then stole the old man's gun and ran off. Next installment, next incident! All joking apart, everyone knows about Geoff's involvement in the anti-poaching efforts, and I think we may be in some sort of danger, but it's probably my overactive imagination."

It is not just Vicky's imagination.

《•》《•》《•》《•》

Like many villages along East Africa's coast, Mkwaja Village has a long, commercial history (in its case going back to the ninth century when Arab and Omani traders first used it as an outpost for the export of slaves from Tabora to Zanzibar via the port of Saadani, then East Africa's most important slave trading centre).

First Germany, then Britain abolished slavery. They also chose Dar es Salaam as Tanganyika's capital and, with that decision, officially sidelined Saadani. Unofficially, some Tanga-based traders, mainly Arab, continued to take full advantage of their existing trading networks and traditions, all the way to Tabora and back. Only now they focused on exporting illicit ivory—made more lucrative after moves to protect the dwindling elephant populations.

By the time Geoff and Vicky arrive, Mkwaja Village consists of about 800 people. At face value, like other villagers along the coast, they make their living primarily from prawn fishing. Behind the scenes, many supplement their meagre incomes by helping powerful smugglers to transfer illegal tusks and stolen cattle onto boats moored off the isolated Mkwaja beach before heading to Kenya and Zanzibar.

"What news of Mkwaja's new ranch manager, that nosy Englishman?" the bosses ask.

"He has hired rangers to protect the wildlife."

"Mkwaja beach is also under surveillance."

"And he is not afraid to bring in the authorities. Have you seen today's *Daily News*? It says, 'The new manager of Mkwaja intends to halt the ivory poaching.'"

Not amused, they plot their countermeasures. A few days later, government officials in Tanga and Dar es Salaam are informed, "based on direct observation by Mkwaja villagers," that Mr. Fox himself is an ivory poacher. This, too, is printed in the *Daily News*.

"Foxey, do be careful, please," Vicky pleads. "As Peter said, these people are dangerous."

"I can't just sit by and let this happen right under our noses. But I will get all the help I can from the authorities. For example, they are now allowing me to form a *mgambo* unit right on the ranch."

"What's a *mgambo*?"

"It's a militia made up of government-trained, auxiliary police. They are legally permitted to carry firearms."

"Will they be effective against such powerful people and their big weapons?"

"That's the best I can do."

"How will you know which part of the beach the boats will come to? And what about all that bush and its cover?"

"We've jointly engaged a team of village informers. They can direct the militia to where the cattle are tied up in the forest, waiting to be loaded under cover of darkness."

Vicky is thinking of all the windows at Mkwaja Ranch. They don't have iron grilles, let alone glass—just mosquito gauze—but she knows better than to try and stop Geoff when he's on one of his missions.

"As if the ivory poaching business isn't enough," Vicky writes to Libby, "the general manager of Amboni is off within a year. His wife, who I really like a lot, is having an affair d'amour with a harbour pilot. The latter hot gossip is the product of the worst Tanga yacht club scandal-mongery. In short, Geoff and I venture into our nearest metropolis, about sixty miles away, less and less, in case it should disrupt our 'peace.'"

Dr. Crippen's Handcuffs

In the end, strapped as they are, the police department agrees to Geoff's request to post two policemen at Mkwaja Ranch. They duly move into the little police station Geoff has built for them, complete with its own tiny lock-up.

The Mkwaja police station helps Geoff to process all the necessary documentation related to petty theft right there on the ranch, rather than having to drive thirty miles to Pangani on an appalling, black cotton soil road, all but impassable for three months in the rains.

Unfortunately, the policemen have no handcuffs.

"So out came the handcuffs once used on Dr. Crippen, the first murderer apprehended by the use of radio." Geoff is proudly brandishing an ancient pair of handcuffs in front of visitors from Mufindi. "So, Dr. Crippen's handcuffs will be used by the Mkwaja police station." (Little does he know it then, but those same cuffs will in the following eight years be used for apprehending and constraining poachers, cattle rustlers, petty thieves, and even a murderer.)

"How come you have Dr. Crippen's handcuffs in the first place, Geoff?" one friend wants to know.

"Do you remember John Gray [a fellow settler in Mufindi]? When he was at Oxford, he shared his rooms with the son of the High Court judge in London who tried Crippen. As I said earlier, Crippen was the first murderer apprehended by the use of radio. He supposedly killed his wife, before boarding a ship to Canada with his girlfriend, who was dressed up as a boy. His escape was big news. The ship's captain recognized him and, using radio for the first time, sent a message ship to shore. London detectives boarded a faster ship. They arrested Crippen as he set foot in Canada, brought him back to the UK for

Dr. Crippen's handcuffs on Gordon
Breedyk — key with Evelyn Voigt!
(Geoff Fox)

trial (on evidence of human body parts buried in his cellar), convicted him, and hanged him for the murder of his wife.

"He was wearing these handcuffs when they brought him into the Old Bailey. The judge asked if he could keep the handcuffs as a souvenir, and later gave them to his son, who then passed them on to John Gray. Subsequent sleuthing discovered that the body parts were those of a man and not Crippen's wife. Two years ago, a television program reported more evidence to support Crippen's innocence — on the charge of murdering his wife, that is.

"His American wife had actually escaped to the U.S. From there, she wrote a letter to the junior minister responsible for the case, Winston Churchill. He put the letter in his pocket and, perhaps, forgot about it until after Crippen was hanged. The letter said that she was alive but would not come to England to attend the court.

"Mrs. Crippen had a number of boyfriends among the many lodgers who stayed with them. Fellow residents constantly heard the Crippens fighting about her infidelity. Assuming then that the parts belonged to one of the lodgers, and that Crippen was responsible for the murder, I don't think injustice was done. They just got it wrong. Anyway, these are Dr. Crippen's handcuffs. According to their number they are 100 years old."

Geoff walks over to his friend. "Why don't you try them on?" With that, he shackles his friend's hands, throws the key to his wife, and says, "Up to you when you let him go."

CHALLENGING
THE VETERINARY ESTABLISHMENT

"Now, back to cattle rustling at Mkwaja," Geoff tells his friends. "All our herdsmen are Wagogo (or Mgogo, singular). They have a long tradition as pastoralists in the central region of Tanzania. It is like having our own family around us, and we are not really nervous on the ranch. That is our territory."

"Speak for yourself, Foxey. I am scared," says Vicky.

"Going into the Mkwaja village isn't much fun," Geoff acknowledges. "People scowl at us. They are clearly thinking, 'Why should this white *mzungu* interfere with what we have been doing all these years?' By now, of course, I am already trying to stop people from cutting down all the mangroves and large forest trees growing on the ranch—for sale to Zanzibar or making dugout *ngalawas* (outrigger boats). I also regularly monitor Mkwaja Ranch for game poachers, as well as trying to come to grips with the cattle rustling."

"And I am having nightmares," says Vicky. "But at least I have something to keep my mind off all this: research on how to reduce cattle mortality from a virulent disease called *anaplamosis marginale*, supposedly transferred by ticks."

"Something else doesn't make sense, Peter," says Geoff at his next meeting with his boss. "Vicky knows what a tick infestation looks like. She's had many on her cows in Mufindi. But there are hardly any ticks to be seen on the Mkwaja cattle."

"As far as the scientific community is concerned, anaplamosis is transferred by ticks," Peter says definitively.

"As far as Mkwaja is concerned," Geoff echoes, "anaplasmosis is clearly a problem. The cattle are dying at unacceptable levels, and I suppose it only takes one tick to infect the cow."

"On the other hand," Peter acknowledges, "dipping the cattle doesn't seem to be helping. So, Geoff, see what you can do."

"STRUCTURAL ADJUSTMENT"

Meanwhile, Structural Adjustment dominates the national and urban economic climate in Tanzania. Vast state enterprises, known as parastatals, which previously controlled inputs to, and marketing of, products are to be streamlined for sale; government structures rendered leaner; the civil service reduced. In anticipation, donor funds pour in (unfortunately some thereby increasing Tanzania's foreign debt). Investments, foreign and domestic, begin to take root.

TICKS OR
TSETSE FLIES?

"I think we may be on to something," Geoff tells Peter a little while later. "You know how Vicky digs deeply into detail, whereas I do mostly guessing jobs?"

"Self-deprecating doesn't become you, Geoff."

"Seriously, Peter. Vicky has looked into all our veterinary books and discovered that anaplasmosis once contracted by a cow remains in the cow. If the cow survives, the cow becomes a carrier. This means the cow carries the disease in a so-called premunitive condition (the live parasite balanced by antibodies), which actually protects the cow from further infection from ticks. However, under stress, the cow's immunity can break down, even without a new tick bite. The live parasite then increasingly takes over, finally killing the cow. Post mortems and ranch laboratory tests will clearly show its cause of death as anaplasmosis, but—and this is the kicker—not necessarily from infection by a new tick bite."

"You realize this goes against current scientific consensus, don't you?"

"Yes," says Vicky. "Still, whichever way we slice this one, Peter, we believe that tsetse flies and not ticks may be causing the anaplasmosis mortality. As you know, tsetses transmit trypanosomiasis or tryps (sleeping sickness in humans)—a chronic, slower developing disease, which stresses the cows, breaks down their immunity, and leaves them vulnerable to the latent anaplasmosis parasite. This, in turn, causes full-blown anaplasmosis—an acute disease, from which they die."

"I realize that Vicky and I have only just arrived from Mufindi," Geoff adds. "I know we're not scientists. But, Peter, nothing else makes sense, given the impossibly high rate of mortality and low levels of tick infestations."

Peter thinks a while. Then he says, "I suppose we should look into it further. Although, from a veterinary viewpoint, I'm still skeptical."

《•》《•》《•》《•》

It turns out that Mkwaja Ranch has four species of tsetse, probably not found together anywhere else in Tanzania, each with its unique habits and habitats: forest, open savannah, one active early morning, another attracted by movement (all by smell), one species very large, another very small, etcetera. "Absolutely fascinating and, from an entomological standpoint, exciting," Geoff and Vicky agree. The more they look into the issue, the more convinced they are that herein lies the key. But all the veterinarians they contact continue to pooh-pooh their idea.

"Not possible," they say. "Only ticks transmit anaplasmosis."

"At least hear us out," Vicky answers. "In theory, doesn't it make sense? Take a cow carrying anaplasmosis in a premunitive condition (i.e., where the cow has a low-level anaplasmodic infection with balancing antibodies that protect it from the severe version of the same infection). Theoretically speaking, could it not pass antibodies on to its calves before weaning?

"We've noticed that, in accordance with long-standing Mkwaja Ranch policy, calves are not dipped at all while still suckling. During this time, presumably still protected by their mothers' antibodies, they are deliberately exposed to tick-borne diseases and therefore could, arguably, acquire their own premunity (carrier status) against anaplasmosis. Yet, during the same period, they do not succumb to this disease.

"At the same time, we've also observed that normal, healthy calves have no visible ticks on them, despite not being dipped in an acaricide. Our herders are counting the ticks on calves, and for these eight or nine months before weaning, they really only see ticks on them when they are sick for some other reason (and become literally infested with ticks). This, surely, would suggest that healthy calves possess some sort of tick repellant when they are young. Where an adult cow without premunity might well have died, these calves survive.

"However, during weaning—a stressful time—calves still confined to weaning enclosures (with no ticks) do, indeed, succumb to anaplasmosis, demonstrating that they were previously carriers.

That does seem to support our theory, doesn't it?" Still no takers. The scientific community remains skeptical.

《·》《·》《·》《·》

"We can't give up, Foxey!" Vicky has just heard that, yet again, no one is listening.

"Absolutely not, Mrs. Fox."

During a trip to look at Boran cattle in Kenya, Geoff and Vicky put their theory to a veterinary immunologist at the International Laboratory for Research on Animal Diseases (ILRAD) in Nairobi, i.e., that "carrier" cattle are not dying suddenly of anaplasmosis transmitted by ticks but from the stress of being infected by African tryps, transmitted by tsetse flies. He does not dismiss them.

They also attend the twentieth International Scientific Council for Trypanosomiasis Research and Control (ISCTRC) in Mombasa from the tenth to the fourteenth of April 1989. There they meet some of the top scientists and veterinarians in the field, including Dr. Alex Wilson, previously the Director of the Zimbabwe Veterinary Services, now representing Coopers Animal Products. His paper cites a small-scale research project in Zimbabwe that reduced tsetse infestations by dipping cattle in a synthetic pyrethroid called Deltramethrin. Geoff and Vicky accost him.

"We would like to reduce our tsetse flies on a large scale at Mkwaja Ranch," they tell him.

"How large?"

"Fifty thousand hectares. Or about 125,000 acres."

Unlike other veterinarians, he is open to the possible link between anaplasmosis and tryps. Not only that, he also declares himself "positively delighted" to conduct a large-scale, commercial experiment to test his company's product, Decatix, on Mkwaja Ranch. They return to Mkwaja together.

50,000-HECTARE EXPERIMENT

"May 5, 1989. Dear Libby . . . We are starting a very interesting project to try to clear Mkwaja of tsetse flies this year, but meantime Geoff has been incredibly busy proving to everyone that the animals are getting sick from early breakthroughs of trypanosomes because of our problem with Samorin (a prophylactic drug that has been used for thirty years, but which now has become less effective).

"He has set up a whole lot of experiments with Packed Cell Volume (PCV) to test the cows' anemia red cell count, done every week followed by tests for tryps and he now has conclusive proof that we have to use Samorin once every five weeks instead of every two months to be effective, and that at this increased rate it may be toxic. Now all the big drug companies are getting embroiled in the discussion, one selling the new deltamethrin insecticide, and M&B defending their prophylactic Samorin. Interesting.

"All the roads are impassable, just a sea of mud. We took a guest to visit the beach and ended up with two four-wheel-drive vehicles stuck in the mud. One we managed to winch out. We then had to use it to pull the other one free.

"In Mufindi, the sheep have had nasal worms and the horses are dying of African horse sickness. War. I finally managed to get some vaccine for the latter but only after I had already lost seven out of twelve. Heartbreaking. I hope the rest survive. I also finally managed to get treatment for the sheep.

"Some important guests were supposed to fly into Ruaha, so the supplies vehicle was sent across the river, which promptly rose, never to go down again for the duration of the rains. The ferry was unable to operate, leaving Christopher with no supplies vehicle and, in fact, no transport at all. All the tourist permits ran out and they had to leave the country."

VINDICATED

"September 1989. Dear Libby . . . Breakthrough! To cut a long story short, the total population of tsetse has declined by 75 percent in the first three months!"

More specifically, according to the Summary of an article later published in a scientific journal by "R.G.R. Fox, S.O. Mmbando, M.S. Fox, and A. Wilson: A large cattle ranch was established in 1954 in a heavily tsetse-infested part of northeast Tanzania. Trypanosomiasis was controlled for thirty years by prophylactic drugs but in 1988 drug resistance seemed to be developing as cases of trypanosomiasis were being confirmed four or five weeks after treatment with iso-metamidium chloride (Samorin). Herd health had deteriorated and productivity was uneconomically low. In order to control the tsetse population, 8,000 cattle, grazing over 155 miles[2] were regularly dipped in the synthetic pyrethroid deltamethrin (Decatix Cattle Dip and Spray formulation). Within a year, the tsetse population, as monitored by traps, had decreased by more than 90 percent. Disease mortality decreased by 66 percent and a range of productivity measures such as calving percentages and weaning weights were raised to levels above those prevailing before the decline in herd health."[50]

Geoff and Vicky are vindicated! Cattle mortality from all diseases has declined by 66 percent, trypanosomiasis also by 66 percent, and—wait for it!—tick-borne anaplasmosis by 83 percent! Even hyena kills (on sick and recumbent cattle) have dropped by 74 percent. The calving rate has risen by 33 percent to 77 percent and weaning weights have increased by 17 percent. Abortions/stillbirths have dropped by 40 percent and pre-weaning mortality by 68 percent. Success!

《•》《•》《•》《•》

"More good news, this time from Mufindi," Geoff says. "Perhaps the Mufindi forest will survive after all. Apparently, the Tanzania Forest Conservation Group has finally started its work with the communities and the district council to conserve forests in Lulanda and Lugoda-Lutali.[51] Just in the nick of time, I think. Apparently they are going to come up with some sort of joint forest management scheme between the communities and the government. Sounds like a lot of paperwork to me, but at least something is finally happening." Vicky agrees, although Mufindi seems a long, long way away.

---

50   R.G.R. Fox, S.O. Mmbando, M.S. Fox, and A. Wilson, "Effect on herd health and productivity of controlling tsetse and trypanosomiasis by applying deltamethrin to cattle," *Tropical Animal Health and Production* 25, no. 4 (1993), 203–14.

51   For details, please see **http://www.tfcg.org/docs/project_udzungwas_s.htm**.

《•》《•》《•》《•》

"Not only are the Mkwaja cattle now being dipped every two weeks in Decatix, and injected with Samorin into their necks (only for the first three months of the tsetse control project), but they are also rotated in an even and regular pattern all over the ranch," Vicky writes to Libby. "This exposes them to all the tsetse varieties as live bait during the time in which they are partially protected by the Samorin. After three months, Samorin, which has become ineffective and even toxic to the cattle, is stopped.

"Within twelve months, the tsetse population on Mkwaja has collapsed to 5 percent. In other words, it has fallen by 95 percent! I know you could have concluded that on your own, but I just had to repeat it. It's all so exciting.

"Some residual tsetse flies do survive in the thicker bush and forest areas inaccessible to cattle. The particular aggression of one tsetse variety, attracted both by odour and movement, leads to its total demise."

Mkwaja productivity parameters are going through the roof. The total cattle count has increased from 10,000 to 14,000. This allows Geoff and Vicky to cull any animal still retaining its old Zebu characteristics (humps, pendulous dewlaps, droopy ears, long horns) until in very short order, Mkwaja ends up with mouth-watering Boran, all selected out into different herds according to colours: brown, white, and black.

Mkwaja Ranch has become the first large-scale commercial demonstration of tsetse control since the war against the tsetse was first waged in 1922, and the first ever virtually to eliminate the tsetse.

Everything is minutely recorded, so Vicky ("the academic in our family," to quote Geoff) writes a scientific paper for presentation at various tsetse and trypanosomiasis conferences, in Arusha, Mombasa, and Yamoussoukro, the capital of Côte d'Ivoire ("a magnificent venue, built with marble imported from Italy by the president at the time," again from Geoff.)

The scientific paper also unleashes a maelstrom back home. In the first year after its release, Mkwaja has 168 tsetse and tryps experts coming to see the results on the ranch for themselves. They hail from all over the world, from as far afield as China, Romania, Greece, the UK, and Canada. This means feeding all of them, even though the Foxes live about sixty miles from the nearest shops.

Vicky with the Mkwaja Ranch laboratory team.

Geoff and Vicky at tsetse and trypanosomiasis conference.

LUCKIEST PEOPLE ON EARTH

"October 1989. Dear Libby . . . The good news is that after all the rains, the dams are full. The bad news, just joking, is that crocodiles in the wild travel considerable distances overnight. Can you believe it? They surprise us time and again in Mkwaja. Geoff builds the catchment dams in areas without any signs of crocodiles for many, many miles around. And yet, within three months of filling up, a crocodile will make itself at home in the new dam.

"Speaking of dams, we have two herdsmen who against all evidence to the contrary say that they are the luckiest people on earth. One was washing beside a dam one day when a crocodile grabbed his arm. He somehow managed, with his foot, to stamp on the crocodile hard enough to pull his arm out, unfortunately scraping all the meat off it in the process. So, we delivered him to the Pangani District Hospital.

"Then a hippo picked up the second herdsman, crushed his pelvis, and damaged a number of internal organs. He, too, was sent to the Pangani Hospital. Both survived and returned to the ranch. Their outlook? Enthusiastic! They walk around with enormous smiles, happy to be alive, broadcasting how lucky they are and delighted to be herding again."

Green Turtles at Risk

"October 1989. Dear Libby . . . We now know that our beautiful beach is not just a hatching area for the green turtle, it is one of the last significant breeding beaches in East Africa. Apparently there are no more hatching grounds all the way south to Mozambique or north up to Kenya, although Zanzibar has a few. This is tragic, particularly since everyone seems to be after the turtles.

"The villagers fancy their eggs and meat (including that of the nesting females). Civet cats, with their sensitive noses, and possibly even honey badgers dig up their eggs. We see more and more dead and damaged turtles washing up on shore after foreign prawn trawlers have passed through. Time for us to do some serious research on how best to protect them. Did I say time? What time? We'll just have to make some, won't we?"

Outsmarted by Lions

"The lions have outsmarted us again, Peter." Geoff is attending a Mkwaja management meeting.

"And we were doing so well," Peter says glumly. "What is it this time? Actually, Geoff, before you answer that—how about a quick rundown of what you have tried so far, for the benefit of those who may not know?"

"Historically, the lions accounted for about 250 cattle deaths a year. Soon after our arrival, we decided to pattern our cattle enclosures after Tanzania's greatest pastoralists, the Masai. They traditionally build their homes in a circle around a central cattle enclosure for increased protection against predators. We followed their example and relocated our cattle into night paddocks surrounded by herdsmen's houses. For two years, lion attacks decreased dramatically. Then the lions developed a new system. Instead of killing heavy adult cows and eating them within the enclosure as they used to, they started taking younger cattle, light enough for them to carry over the protective fencing and consume in the safety of the bush beyond."

"Thank you, Geoff. Any thoughts?" Peter is again addressing the team. Little does Geoff know it then, but he will never solve the lion problem during his watch on the ranch.

PIONEERING SONS

"November 1989. Dear Libby . . . I can't believe how long it's been since the boys started developing our highland farm. Peter and Sarah are now in Ruaha managing the River Lodge full time. Bruce, being the farmer in the family, has relocated to the farm with Jane. I must say, life is pretty tough for the children at this stage, as there is no money, and anything that they produce on the farm is sold to finance development of the farm or to keep the Ruaha lodge in food.

"For that we need an enormous quantity of vegetables every week. We can, in season, buy tomatoes, potatoes, onions, fruit, and eggs, either at the Iringa market or on the main road between Mufindi and Ruaha." (As you drive along the Tanzam Highway, you can see *debe*s [four-gallon tins] of tomatoes, potatoes, or onions at the side of the road, in some cases also beautifully woven baskets and mats artistically draped over thorn trees. Such offerings usually denote a surviving *ujamaa* village, founded roadside for ease of access to transportation and markets.)

"What we cannot buy, we have to grow ourselves: fennel, leeks, lettuce, various salads, rhubarb, cauliflower, broccoli, Brussels sprouts, parsnips, baby carrots, sugar peas, fine beans, runner beans, broad beans, beetroot, *courgettes*, and butternut and other squashes.

"All building materials still require permits, with the requisite monthly visit to Dar to apply for permission to buy items as basic as cement, shower curtains, even nails. And groceries are still so scarce that 'supermarket' shelves remain virtually empty except for Chinese goods.

"With government permission, the kids can buy flour, sugar, margarine, rice, and cooking oil. As for the rest, they have to produce it themselves. Hard work! Especially given that they themselves are almost on a starvation diet to make sure there is enough for the camp, not to mention money for all the buildings (barns, slaughterhouse, stores, staff accommodation) and infrastructure (dams, farm roads, pastures, fencing, power supplies), as well as equipment. The list is endless. And still they all enthusiastically pitch in. How proud we are of them."

CENTELLA REVISITED

"Geoff! You won't believe this letter!" Geoff and Vicky are on their way back to Mkwaja Ranch from one of their rare visits to Tanga and the post office. With Geoff at the wheel, Vicky is taking advantage of the ride home to sift through the mail.

"Good news or bad news?" Geoff asks.

"Good, I think. It's the *Centella* folk in France. The new owners are finally replying to our letter from goodness knows when."

"What do they say?"

"They're apologizing for not communicating with us earlier, etcetera, but wonder if we could deliver huge quantities."

"That could be very lucrative. Let's get the boys on to it."

"In the end," Vicky writes Libby, "*Centella* proved to be too light to be remunerative. A tea chest of uncrushed dried leaves weighs only about seven kilograms. Madagascar, where *Centella* is virtually a subsistence crop, presumably accepts very low returns on their investment. We can't afford to. Laroche will have to look elsewhere."

HIGH DRAMA AT MKWAJA

"March 30, 1990. Dear Libby . . . This is supposed to be a backwater, but life seems to be full of drama, crisis, and turmoil. When we came back from local leave, we found our acting manager very enraged and frustrated with twenty-one missing cows.

"Geoff decided there was only one answer: to mount an offensive campaign. Traps were set and inevitably came to grief with the thieves arriving and getting away with two cows. Fortunately, one of the cows escaped and came home to sound the alarm with its telltale rope on a back leg.

"Infuriated field assistants set off to get their revenge. With the help of the village chairman, they caught two of the men known to be involved, bundled them into the car and 'persuaded' them to name the others—but only after Geoff suggested that the assistants stage a conversation just outside the car (in other words, within hearing distance of the thieves) about not bothering to waste a bullet or even a car trip to the police station. Why not just dump them in the sea?

"After that, everything spilled out, including the whereabouts of the thicket in the depth of the bush where for years they had been tying up stolen cows. Three of the thieves ended up in jail and one escaped into the bush in only his pants just as they arrived to catch him. High drama.

"Now a trap has been set for another ring of thieves. Unfortunately, rumour has it that an assistant is involved. I think when we leave here, just for a change, Geoff should set up as a private detective."

"Whilst we were away, they also had a very exciting episode in the elephant poaching drama. Some friends of ours in Tanga stumbled upon tons of ivory tusks buried in the sand on an isolated island off Tanga. It seems there is some local, high-level involvement, never caught, of course. The people brought in to dig out the ivory took five days to recover it all, and rumour has it that some was actually stolen from the government's ivory storage room. The rest was poached fairly recently, I suppose, but none very recently. There seems to be Arab involvement."

《·》《·》《·》《·》

"We'll have to lay low for a while with further shipments."

"And who's going to make up for all our lost ivory?"

"That nosy Englishman on Mkwaja has to go, one way or another."

"I'll get my contacts in Mkwaja village onto it. We may need to offer a large reward to solve that problem, if you know what I mean."

"For now, let's just stir up resentment against him in the village."

"Not to forget our links into government."

"That way, perhaps the problem will solve itself."

Vicky and some of her students, the herdsman's children.

STICK FAMILY

"The good news, Geoff, is that thanks to you, the cattle rustlers are now in prison. The bad news is, I've just had a visit from the wife of one of them. She's here with her starving children. They look like a stick family. They are so thin. It turns out that our imprisoned herdsman is their only breadwinner and she has tuberculosis."

Vicky looks after the whole family for some months, until Geoff asks the prisons and police authorities if they can release the father on compassionate grounds to care for his children. They agree.

"The father came as far as the ranch, then ran away because he thought his family was better off with us," Geoff tells friends. "I heard he was heading toward the train station. This was not on, so I sent a posse after him . . . and I had to rehire him as a herdsman."

DEEP MUD AND HIGH PRAISE

"Now to the ranch: It's all a wonderful success, with this last financial year's mortality rate halved from the previous one. Next year we should halve it again, if we're lucky. The weaning weights are up 17 percent; the calving rate up about 33 percent; the cattle growth rate is just romping away, with graphs going up to heaven. The chairman/owner of Amboni from Switzerland arrives in a couple of weeks, so he should be pleased. Geoff is very busy getting all the figures ready for him.

"Then we have a big meeting at the end of May with the number one world authority on the tsetse fly, Glyn Vale. He stayed here at the

After Decatix, calves show an increased weaning weight.

Geoff, tsetse project, Mkwaja.

beginning of the project and is a very nice person. We hope to have some sort of a paper written up by then, authored by the whole ranch team but nobody involved with any commercial interest to colour the picture. You can't always trust scientists not to slant the figures to support their product, as the ranch has already learnt to its cost. Anyway, Coopers—who produce it—should be pretty pleased at the outcome, even if the tsetse fly is not completely cleared."

"I am coming back to the UK again this year. We are about to embark on a new line—processing deep-frozen food—and I need some lessons in butchery, etcetera. Also, I think it's time I had a medical checkup to find any bugs I may have picked up over the years."

《•》《•》《•》《•》

"May 1, 1990. Dear Libby . . . The weather seems to have gone mad here. We had the rains arrive a month early; and it just never stops. The whole place is a quagmire of deep mud. No one can get on or off the ranch except by four-wheel-drive tractors.

"Even the Swiss owner had to be met by tractor. He certainly couldn't stand on ceremony, bouncing around on a trailer in a sea of mud. Actually, I think he really rather enjoyed the experience, but it palls a bit after a couple of months, stuck in a muddy morass for hours, being eaten alive by millions of half-starved mosquitoes.

"Yesterday, we tried to reach the farthest section of the ranch and sank axle deep in mud just as we arrived. We hailed a few passing herdsmen and managed to push ourselves out but we were covered in a thick layer of black mud. It was quite revolting. We started off again. On the way back, the exhaust went. The car finally spluttered to a halt. It simply refused to move. We had a beautiful walk home for one and a half hours through the moonlight.

"On the plus side, the losses of cattle were halved last year, the growth rates shot up and still seem to be shooting up, the calving rate is way up and the ranch was even given a prize for beating our optimistic target. The Big Boss was delighted, so we are just keeping our fingers crossed that it all continues and no great scourge hits the ranch. It was just wonderful to show people fat, sleek, healthy cattle.

"Geoff has signed on for two more years, but the owner is putting pressure on him to stay longer. Geoff, for his part, can't wait to help the children with all the amazing Foxtreks development.

THINGS TAKE OFF FOR THE FOX BOYS

"The boys are just taking off. Christopher has a concession to manage a hunting block, with a French hunter bringing in the clients, and Christopher managing the camp side of things from Ruaha. The idea is to create a buffer zone for wildlife protection next to the Ruaha Park, keep the poachers out, and share money from the hunting with the nearby villagers, so they will feel it is in their interest to help prevent the poaching. The hunting will be controlled very strictly, with no unscrupulous hunter allowed to shoot more than his permit specifies.

"We have just finished designing a processed food factory for Mufindi, to prepare frozen vegetables, fruit, even strawberry jam,

All grown up—Christopher, Peter, Geoff, Vicky, Bruce, Alexander.

as well as sausages, bacon, ham, pâté, lamb, pork, beef, and chicken (having first grown the animals!) for Ruaha, including ice cream and sorbet. Peter and Sarah will even freeze milk, cream, everything. First, they will separate the milk, and then they can freeze the cream and skim milk for use in the camp.

"All the homemade goodies from the freezer are to be packed for transportation to the camp in big wooden boxes lined with styropor sheets, with the frozen meat packed around ice cream containers in the centre. We already have a deep-freeze container.

"Then, of course, there's our new interest in buying an airplane, and, as if all that weren't enough, Christopher is negotiating for a tea plantation with a mini-mobile factory. The village where we have our farm has 4,000 acres somewhere near the escarpment. Geoff will have a look to see if it is suitable for that, and if it comes off, will invest in it as a joint venture, for which we would hope to get an enormous loan. The boys are really developing things.

"In the meantime, here at Mkwaja we are all madly preparing a handout for the meeting we will have on the ranch at the end of May. The world expert on the odour attractants used to trap tsetse for monitoring counts is coming here, with the Tanzanian tsetse and pesticides researchers, and the Coopers (Burroughs Wellcome) vet, Alex Wilson, who sells the chemical."

《•》《•》《•》《•》

"September 12, 1990. Dear Libby . . . We had a fabulous, albeit busy, six weeks in the UK. Bruce and I rushed around trying to become expert cheesemakers, butchers, gardeners, silkworm rearers, etcetera. It was actually very interesting, including visits to Kew Gardens, a butterfly company, and Crawford College, where a lady teaches cheese-making. That was hilarious, as Bruce and Jane came too, and we stuffed our brains full of knowledge for twenty solid hours over two days.

"Kew Gardens is still like something out of *My Fair Lady*. The visit ended with 'Albert' giving me four pounds of rosebuds for my mum's birthday, so I later sent him some Devonshire cream.

"When we came back to Tanzania, Geoff finally took some leave. We borrowed a house in Mufindi and went each day to 'empire build' on our Highland farm.

"We tramped miles up hill and down dale, all round the land — 1,250 acres — none of it flat! It was amazing how many sites for dams Geoff found! There are three main streams running through the land and a very nice spring for drinking water. Our four new horses are all rideable now. They will be a good way to oversee the farm. The boys have finished one house and should complete the second very shortly. They are only temporary ones, eventually to be converted into an office area. However, they're quite substantial enough for the boys.

"As we sat on top of a large, granite rock surveying 'our bit of Dartmoor' at the end of the day, we thought of Karen Blixen's *Out of Africa* — I have a farm in Africa."

《•》《•》《•》《•》

"October 14, 1990. Dear Libby . . . We are having a letter-writing session today, as tomorrow we have seven managers from government-owned ranches arriving for a two-day visit and they can post them for us when they leave.

"They are going to be very interested in how the Decatix is working. It is, in fact, still doing really well. More successful results come in each month. We hope the government will pass it soon for general sale throughout Tanzania.

"Actually, the visitors will be able to post our letters in Dar es Salaam! The weather is still quite pleasant, not too hot yet. The garden looks a lot healthier, with masses of colour, now that our sheep are safely within the confines of an electric fence. The cool months will take us up to November.

"We have found large deposits of fossilized shells about five and a half miles from the sea, at about 100 feet above sea level. They are mainly giant oyster shells, but also razor shells. An expert at the London British Museum dates them at a minimum of seven million years old. He is keeping my sample at the museum. And now I use them as soap dishes and ashtrays. There's one huge one that serves as a doorstop on the farm. I'll have to put them away before somebody steals them.

RAM CHOPS

"'Ram Chops,' our chief breeding ram, is now, at last, under control. He has been a source of great entertainment for the past year but was beginning to become a positive danger. Unsuspecting guests would be seen sprinting down the paths with Ram Chops in hot pursuit. Geoff was often to be observed going to "teach him a lesson" but returning bruised and tattered and muttering dark threats involving cooking pots.

"Finally, I almost met with a nasty accident when he pounded after me from the bottom of the garden, gaining on me by the second. I reached our minute mulberry tree and tried to hide behind it but, after a couple of circuits, I sprinted for the casuarina tree. That gave me a few moments' rest and then I just managed to make it to the house and slam the door in his face. He attacked the bars on the dining room doors in silent frustration.

"Out came our electric fence, which our electrician set up, and with all available hands we set out to try and entice both Ram Chops and his entourage inside. After evading all our miserable attempts with a series of full-blooded charges, which either put all us adversaries into full flight or clawing our way up the trunk of a tree, all seemed rather quiet.

"As I stopped to take stock of our progress, I noticed there were only two of us left in the contest. In response to my call, I located two of my helpers up trees and one flattened along the roof of the sheep house. I'm happy to say that our task has been accomplished and all seven sheep are at last confined. Said sheep are more trouble than all 12,000 cows. (Yes. We're hovering at 12,000 cows on Mkwaja after sales!)"

《·》《·》《·》《·》

"February 16, 1991. Dear Mum," Geoff writes to his mother, "in Harare, Vicky and I travelled extensively, visiting a Highveld cattle ranch, attending tsetse meetings, etcetera. Our friends (Jack and Pat), Vicky, and I went to the races in Harare, where, of course, money was lost. Jack and I put our money on the most attractive jockeys in the ladies' race. His came in last and mine second to last!

"In Mufindi, we did the rounds of friends and spent many hours tramping around the farm with Bruce, making grand development plans without the money for them! Sadly, the cows have got a disease that has decimated the herd and left us with a few rubbishy ones, so we will have to start all over again, once the vaccine for the disease has arrived, by bringing in about twenty Friesians from Njombe.

"Bruce is very depressed over it, but the sheep seem to be okay, and Bruce is busy with a large cinchona nursery for next year's planting. Peter's house is now nearly complete, and all of them, Peter and Sarah plus Bruce and Jane, have moved in.

"The main objective now is to build a food processing factory that will freeze certain vegetables for Dar es Salaam, make cheese, hams, sausages, etcetera, and produce dried fruit (mainly tropical) for mueslis and similar health foods, for export.

"Christopher is extremely busy with his hunting camp project. He has been allocated a number of useful hunting blocks for his French clients this dry season, and his role will be to provide luxury hunting camps (five of them) and all the service and food for them during the whole season.

"This will be an enormous task, as, although three camps will be north and west of Ruaha Park, one will be in the Selous Reserve and another will be near Lake Manyara, West of Ngorongoro in the north, so the logistics will be horrific. By June, he will need about thirty new tents and all the equipment, teams of men organized to build up the various camps, and a working system for regular food supplies.

"As Christopher will be so involved in this venture, and as he feels better working solo, we have decided that he run the hunting lodge project as his own, but under the nominal umbrella of Foxtreks Ltd. He should be earning a lot of money if everything goes as planned.

"Peter will take over the whole Ruaha camp operation, at the same time as flying the Friends of Ruaha plane, mainly for anti-poaching

Peter Fox piloted the Ruaha plane for ten years on a voluntary basis.

operations. We are still hoping to get a Cessna 206 (or 210) for Peter to fly on charter. This is a six-seat, single-engine plane, which could be useful for transporting Christopher's clients. If the authorities permit us to operate it out of Ruaha, it will be very convenient.

"I wonder how Alexander is getting on at college. He MUST pass his course with high grades if he expects to go on for further training. There's no other way for him to get a work permit out here. Please tell him that Vicky and I do NOT sanction any use of cars or motorcycles that do not keep STRICTLY within the law."

"P.S. Dear Gelly, this is Vicky. I just wanted to add that we are very sad to see ever more foreign-owned ships, mainly Greek and Japanese, trawling for prawns up and down the coastline, very close to shore. They never land or come into port. They don't need to — what with cold rooms on board for their preferred catch, and an ocean as waste bin for anything they want to discard. This includes myriads of turtles and fish.

"The commercial prawn fishing is threatening to destroy what used to be a thriving little prawn industry in all the villages along the coast, whereby Arusha merchants and restaurants distribute iceboxes to the villagers, for daily filling with prawns and prompt delivery back to them.

"The trawlers are completely ruining this, despite government efforts to stop them. They are also threatening the green turtle's nesting cycle because they don't put a mesh in front of the shrimp nets to prevent sucking in the turtles. Heartbreaking.

"We're still in negotiations with the villagers and authorities on how to save the turtles. As I wrote earlier, our tiny beach is a key hatching area for their little ones. We despair if we will ever get there, but soon (fingers crossed) we can start up a protection project. This can only be done with everyone's co-operation. Alone, we would get nowhere.

"We went out in a very faulty rubber boat one day. As we approached a trawler, a hostile, glaring, European man stared down at us. He probably thought we were going to arrest him for fishing in national waters. Unfortunately, we couldn't stay long. Our boat was leaking too badly!"

CHRISTINA DENIED

Christina Mvinge, who as a five-year-old ran away from Geoff on the tea plantation for fear that the white man had come to steal children, is now about to graduate from Standard 7 at primary school. She has finished top of her class and, miracle of miracles for someone from such humble beginnings, she has a chance to go to secondary school.

"Impossible," says her father, still firmly rooted in his customary sense of propriety. "I will not pay for you. Girls don't need to be educated. Now, go and help your mother in the house and in the fields. There's also water to fetch. And wood. You need to learn how to be a good wife. That's much more useful."

MKWAJA BATTLES WON AND LOST

"January 9, 1993. Dear Libby . . . The only good news of the year is that we have won, for the time being, our five-year battle against poaching. There were twelve animals in all, some protected and half of them females. Geoff took their heads to use as evidence against the poachers, who were caught red-handed, stuck in the mud on ranch land. They were caught red-handed, stuck in the mud on ranch land. The case, in Tanga, is pending, so we hope that they will end up on the other side of the gate in the jail.

"Christopher is also fighting the ivory poachers, who have started up once again in Ruaha. He infiltrated their group, so in the end, their own people turned and gave evidence on behalf of the Game Department. Again, the poachers are mostly Arabs. It's all very hush-hush at the moment."

《•》《•》《•》《•》

"Time to move. Offer the reward, but tread carefully. We can't risk being linked to whatever happens to that pestering Englishman."

"May he have double torment."

"In the meantime, dip what we whisper to the authorities in honey."

《•》《•》《•》《•》

"February 27, 1993. Dear Libby . . . We are gradually exploring the area and found a good place to plant our arboretum of fruit and spice trees — my next project. The area is an ancient riverbed shaped exactly like a natural bowl and frequented by buffaloes, with opportunities for a series of small ponds to improve the soil for plants."

《•》《•》《•》《•》

Tanzania's economy is finally on the upswing. Consumer goods start crowding erstwhile empty shelves, visible but not necessarily available to the average Tanzanian, who has yet to feel the benefits from Tanzania's increasing gross domestic product. Even as some Tanzanians prosper, huge swathes of the population are still suffering. This disappoints donor agencies, given the obvious economic momentum in urban areas, with burgeoning construction, investment (both foreign and domestic), and tourism. Give it time, say stubborn proponents of the trickle-down theory.

《•》《•》《•》《•》

FOX GREEN TURTLE PROJECT

The Foxes' Green Turtle Conservation Project eventually gets off the ground in 1993 (and will run for about ten years along the five-mile beach, initially funded by Amboni, later by the Fox family).

"We spent years researching ways of protecting the eggs and the hatchlings," Geoff remembers. "Nothing worked until we were forced to physically remove the eggs from their nesting sites along the beach, relocate them in a secure area near a ranger post, buried in deep beach sand, in the same cluster as they were laid originally, with

Releasing baby green turtles.

the numbers of eggs, dates, hatching and release times, all recorded. Funding continued out of our own pockets once Amboni withdrew.

"They always hatch out at night," Geoff marvels. He is showing visitors around. "Somebody must say, 'Ready, get set, go!' as they all come out at the same time. Within minutes, the show is over, and they are running around searching for the ocean. We put them in buckets and release them just a few yards from the water, so they don't have far to crawl to the sea. This minimizes their exposure to predators."

Looking back on the project many years later, Geoff will note that green turtles supposedly remain at sea for fifteen years and then return to the spot where they were born, to lay their eggs. "Scientists suspect that they navigate by the stars, which possibly imprints in their memory where they need to return to for laying eggs. We released them in daylight, so we're not sure if they will return. We also likely affected their sex ratio balance, since James R. Spotila et al. have observed that the temperature at which eggs are incubated impacts on the sex of the hatchling.[52]

"On the other hand, with our intervention we were able to rescue thousands of hatchlings, which is thousands more than before because, until our project, predation was reaching 100 percent. (This is confirmed by German researchers in 2001 who estimate that 9,630 eggs were collected by the project between 1993 and 1999, with 8,147 hatchlings launched into the ocean.[53])

"The project continued for ten years, but I think such direct intervention in nature is not the National Parks policy, on the assumption that nature doesn't need any help. In my view, this is not correct. One example is the relatively few buffalo, but too many lions, now found in Ruaha Park.

"The strength of buffalo to combat lions is in their numbers. In Ruaha, when 'bushmeat' poachers greatly reduced their numbers, they stood no chance against the lions. Now the lions feed on giraffe, an animal they usually avoid because of the lethal punishment giraffe can exact with their strong necks and legs. It's all very sad. The giraffe are so tourist friendly.

"This is my way of saying that I don't believe that the TANAPA policy of always leaving nature to fend for itself is fully correct. I would shoot the lions in Ruaha, or dart them and translocate them somewhere else to achieve a better ratio. The bordering villagers are also unhappy about the increasing number of lions.

"I remember Ruaha Park Warden John Savidge facing the same dilemma, only with Ruaha elephant, in the early 1970s. At first, the new Ruaha National Park had very few elephants. But, as the elephants recognized the relative safety within the park borders, compared to the rampant poaching beyond, they soon took refuge there.

"At one point, there were 40,000 of them in the park. Uprooted, ringbarked, and broken trees became a common sight. Changes to Ruaha's natural balance particularly affected browsing animals (which

---

52   James R. Spotila et al., "Temperature dependent sex determination in the green turtle (*chelonia mydas*): Effects on the sex ratio on a natural nesting beach," *Herpetologica* 43, no. 1 (1987): 74–81.

53   For more information see: *Tanzania Wildlife Discussion Paper No. 30*, for Wildlife Division, Deutsche Gesellschaft für Technische Zusammenarbeit (GTZ Wildlife Programme in Tanzania, 2001) [*sic*].

eat leaves and twigs rather than grass) such as kudu and the black rhino (in fact, more of a browny grey), and destroyed the riverine forest that sheltered smaller bushes that could not survive without shade. John wanted to cull the elephants. His request was denied.

"The poachers increasingly ignored the Ruaha Park boundaries and, in about ten years (mid-1970s to the mid-1980s), reduced the elephant population by 32,000, down to 8,000. It was horrendous to witness. Vicky and I alerted Marcus Borner of the Frankfurt Zoological Society. He conducted an aerial count, which confirmed that the elephant situation throughout Tanzania had reached disaster levels by the mid-1980s, with critically low populations resulting from rampant poaching.

"The situation was addressed in the nick of time by the director of wildlife at the time, Costa Mlay, who, assisted by overseas funding, rescued the elephant population throughout Tanzania with his highly successful, nationwide offensive (Operation *Uhai* / Operation Life) conducted jointly by the Wildlife Department, the military, and the police.

"The poachers all went to ground, and the ivory trade was interrupted. Its success rested on covering all animals, not just elephants. Sadly, it came too late to save the rhino, which is clinging on by its 'fingertips.' Just a few still survive in one or two areas. The elephant populations recovered."

(By 2012, there will be about 20,000 to 25,000 elephants in Ruaha, which Geoff will consider to be about right. But by then, history will be repeating itself, with tusks leaving Tanzania by the container load, decreasing transparency about elephant population sizes and poaching-related mortalities, and rising proportions of elephant mortality attributed to illegal killing [from 22 percent in 2003 to 63 percent in 2009 in the Selous]; and with data values generally unavailable for western Tanzania, where illegal killing of elephants when previously reported was as high as or higher than in the Selous.)

OF FRIENDS AND ENEMIES

Meanwhile, back on Mkwaja Ranch in March 1993, Vicky writes, "Dear Libby. . . Taking all the problems head-on from the beginning and prevailing has been great, but we have made a lot of enemies among those whose livelihoods have been affected. Our situation remains fairly hazardous. Yet somehow one gets used to it. Except I do still sometimes wake up Foxey, screaming and pummelling him (probably dreaming about unwanted visitors). Ours is a very open house. The windows have neither bars nor glass, so we are fairly vulnerable. Anybody can come in at night.

"We have also made a lot of friends. Juergen Goebel, Peter Schachenmann's successor as general manager of Amboni, and his wife, Sybille, are roughly our age. They often come to visit us at Mkwaja Ranch [and will continue to periodically visit Mufindi in years to come], and we're about to head off for a little trip to Zanzibar with them."

Zanzibar's relationship with mainland Tanzania remains complex. From their hotel, the Foxes and Goebels look out onto the beach where Arabs were slaughtered in 1964. Today, a young Arab father is rendering the sand equally red, only in his case by spreading out a scarlet towel. He removes his white kanzu to reveal neon trunks, and generates new screams, this time screams of laughter from his sun-brushed little girl chasing her beach ball.

Yesterday, their taxi driver praised the Revolutionary Party for maintaining its stranglehold on Zanzibar. He chuckled as he spoke about veterans of the revolution and their offspring still controlling prime land and political power, but saved his loudest laughter for a graphic description of the original revolutionaries subjugating Arab women. Strange how many well-intentioned revolutions simply reverse discrimination.

JANE TAMÉ

"The Goebels have introduced us to Jane Tamé," Vicky writes to Libby. "She is a British lady in Tanga, whose late German mother-in-law was the honorary German consul in Tanga. Jane has inherited full responsibility for taking care, not only of the graves of German soldiers and their Tanganyikan counterparts, the *askaris*, in Tanga, but also for ensuring that annual pension payments are delivered to the few remaining *askaris* who in WWI fought with von Lettow–Vorbeck."

《·》《·》《·》《·》

Rather than surrender Tanganyika to Britain at the outbreak of World War I, Col. Paul Emil von Lettow–Vorbeck (1870–1964) convinces the German governor to allow him to fight the Allies. His aim is to prevent the enemy from engaging in Europe by embroiling them in East Africa.

The first significant battle, the Battle of Tanga (or the "Battle of the Bees" referred to earlier), sees the Germans routing the British, despite being outnumbered eight to one. Streets and beaches are strewn with casualties: 847 British dead and wounded, and 147 on the German side, all cared for tirelessly by German doctors and their African orderlies.

The morning after their defeat, British captain Richard Meinertzhagen returns. He carries a white flag, medical supplies, and a letter from the disgraced British general (A.E. Aitken) apologizing for shelling the Tanga hospital. In keeping with what is sometimes referred to as the last of the gentlemen's wars, German and British officers then share a bottle of brandy as they discuss how best to care for the wounded.

Hugely outnumbered, with about 3,000 German soldiers and 11,000 *askaris* ultimately fighting against approximately 140,000 British troops, von Lettow–Vorbeck resorts to what will be referred to as the greatest and most successful single guerrilla warfare operation.[54]

《·》《·》《·》《·》

Almost eighty years later, Geoff's new boss, Juergen Goebel, and his wife, Sybille, invite Geoff and Vicky to Tanga for the annual tribute to fallen German soldiers and Tanganyikan askaris, which concludes with the laying of wreaths on the graves of officers in their respective cemeteries in Tanga. Their new friend, Jane Tamé, always holds a small tea party afterwards, and uses the occasion to pay the remaining askaris their annual pensions on behalf of the German embassy. This year, there are only three.

"How old were you when World War I broke out?" Vicky asks one of them.

---

54 For a fascinating account, please see Charles Miller, *Battle for the Bundu: The First World War in German East Africa* (London: Macdonald & Jane's, 1974).

"I was just an adult," he replies. By Vicky's reckoning that would likely make him sixteen years old then, and approaching his hundredth birthday as they speak, literally living history.

"Were you wounded?" Vicky asks.

"Yes," he says. "But it was my own fault. I blew myself up with a bom bom."

"A bom bom?"

"You don't know what a bom bom is?"

"No. I'm sorry, I don't."

A "bom bom," it turns out, is a mortar.

"Were you well cared for when you were wounded?" asks Vicky.

"We had better medical care then than we do now."

《·》《·》《·》《·》

Jane Tamé herself is barely surviving on a miniscule stipend, in an old, German-built house in Tanga. She also still owns a small cocoa farm, beautifully situated under the slopes of the Usambara Mountains, where German settlers first discovered African violets at the turn of the nineteenth century. But she no longer has the funds to make it profitable.

In recognition of Jane's long-term contribution, not only to the memory of the German soldiers, but also to the well-being of the *askaris,* Juergen Goebel and others in the Tanga community contribute toward her upkeep. Geoff determines to draw the German ambassador into the debate on his next trip to Dar es Salaam.

"How can I help you?" the ambassador says, handing Geoff his card. It reads: "Dr. Enno Barker."

"First, congratulations on being British," Geoff answers in his best Queen's English. They both laugh.

"My grandfather was British," the ambassador explains. Geoff then fills him in on Jane's history. "In short," he concludes, "I wonder if you could somehow arrange for the German government to look after Jane Tamé, the British lady who is looking after the German army." More laughter. "In fact, Jane's mother-in-law was once the honorary German consul in Tanga," Geoff adds.

Before leaving, Geoff lends the ambassador a pictorial history about von Lettow–Vorbeck and his campaign. "A British author," he says, "but very complimentary."

"A nice guy," Geoff debriefs everyone later. "He really tried hard, but in the end, the embassy's hands were tied. There was an embassy grant for supporting expatriates in difficult circumstances, but it could only be spent on Germans. Try as the embassy might, they couldn't find a loophole in the regulations."

Economics of HIV/AIDS

In his 1993 article, "Modeling the Macroeconomic Effects of AIDS, with an Application to Tanzania," John T. Cuddington analyzes the impact of AIDS on the Tanzanian economy and per capita production. Without decisive policy action, he projects that AIDS may by 2010 reduce the gross domestic production of Tanzania, already among the poorest countries in the world, by 15 to 25 percent in relation to a no-AIDS scenario, with per capita income levels falling by up to 10 percent by 2010.

High-Profile Mkwaja Visitors

Dr. Ulrich Albers, chairman of the Schoeller group and owner of Amboni (as well as sundry other enterprises around the world) is visiting Mkwaja. Originally German, he first went to Switzerland at the end of World War II to work for a Swiss, Schoeller, who owned several yarn factories in Europe. Schoeller soon looked upon the young German as a son and eventually left everything to him.

Dr. Albers invariably wears long-sleeved, blindingly white shirts to guard against sunburn at Mkwaja. On one occasion, he is sandwiched between Vicky and Geoff in their Toyota pickup when it gets bogged down in black cotton soil.

"Quick as a flash," Geoff later jokes with friends, "Vicky leapt out to push. And Dr. Albers felt that, as a lady was doing so, he should as well. However, Vicky was experienced. She didn't stand directly behind the rear wheel! We had to wash Dr. Albers, chairman of Amboni, etc., etc., down in the sea. His glorious white shirt pristine no longer." Then adds, "Albers certainly knows how to earn my respect."

"How's that?"

"By telling me very early in the visit how lucky they were to have me — something Brooke Bond would never have said!"

"How did the Foster brothers [of Kenya polo fame] visit go?"

"Great fun. When told that they would be taken to the beach ('our get-away-from-everywhere place'), the two old boys (by now in their late sixties) put on their shorts, their belts, and their sheath knives like little school kids preparing for an outing.

"By the time we got to the beach," Geoff laughs later, over drinks with friends, "they had already raided our lime tree and picked all sorts of lethal-looking mushrooms along the way. Once there, they enthusiastically worked their way along the beach, with their knives prising oysters right off the rocks, giving them a good squirt of fresh lime juice, and relishing the results. Heaven."

A BOUNTY ON GEOFF'S HEAD

"May 6, 1993. Dear Libby . . . We are still fighting the battle of the beach plot. It's absolutely amazing that some people will go to such lengths to prevent us from getting the land. They (just one or two influential 'baddies,' we think) want to continue with their poaching and ivory smuggling in conjunction with some Arabs based in Pangani and Tanga. Geoff has been warned by an informer to expect a bullet in his back!

"Of course, if we settle on the beach plot, they can't do it (poach, I mean). Their tactics are convoluted and long term (including paying voters).

"An opposition committee of twenty respected elders are now setting up to rally support for our land claim, and the district commissioner has set a date for the entire village population over eighteen years old to vote on the issue next week. The 'baddy' and his cronies are once more trying to bribe the villagers, so we really don't know if we'll get the plot or not.

"We are most intrigued to see how the villagers will vote. We do hope we get it, or all we have worked for against poaching will be for nothing. On top of everything else, Geoff is to be a witness at the trial of an Arab poacher and three wildlife scouts. This will make him even less popular, but it's time these people found someone to stand up against them. No one else dares to."

《•》《•》《•》《•》

"July 20, 1993. Dear Libby . . . Life here is still rather dramatic. The main case against the Arab caught poaching with three wildlife game scouts and a government lorry is supposed to start mid-September, only nine months after the event! Geoff has to appear as a witness, as he caught them. They shouldn't get away with it, but I expect big money will change hands. Still, we do have the animal heads as exhibits.

"The police have already tried to drop the case on a false claim that Geoff refused to be a witness. Expletive deleted! Luckily, the regional game officer got the public prosecutor to reopen it, saying that he would resign if the poachers got away with this kind of influence.

"The second case involves a really bad hat who has been behind many cases of cattle theft. His favourite trick was to get his cows driven close to our ranch cattle when there was word of a cow about to give birth. Its newborn and as yet unregistered calf was stolen and given to a lactating cow in the village herd. Meanwhile, our ranch herdsman was paid to say that the ranch cow had aborted. Clever.

"He went too far the last time, when he slaughtered an adult Ranch cow that had been branded. We managed to find quite a few witnesses willing to testify not only to this, but also that he sold some of the meat and gave the rest to his supporters. Infuriating, but at least he has been taken in for questioning for the first time ever.

"Geoff is very proud that he at last has a value — is worth something! The local witch doctor has told him that the baddy offered him 60,000 shillings (equivalent to about £60 — about $140) to kill Geoff, but that he refused because he knew the thief was in the wrong. The poachers also asked the witch doctor to poison Geoff. Again, he refused. This rum character, would you believe it, is very religious and has even been to Mecca. He has also been keeping all kinds of stolen cattle on his coconut *shamba* and helping to send them to Zanzibar. Even worse, he killed someone, buried him, and planted a coconut tree over the corpse. The perfect murder.

"Let's hope his sins have at last caught up with him. I doubt it, though. He managed to bribe our resident policeman, who is also involved in another case where he, the policeman, took material and money from a herdsman as a bribe for keeping quiet. It's all a bit out of hand. We're not sure if these cases will be tried honestly. I'd love him (the baddy) to be caught on a charge of bribery, but the low wages around here ensure that it's such a great temptation to accept bribes, and the baddy is very rich.

HOW ELEPHANTS DON'T LEARN

"The ivory poachers are trying to get rid of me," Geoff later jokes over drinks with their naturalist friend, Manfred Brandt. (According to Geoff: "a bird nutter and charming.") "Instead, I will get rid of them." He laughs. Vicky cringes. "They say that I am worth 60,000 shillings, which is the only value I have ever had." Then, more seriously, "Although we have had to make enemies of poachers and cattle rustlers, tree fellers, and canoe makers to protect Mkwaja's fauna and flora, we actually experience no personal threat."

"And the 60,000 bounty? What is that?" Manfred asks.

"As I just said," Geoff beams, "the only value I have ever had!"

Talk eventually turns to Manfred's work. He is exploring how a project by his employer, the European Union, might best protect the flora and fauna in the coastal strip around Mkwaja.

"There are only about forty precious, coastal elephants left in the whole ecosystem," Geoff says. "Elephants have a very fast way of learning where they are safe, so they hang around in the forest close to our house because they know it is the only protected place."

"Eating my vegetables and pushing down my papaya trees, more like it," Vicky interjects. "It only takes a few to do a lot of damage."

"They occasionally move toward the beach and break down coconut trees to eat the soft middle part," Geoff continues, ignoring Vicky. "What probably saves their lives is the villagers protecting their crop by immediately shooing the elephants off with birdshot, akin to spanking them on their backsides. This way, the elephants learn to avoid the villagers' land because they know where they were at the time of discomfort.

"Just as small boys herd cattle up-country, so the coastal children in homesteads bordering the game reserves guard the crops against intruders. They sling stones at offending bush pigs and baboons from the vantage point of accommodating tree branches and stumps.

"Elephants are another matter. When they are sighted, the children call for help to the adults. Tragic is when villages bring in game scouts to kill the elephants. Before the scouts can respond, the elephants have moved back into the bush. Tracking them down takes time. This distances the elephants from the scene of the crime. When the scouts finally find them (sometimes two weeks later), not only do they risk shooting at the wrong ones, it also teaches the offending elephants nothing."

THE "ISLAND"

The early 1990s see Foxtreks searching for a beach-side property within range of Dar es Salaam to offer their guests coastal as well as highland and game park experience. They finally ask Werner whether his earlier offer of doing something commercial with his peninsula is still open.

"Wonderful idea, Geoff!" Werner replies from retirement (at eighty) in Canada. "You know I have always dreamed of having a small tourist facility on the 'island.' But I am too old now to start one up myself."

"We'll have to move quite quickly," Geoff answers. "I hear that an Italian investor is already taking steps to do the same thing, and a geologist has also made a claim to exploit the beach sand, which contains some mineral of interest."

In the nick of time, Peter Fox discovers that the title and all references to Werner's ownership have been removed from the Lands Office. With a photocopy of his original Letter of Offer, ownership is once more restored to the Voigts. The two families then reach an amicable agreement, retaining Voigt land, and having "Fox Enterprise" build on it. The Voigt land is designated as 547 yards of the tip, measured from the high tide mark. The Foxes apply for ownership of the rest of the peninsula, about five miles long, stressing their interest in protecting its flora and fauna.

《·》《·》《·》《·》

". . . Must rush off to the tune of a tummy rumble, elephant, I think," Vicky writes to her parents from Ruaha in July 1994. "Yesterday we watched a leopard drag its kill up the bank from the top bar. Very spectacular, with a hyena trying to get the meat, too." And later, to Libby . . . "We just spent eight glorious days in Ruaha and saw almost everything from the camp. There were many sightings of leopard last month. A second kill happened not far from the camp, involving a lioness and her three large cubs. That night, a leopard was spotted eating from the same kill and being attacked by the lion, only to have hyenas homing in on the kill, too. Very exciting viewing. The visitors really seemed to enjoy it all.

"A well-known photographer, Simon Trevor, producing a film for BBC in Ruaha, witnessed a fish eagle catching a big catfish in the water and taking it to a sand bank. There, a crocodile emerged, chased the fish eagle away, and grabbed the fish for himself. The fish eagle perched on a nearby branch and, as the crocodile was wriggling back to the river with his prize, a gaggle of very noisy Egyptian geese disturbed and harassed the crocodile, which let go of the fish. The fish flopped its way back into the river. The BBC photographer's end shot would have been the fish eagle still sitting there wondering whatever happened to his dinner — but he had left his camera behind.

"The week was marred only by the water pumps breaking down the minute after Christopher left the camp in our tender care, and two days later, the sole supplies vehicle almost wrote itself off when the steering went and it wrapped itself around a tree. The good news was that it's the only fully insured vehicle. All the rest are third-party insurance only. The pump came back repaired after a couple of panic-stricken days, and we managed to make do, just.

"Now we're back to the grind at Mkwaja again, and to the rather terrifying task of writing a paper on the effects of Deltramethrin (Decatix). A friend is staying and leaves the ranch for Dar es Salaam by train tonight, so I can send this back with him for mailing."

《•》《•》《•》《•》

"July 19, 1994. Dear Libby . . . Our generator packed up this morning, so we haven't yet managed the usual 'Fox Chat Show' (that's what people call our twice-daily family radio call. Apparently all sorts of friends tune in to hear the latest!). That means we don't yet know what happened at the district meeting, which finally went ahead yesterday. Can you believe that we drove all the way to Tanga for the prime minister's dinner, only to find that it has now been rescheduled to the ninth of December? Better be a good meal.

"We are visiting the island again, seriously, for a week at the beginning of January just before I fly off to England. Geoff has made intricate plans for the beach cottages. They will have foldaway frond gauze doors stretching across the window of the room, just the same as the ones on the ranch. That way they can be closed for security at night and kept totally open by day."

《·》《·》《·》《·》

"September 2, 1994. Dear Libby . . . There has been so much drama and action here. The coastal politics are almost impossible to understand, but it often boils down to 'we'll do anything for money.' Our policy is still one of avoiding bribery. This is causing us more and more hassle. The problem is that the people are SO poor. The latest episode in our attempt to buy the beach plot as a buffer against poaching has the village chairman trying to do a deal with some new, ex-Kenya people, who want to waltz into Tanzania, with no effort at all, offer money to the unscrupulous village chairman and a couple of others to take the plot from under our noses. Geoff managed to catch the village chairman on the beach conspiring with these people without the knowledge of the village committee. All hell broke loose. The chairman immediately tried to bribe committee members with huge sums of money to vote against us. As one of them said to us, 'What can I do? I can't afford not to take this money.'

"Geoff and I made a quick trip into Tanga to ask the regional commissioner for his help. He will, we hope, step in and try to put the village back on the tracks again. It is so difficult to operate against corruption.

"I think we will get withdrawal symptoms from lack of drama when we return to England again."

Mkwaja for Sale

"September 22, 1994. Dear Libby . . . Mkwaja is for sale!! Dr. Albers is retiring. His son isn't interested in retaining Mkwaja Ranch. He wants to sell it and help pay off Amboni's huge loan. We are to find a buyer. It's rather unsettling, not knowing how long our job will last.

"Advertisements are going into the *Farmers Weekly*, *Financial Times*, and *Country Life*, probably the October edition. Several hunting companies have expressed strong interest, which worries us — after so many years of wildlife protection on and around the ranch.

"Ah, well, the next few months will be interesting. There will probably be prospective buyers from all walks of life—most likely tourism development, game ranching, or cattle ranching at our door. We can but test our patience."

《•》《•》《•》《•》

Their first visitor is Uhuru Muigai Kenyatta from Kenya, the son of Kenya's first president, Jomo Kenyatta, and, like his father, a long-time Kenyan politician. (He will become Kenya's deputy prime minister in 2008 and later the new president, but also stands accused of crimes against humanity by the International Criminal Court for orchestrating violence that left more than 1,200 people dead after the 2007 elections.) "He was charming, wasn't he," Geoff says after his stay. Vicky agrees.

《•》《•》《•》《•》

The only other potential buyers who come are hunting companies, mostly from Arusha. After all their dangerous efforts to quell the rustling and stop the poaching, the Foxes now face the possibility of Mkwaja Ranch's falling into the wrong hands.

"Imagine allowing hunters to come and start shooting all the animals we have so painstakingly been protecting over the years," Geoff worries.

"Especially that awful Englishman from Zimbabwe (later up for murder in England)."

"Of course. But I will act in the best interest of Mkwaja itself."

WHY NOT A NATIONAL PARK?

The Foxes ask for a meeting with the director general of Tanzania National Parks, David Babu. "In short," Geoff says, after a long exchange, "we propose that the Mkwaja Ranch be turned into a national park for all the reasons you know so well: its unique variety of wildlife, its exciting range of coastal forests (five distinct types), and its singular status in having a game area reaching the ocean, where sable antelope, buffalo, and reedbuck graze right down to the beach. I needn't tell you, sir, how unusual and unlike any other park in Tanzania this is."

"And your proposal fits right in with TANAPA's long-term vision, as well as with Saadani's status as the first game reserve (as far back as 1969) to try and reconcile the interests of game and bordering villagers."

David Babu's successor, Lota Melamari, is equally excited by the two-pronged proposal: first, to merge Mkwaja Ranch with the smaller, Saadani Game Reserve (half its size and on Mkwaja Ranch's southern boundary, thereby tripling Saadani's reach); and second, to transfer the enlarged reserve to TANAPA as a fully-fledged national game park. Unfortunately, the Wildlife Division has no money to speak of.

《•》《•》《•》《•》

To the rescue comes their naturalist friend Manfred Brandt. Having seen Saadani's potential for himself during his many visits to Mkwaja, he applies to Brussels for money to help the Tanzanian Wildlife Division buy Mkwaja Ranch. Brussels agrees in principle. In practice, they need a project framework, since their regulations do not permit money to be paid directly to an individual (in this case, Dr. Albers, owner of Mkwaja Ranch).

As luck would have it, some other long-time friends, Mary and Wolfgang Schaeffer, visit Mkwaja shortly afterwards. Following many years in Tanzania, they have recently moved back to Germany, where Mary is now the Tanzanian country director for the Deutsche Gesellschaft für Technische Zusammenarbeit (German Technical Cooperation Organization [GTZ]).

Over beers on "their" beach ("one of the last significant breeding grounds for the threatened green turtles," as the Foxes never fail to stress!), they ask her to help them out with a project to satisfy the European Union (then the European Economic Community) if possible.

"It would be marvellous if we could leave something permanent to stop all the poaching from starting up again in a big way. Otherwise, it will all begin again once we go."

Mary cannot, and of course does not, respond immediately. Meanwhile, the fate of the elephants hangs in the balance.

DREAMS OF A LAZY LAGOON
ISLAND LODGE

"September 22, 1994. Dear Libby . . . Our 'island' land applications in the Bagamoyo area, about forty-five miles from Dar es Salaam, are through the villages' meeting and now at the district level. In the meantime, we have been given permission to go ahead on Helga and Werner's land. It is only five acres—not an awful lot, but by far the easiest way to go.

"It is on the tip of a peninsula and beautiful in its isolation. We have already organized hundreds of palm trees, Indian almond trees, and casuarina trees to be planted. The palms and almonds have apparently survived, but the casuarinas have died. Casuarinas are normally the easiest of trees, so they must have been transplanted too late.

"We have also put a down payment on a *mashua* (small dhow) sailing boat for taking supplies to the island (really a peninsula but way out to sea). Craftsmen are just assembling the materials in a fishing village about half an hour's drive from here (Mkwaja). It is really quite an exciting development and takes our minds off this one. The nails to make the boat have to be fetched from Zanzibar, as they are special ones used since way-back-when for building dhows.

"All the boys are set to get into top gear. There is a down payment to be put on a large dhow next week. This will be built in a boatyard on the mainland, opposite the 'island' camp, or 'Lazy Lagoon Island Lodge,' as the surrounding area is known as Lazy Lagoon. The only

Oops! The tide went out! (Foxtreks boat made in Mkwaja Pangani
and sailed down to Lazy Lagoon.)

time I may have mentioned Lazy Lagoon to you would have been in connection with the annual Lazy Lagoon / Dar es Salaam race."

The "Lazy" race always begins in Dar es Salaam. The first leg involves sailing to the Lazy Lagoon peninsula, where the sailors stay for the night before completing the race back to Dar the following day. Usually they all share a great big barbecue on the beach. Then some of the sailors retire onto their boats to sleep; others just use camp beds on the beach. But when Alex and Johno from Mufindi participated one year, they noticed several lion prints below the high tide line on the peninsula. That meant the lions were still around, so everyone retired to their boats.

A few days before, Vicky and Geoff had spent an enjoyable week camping on the island with Mike and Debbie Ghaui and Alex and Liz Boswell—exactly above the spot where the lion tracks are found!

"Alex had brought down his boat (which he had built together with Johno Beakbane) and, as my (Company) Land Rover was bigger than his vehicle," Geoff later tells friends, "I volunteered to launch it on its trailer into the sea. However, the problem was that it was SO full of crates of beer (mainly), and everything else needed for a week's camping for us all, that it wouldn't float off the trailer until I had reversed well into the sea—with the water around my knees as I drove backwards. Finally, at considerable water depth, we got the boat off its trailer. But by this time, my engine had understandably cut out! The tide was coming in. We were stuck!

"At that moment, Mike and Debbie Ghaui appeared, saw our dilemma, and convulsed into laughter! A rope had to be found, and two cars. Then, with considerable difficulty, they towed my car out of the sea.

"A fun week was had by all—eating oysters off the rocks served in every possible way until we were sick of them. Of course, when the time came to return to Mufindi, we had enormous difficulty in starting my Land Rover; all the electrics had rusted. The workshops manager, David Macdonald, was most understanding—blaming the salt air in Bagamoyo!"

《·》《·》《·》《·》

The Foxes' youngest son, Alexander, still studying abroad, is designated to build an ecolodge on Lazy Lagoon after his return. According to a running Fox family joke, Alexander declared when he was still very young that he wanted to go to college, after seeing his oldest brother, Christopher, marry very late, while the next two, Peter and Bruce, found their wives early, at college.

At one a.m., the Foxes' phone rings. It is Alexander. He is calling from Dallas, where he is taking aeronautical engineering (very helpful, since the Foxes are also toying with the idea of starting up their own air company).

"Hi. Guess what?"

"Mmm . . .?"

"Jeanie has agreed to marry me, so I no longer need to go to university. Oh, and by the way. Can you come to the wedding?"

Half asleep, they treat it as a joke and tell him to shut up.

"I'm serious," he says.

So, Vicky, Geoff, and his mother fly to Dallas. ("Since then, Gelly has had great admiration for American immigration officers," Geoff reports back to Mufindi friends, "because they wouldn't believe she was my mother. They thought she was my sister! Once through immigration, we looked out for the 'tiny, little car' they had told us about. It turned out to be a stretch limo, hired for their going away to a hotel after the wedding. The limo, its windows of tinted glass emblazoned with "Just Married," later stopped traffic after their wedding, when Alexander stuck his hand through the sunroof waving a pair of ladies' knickers.

"The wedding was scheduled for the next day. It soon transpired that the stretch limo and a pastor to officiate at the ceremony were the only two things Alexander and Jeanie had arranged for the occasion. Vicky and Mum to the rescue: decorating, ordering food, etcetera, etcetera, late into the evening. At the party, an aged man fell in love with my mother. It was delightful watching the two oldies.

"One of Alexander's classmates said, 'Your son is amazing. He's the only person we have ever heard of who told a tutor that he had made a mistake. The tutor had instructed us that 'Mathematically, this, that, and the other is the way it works.' Alexander said, 'That can't be right, for this, that, and the other reason.' The tutor acknowledged his mistake."

《·》《·》《·》《·》

Each of the two older boys in turn will take his gap year off to manage and continue building the Ruaha River Camp, before returning after college to devote himself entirely to the business. Christopher transfers to Mwagusi, allowing Peter to take over the Ruaha Camp. (Much later, when someone in the Ministry of Tourism has to prepare a management plan for Ruaha, they will include a lodge, so the Foxes have to upgrade the Ruaha Camp.) Bruce comes to the farm in Mufindi and Alexander concentrates on Lazy Lagoon.

After camping rough on the island for a few months, Alexander and his new bride, Jeanie, move in with their friend Joe on the mainland opposite Lazy Lagoon peninsula. For nearly two years, Joe has to tolerate their chaos, which includes a Jack Russell terrier and his best friend, a wild boar named "Piglet." They are inseparable. Alexander and Jeanie regularly go for evening walks up and down the beach, where Piglet and the Jack Russell take turns chasing each other, until the time comes when the Muslim fishermen ask them to cease this activity because the pig is defiling their beach.

So Alexander and Jeanie transfer back to the "island." There, the two buddies continue to cavort up and down the beach together. Years of rough living pass, first waiting for permission to build and then building the Lazy Lagoon Lodge. By that time, Piglet has grown into a huge, massive boar, still trying his best to chase and catch the Jack Russell, which, being faster, easily manages to nip him.

One evening, during the annual "Lazy" race from Dar es Salaam, everyone is sitting on the beach in moonless darkness—other than pinpoints of light from houses on the mainland across the bay, and

"Piglet" or *Tundu* (bush pig), rescued as a baby,
sleeping under Alexander's arm (bush piglets are born striped).

their campfire—when Alexander and Jeanie's mature and massive wild boar quietly emerges out of the darkness to join the party. The racers haven't been forewarned.

"Shock and awe," Geoff laughs later, "until Alexander introduces his Piglet, and shows them that all it takes is one little finger scratching him on his neck behind the head for him to collapse in bliss. Piglet gradually joins a wild sounder of pigs on the peninsula. Sadly, he brings his new chums 'home' into the camp with him. This upsets the camp Dobermans. They chase off the interlopers, rendering Piglet increasingly aggressive.

"Tourists often go for long walks along the beach, accompanied by the dogs. When they sense bush pigs, the dogs go into the undergrowth after them, and often re-emerge with gargantuan Piglet in hot pursuit. On two occasions, Piglet threatened the nearest target, a human being, so, sadly, he had to be shot.

"Incidentally, as a general rule, bush pigs like to live in close proximity to water and mud. There is no still water on the island, so the bush pigs there have adapted to getting all their moisture from the vegetation.

"Speaking of pigs," Geoff adds. "Did I tell you when I was made to sleep with a pig?

"At our house in Lugoda, Vicky had started pig-keeping when her sow sat on one of her newborn piglets, dislocating a limb. An English general practitioner had very recently come as a locum while our company doctor was away on leave. When Vicky walked in with her piglet, he tried not to show surprise and examined the 'patient' on his surgery couch, declaring nothing broken and to come back tomorrow if there was no improvement. As Vicky carried her piglet out, she passed Liz Boswell carrying her new child in.

"Piglet was put in a box in the airing cupboard just outside our bedroom door. Almost precisely, every two hours, the damned thing squealed for its bottle. Vicky jumped out of bed to feed it on demand. At some stage in the night, she decided to feed it in our bed without turning on the lights to disturb me and, after one early morning hour's session, I told her to turn on the lights as something wasn't quite right. She did. I was not wearing pyjamas in those days and was BLACK with pig shit—all over! We had to exchange the bath water twice before it all came off."

A DRAMA A DAY

"May 23, 1995. Dear Libby . . . Geoff and I are also still in limbo at the moment, with a drama a day as usual to prevent us getting too complacent. The field has narrowed to three who appear to be serious about buying the ranch: Two Irishmen, one with a 300-acre farm in Scotland (dairy, I think) and the other, who has already sold his farm. The third is a German businessman who wants to sell 11,000 cattle to Lebanon. Madness.

"He is thinking of transporting everything from tiny calves to old bulls. Can you imagine marching suckling calves sixty miles to Tanga and then hoping the calves can find their mothers on board the ship? I couldn't believe that our general manager could even contemplate such a deal. Unthinkable cruelty.

"Also, imagine having improved all the standards of Mkwaja animals for up to seven years, just to see them all going into some pot. Well! I think we have managed to scotch that one with some judicial hinting to the government livestock people that Tanzania's sole Boran genetic bank is about to be exported out of the country. They are of course on our side and will back our advice to the general manager that we should at least keep the breeding cows and their suckling calves. We will try to save as many young heifers as we can. Anyway, let's hope the ranch is bought as a whole.

"We have bought Bruce some of the Charolaise-crossed and Jersey-crossed Boran, a few straight Boran heifers, twenty in all, some of them in calf to artificially inseminated Friesian bulls. Our ranch's artificial insemination scheme, supported by the Dutch in Tanga using, initially, 1,000 of our best breeding cows, has enabled them to buy all our really beautiful progeny and they are VERY pleased with them. We now have over 700. The place is just littered with crossbred calves; last month more than 100 were born.

"The drama over drugs stolen whilst we were away in Dar es Salaam is now so complicated that we need Sherlock Holmes to point his finger at the culprit. All the suspects are busy collecting evidence against each other. The laboratory storekeeper's daughter was the mistress of Geoff's "best" assistant, who was in charge of the ranch at the time.

"The assistant to the laboratory assistant was at first accused by the laboratory storekeeper's daughter of taking the keys from her.

Then she changed her mind and said she gave them to her lover, the Best Assistant. Now Best Assistant has come back with an impossibly complicated story, with 'evidence' and 'witnesses' that supposedly include boxes from the drugs apparently thrown into a river, teachers from two different schools, the assistant laboratory's assistant, and of course the storekeeper's daughter. To cap it all, a letter just came from Best Assistant's previous employer saying he isn't trustworthy. Geoff and I are quite confused.

"The seventy-one steers stolen whilst we were away (on top of everything else) took a month to track down. They are about 125 miles away, in Chalinze. We have recovered thirty-nine, in all. During the course of their recovery, two Masai thieves were shot dead by the government stock theft prevention people, which was rather a devastating punishment.

"Whilst I was in England, one of the rangers caught some poachers on the ranch. One poacher swung a gun onto him so, in self-defence, he fired first and shot the poacher dead. The rest of the gang ran off. Geoff, following lawful requirements, had to inform the police. They made what seemed to be a half-hearted attempt to find the body (half-hearted, I think, to save the ranger) and, thank heaven, dropped the case when they didn't find it."

《·》《·》《·》《·》

"November 12, 1995. Dear Libby . . . Geoff has signed on until next March. We will be back in the UK on leave in February and for good in July. Mum is now very blind and needs us to look after her. After eight years at Mkwaja, we are rather sad to have to leave. Bruce and Jane will take over Mkwaja in January, if the terms are good enough."

FIRST MULTI-PARTY ELECTION

In November 1995, President Mwinyi (nicknamed Mzee Ruksa ["Everything Permitted"]) cedes power to the winner of Tanzania's first multi-party elections, President Benjamin William Mkapa, initially nicknamed "Mr. Clean" and "The Iron Broom" for his anti-corruption political campaign platform. How differently things would turn out.

OF BEACH BATTLES AND BACON

Vicky's November 12, 1995, letter to Libby continues: "Jane is doing well with her Mufindi ham, bacon, sausages, etcetera, and doesn't really want to give it up, so they may come to manage the handover of Mkwaja on a part-time basis. Goebel has only to make up his mind.

"Approval for the Bagamoyo / Lazy Lagoon area is nearly through. The Region has agreed, which is a great relief. Now the environmental impact assessment all rests on whether it is an island or a peninsula, so we have to fight that one next.

"Life on the ranch is much as usual: amazing drama followed by relative tranquility. We were getting cattle rustled every other day, and sometimes in large numbers, so Geoff mounted a campaign to combat the problem. He put out an enormous reward for information leading to the capture of one of the boats used to ship stolen cattle to Zanzibar. It was astonishingly successful. The ranch-based police force joined hands with the rangers to set up an ambush on the beach, close to where our Lazy Lagoon boat was made.

"The rustlers in a large *mashua* with engine arrived and started to load the cows into the boat. Springing the trap, our guys were then shot at. A gun battle ensued on the beach. Our people only had birdshot, as Geoff didn't think that would kill anyone."

Geoff, looking over Vicky's shoulder as she writes, assumes a Churchillian posture and intones: "Together with my rangers, *mgambo* [militia] unit, and my cattle section watchmen, we now had a little private army, with which we engaged our Zanzibari friends on the beaches. None of my men were injured, but at least one of the Zanzibaris was hit." Vicky giggles and keeps writing.

"Apparently there were screams of, 'I'm dying!' from someone in the boat. One of the rustlers was abandoned on shore. He was so scared that he fell to the sand in a dead faint. The police arrested him and he immediately told all. Later, we dropped our policemen and the rangers off to arrest a second suspect who had, as it transpired, been slightly wounded. According to him, the boat owner was wounded in the head and died en route to Zanzibar. We later heard that he was tipped overboard on the way back to Zanzibar to avoid answering any embarrassing questions. The wounded man was dispatched to the village dispensary to have all the birdshot removed."

"Did you add that when he was presented in court, the pellet marks peppered on his body were used as evidence of his participation?" Geoff asks. "And that he turned out to be a notorious cattle rustler, twice caught and twice released? What you probably shouldn't add is that when the court again released him, the district commanding officer advised me in future to 'bring them in a box, because I don't trust the magistrate.'"

SOLD!

"Vicky! This is unbelievable!" Geoff is rushing in from a meeting with the Wildlife Department in Tanga. Vicky's heart sinks. So much has happened this year, she cannot bear more bad news.

"Okay, Geoff. I'm bracing myself. What happened?"

"Remember our discussions over beers with the Schaeffers on the beach last year? About how the Wildlife Division needed a 'project' so that they could buy Mkwaja? Well—"

"Have a heart, Foxey. Stop stalling."

"GTZ has just approved a community wildlife management project all around Mkwaja! This will allow Brussels to release the EU money to the Wildlife Division. They can then pay Dr. Albers in Zurich. And everyone is happy."

"Except Vicky."

He sympathetically hugs her.

"Now we have to sell off the cows very, very fast, and our only buyers are butchers in Dar es Salaam. So there goes Tanzania's national Boran cattle herd, painstakingly built up and improved as a result of the tsetse eradication program; off to the butchers."

"At least we have saved the cream of the herd by selling it to various government ranches. Too bad we don't have the money or we would buy them all."

Dr. Albers thanks the Foxes and gives them a return air ticket to Tanzania.

MKWAJA FAREWELL

"March 3, 1996. Dear Libby . . . A container is to be dispatched tomorrow and arrives here at noon. We then have three hours in which to pack it with all our belongings in preparation for leaving Mkwaja—three hours before they start charging demurrage. Then, at 5:30 p.m. Friday, they tell us that there isn't a ramp on the lorry. I suppose they thought the container could fly onto it! Anyway, Geoff has managed to arrange something. By Wednesday, I think I'll need to replace my hair appointment with a visit to a psychiatrist!"

《•》《•》《•》《•》

"That's that, then," says Vicky as the truck loaded with their goods in a container finally trundles off. "Time to say all our goodbyes and go to Mufindi for a while."

"After that, UK here we come, to look after the old ladies [Micky and Gelly, Vicky's and Geoff's widowed mothers, respectively]."

"Well, at least we won't have a drama a day in England. And think of all that lovely cheese."

"And chocolates!" says Geoff.

"But we will miss Mkwaja, won't we?"

"That we will."

Vicky and Geoff agree that their time on Mkwaja Ranch has been the happiest and most exciting time of their lives—that and the walking safaris. Vicky loved everything to do with the cattle and research, not to mention teaching. Despite cattle ranching, despite Foxtreks demands, despite research documentation and follow-up, despite catering for streams of scientists visiting Mkwaja, and now potential buyers, Vicky's "school" grew to ten children "to supplement their primary school for two hours a day," as she wrote to Libby. "Their ages ranged from seven to thirteen, but the standard at Mkwaja is way behind English schoolchildren and even behind other parts of the country."

"Vicky, being Vicky, never says no," Geoff adds to the letter. "Just like in Mufindi, being the only teacher in the community (with a double teaching qualification), she set up her school at Mkwaja Ranch on a voluntary, unpaid, basis. All told, she has so far kept it up for more than twenty years. The kids loved her. When they heard we were leaving Mkwaja, all her ranch schoolchildren wrote lovely letters thanking Vicky for teaching them."

"You don't get that kind of appreciation from schoolchildren in the UK," Vicky concludes.

For his part, Geoff had relished being in charge of a vast area of the coastland and given total freedom of action by Amboni. He'd had to protect, not only the wildlife, but also the forests. He extensively managed to stop the felling of large trees and mangrove forests supplied to Zanzibar for dugout canoes and roofing, respectively; the massive rate of cattle rustling; and also the very heavy game poaching on and around the ranch. And, of course, he had his favourite toy: a bulldozer.

With it, he created a network of ranch roads and game-viewing roads, as well as constructing catchment dams so they could spread the cows around the ranch and, in the process, also provide water for the wildlife. But, perhaps Geoff and Vicky's greatest satisfaction came from joint pioneering of their successful tsetse eradication project and its amazing consequences.

"We were lucky," they agree, toasting each other. "However, time to move on."

BOUND AT GUNPOINT

After Geoff and Vicky's departure, son Bruce and his wife, Jane, take over Mkwaja management. Bruce's role is to oversee the transfer of the ranch to the Wildlife Division and, less pleasant, to sell off all the cattle. Under his watch, the rustling is completely wiped out, after two of his men, sent to Zanzibar, manage to catch the thieves and present them to the authorities.

A continuous stream of butchers and cattle buyers select, weigh, and purchase cows to meet the butchery requirements for Dar es Salaam. (It breaks Vicky's heart. "We had built the ranch stock up to mouth-watering levels of quality-grade Boran after the tsetse eradication project, and there they now are, selling everything off to the butcher, including pregnant breeding cows.") A massive loss for Tanzania; a huge sadness for Vicky and Geoff.

Three buyers turn up one day on a motorcycle. Bruce duly weighs a number of cows, before going back to finalize the paperwork in the ranch office. As he is writing out the sales documents, the "buyers" produce a gun. Quick as a flash, Bruce leaps up and grabs one of them, using him as a human shield between the gunman and himself. Unfortunately, the third man, to one side of Bruce, produces a knife.

They tie Bruce up with rope, take the safe keys, and make their escape with pockets full of cash.

Trussed up, Bruce helplessly watches them through the window. He can see them trying to start up the motorcycle right in front of two seemingly bored police, sitting outside the smart police station that Geoff had built for them, twenty paces from Bruce. The motorcycle takes some time to catch, then all three robbers jump onto it and drive past the two policemen.

Their gun, though visible, isn't noticed. When Bruce finally frees himself, he manages to phone through to a friend at the Kwamsisi cotton farm farther inland. By this time, unfortunately, the thieves have already passed through on their way to the Chalinze/Korogwe road. They are ultimately traced to Morogoro by the son of one of Geoff's field assistants and by the other two police officers from Mkwaja. At least one of the thieves is later killed during another robbery in Morogoro.

Starving under Grass Too Tall to Eat

At Mkwaja, driving cattle was routine procedure. Geoff and Vicky trekked cattle to Amboni Sisal Estates every month, from Mkwaja cross country to Korogwe and then to Tanga through all the sisal estates; also on a number of occasions to Vipingo, north of Mombasa. However, the longest cattle trek is undertaken by Bruce, after he and Jane finish their Mkwaja assignment.

While Jane heads back to the Highlands Farm in Mufindi, Bruce remains behind to transport 1,100 heifers that he has bought with a Dutch loan as part of the Mkwaja cattle sell-off. A third of them are trekked to Bagamoyo, where their descendants still live.[55]

Bruce loads another third of the cattle onto a nearby railway in cattle wagons, which, on their way south to Ruvu, promptly derail. The last third are trekked directly to Ruvu where Alexander is awaiting them all. Together, they then walk all the Mufindi-bound cattle

---

55   The Bagamoyo cows include one purebred Boran given to Vicky as a present by Amboni, and six Boran/Friesian crossbred heifers given to Vicky and Geoff by Tanga Dairy project staff in recognition of what they did for a Dutch-assisted dairy project in Tanga. (Over a number of years, they artificially inseminated more than 600 breeding cows with Friesian semen provided by the Dutch. This project was most successful, literally created the Tanga Dairy Scheme and, to this day, regularly delivers milk in tankers to Dar es Salaam.)

south to a station on the TAZARA Railway Line. Both groups have to cross the mighty Wami River, so Bruce quietly selects a time when no trains are passing and drives them over the railway bridge. The cattle are then transported in TAZARA railway wagons—half to the Mufindi pulp and paper mill at Mgololo station, below the Mufindi escarpment, and the other half offloading long before, at Mpanga. From there, they trek cross-country over difficult terrain without tracks and through many rivers to the Foxes' newly acquired land at Kimbwe, right below the escarpment.

Then the rains fall. The Mwenga River floods, and the cattle are stuck for several months, starving under grass too tall to eat. Mortality is very high, there also being no dipping facilities; but, a year after they first set off, the Foxes' nucleus breeding herd finally reaches its destination, Maganga Highland Farm, to be crossed with Holstein bulls, purchased from Kitulo Dairy Farm near Mbeya. Several bulls and breeding cycles later, Vicky will have, in her words, "what looks like a Friesian dairy herd."

"Which happily gets her up at six-thirty every morning for milking," says a pampered Geoff, "after she has brought her husband his early morning tea in bed!"

WERNER VOIGT'S LAST VISIT TO AFRICA

Meanwhile, after ten years in Canada, the Foxes' German friends, ninety-year-old Werner Voigt and eighty-year-old Helga, are preparing to see their beloved Tanzania one more time before he dies—the farm, the island, the Foxes, and other Mufindi friends. Today they are in the doctor's waiting room, about to get their shots.

"Werner and Helga Voigt," the nurse calls out. Their daughter Evelyn's husband, Gordon, helps Werner to his walker. Evelyn hands a cane to her mother, Helga (still sprightly, although almost bent double with osteoporosis and osteoarthritis).

"There must be some mistake," the nurse says uncertainly. "I'm looking for the folks who are going to Tanzania."

Once in Tanzania, the Voigts are warmly welcomed to Lazy Lagoon by the Foxes' youngest son, Alexander, and his wife, Jeanie. The Voigts feel a little odd being guests on their own "island," even as they admire the young couple's stamina. Jeanie, with her halo of honey curls, her eyes a deep, glacial blue, seems to have seamlessly transplanted from the United States to camping on a peninsula in Africa. She has even mastered her "island oven" (a hole in the sand filled with embers) enough to bake Alexander his favourite birthday cake. "Chocolate," they both say in unison, these enthusiastic child-adults. Alexander is systematically preparing to bring his dream lodge to life as soon as permits are granted.

Tonight, the men will stay on the "island," not a mean feat for ninety-year-old Werner. The women will overnight on the mainland. When the guys return the following day, Werner is sporting an impressive bandage.

"A close encounter with Tess [Alexander and Jeanie's Doberman pinscher]," Gordon explains. "We had a hard time stopping the bleeding because of the anticoagulants for Werner's dicky heart." Gord and Alexander look a little sheepish. It turns out that the only sterile gauze available on the island, or approximation thereof, was a box of Tampax, which they had duly dismantled and put to effective use.

Coastal humidity gives way to crystal, highland air on the Voigts' onward journey to Mufindi. With every puncture, every pothole, every setback, Werner gets more enthusiastic. "Now, this—" is his constant refrain, "—this is Africa!" Palm trees and baobabs yield to clumps of virgin forest and eucalyptus, interspersed with sheets of emerald tea, and, finally, to the Fox Highland farm. Behold a plethora of buildings, rambling berths for welding, storage, and machinery, not to mention the piggery—with its "honeymoon suite" for breeding and a hundred piglets—also kitchens where Bruce's wife, Jane, competently churns out endless supplies of ham, sausages, and bacon.

Soon it's Club Night in Mufindi. Helga and Werner tread the same stone steps past the same mown lawns to the same front door, under a new sign: "Golfers, please remove spikes before entering." Daughter Veronika's painting still hangs on the wall, a dramatic tableau of Masai, lion, and cattle painted when she was only fifteen. Everyone in the club seems protective of it, wants to know how she is. (For the record, she is still producing brilliant work and can be found at **http://www.veronikahart.com**. One Thanksgiving, a young niece was asked to check the website during a family gathering and spelled Veronika with a "c." Turns out that Veronica Hart with a "c" is a porn star.) The billiards table has been replaced by a satellite television. They pause just long enough to register that Canadian Donovan Bailey has won the 100 metres at the Olympics.

At last the Voigts arrive back on their erstwhile farm. Today's gracious host is Dunstan Ndamugoba (the first officer-in-charge of the Government Tea Research Station, formerly the Voigts' farm). The initial order of the day is supposed to be tea and *maandazis* in their former living room. But the Tanzanian donuts will have to wait. There are too many folks mobbing Helga and Werner at the car, too many friends to greet, to laugh and to cry with, friends they never thought to see again. Mzee Mpiluka from Lwanga village is here, with his wife, siblings, children, and grandchildren. There are Taina, and Ena, and Tugurime . . . now almost blind. Mzee Shabani. There's Kaziimpya, and Oresto! Charles, the only one allowed to drive Werner's tea truck (other than Helga) is a riot, dancing up a storm. At one point, Charles's father takes Gordon and Evelyn aside.

"I understand that in Europe they lock old people away. I want you to promise me that you will never lock these two people away. You must promise." It is not a request. It is an order. They promise. He relaxes somewhat, but not completely.

Oresto, their former cook, has turned up. Damp-eyed reunion. Apparently, when he heard of Werner and Helga's visit, Oresto asked Dunstan whether he could help prepare the meal and, more than that, requested that he be allowed, for old times' sake, to serve Werner and Helga personally. And so the day unfolds in dancing and speeches, including Dunstan's formal announcement that a new laboratory has been designated the Werner Fritz Voigt Research Laboratory.

Then on to Lwanga and a visit with close friend Mzee Mpiluka and his family. They spill out into the courtyard to a concert of blessings and welcome in eight-part harmony followed by more tributes:

Jesaya's son, Saidi, offers Helga a small, handwoven basket. "This is for you," he says. "You may not remember me. I am one of the many children who came to your farm with our mothers when they did business with you. I never left the farm but you gave me a sweet, or an old tennis ball, or a little shirt. And in all the years, I never said thank you. So, I would like you to have this basket. It comes as a thank you, not just from me, but from all the other kids you helped over the years."

Soon Mufindi recedes, and the Foxes' Ruaha River Camp beckons. They find fellow guests watching lions across the water from their verandas. Pre-dinner drinks are served under blazing African stars: brilliant, countless, overwhelming. Lions still roar in the distance.

Son Peter and daughter-in-law Sarah Fox, each in their own way are coming to grips with life in Ruaha: Peter of the dreamy look, the fixer, the one who can lose himself healing machines. He was the kind of kid who could do the Rubik's cube in seconds flat while others struggled unsuccessfully for days. How gently he cradles his sleeping son; Sarah competently solving a dozen mini-dramas each atypical River Camp day as hippos bellow, Egyptian geese honk, leaves rustle, the wind sings.

At breakfast, Peter and Sarah's four-year-old daughter, Rachel, is fascinated by a little doll the Voigts have brought her from Canada—and oblivious of the elephant browsing just beyond a three-foot retaining wall. The doll is exotic, the elephant routine.

Now they're off to Christopher's luxury tented camp on the banks of the Mwagusi Sand River, where Christopher and Werner, both strong, self-contained men, tap into each other's gentleness and Africa's splendour.

Today's rising sun burns red beyond canvas tent flaps, silhouetting trees in pre-dawn drama. The sky lightens ... now blazing orange over hills of cobalt and water holes of glowing amber. Now blistering turquoise, rendering distant hills in palest lavender, while water holes, since dappled brown and blue, reflect another perfect Mwagusi morning.

A lilac-breasted roller takes off, mauve and indigo in iridescent flight beside the game-viewing vehicle (a converted truck with seats in the open back) as Ruaha's vistas offer here a dash of red from toothbrush trees, there the yellow of busy weaver birds. A sudden stop, seemingly in the middle of nowhere, and Christopher—master of the dramatic gesture—has done it again. Before them is the unlikely sight of a table set for breakfast in the wilderness, complete with linen and china, cinnamon rolls, fresh orange juice, and eggs of their choice.

"When are the buffaloes coming?" someone asks.

"They should be here soon."

"Perhaps we should get ready."

"Which buffaloes?"

It turns out that at ten-thirty or so every morning, a huge herd of buffalo frequents this particular watering hole in the sand river. Sure enough, a single, old male—head almost hidden by half a dozen tick birds—lumbers onto the sand, stops to smell the air, continues to the water, and drinks deeply. In ones and twos, and finally by the dozen, the rest of the teeming herd follows.

Christopher infects the party with his undying enthusiasm. "Look! Look over there! See how the light falls on them. Stunning." You would think he had never seen a buffaloe before. Despite decades in the bush, each vista, each animal still a miracle ("blackbird has spoken, like the first bird").[56]

Later in the day, a group of elephants registers on his enthusiastic radar, moving as gently as shadows over sand. A young female intently sucks water from a hole created by tusks larger than hers. Others, already on their way out of the riverbed, reflect golden, evening light. A large male silhouetted against the pale clay bank lifts his trunk to smell the air. Giraffe and waterbuck, and some zebra, are approaching, slowly, to take their turn at the water hole kindly created by their tusked benefactors.

《・》《・》《・》《・》

> *Yesterday, he met a lion strong and powerful*
> *"Who is the king of the jungle? Tell me, who is king of the jungle?*
> *Tell me, tell me truly, and I will bow before him."*
> *He stood before that lion, that mighty lion,*
> *sleek and sated from a recent kill*
> *with baleful eyes barely open, but alert.*
> *Before the lion, he stood.*

---

56 From "Morning Has Broken," a hymn written by Eleanor Farjeon in 1931 and later popularized by Cat Stevens.

Today, he meets an elephant, tall and powerful,
"Who is the king of the jungle? Tell me, who is king of the jungle?
Tell me, tell me truly, and I will bow before him."
He stands before that elephant, that wise old elephant
Who dug out watering holes where others might drink,
Who brought down branches whereby others may eat,
created pathways where others may tread,
Before the elephant, he bows.

Senior guide Saidi stares intently at the ground, his brow furrowed with concentration. Where most can at best make out scattered hoofprints and something that might resemble a claw mark in the dust, this wise and aging tracker, in unselfconscious absorption, is clearly reconstructing a thousand dramas indelibly imprinted just for him in the same grains of sand.

Saidi Masonda was tracker to Jonny Niblett, then later to Geoff and taught all of the Fox boys the art of tracking as well as the feeling of, and love for, the African bush. When hunting was suspended, he was engaged to shoot elephants for a dealer, as the "gun" in the bush—in other words, working for the guy who gets other people to shoot his elephants for him. Saidi was caught.

Christopher (whose earlier school reports always had the same comments from his English teacher: "He writes good essays. But I wish he could write about someone other than Saidi.") was determined to help him get released, and promised the authorities that he would personally employ and be responsible for Saidi. "That they allowed this is very bizarre, because the law is the law. But the police trusted Christopher, and he was able to obtain Saidi's release," Geoff remarks. "And will employ the old man for as long as he wishes to work."

《·》《·》《·》《·》

Christopher has insisted on joining the Voigts for today's game-viewing drive. They are just about to find out why. He stops the truck, goes over to Werner's side of the cab, and says, "Werner, would you like to walk to the elephants?"

Werner fiddles with his hearing aid.

"We will walk together to the elephants?" Christopher repeats more loudly.

"No," says Werner (getting in and out of the vehicle is a painful and demanding exercise at ninety). Short pause. "Maybe." Micropause. "Yes. Why not?"

His mind made up, Werner gets out of the car with the alacrity he otherwise only musters for liquor stores and urgent bathroom breaks. And off they go, Christopher, this thirty-two-year-old child / man of nature with his "adopted grandfather" Werner Voigt leaning heavily against him. Two lone figures in that vast landscape, the youngster solicitous, the elder trusting, both of them relaxed, at peace, and in a world unto themselves, moving slowly toward several wild African elephants.

Without a word, Saidi positions himself behind a bush, ready to create a diversion if necessary. There is some trumpeting from mothers with calves. Some mock charging from the distance. And then the elephant nearest to the two humans charges in earnest to within five metres of the tiny figures, paws the ground, flaps his ears in irritation, trumpets antagonistically, retreats, turns and charges again, and again. If Werner has to go, everyone knows that this is the way he would choose. Even so, friends and family watch from the safety of the viewing vehicle with their hearts in their mouths. After the elephant finally retreats, the old man and his young friend slowly wend their way back.

"How was it?"

Werner ignores the question. He has eyes only for the video camera.

"You got it?" Yes, the photographer "got it": eleven dramatic minutes of video, which will comfort Werner in the last six months remaining to him after his return to Canada. Indeed, his last conscious act on his deathbed is to hold ever closer to his fading eyes the picture of the elephant towering over them.

DEFYING DYNAMITERS

Alexander and Jeanie are increasingly frustrated. Their frequent and constant representations to district authorities fall on deaf ears when it comes to the destruction of Lazy Lagoon's reef by men fishing with dynamite (easily accessible from quarries for cement and road projects). Alex and Jeannie often give chase to would-be dynamiters.

"They sailed off in an *ngalawa*, a dugout sailing boat, with

Alexander and me in hot pursuit," Geoff tells friends after one such occasion. "When we caught up with them and grabbed their rigging, one of them produced a very large and sharp knife. We considered our options and promptly let go."

Explosions from sticks thrown into the sea are not only indiscriminately stunning and killing the fish (for dynamiters to scoop up) but also crushing the surrounding coral and anemones, crucial to long-term marine survival.

Lazy Lagoon's reef has always been a valuable breeding nursery for myriads of fish. Its once blinding palette of neon pinks, oranges, purples, and indigos is now fading into dirty greys, except for the black of marauding sea urchins. Vital rock pools are emptying. The odd moray eel still survives, and, for some reason, the dramatic scorpion fish (also called feather and dragon fish). But there are ever fewer baby zebra fish, angelfish, neons, pipefish, and crayfish.

Sponges and anemones, once reflecting the colour wheel in their profusion, wither and fade. The erstwhile click of countless crabs scrabbling over oyster beds hushes. A few solitary mudskippers bear diminishing witness to earlier, teeming colonies. And, as Peter Voigt often points out, Lazy Lagoon's receding shoreline itself can be attributed—among other factors—to the demise of large shoals of parrotfish. Not only did they provide rainbows to bewitch the snorkeller and delicious eating for the gourmand, but they also played a key role in creating beach sand by grinding up and excreting small rocks harvested from crevices along with their smorgasbord of algae.

Finally, Alexander seeks higher support from the minister and the director of fisheries. Amazingly, the Tanzanian navy responds. Tiny it may be, but it does have military authority. Marines raid all three villages on the mainland near Lazy Lagoon and arrest any fishermen with unlicensed dugout canoes.

"In other words, all of them," Geoff continues. "These hapless traditional fishermen were marched off to court, charged, fined, and warned that, if they did not stop the dynamiting, the navy would return and repeat the exercise. It was a drastic, but effective, step.

"The fishermen in all three villages knew who the dynamiters were; many of them came from the mainland and even Zanzibar. They also knew that dynamiting was reducing the fish stocks near land and forcing them to fish ever farther afield in waters too dangerous for their light craft. Without the backing of the navy, they could not have challenged the dynamiters, for fear of reprisals. This way, they could legitimately plead desperation. The dynamiters left."

MKWAJA LINKS WITH SAADANI GAME RESERVE

In 1996, the Wildlife Division officially expands the Saadani Game Reserve to include the southern half of Mkwaja Ranch (with the northern part still holding the dwindling Mkwaja Ranch's cattle stock, which son Bruce now has the thankless task of selling). Meanwhile, GTZ concludes that seasonal migratory mammals like sable antelope, kudu, eland, buffalo, and elephant need a larger area for protection, threatened as they are by commercial meat poachers, deficient land use practices, and burgeoning tourism along the coast. Rather than benefiting from the new reserve, neighbouring villagers are also suffering. For all of these reasons, GTZ sets in motion plans for expanding investments to help both the communities and migratory mammals, with money channelled through the budget-deprived Wildlife Department.[57]

《·》《·》《·》《·》

On a high about Saadani, but with mixed feelings about leaving Tanzania, Vicky and Geoff bid a nostalgic farewell to Mufindi. The time has come to be with their aging mums, Micky (almost blind by now) and Gelly, in the UK.

"See you soon, Mrs. Fox," Geoff calls as Vicky heads toward Immigration at the Dar es Salaam airport. He is staying behind for a few more days to tie up some loose ends.

Little do they know it, but their life is about to change forever.

---

57 For more information: Saadani Conservation and Development Programme (SCDP), **http://www.saadanipark.org/history.html**.

PART FOUR

Breaking the HIV/AIDS Stranglehold

(1998–2012)

Catastrophe

Hours before Geoff's scheduled flight to retirement in the UK, the phone rings.

"Hallo?"

"Hallo, Geoff. Rick here. [Rick is wildlife artist Mike Ghaui's younger brother]. There's been an accident. It's Bruce."

"Is he okay?"

"No details yet, I'm afraid, except that he's hurt."

"I'm on my way to the airport shortly. Should I cancel?"

"No need for that, I don't think. It's all under control. He's being cared for at the company hospital, and Jane [his wife] is there."

Geoff proceeds to the UK, only to find out that Bruce's condition is critical. "Can you help?" Jane gasps over the phone. "The Aga Khan Hospital says that, if he's going to walk again, he needs to be treated in the UK immediately! British Airways in Dar are being very helpful. But they need authorization from London to take on a medical emergency case. And London is stonewalling us. Please see what you can do at your end. We're running out of time!"

"And that is when," as Geoff will later put it, "I ran into the intransigent 'female boss of British Airway's medical team' in London."

"May I help you?"

"Yes, please. This is an emergency. Our son needs urgent medical treatment in the UK. There's a BA flight scheduled to leave Dar es

Salaam today. If he's to walk again, he has to be on it. We understand the crew needs your authorization to take him."

"We're glad to be of service, sir. Now, can you fax me the fully certified details of all his injuries, the qualification of the doctor accompanying him, and the registration number of the ambulance that will meet him in London?"

"Ma'am, time is of the essence. It would take too long to get all that to you. The BA flight is about to leave." Indeed, as he was speaking in the UK, in Dar es Salaam the engines were warming up and the plane was ready to go. "If my son doesn't get on it, he may never walk again. It will be too late. Please."

"We have our rules."

"Is there anything you can do, please?"

"We have our rules."

And so it continues, with her, in Geoff's words, "blocking, blocking, blocking and the plane almost going, going, going."

BA finally relents. Jane and Bruce's brothers get him onto the plane, with Bruce taking up three seats, Jane a fourth, and a volunteer Dutch doctor a fifth. Their fellow passengers are wonderful. They take over the care of the toddlers.

Only much later do the details of the accident itself emerge. It turns out that Bruce was driving from the Highland farm to pay monthly wages at his other two estates, along a road that is treacherous in the rain, when his truck slipped and crashed down a precipitous slope. A rock crushed in the roof, squeezing Bruce through the front windscreen. Even as he slid down the steep slope, Bruce was apparently more concerned about the cash he was carrying to pay the employees on the farm below the escarpment than about himself. As soon as he could, he gave the money to one of his employees and said, "When I get back up there, I'm going to count it again!"

It took several men to carry him to the road. One of them then ran three miles to where they knew someone had a motorcycle. With that they rode some six miles to Luhunga village and hailed a *dalla dalla* (a mini bus, used for public transportation, often costing a dollar). Somehow they got Bruce into it. And, finally, off they bumped and slid, only to run out of petrol. After five hours, Bruce finally arrived at the Unilever Tea Company hospital. The next day, he was flown to the Aga Khan Hospital in Dar es Salaam — and from there, at last, to the UK.

Two surgeons are on standby in Bristol. Vicky stays with Bruce to enable Jane to catch up with some sleep. The operation takes ten hours. He is put on his face, despite broken ribs, which could puncture his lungs. But the surgeons have no choice. They need to insert two titanium rods into his back. All told, Bruce has five broken vertebrae (one "exploded"), three compound broken ribs, and a broken arm that was flapping around. Yet after he comes to in his room and sees Vicky sitting there, he is still strong enough to call out: "Nurse! My mother cannot be expected to sleep in the chair."

"I tell you what, Bruce," the nurse answers. "You sleep on the floor, and your mum can sleep in your bed!"

"That is the measure of Bruce," his proud father will later tell friends, still shaking his head in amazement. After two days, some university buddies arrive and have a party around his bed.

"What about Sister?" Bruce asks.

"Don't worry," he is told. "We've bribed her—with a cake."

Seemingly Endless Years of Separation

The indomitable Jane at his side, Bruce sets an extraordinary example, stoically adjusting to his abrupt displacement out of Africa and into a wheelchair. Unlike his fellow patients, who are receiving compensation for their accidents, Bruce has to earn a living, now from his new base in the UK.

Foxtreks readjusts accordingly. Peter is to retain overall direction of Foxtreks; Alexander, among others, responsibility for Lazy Lagoon and Mikumi. Bruce and Jane take on international Foxtreks marketing.

"Huge thanks to Jane and also to her parents, who have been really great," Geoff will regularly acknowledge over the coming years. "Whenever Jane and Bruce travel to trade fairs around the world for marketing, their kids stay with Jane's parents nearby. Jane's father, a skilled handyman in his retirement, has changed their whole house to be wheelchair friendly. They are all fantastic."

In addition to international marketing, Bruce also continues to direct Highland farm operations remotely and, increasingly, the planning of new Foxtreks ventures. (Not to mention daredevil skiing on special para-skis down black diamond ski slopes in the U.S. whenever he can fit it in.)

Bruce at Breckenridge Ski Resort, 2009.

As for Geoff and Vicky themselves, rather than retiring to England together as planned, they now find themselves living two continents apart—Vicky as caregiver to the mums in England, and Geoff as on-site manager of the Highlands operation in Mufindi (under Bruce's continuing direction from the UK, thanks to email and the web). "One day, I decided to teach the cook how to make crème brûlée," he writes of an early attempt to improve the Highland Lodge cuisine. "It then was served in a rather large bowl—with the result that one of the guests turned white and went out to be sick! So now I don't interfere in the kitchen!"

To his mother, Gelly, he later writes: "I can't wait for Vicky to come so that I can catch up with all her news. I haven't seen her in FIVE months. I don't know yet how long she will be able to stay. Perhaps I should throw away her return ticket!" Behind the joking is as desperate a declaration of love as stiff-upper-lip-and-don't-let-on Geoff will allow himself.

And still they share the fruit of their earlier work in Tanzania. For example: "Great news, Vicky. The expanded Saadani Reserve is at last scheduled to become a national park! And the GTZ project has finally been approved to help the surrounding villages to benefit from increased tourism, and the game to benefit from improved wildlife management."

Unbeknownst to them, the pattern is now set for almost seven seemingly interminable years of long separations interspersed with brief reunions (for a total of about four months per year) either in Tanzania or England, the latter inevitably filled with shopping to buy crates full of replenishments for Foxtreks (not to mention eventually converting the derelict stables beside Micky's house into a self-catering cottage for Vicky to manage on the side).

Letters from Geoff help Vicky through bouts of emotional

exhaustion, as do brisk walks over Dartmoor, and the piano when she can. "Time to get on with the day," she will scold herself; "time to check on the cottage . . . new guests arrive tomorrow . . . they all do seem to love it here . . . leafy lanes, open moor, and carpets of bluebells in spring—how could they not?"

When she feels she might lose herself in sadness, Vicky works hard toward her final piano certification, its rigour an escape, but also a wonderful bond with her ninety-year-old mother. Blind as she is, Micky still plays beautifully. Speaking of playing, the two old girls remain a riot . . . never fail to amuse . . . although even irrepressible Gelly is now beginning to show some signs of decline.

So the years slip and drag and tug and meander by with the wind in her face and the gentle moorland mists as she gallops . . . the gardening, the cooking, the children visiting, the children's children, the learning to train sheepdogs—and, always, the mirage that is Tanzania, beckoning, briefly immersing, then abandoning her again until the following year. On good days, and there are many, giggles with grannies; on others . . . *Oh, Foxey, how did it come to this?*

At first, Vicky manages to care for both mums in their respective family homes—lovely stone structures, parts of which have seen 400 years or more, with gardens in summer a riot of rambling roses and fresh vegetables; the faint sound of sheep carried on the wind, otherwise a peaceful silence. But as time erodes Micky's and Gelly's health, they all move in together (anything to avoid confining them in a nursing home, although Micky does eventually go into residence for short periods of respite care).

Mufindi Highland Lodge.

283

"Perhaps at times they might have thought it more comfortable in the nursing home," Geoff will joke in later years, usually with a big smile for Vicky, who inevitably braces herself for what is coming. "Especially after Vicky's mother was left sitting on the commode all one night. At eight a.m. the next day, Vicky got out of bed and went down to make breakfast for her mother. A friend, who came in to help get her mum up in the mornings for half an hour or so, found Micky still sitting there from some eight hours before. 'I didn't mind,' said Micky. 'I just went to sleep.'

"I have never let Vicky forget it," Geoff grins. "And, with this experience, I tell her of my great fear that I, too, may be bedridden one day and forgotten. She's already showing signs of it. 'Would you like a cuppa?' she asks me. And there will be this great anticipation on my part for that cup of tea. Three hours later, she'll come back into the room and say, 'Was there something I've forgotten?'"

IMPORTING SHEEPDOGS

"Look at that poor shepherd," Vicky says to Geoff on one of their reunions in Mufindi. "See how he has to run madly from side to side to try and keep the sheep in check." Over time, Vicky has dramatically increased her flock of six original Corriedale sheep from the Kitulo Plateau, added a few black-headed Persians to speed up expansion, and used only pure Corriedale rams for breeding. Almost purebred they may be, but the Highland Farm sheep don't stay in paddocks. Instead, they roam on hillsides, making it very easy for them to wander off and get lost.

"Geoff, we need a sheepdog to help our shepherd. It's too much to ask of him alone."

"Agreed," says Geoff, so pleased to have Vicky home that just about anything goes. "There must be some in Tanzania."

"No, there aren't. I've checked everywhere. We'll just have to buy one in the UK."

"Gulp."

"I know, Foxey. It's not going to be cheap." A friend of theirs in the UK is a shepherd, also one of Britain's top sheepdog trialists and, in fact, owner of the southwestern champion, whom he uses for breeding. As luck would have it, he has one adult (Breeze) and one puppy (Storm) for sale—both well-bred border collies.

Once back in England, Vicky and Storm are duly trained, not only by the shepherd but also by Vicky's newly acquired and well-trained Breeze. All three travel to Tanzania together on Vicky's next visit, Storm and Breeze (at vast expense) to form the nucleus of Vicky's breeding stock—the first working sheepdogs ever in Tanzania.

"With great pride, I took our shepherd and Geoff out to the sheep, where Breeze and I would show them how to handle a sheep-dog." Vicky giggles as she later relives her first demonstration, over a cup of tea with friends. "First I took five sheep down to the bottom of the field and walked back up to the post where Breeze was sitting obediently awaiting my command to go and fetch the sheep and complete the trialling course. [This entails sending the dog on the outrun, collecting the sheep, taking them through a central gateway, passing round the shepherd's post at the top, taking the sheep through the Maltese cross in two directions, bringing the sheep to a central shedding circle, choosing two sheep to separate from the three others, and completing the course by putting the sheep into a pen and closing the gate behind them.]

"Breeze obediently ran to the bottom of the field. His outrun was perfect, but by the time he got there, there wasn't a sheep in sight. Never having seen a sheepdog in their lives before, they had scattered in terror. This left both Breeze and me nonplussed. As for Geoff, still smarting from the expense, he was not impressed."

Within a few weeks, both the sheep and the farm shepherd are well enough trained, not only to do the normal herding but, on occa-sion, to entertain the Highland Lodge guests with a full sheepdog trial show. Gradually Storm also becomes a very good sheepdog. This revolutionizes the life of the shepherd, who gets a lot of kudos from the sheepdog trial and can control his flock of 400 sheep with much greater ease. The mere presence of dogs also prevents the sheep from being stolen, as folks are now nervous about coming too close.

"See, Foxey? A great investment, after all."

BOOM AND BUST

Many entrepreneurs are benefiting from Tanzania's economic liberalization, particularly those with access to foreign exchange and the courage to take investment risks — witness burgeoning supermarkets overflowing with imported consumer goods, and high-rise structures changing Tanzania's urban skylines. (These unfortunately also include growing numbers of hotels and businesses owned by corrupt officials.)

However, benefits are still not trickling down. Small farmers in particular continue to hurt across the land, as reflected in the general stagnation of agricultural production — not surprising, since they produce almost all of Tanzania's staple foods: maize, millet, and paddy.

How did things go so wrong? Wasn't economic liberalization supposed to stimulate Tanzanian agriculture, increase agricultural yields, up labour productivity, raise production and incomes? In theory, yes; in practice, well, no. Over and above the distortions caused by structural adjustment, culprits include everything from bad weather and the war with Uganda; a cholera outbreak; the fluctuations in donor support and conditionalities; depressed national prices, leading to cross-border smuggling; rising corruption; decreasing demand for traditional export crops such as sisal; and, of course, the lingering fallout from forced villagization.

SHE SHALL BE CALLED FELISITA

Into this world — not far from the Fox farm geographically, a universe away economically, but soon to cross their path dramatically — is born a little girl.

"She shall be called Felisita," her mother says, and, because her father is already lacking in energy, he agrees. Felisita's parents have a tiny plot of land in rural Mufindi. Like their forefathers before them, they have — until recently — lived independently and with dignity. In good years, they can put aside extra maize for bartering . . . perhaps against a new shirt, or a *khanga* (Tanzanian sarong), or extra oil and salt.

Each day, as Felisita's mother walks to and from the fields to hoe, to furrow, to seed, to harvest, to water, to cook, to clean; each day, as she forms her pots of clay, and sings her songs of perseverance, Felisita is tied firmly on her sinewy back, comforted by her warmth and lulled by her movements. She feels secure. Sometimes she is handed to her step-grandmother. But mostly Felisita is where she feels best, on her mother's back. Like others, she gradually starts crawling, walking, even running. Unlike others, she isn't growing much and remains very thin.

Theirs is a life removed from national politics, except, briefly, in October 1999. That is when, with fellow Tanzanians, rich and poor, urban and rural, sick and healthy, young and old, socialist and capitalist, supporter and critic, they stop in their tracks. Mwalimu is dead. Although Felisita knows that something important has happened, she is of course not old enough to understand how important this milestone is to her young country.

MWALIMU'S HERITAGE

On his death, the first president of Tanzania is still the chairman of the CCM party, still revered in much of Africa as one of the continent's greatest visionaries in history, still a "world hero of social justice" (in the words of the later president of the UN General Assembly, Miguel d'Escoto Brockmann), and still, in the view of many international critics, the man who bankrupted Tanzania economically.

"I was struck by, and am still pondering, the extraordinary contrast between the easy international generalisations that Nyerere had not served his people well and the profoundly different judgment of Tanzanians themselves to which this letter gives evidence," Canadian Cranford Pratt posts online.[58] (Author of *The Critical Phase in Tanzania, 1945 to1968: Nyerere and the Emergence of a Socialist Strategy* [1976], Pratt has written extensively on Tanzanian politics and economy. He was the first principal of the University College, Dar es Salaam [from 1961 to 1965], has travelled back extensively, and is now professor emeritus of political science at the University of Toronto.)

"Following the death of Julius Nyerere," Pratt's blog continues, "there were, internationally, many expressions of the respect and affection that he had long commanded.

---

58   Cranford Pratt, "Julius Nyerere: The Ethical Foundation of His Legacy," *The Round Table: The Commonwealth Journal of International Affairs* 89, 355 (2000): 365–74.

Nevertheless there intruded into retrospective articles, critical and sweeping judgments that after all Nyerere had not served his people well. As I was reading them, we received a moving letter from someone who had long been a close associate of Nyerere and who had returned to Tanzania to be present at Nyerere's funeral. She wrote:

> It was very sad but also awesome. The people went in their hundreds of thousands—more—wherever the coffin was. For the most part they stood in quietness. The grief was palpable. Honestly, millions of Tanzanians were involved because they wanted to be—to have some way of expressing their feelings. The police just stood back and let them go where they wanted to, only gently keeping a path clear when necessary. Some people were crying but there was none of the formal wailing. For the most part it was the quietness, the standing in sorrow and slow movements afterwards which made me want to cry, at the same time as it stopped me from doing so. There was no pushing or shoving. I really cannot express their feeling or mine resulting. It was a depth of community mourning in which there was nothing formal or forced. It was individual as well as a coming together.

". . . What were Tanzanians in their millions responding to which the international commentators were ignoring? The short answer is that Tanzanians have no doubt that for over forty years they had in their midst a leader of unquestionable integrity, who, whatever his policy errors, was profoundly committed to their welfare. That is the short answer and it is a good one. The long answer, itself a footnote to this short one, focuses on Nyerere's commitment to the welfare of his people. This commitment had generated the remarkable effort beginning in 1967 to accomplish a socialist transformation of Tanzania. These socialist initiatives have been the primary focus of the criticisms of Nyerere's leadership levelled by western economists, governments and development agencies. Yet these initiatives emanated from that very commitment of Nyerere to his people's welfare, which they so movingly acknowledged in their final farewell to him. It is in the different readings of the significance of that commitment that we can discover the reason for the contrast between the dominant western judgment of Nyerere and the judgment of his people.

"I am not suggesting that Tanzanian socialism was in fact a great success and that this is recognised by the vast majority of Tanzanians though not by most Western observers. That would be naive and severely inaccurate. Rather I am suggesting that while many of Nyerere's policy initiatives failed, they rested on an ethical foundation and on an understanding of the challenges which Tanzania faced, which were vastly more insightful than anything offered by his critics. Perhaps, ordinary Tanzanians have always recognized this truth."[59]

FOX CHAT SHOW

Post-Mwalimu economic liberalization sees the Foxes now flying their own light aircraft from camp to camp, expanding into new game parks across Tanzania. Their Highland Farm activities mushroom, as does the Foxtreks workforce—still sourced from surrounding villages. Vegetables, dairy, and meat supplies no longer have to be bused to the game parks. A huge relief, since the more reliable buses tend to be owned by Muslims, who will not agree to carry pork products, and the less reliable buses have a nasty habit of malfunctioning, risking delivery of produce defrosted en route. Although this, in fact, has only happened once, the worry is always there, especially without a telephone service.

"Few people would believe that for forty years we happily survived without a telephone," Geoff will recall in later years (right after complaining about the daily bombardment of email messages). Actually, in those days, it was bliss to write a letter and know that you weren't going to get a reply for two to three weeks. How email has changed the world—for the worse!

---

59   Ibid.

"However, we did eventually communicate around our tourist camps and lodges via a radio call system—gradually dubbed by those listening in as the Fox Chat Show (which should be preceded by the theme tune of the British radio series, *The Archers*, some friends suggested). The call had to be at specified times: in our case at 7:00 a.m. and 4:00 p.m. every day, which rather tended to tie you down.

"I remember calling Jenny one morning—Jenny Coxell, a very efficient young lady working for us in the Ruaha River Lodge. To give Peter and Sarah some leave in the UK, she was landed with the temporary management of the Ruaha River Lodge after barely four months on the job.

"'Good morning, Jenny,' I began, when everyone had reported in on the radio. 'I just want to let you know that a large group of visitors from Saudi Arabia are on their way. They aren't very happy, having been fed pork last night, and want to know what you will serve them. But don't worry, we've slaughtered a sheep and sent it down with them, including the sheep's eyes, which is, of course, a delicacy for you to prepare.

"'They have also asked me what entertainment you could provide, so I assured them that they were in luck because we had a resident belly dancer in Ruaha. Don't worry too much. Just find something flimsy and see-through, and I'm sure you will be great.'

"Jenny nervously asked about exact numbers and times, at the end of which I put her out of her misery by saying, 'April fool!' It was indeed April first. She growled back, 'Geoff, your time will come.'

"Before all our camp and lodge bookings could be made through these radio calls, visitors used to just turn up. That was normally manageable, provided you had enough food and drink. But one Christmas, when Christopher was on his own at the Ruaha River Lodge, some 100 people arrived. There were only sixty beds available. Undaunted, Christopher found mattresses and told people where they would spend the night. I imagine it was very exciting not knowing with whom you would sleep.

"Nowadays," Geoff will conclude, "bookings and other futile email messages tie you down to a computer all day. It is also amazing how almost every square metre of Tanzania is covered by mobile, unlike the UK, where several areas are still off the network."

MAMA REHEMA

Still off the Fox network, but destined soon to run into them again, is Christina. She now has her own little daughter, Rehema. And, as custom dictates, she is more often than not referred to as Mama Rehema. Then Rehema's father falls sick. He is often in hospital. Mama Rehema does everything in her power to help and is even widely credited with bringing him back from the brink of death.

"I have given you nothing but work," her husband says one day. "Yet you still joke and laugh. How do you do it?" Mama Rehema wipes her brow, continues pounding maize for *ugali* in its wooden receptacle, and laughs some more.

"You are my hero," he tells her in the privacy of their little home, as the fire burns beneath the cooking pot, and smoke curls into the grass thatch above them.

These are rare words, seldom spoken aloud man to woman. Life is good.

Not so in Little Felisita's family. She is old enough to notice that her father is losing weight; that sores are starting to cover his body. She sees how he tries to hide them from others. How friends no longer visit. Her family, it seems, is living behind a wall that she cannot see to break down.

TANZANIA DECLARES WAR ON HIV/AIDS

"We must openly declare war on this killer disease," President Mkapa tells his people on the cusp of the new millennium. He is referring to HIV/AIDS. "Let us not feel shy to talk about it." One in eight Tanzanians is now HIV positive. About two million people (equivalent to almost everyone in Toronto, or to a quarter of those living in London). Of those, roughly 600,000 have full-blown AIDS. Unlike other diseases that target the weak, HIV/AIDS is killing the family breadwinners—subsistence farmers, teachers, nurses, doctors, labourers, government workers; this, in one of the world's poorest countries.

In desperation, government, business, and civil society organizations come together under the newly established Tanzania Commission for AIDS. They agree, with international

291

donor backing, to a single blueprint for nation-wide prevention, care, and support, giving highest priority to lowering the
stigma of AIDS, school-based prevention, and blood safety.

Putting these reforms into practice is another matter,
especially in a cash-strapped nation whose social fabric is
unravelling — no, tearing — as exhausted survivors try to
meet family obligations adhered to since time immemorial.
The task increasingly rests with those too old and too young to
die from a sexually transmitted disease. Those usually seen as
too weak to bear such a burden now must care for the sick, the
dying, and the infants — their own, as well as those of siblings
and cousins — and often in secret, for fear of stigmatization in
a world of disease without a cure.

FADING DREAMS OF RETIREMENT

Geoff and Vicky, meanwhile, are watching their dreams of early retirement fade in direct proportion to the growth of various Fox enterprises
and the extended care now needed for aging mums in the UK.

"Whatever happened to our idea of building a house and keeping
a few cows in our golden years?" Geoff asks Vicky. She is on another
of her precious visits to Mufindi, and they are trying to catch their

breath before heading back down
to host new guests at the Mufindi
Highland Lodge. "Instead," he
continues, helping himself to
homemade popcorn, "here we
are, in 2003, still expanding our
business."

"At least we are keeping our
word to the villagers," Vicky counters, sipping her drink. "We said
we would bring employment."

"Employment. That reminds
me. Another politician in Mikumi
is pressuring us to hire locally, even
though I've told him about our
pact with host villages in Mufindi."

Ninety-year-old Micky at the piano.

"How many folks are we employing right now?"

"Counting estate workers in Igoda, Ibwanzi, and Chogo villages, as well as in Ruaha, Lazy Lagoon, the office in Dar es Salaam, and Mikumi, several hundred," Geoff answers. "I keep telling the politicians that I like to think of us Mufindi folk as a big family, that employment is our way of giving back to our home community, and that our employees are from one of the poorest areas in Tanzania."

(Giving back, or tithing, has been a long Fox tradition—perhaps going back as far as George Fox, founder of the Quakers. The Foxes were all Quakers down to Geoff's parents' generation, when Gelly and her three other sisters crossed their Meeting House elder by not marrying Quakers, considering their options too narrow. Geoff's adventurous and favourite uncle, enlisted during World War II and was immediately excommunicated [the Quaker movement forbidding Friends to sign up]. After the war, when he became a director in the family firm [Fox Roy Merchants], they invited him back [in Geoff's view, "no doubt to contribute toward the finances of their local Quaker group"]. However, Gelly's first cousin, Joan Fox, the only close family member still alive, remains an active Quaker to this day.)

"But are we giving back enough?" Vicky muses. "So far only those directly employed by us are benefiting. Mind you, Foxey, if we count their families, we must be up to well over 1,500 beneficiaries."

"Even so," Geoff answers, "you're right. We need to do more. But what?"

I HAVE NO FATHER

The answer arrives early one morning soon after their exchange. As usual, men and women are lining up to register for work at the Fox Highland Lodge and Farm, a skinny, fourteen-year-old boy, dressed in rags, among them.

"You're too young to work, child," Geoff says. "Tell your father to train you to become a mechanic, or a driver, or something. Then you can come back, and I'll hire you."

The boy straightens his bony shoulders, tries to look strong, and says: "I have no father. I have no mother. Eight of us now live with my grandmother. I am the oldest and she has sent me out to find money."

"*Pole sana*," says Geoff, using the all-encompassing Swahili word of empathy that is impossible to translate. "We are not allowed to employ children. It is against the law."[60]

"You should have seen his eyes just before he turned away [with a small gift of money in his pocket]," he later tells Vicky. "If she's lucky, his old grandmother can still grow enough food for all of them, assuming even the little children help. She is too old to find employment, but she also needs money to repair their thatched roof before the rains, to buy clothes, soap, school uniforms, and so on."

"That dreadful disease strikes again," Vicky comments. "Remember the visiting researcher at the lodge the other day? He said that he was running into whole villages toward the Uganda border with only grandmothers and grandchildren surviving."

"I wonder how bad the situation is here in Mufindi."

"Why don't we check with the district medical officer?"

To their horror, the Foxes find not only many grandmothers caring for their orphaned grandchildren in the villages all around them, but also very young children without any supporting relatives trying to feed and care for their even younger siblings. Here's an answer to what more they might do. They could build an orphanage. ("Imagine," Geoff will exclaim in later years: "In those days, we really were naïve enough to think that an orphanage could solve the problem!")

ANOTHER WAY OF GIVING BACK —BIRTH OF THE FOXES' NGO

When Geoff's mother, Gelly, passes away in the UK, the Foxes decide to circulate small appeal leaflets about the Mufindi AIDS orphans at her funeral. They do the same at Micky's memorial service, seven years after Vicky first went to the UK to look after her. Gelly is laid to rest beside Jimmy, and Micky beside Josh. Both in the grounds of the same little stone church in Sheepstor, where Geoff and Vicky were also married, and the White Rajahs of Sarawak are buried.

"This way, our parents who were so supportive of our ventures in life, remained so, even in death," Geoff and Vicky tell family and friends. "Altogether, they raised £4,000 (just under $9,000) toward our dream of a Mufindi orphanage."

60　In those days, it was illegal to employ children under the age of eighteen. The law has subsequently changed to permit employers to hire youth for limited hours each day.

《•》《•》《•》《•》

Back in Tanzania—together at last, after seven long years—Geoff wastes no time before meeting with his accountant to set up the Mufindi Orphans Initiative.

"You do realize, Mr. Fox, that registering a charity will entail approvals at every level of government: village, district, regional, and national."

"But that could take years, and some of the children are already desperate. Isn't there another way?"

Enter the Luhunga Ward Councillor (*Diwani*). So enthusiastic is Mr. Nyaganyilwa that he personally goes down to Dar es Salaam to facilitate the registration of the non-governmental organization (NGO). Not only that, but he also becomes (and will remain into the future) an active committee member of the new Foxes Community and Wildlife Conservation Trust (FCWCT).

"It rather embarrasses me that our NGO uses the name 'Fox,'" Geoff later tells his friend Bob Ellis, who has by now retired from Mufindi to Oregon. "But I was advised that people familiar with our name would feel reassured that their donations were in safe hands. Now we're stuck with it! We also needed an all-encompassing, single charity to serve not only the orphanage, but also our other activities."

"Which other activities?" Bob wants to know.

"Broadly, protecting the environment and reducing poverty. More specifically, protecting the future of wildlife, reducing poverty, and increasing community health (as you know, wildlife is wholly dependent on the communities around them). And most specifically, high-level environmental lobbying for wildlife preservation, and setting up the HIV/AIDS Orphanage in Mufindi. So, Foxes Community and Wildlife Conservation Trust it is."

Geoff pauses before adding, "By the way, Bob. How about registering a sister charity in the United States (Mufindi Orphans Inc.) to help raise funds for the orphanage?"

《•》《•》《•》《•》

"Bob accepted on the spot!" he tells Vicky after the phone call. "And, as we speak, I bet he is already applying his considerable business acumen to the task."

Meanwhile, son Bruce and daughter-in-law Jane are registering

"Orphans in the Wild" in the UK. Marion Gough (incidentally, Evelyn's secondary schoolmate from Iringa) enthusiastically takes on the burden of fundraising, with a view to shipping large containers of donated items to Mufindi, filled with precious donated items, ranging from crucially needed clothes and medical supplies to surplus dental equipment.

EVA

A little girl of eleven living near the forest has never heard of the Foxes. Neither does Eva know how closely she will one day work with them. Right now, she is busy caring for her grandmother *Bibi*. Just like she looked after her mother before her. Not a day has gone by without memories. Sometimes they are memories of those magical early years before Mama got sick, when the three of them always joked together. Sometimes they are memories of those heavier later years, when, although she seemed to fade a little more each day, Mama could still join in. But worst of all are the memories of that heart-stopping moment when Mama said, "At least you will have *Bibi* to look after you when I am gone, my child. She adores you, you know."

"Mama, please don't say such things. Please," Eva had cried, automatically running to help *Bibi* remove a bundle of firewood from her head, and then watching as she carefully unknotted her *khanga* cloth to reveal some spinach-like *mchicha*. "Look what I found near the forest today."

Eva's mother had just smiled and stretched out her arms, as though to hold them both. Then, quietly, "*Bibi* will need all your strength, Eva." Such a short exchange, but still deeply etched in Eva's mind more than a decade later as she cradles her *Bibi*, trying to coax a little *uji*, maize meal porridge, past her lips.

《•》《•》《•》《•》

"Phew! Thank goodness that's done, Vicky!" The Foxes' NGO is now formally registered as a charity at last. "We can finally sink our teeth into actually getting on with building the orphanage."

"And none too soon," Vicky answers. "Not a day goes by without hearing of someone else who has died, and seeing folks wasting away.

Not that they ever admit to having HIV/AIDS, but it's written all over their emaciated bodies."

"Imagine the children left behind! I can't wait to get started."

"Well, Foxey, thanks to the village, we have land and people eager to work. Thanks to fundraising in the UK and the US we have some money. Not a bad start, I would say."

"Things really do seem to be coming together on every front, don't they, Mrs. Fox?"

"You mean the good news, too, about the Mufindi Forest Initiative?"

"Yes. I'm also rather pleased about that! I hear that the communities in our area have finally signed joint management agreements with the government to stop all logging there. At last count, I heard that sawyers were buying licences to cut down one tree and routinely using the same licence to fell up to 100 trees."

"Poor forests."

"And water catchments. And downstream communities. At least now there will be some recourse against illegal logging."

"Only if they can find other ways of making money."

"Apparently, the Initiative is also helping them to do that."

HELGA VOIGT'S
LAST VISIT TO TANZANIA

Soon an emotional reunion is taking place with another grandmother, this time at the Ruaha River Lodge, where Geoff is hugging his old friend Helga Voigt, now eighty-eight. She is on her final visit to Tanzania with her daughters and friends from Canada. "There's where Vicky and Evelyn carried rocks on their heads to prove that they could work as hard as any male," Geoff says pointing upwards. "There's where the water pump broke down, forcing the men — for the first time in their lives — to carry water. 'It's hard work,' they said. 'We thought, because it's women's work, it must be easy.'

"'Now, will you tell your wives how much you admire them?' Vicky joked. They just laughed."

Halfway up the *kopje* toward the eyrie that is the Baobab Bar (Gordon's favourite bar in the world), hyraxes block the footpath. They look like a cross between a groundhog and a teddy bear, with the hind legs of a rabbit and the agility of a klipspringer antelope. More hyraxes gather not three feet from where some fellow tourists are relishing wine and ice-cold beer ("Yes, Geoff," Helga jokes, "with the condensation running down the outside of the glass!"); other sun-bleached reminiscences of the day include the rare sighting of a pregnant cheetah.

Below them, as far as the eye can see: the Ruaha River, baobabs, animals, and even distant rainstorms falling like lace curtains, now in blues and greys against the evening sky, now gilded by the drama of a blood-red setting sun.

Supper was to have been a barbecue under the stars. Instead, a short shower forces them into the Fox lodge's thatched dining area. Pre-dinner drinks are served beyond a canopy of flying ants — termites — enjoying their short-lived wedding flight after the rain. Already some have landed on the floor, shed their wings, and walked off in pairs, one leading the other, to found new colonies. A gourmet dinner follows.

The next day, several people in Helga's party favour game drives. Others prefer the solitude of private verandas, enveloped by the teeming silences of Africa. Even the river seems thirsty today, although the rains have finally started. Elephants are beginning to follow the sweetness of new shoots farther inland. Only waterbuck remain. And birds, gracefully sweeping the sky with dance and display. One lands on a nearby twig. It preens. It struts. Its tail glows turquoise, as veins beat a delicate tattoo under its neon-tangerine throat (where are the birdwatchers when one needs them in this heat-drugged Ruaha at noon?).

Lazy Lagoon Revisited

All too soon, Helga's party has to bid farewell to the Foxes in Ruaha and head back toward the coast. Their flight begins with the pilot checking out some vultures wheeling overhead (to make sure they are out of harm's way) and taxiing the light aircraft past a giraffe, its tongue seeking rain-swollen leaves at the edge of the runway. Lions shrink beneath them as the plane rises. Are they part of that twenty-one-member pride seen the day before?

A kaleidoscope of Tanzania, etched in fragments of Foxtreks

memories, rewinds their earlier journey, this time from Ruaha, over Iringa and Mikumi, back to Dar es Salaam. And finally by bus on to Mbegani, from where Werner first glimpsed his "island" eighty years before. Only a short boat ride, and then, at last, they are there.

"The Lazy Lagoon eco-lodge is amazing," Helga enthuses. Alexander Fox has managed to tread very lightly on "island" flora and fauna even as he caters for the creature comforts of tourists. Spacious the dining and gathering areas may be, but they do not overpower. Neither do the

Lazy Lagoon … miles of beach.
(Gord Breedyk)

twelve individual guest cottages, luxurious yet authentic with their Zanzibari-style furnishings under traditional palm-frond thatching. Each overlooks the Indian Ocean to absorb every available breeze in this world of sand, sea, and sumptuous meals — of an evening served on the beach under African stars. Bliss.

"WHEN I GROW UP, I WILL HELP OTHERS LIKE ME"

Back in Mufindi, eleven year-old Eva's grandmother has given up her exhausted hold on life. Eva moves in with cousin-sisters and brothers in the village. Almost immediately, her foster parents fall sick and, ailing themselves, can no longer care for Eva. She moves to more distant relatives, closer to the Fox farm. Again, AIDS drives her out.

These are difficult years for everybody, given layer upon layer of overcrowding in cash-strapped foster homes: some of them warm and welcoming despite it all, others not. Regardless of the welcome, Eva is always acutely aware of being the outsider, of being an extra mouth when they can hardly afford to feed their own. The only thing she can do in return is to serve them well while under their roofs and eat as little as possible. Touched by someone's unexpected kindness toward her one day, Eva vows, "When I grow up, I will help other children like me."

A few miles away, Felisita is still tiny for her age, but what she lacks in size she makes up for in determination. Nothing seems to stop her. Her mother is grateful, for she can no longer manage all the work. Felisita is supposed to be in school. But how are they to afford her school uniform? And who will help fetch the wood and water? Who will keep the fire going under the *uji* and potatoes? Even now, Felisita is blowing the embers and rearranging pieces of wood more evenly between the fire stones.

"Don't forget to give it a good stir," her mother calls. Felisita notices Mama's voice is not as strong as it used to be. She worries.

SAADANI GAZETTED AS NATIONAL PARK

Several hills farther on, the sound of a ringing phone still shocks the Fox household. One never knows. Geoff picks up. It's Alexander, their Dar es Salaam-based son and king of schmoozers.

"Good news, Vicky!" Geoff tells her at last. "Alexander says it's official: Tanzania has finally gazetted Saadani as a full-blown national park!" Vicky, who is putting on her gumboots before heading out for her evening tour of the farm with Julius, stops, drops the boot, rushes over to Geoff and takes the phone. "Brilliant," she shouts. "Brilliant! Brilliant! Brilliant!"

"Brilliant, indeed!" Vicky and Geoff hug and laugh. "Even if it took more than a couple of years to happen." In fact, it's about a decade since the proposed sale of Mkwaja Ranch prompted the Foxes to facilitate the merger between Mkwaja and the Saadani game reserve, thereby tripling its size.

《•》《•》《•》《•》

Recent visitors to Saadani, now staying at the Fox Highland Lodge in Mufindi, bemoan disappointing game sightings in the new national park, although they do agree that it does live up to its exotic status as the only park where the bush meets the beach. They just wish they had seen more of its wildlife.

"When the Ruaha Park was first created in 1964, there was almost no game there, either," Geoff responds over drinks. "And now look at it! Vicky—pregnant with Christopher at the time—and I travelled through Ruaha in November 1963. We walked all day and saw nothing but a hyrax. Today, there is game everywhere, apart from rhino (which were eliminated in the early 1980s) and buffalo (which have been badly reduced, initially by the bush-meat trade and then by a burgeoning lion population).

"Watch out! Geoff's on his favourite soapbox," someone jokes.

"No problem, Geoff. We're listening."

Geoff needs no further prompting. "All you need is a breeding nucleus, protection, and time. John Savidge agrees. He was Ruaha's park warden for eight years, succeeding Ruaha's first warden, 'Steve' Stephenson. At that time, John knew of only a single pride of lion and some zebra across the river. He couldn't believe that Ruaha is now crawling with wildlife.

"Saadani has the same potential. I know that the breeding nucleus of an exciting variety of wildlife is there. It just needs time and protection against poachers, especially by TANAPA. Sadly, while camping there, members of our family have recently heard shooting at night. There doesn't seem to be the same enthusiasm about protecting the area as when we were at Mkwaja. Now folks seem to see it as just a job, as in 'why go out and risk your life for animals?'

"Mind you, conservation has to be balanced with understanding how harsh life can be for people living on the outskirts. I remember on one of my safaris passing a small settlement with what was left of its adjacent maize *shamba*. It was supposed to feed them for a year. Instead, a large herd of elephants destroyed it in a single night.

JENNY PECK
MEETS GEOFF KNIGHT

Continents away, at about the same time, a young student named Jenny Peck is rushing to a meeting on the University of Kansas campus in America. With long chestnut hair flying behind her, she bursts into the room. Geoff Knight stands up to greet her. Little do they know it, but their lives, too, are soon to mesh with those of Geoff and Vicky.

"Hi. You must be Jenny, president of women's rugby, right?"

"And you must be Geoff K, president of the student hockey team and Emily's 'cool brother.'"

They both laugh. Jenny has recently recruited Geoff K's doting sister onto the girls' rugby team. After chatting for a while about their respective sports programs and studies (anthropology, biology, and mathematics), they go their separate ways. He has a girlfriend. She is seriously involved with another man. Every once in a while they bump into each other. There's always lots to chat about. Not just hockey and rugby, but also music (he plays guitar and banjo, she the viola) and dreams. Jenny's is to go overseas with the Peace Corps.

"That's awesome!" Geoff K enthuses.

"Glad you think so," Jenny says. "My boyfriend is less than impressed. In fact, it may be our undoing."

Geoff K's adrenalin spikes. His own relationship hasn't worked out and he finds it increasingly difficult to resist Jenny's sparkling eyes, infectious energy, and boundless warmth. They start spending more time together, ostensibly working on the Peace Corps' long, drawn-out application process for Jenny.

The day Jenny finds out that she is going to Tanzania, Geoff K says: "I've always wanted to do something different than Kansas. I'm coming, too."

Had Jenny been rejected by the Peace Corps, Geoff K would have asked her to marry him then and there. As it is, he doesn't want to put her in a difficult spot by not letting her have her Peace Corps experience. So they agree that he will stay on at the university, coaching hockey and finishing his degree. "This way I can wait to find out which village they send you to. Otherwise, I might end up on the other side of Tanzania."

PRESIDENT KIKWETE

On November 5, 2005, Tanzania elects its fourth president, Jakaya Mrisho Kikwete—once more on an anti-graft platform. Distraught communities, struggling to feed their orphans, pray that he will live up to his promises better than his predecessor. They are tired of new high-rises and luxury hotels blatantly being financed by civil servants and politicians with relatively tiny official salaries.

MAMA REHEMA'S AILING BABY

Mama Rehema is among the desperate. In her case, it's because medical bills are threatening to overwhelm her little family. She finally has a second child. But something is terribly wrong. Instead of gaining weight, her baby is thin. Instead of bursting with energy, her baby is still. Instead of smiling, her baby whimpers.

Yet again today, Mama Rehema sets off on the long journey to a hospital. First she walks for hours to catch the bus. Another few hours pass before she is deposited at the turnoff to Mdabulo—hours she should be spending working on the *shamba* to grow their food, or fetching water or wood. Then more walking before she finally reaches the hospital. Each time, it is the same story: A brief examination, followed by medicine—which she can hardly afford—then some short-term relief. And finally back to the clinic again for another round. At least her first-born, little Rehema, is thriving.

ORPHANAGE FOUNDATIONS

"Welcome to the future Igoda children's village!" Geoff says. He and Mary Ellis are walking "on a beautiful hillside about a half mile, as the crow flies, from both the Fox Farm house and Igoda village,"[61] she later reports back to the United States. Bob's wife is on a site-visit from Oregon, where Mufindi Orphans Inc. is now successfully raising funds for the Foxes' NGO.

Yesterday, she presented a Certificate of Directorship to Julius Mdegela, long-term Fox employee, now farm headman and NGO champion. (Also, incidentally, the same Julius who helped Vicky with the coffee farm below the escarpment decades earlier and has helped Geoff to find and prepare their mutual burial site.)

"We've lots to show you, Mary!" Geoff enthuses. He is in his element. Decades of living in Mufindi and fluency in Swahili, not to mention excellent relationships with Igoda elders, are standing him in good stead as he plans and supervises construction in one of the

---

61 Geoff Knight, Project Administration Manager Foxes' Community and Wildlife Conservation Trust (Tanzania), Habari Ya Mufindi, Quarterly Newsletter 1, no. 1 (31 March 2006), **http://www.mufindiorphans.org**. The quarterly newsletter is designed to inform donors about progress made in the implementation of the Mufindi Highlands Orphans Project in the Mufindi District of Tanzania, East Africa.

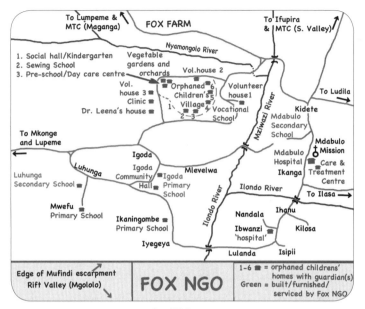

Fox NGO map.
(Evelyn Voigt, based on Geoff's sketch, 2013)

poorest regions of Tanzania.

"Here's how folks level the ground when they have no heavy equipment, not even a wheelbarrow." He points to where villagers are dragging heavy hessian sacks, filled with rocks, back and forth over the site.

"And remember the massive rocks that used to be here? Well, they had to be removed to make way for our orphans' houses on their sites. Dynamite? No, I would blow my fingers off! Instead, Vicky found the solution in an old history book. Fire and water! We burn the rock all day under a hot fire and then, in the evening, pour drums of cold water over it. The sounds of the stone cracking are like gunshots. Two days of sledgehammering follow before the process is repeated—until there is nothing left except for broken pieces that are then used for building."

"Brilliant," says Mary.

"As you can see, the dormitories will circle around the head of a small valley." Geoff is now pointing at six house sites. "That way, our 'Children's Village' can look and feel like any other hamlet around here, with orphans as closely linked to their communities and traditions as possible. We are trying to set things up in such a way that as the children get older, they can comfortably reintegrate into normal

Cracking boulders using hot and cold water, in the absence of heavy machinery, at the Foxes' Children's Village site.

village life. That's why we now prefer to call it the Igoda Children's Village, rather than 'orphanage.'

"We've already identified a candidate for the position of matron to oversee the Children's Village startup and health-care planning. She is a trained Tanzanian nurse. Better yet, she grew up in Mufindi as part of a well-respected family living close by, so she will likely stay a long time. This is a deliberate strategy. We can't have parental figures coming and going. That would be too hard on children already orphaned by HIV/AIDS. Yet these are all just stopgap measures. It's not enough simply to house children affected by HIV/AIDS. There's also education to think of. And health care. What the NGO needs is lasting solutions so we can work more systematically in all these areas."

Miracle Sponsors

Little do the Foxes know it, but help to do just that is on its way in the form of two Canadian couples touring Tanzania. Like other Highland Lodge guests, they love Geoff's stories. His growing fixation with the NGO is also infectious. And, of particular interest to the wives, would be a chance to tour a typical school.

"Why not join me on my rounds tomorrow," Geoff offers. "I need to touch base with Igoda Primary School anyway about our future HIV/AIDS orphans. We could visit the Children's Village site on the way back."

Ruth James and Anne Pearson are delighted. "A research study in Igoda Village a few years ago," Geoff says on the road the next day, "found that the average woman works sixteen hours a day, whilst the average man works only six hours. Fetching firewood and water are two very time-consuming tasks. So we decided to plant twenty acres of eucalyptus on our farmland near the orphanage over there." As he speaks, he expertly manoeuvres the land cruiser around a deep rut in the track with one hand, while pointing through the window with the other. "They will provide the hard-pressed Igoda women with an ongoing supply of firewood and house-building material."

"Why eucalyptus?" Anne wants to know.

"Eucalyptus doesn't die after felling," Geoff answers. "It recoppices, or regenerates. Many thousands of additional, potted eucalyptus seedlings are now in the hands of villagers to plant nearer their houses. Three deep well hand pumps are also already under installation so the women won't need to walk so far to get water, but many more are needed.[62] Since much of the care for orphans is falling on grandmothers these days, the NGO is also looking at other ways of helping them to keep their grandchildren at home."

Ruth and Anne witness how Geoff's plans for the NGO are clearly anchored in strong community support and decades of Fox experience. And the Igoda schoolchildren are amazing—a sea of smiling faces despite walking miles on empty stomachs to reach these crumbling and overcrowded facilities.

Of 506 children currently registered, the head teacher shows them his figures of fifty-four children who have no parents. Another 166 have lost one parent. And there are even twelve-year-old "heads of their household" looking after younger siblings who have to grow their own food. Despite all this, the children look cheerful.

"What do you think?" Ruth murmurs.

"Definitely," Anne replies. About to retire, the two experienced teachers are looking for opportunities to contribute, recognize potential when they see it and, as luck would have it, are not lacking in resources.

Geoff does not know this when he says, "What our NGO needs is somebody like Bill Gates to take an interest and help us with

---

62   Geoff Fox, Habari Ya Mufindi, Quarterly Newsletter 2, no. 3 (September 2007), **http://www.mufindiorphans.org**.

Miracle workers Anne Pearson and Ruth James in Mufindi.
(Foxes NGO)

operational funds, so we know that we won't leave the orphans high and dry at some point, not to mention help us do all the other things we have in mind."

"I know someone who might help," Ruth James replies.

"And who might that be?"

"My husband." It turns out that Don James has built up the Canadian franchise for Harley-Davidson motorcycles and frequently gives back to the community.

With his backing, the "Teenage Grannies" as Geoff soon fondly calls Ruth and Anne ("because they are such fun and always giggling") pledge an amazingly generous annual donation to support NGO operations and maintenance for ten years.

"That should give us all time to get our feet under us and start handing things over to the Tanzanians," a beaming Geoff later tells Vicky. They are on a short walk — still their long-time daily ritual, if at all possible.

Today it takes them through a remnant of virgin forest, smelling faintly of sodden wood. Around them, thriving in damp nooks and crannies, behind peeling bark, are intricate miniature gardens of mosses and tree orchids. Above them, windswept branches creak and sway gently, while buckled roots break up fertile ground beneath. Only the muted calls of pigeons, the harsh cry of a Livingstone's turaco — crested, green, a splash of scarlet on its wings — and eternal cricket stridulations enliven the forest's otherwise cool, dark mystery. Timeless. Beside them now, still water. Not a ripple. Refreshed, they return, Vicky to run the farm, and Geoff to chat with guests in the lodge, two of whom suddenly ask if they could be married there.

First Highland Lodge Wedding

The first Highland Lodge wedding, a very small and relatively impromptu affair, takes place in the "secret" garden (a profusion of tropical and temperate blossoms in rainbow colours among ferns, caves, rocks, and palms morphing into a croquet lawn). The bridegroom, a Peace Corps field director, has arranged for the lady district commissioner to officiate.

"Being polite, I asked her if she would like to drink something before we start," Geoff later recalls, "to which the district commissioner responded: 'Yes, please. Have you got a Ballantyne's whisky?' and promptly kicked off her high heels and started the ceremony—with support from her 'district office assistant' (a.k.a. Geoff Fox).

"She then explained that she first had to tick a box asking whether the bridegroom (brides not being given the choice) wished to have a monogamous or polygamous marriage. The bride swung her head and fixed her groom with a hard stare. There followed a moment's silence, whereupon I interrupted (Vicky and I were sitting in directors' chairs as witnesses directly behind them). 'I feel I have to explain. In Tanzania, if anyone committed to a monogamous marriage takes another wife without divorcing his first, he is breaking the law; whereas, if he chooses a polygamous union, he will not be breaking the law.'

"The bride continued her hard, fixed stare. This seemed to wilt the groom into replying quietly, 'monogamous.' All lodge visitors had been recruited as wedding guests. They performed admirably, dressing up for the occasion.

"I couldn't resist arranging for the honeymoon cabin girl to slip a very large, rubber tarantula in between the sheets of the double bed. This wasn't discovered until around two in the morning. I later got the impression that the Americans were not exactly amused. It was dark. The generator was off."

OF SNAKES AND SCORPIONS

Vicky to Libby: "I had a fright last weekend when I was in Ruaha. As Andi, the barman, was coming out of the bar, I walked straight over a snake and he stood on it without shoes on. It bit him. His foot swelled up. The Tanzanians cut into the bite and strapped on the special 'snakebite stone.' I got really worried, but we put a tourniquet on, prayed hard, kept our fingers crossed, etcetera. Thank heavens he was all right. It was very nerve-wracking. Then I walked back into the dining room to find an enormous six-inch long black scorpion. Fortunately, they're not as poisonous as the little ones. What a night."

DELICIOUS CREEPY-CRAWLIES

Meanwhile, little Felisita is celebrating the arrival of some delicious creepy-crawlies. "*Kumbi kumbi!*[63] *Kumbi kumbi* are flying!" She laughs out loud, grabs one by its wings, watches it wriggle to shed them and, once detached, fall into her little *kopo*, tin can, positioned at the ready. As her *kopo* slowly fills with ants, her mouth waters. She is tempted to sample a few, can just imagine their delicious, buttery taste. Tempting. But, no, Felisita decides to take them all home to Mama. Perhaps they will help make her strong. Once there, she carefully transfers her treasures to a clay pot balanced on stones above embers, and watches the precious ants fry in their own fat.

"Mama," the little girl says at last, "*kumbi kumbi!*" Mama smiles.

"Well done, child." Not wanting her daughter to worry about her lack of appetite, she adds: "Now, let's share them with everybody." The little girl sees nothing unusual in this. She is used to such "communality" (although too young to associate it with the traditional *ujamaa* Mwalimu Nyerere once hoped to apply nationally).

JENNY PECK ARRIVES IN MUFINDI

Several miles away, a newly minted American Peace Corps volunteer begins teaching at a secondary school in Mufindi, eyes sparkling, infectious laugh, and brimming over with typical Jenny Peck energy.

---

63   Flying ants.

It is 2006. She is finally in Tanzania, and well prepared for this great adventure—or so she thinks.

What she has not counted on is the horrifying impact of HIV/AIDS on Mdabulo Secondary School. "It's the elephant in the room that's getting to me," she writes to Geoff K, her energy beginning to erode. "Nobody is admitting to the disease even though it's all around us. Just as they said during Peace Corps training, the very mention of AIDS seems to be taboo. Nobody wants to get tested because it is like a death sentence. And even if they are brave enough to be tested, they cannot afford the treatment. Women risk being thrown out of their homes and even physical violence. Quite aside from the social stigma, treatment is a four- to eight-hour bus ride there and the same back at a cost of up to ten dollars [about £6.50]. Most people here live on one dollar [about £0.65] a day. They just don't have that kind of time or money."

"Since nothing can be done right here, it's better not to know," Jenny's colleagues tell her. "And if you do know, it's better to keep quiet. Even when you die, it's better that your family says it was malaria, tuberculosis, or some other disease (which, by the way, are curable, unless you also have AIDS). Otherwise, your remaining relatives will suffer."

"The customary system is falling apart. Before HIV/AIDS, people always took orphans into their own homes and raised them. Now they are overloaded up to the tipping point, where they can no longer take in any more kids, and have started turning them away or treating them as farm slaves." Another day. Another letter to Geoff K. "And there are so many children that need caregivers! As tradition demands, the more affluent are still housing and educating their less-advantaged siblings, nephews, and nieces. Only now, many of them are themselves too sick to keep their jobs—others too poor to take in yet another child or grandparent. Classrooms are without teachers. Not just because of ill health, but also because of funerals, caring for patients, and helping to nurse or take in relatives. And school-age children stay home because they have to grow their own food. Many are living in dangerous situations. Twelve-year-old girls are looking after their brothers and sisters. Their basic rights aren't being met—health care, education, a safe place to sleep, and having someone they can depend on as a guardian. It's all a bit overwhelming."[64]

---

64   Adapted from *Alice's Story*, by Georgia Bagnall. This film was made, produced, edited, and

JUMP-STARTING
THE FOXES' EDUCATIONAL OUTREACH

Meanwhile, now retired, the "Canadian grannies," Ruth and Anne, show Geoff and Vicky how serious they are about helping, not just financially, but also practically. Others might be discouraged by Igoda School's ranking near the bottom of 149 district schools and more than 837 regional schools. Not these two seasoned teachers.

Drawing on decades of experience back home and a natural instinct for consultation, not to mention their infectious sense of fun, they roll up their sleeves and start exploring options with Tanzanian teachers, administrators, students, and Ministry of Education officials — not to mention Geoff (the fixer) and Vicky (the fellow teacher), both fluent in Swahili.

As weeks, then months, go by, the Igoda staff and students are soon fully engaged. How could they not be amid the fun and laughter — but also solid educational expertise — of these two irrepressible pensioners?

Slowly and gradually, the Fox educational outreach strategy takes shape (in consultation with the Ministry to make sure that the NGO does not saddle Igoda School with expenses it cannot maintain in the future).

Igoda School classrooms are to double, from six to twelve, with additional toilet facilities. This will reduce the average class size from ninety to forty-five and make room for orphans not previously able to attend school due to lack of space. The NGO will also renovate old classrooms and convert one into a "teaching library" before starting on improving the water supply, with funds from the African Children's Book Box Society[65] in Canada and supplies, including books, to be brought in by Orphans in the Wild (UK).

"After painting and fully equipping all classrooms, not just the six new ones, we hope that the Igoda School will serve as a role model that other schools in the region will emulate," an ebullient

uploaded by Georgia Bagnall, sixteen years of age, to highlight the plight of women and children in a small community in Tanzania suffering from HIV/AIDS. It is based on actual footage of, and interviews with, the community. http://vimeo.com/61104860

65   http://www.africanbookbox.org/about_us.html

Geoff enthuses at every opportunity.

OF RATS AND CATS AND RUGBY

One such opportunity presents itself in the form of Jenny Peck. Much to the Foxes' astonishment, she has just walked over from Mdabulo. Even more amazing, she arrives with a rugby ball under her arm and a huge grin on her face.

"Hi," she says in greeting when they answer her knock at their door. "I'm your neighbour, Jenny. I hope you don't mind. One of my students told me there were other *wazungu* [white folks] living in this area."

"It was a Saturday," she writes home to Geoff K on December 10, 2006, "and I started missing you, so I told myself I had to get out of my house. So I took a walk to a place called Fox Farms. Met this crazy (eccentric) older couple, which I already LOVE! We talked about my project here. Then for a long time we talked about you. Told them you were coming and about how we weren't sure what you would do . . . and I am so excited to TALK to you about all this! Got a lot of ideas to pass your way. Vicky and Geoff (yes, he's also called Geoff!) gave me a kitten, because I had mentioned rats. Of course, I had the rugby ball with me, so we were best friends right away . . . I miss YOU so much!"

ORPHANAGE GROWING PAINS AND JOYS

Jenny's home is on the distant hill, as seen from the Fox farm.
(Jenny Peck)

All too soon, the Foxes realize that starting an orphanage is more complicated than they first thought, especially since they want to make sure it is fully integrated into the community. Bridging village priorities and overseas funding involves time-consuming, but crucial, dialogue with community leaders. Luckily, Geoff's Swahili is fluent, and he can draw on years of trust between the Foxes and Igoda. Even so, the NGO threatens to overwhelm him, given the ongoing Highland Lodge and other Foxtreks demands on his time.

Then, miracle of miracles—a Canadian doctor and his wife volunteer their services. "Full time," Geoff exults. "And at no cost to our NGO!"

"Welcome to Mufindi," Geoff and Vicky greet Dr. Patrick Ney, wife Kate, and their three children. "You can't imagine how glad we are to see you. And truly amazed that you would volunteer two years of your time."

"We are looking forward to our new adventure in Mufindi," Patrick says. "It is such a beautiful place. And what a great undertaking."

"We'll do everything we can to help out!"

《•》《•》《•》《•》

Shock is the only word to describe Patrick's and Kate's first impressions as Geoff shows them around the project area. Most hospitals within a 100-kilometre radius of Igoda are non-functional. There are only a few dispensaries for 40,000 people, and all of them need referrals from distant medical centres just to dispense pills.

"Here we are at Mdabulo Mission Hospital, the best in this part of Mufindi," Geoff says. Patrick and Kate take in the rusted roofing, the crumbling walls of bricks and mortar, the crowded waiting lines and all but empty dispensary shelves.

"Mdabulo was built seventy years ago by resident Italian priests with connections to foreign funding sources," Geoff explains. "Now it depends on what impoverished villagers can pay for the aspirins and anti-malarials the hospital can still afford to stock."

"You're right, Geoff," Patrick says at last. "Rather than doing clinical work, I should probably focus on helping to rebuild and extend medical facilities." With that, he and Geoff start planning how to convert Mdabulo (one room at a time, as funds permit) into a "referral" hospital, and the little Ibwanzi clinic into a health centre.

Meanwhile, Kate focuses on two major tasks: an NGO census (to get a better picture of the HIV/AIDS status in surrounding villages); and accommodation for the children. Villagers (grateful for the employment) have already constructed three buildings under Geoff's supervision, as well as clearing the ground and preparing the site for the whole complex.

Now the rush is on to complete what seems to be an endless to-do list so some orphans can move in before the first downpour! This way, they will at least have a temporary roof over their heads until they can be placed with relatives. Only children without surviving relatives are to enter the orphanage permanently, and, of these, the most needy first, as identified by the villagers. Negotiations with the elders will add more time to Geoff's already staggering schedule.

MY NAME IS ALICE

Several miles away, Peace Corps volunteer Jenny is becoming ever more despondent about the silence around HIV infection. Then one day she hears, "*Hodi, hallo*," at her front door.

"*Karibu*, please come in," she calls, her Swahili improving by the day. Before her stands a painfully thin woman. Two children, dressed in tatters, peek out from behind her threadbare *kanga* cloth. Jenny smiles. "*Jambo*, hello, Mama. I'm Jenny. How can I help you?"

"My name is Alice," the woman says. She is clearly nervous, but determined. Deep breath. Then, in a rush, "I am HIV positive. I don't know where the father of my children is. He left years ago. I am dying. I cannot leave my children with their grandmother. She is too old. There is no one else. Can you help me get treatment?"

Jenny is dumbfounded. Despite all the taboos, here is one courageous woman willing to look the stigma in the face and say, "I'm not ready to die." But how to help? Already Jenny is dipping into her monthly income of $200 (about £65) to provide a granny with school uniforms for her orphaned grandchildren . . . and an ailing widow to clothe her children . . . Above all, she is promoting HIV testing and treatment. Her motto: "Every conversation is a learning opportunity." But how to help Alice get regular transport for treatment? She walks over to the Fox farm.

Once there, Jenny finds Geoff and Patrick. "No other woman

has dared to speak out openly like this," she says. "Surely her courage should be rewarded."

"You're right. This could set a very significant example to others," Geoff says. Patrick agrees.

"And hopefully justifies using NGO funds to pay her bus fare to the nearest HIV/AIDS treatment centre?" Jenny crosses her fingers.

"Absolutely. An opportunity like this does not present itself often!"

Within a week, Jenny is back. "So exciting," she tells Geoff and Patrick. "Every day Alice brings by one more person and says, 'She is my friend. She also is HIV positive. Can you help her?' I hope we can."

The Fox NGO agrees to pay for their transportation as well. Two weeks later Jenny reports that more and more people are coming forward for testing because they know they will be treated.

She can now also share her excitement in person with Geoff K. He has finally made it to Tanzania just in time to witness the miracle. Together, the young couple marvel as, after only eight weeks, more than 200 people a month are landing on their doorstep asking for bus fares to get treatment.

"Alice is one of my biggest heroes, a true ambassador for good health," Jenny enthuses. "She is changing everything. It's not just that 200 people have started treatment because of her example, but that 200 people a month, and their families, are now being open about their status—unprecedented in an area where HIV/AIDS is such a taboo topic!"

FOXTREKS FLYING HIGH

Also unprecedented is Tanzania's increasing support for private ventures. Combined with steady income from their camps, Foxtreks can now buy more light aircraft. Under son Peter's watchful eye and piloting, this affords easier access by tourists to their equally expanding network of lodges. It helps that Peter can fix anything, including airplanes.

"Peter is an excellent pilot, the best of the lot," according to proud Papa Fox. "By law, all Foxtreks maintenance has to be done by a certified mechanic, but Peter always double-checks their work to make sure they've done it right. He is also a deadpan joker. At Mkwaja, he took up my assistants for their first-ever flights, entered the cloud above, and pretended to be lost, which caused a certain level of alarm.

"Another time, a fellow pilot boarded an aircraft. He sat down among the passengers in his casual dress, as was the norm for bush pilots in those days, pretending to be a passenger. Takeoff time was fast approaching. No sign of the pilot. Seemingly impatient, he announced that if the pilot didn't come soon, he would fly the plane himself—and did.

"On one occasion, with me sitting in the copilot's seat and with two first-time, light aircraft passengers sitting behind him, Peter started to look puzzled, stared at his aviation map, turned it upside-down, and then asked me to pass him a tattered old Shell road map from the side pocket of the door next to me. Looking perplexed, he stared at the map, then craned his neck to peer out of both windows—the epitome of a pilot lost . . . A little while later, he landed perfectly and on time at Ngwazi. Everyone on board, including me, had forgotten that these days, aircraft fly on GPS!

"Ngwazi," Geoff continues, "is where Longstaff once lived, when he managed the estate for, I think, a German owner—although it was Lord Chesham who later sold the land to Brooke Bond. I was told that the Germans used to shoot one hippo from the original swamp annually to keep their family in cooking fat for a whole year. Cyril Dye later dammed the swamp with soil brought in by ox cart.

"More recently, a bull hippo lived in the lake for two or more years, frequenting the sailing club area. It had wandered up the Great Ruaha to the Little Ruaha, past Iringa, then through the Mkewe Swamp that forms the headwaters of the Ruaha River (near Mother Pretorius's; later, the Seventh Day Adventists' farm) and ultimately to Lake Ngwazi. That was quite the journey for a hippo, made gradually over several years. But sadly, just because it frightened the tea company's general manager by emerging in front of his kayak, it was snared and shot. Health and safety!

"*Idara ya Kichaa Cha Unilever* (the Department of Unilever Madness, otherwise known as Health and Safety) has also put up notices everywhere prohibiting fishing, bathing, and washing clothes in Mufindi dams, which we stocked with black bass to provide protein for everyone.

"I love Ngwazi. The climate is beautiful, with its blue lake a mile across each way. We always dreamed of living on the hill behind the sailing club. Happily, however, our good friends Peter Rowland and his wife, Co, now live in an amazing house overlooking the lake behind the sailing club, just where we ourselves once planned to live.

FOXES' "QUAINT OLDE ENGLISH HOUSE" IN AFRICA

Even though the Foxes' dreams of living at Ngwazi never materialize, they are finally able to build their "Quaint Olde English House in Africa" as Geoff calls their gracious stone home at the Fox farm. "It was pretty well designed on the back of an envelope," he tells visitors. "I am not impressed by lawyers and architects! The former write in unintelligible English, and the latter draw in hieroglyphics that no one else can understand—both obviously intending just to protect their jobs. For twenty years, we lived in what was intended as (and now is) our farm office," pointing vaguely beyond recessed windows and the prominent gable, beyond where a sloping English lawn meets African bush.

"It took that long to build up various infrastructures needed for our tourism business, including the farm. At last, while on leave in the UK, we visited friends who lived in a lovely English house, built in 1925. 'We're going to build your house on our farm in Tanzania,' we told them. And, surprisingly, they produced a coloured outline drawing of the ground plan—not an architectural drawing, mind, but it was a great help.

"After juggling a bit and multiplying by one-and-a-half, I drew

Foxes' "Quaint Olde English House in Africa."
(Gord Breedyk)

the blueprint on graph paper. My first manager in Mufindi, Derrick Hester, taught me how to do that. And I have followed his advice for more than fifty years. Being too old to adapt to metric, of course, everything is in feet, i.e., one graph square equals one foot. This makes it easy for artisans to work out various lengths by simply counting the squares.

"And here it is, our '1925 Olde English House in Africa,' brilliantly built by village craftsmen — no planning officer, no building regulations, no architects, no Health and Safety — just freedom. As for the total cost of our large, stone-built, double-storeyed, spacious house, with a covered upstairs balcony, downstairs veranda, and three ensuite bedrooms?" he asks rhetorically: "The price of a reasonably good new car, with stone and sand and timber all from, and around, our farm!

"For a while, I was extremely pleased, but then along comes my oldest son, Christopher, who is now building his own home with considerably more skill than his father. His granite stonework is so skillfully shaped by local masons that cement can hardly be seen. It will be comparable with the best sandstone structures you see in England. I am very proud of what he's done, actually. However, whether we will ever make it out to dinner at Christopher's is, I fear, unlikely. By the time he has finished building, we will be long dead."

Mama Rehema Seeks Treatment

As the Foxes thrive, Mama Rehema's life is about to implode. A year and a half has passed since her second child was born, a child who seems to linger rather than live. Once again, Mama Rehema finds herself walking to the distant hospital. Once again, her tiny, painfully thin child hardly registers among its swaddling. Once again, Mama Rehema is looking up at a doctor.

"Can anything be done?" she asks. The doctor puts one hand on Mama Rehema's shoulder, the other around her infant.

"*Pole sana*, Mama. I'm so very sorry."

Mama Rehema's heart breaks. "AIDS," she says. "How is that possible?" Soon after, much too soon, her baby passes away.

"How is this possible?" she says again, this time to her husband. They have both tested HIV positive. "How?"

"I have been unfaithful," he finally admits.

She stares at him, momentarily shocked into silence. "Why did you not warn me?"

"What could we have done about it? Why frighten you for nothing?"

"But my friend Alice says that a new *msungu* foreigner near Mdabula is helping."

He pauses. "There is more." Deep breath. "I am thinking of taking the other woman as my second wife."

Mama Rehema, always ready with a joke, always laughing, always strong, breaks down. Beyond her sobs she gradually registers Rehema, tiny and terrified, clinging to her. She draws herself up to her full height. "Do that," she says. "But this is my house. We will stay here. You can go and live with her." Her husband looks down in disbelief. She does not lower her eyes in customary submission.

"No," he says, finally. "No. I will stay with you." ·

"On one condition," Mama Rehema responds. "We will go for HIV treatment together. Alice will show us where." He agrees. And that is how Mama Rehema first meets the "new *msungu*," Jenny Peck, and later, through Jenny, the Foxes.

Jenny immediately likes Mama Rehema. Against all odds, this strong woman is still bubbling over with fun and laughter. They now often visit villages together to connect with others once school is over—school and the extra tutoring Jenny offers several evenings a week. One day, a skeletal stranger greets them. Two children shyly peek out from behind her emaciated body. Jenny recognizes Issa and Willy.

It can't be, she thinks. It is.

"Hello, Alice," she says.

RESPITE

Sometimes with Geoff, sometimes alone, Vicky still periodically manages one or another Fox camp, so the kids can go on leave. These are times of hectic administrivia, interspersed with deep, deep regeneration. Today, she is at the Ruaha River Lodge. After a short rain shower, trees are sparkling, impala gambolling, and yellow weaverbirds entertaining. Brilliant feathered architects at work: One whirrs its wings near the entrance of a nest, courts the lady inside. Another has just formed a perfect circle of grass to mark out an entrance for its new home. Still another tests its branch of choice to see whether it can bear the weight of an extra nest. Huge battles go on all day. Not only battles, but strategies. These birds know that snakes will be after their young ones, so they even build emergency exits in new nests—but often continue to lay their eggs in old ones to further outwit their predators.

African Dreamku[66]

Thorn trees rake blue skies
Busy birds weave yellow dreams
Shadows dance

Vicky drinks it all in, relishes her rare moment of quiet. Before bed, she takes one last look at the miracle that is an African sky by night, scans silhouettes of bulbous baobab trees, and sees a single star, seemingly anchored for one stunning moment in the crook of a branch.

Felisita's World

Under the same stars, Felisita's tiny world is crumbling. *Babu*, Grandpa—too old to work—is nodding off under the threadbare family blanket. *Bibi*, Grandma, is moving ever slower. And now even *Baba*, Father, can no longer climb up to thatch their roof. With the dry season in full swing, it is cold at night, but at least there is no rain—yet.

She brings *Baba* a precious potato. He shakes his head and painfully lowers himself onto his sleeping mat. Then, one morning, he no longer moves at all. They bury him quietly behind the house. Felisita's mother does not say much, but she, too, is getting thinner.

Grandmother wails, "Why? Why? Why?"

The little girl helps out where she can. She rubs her grandmother's legs. She digs, she carries, she cooks and cleans. Still it is not enough. On top of everything else, she has to go to school.

---

66   Dreamku, coined by Roswila (a.k.a. Patricia Kelly), are Haiku-like poems about your night dreams. Evelyn's "African Dreamku" was earlier published by *Bout de Papier* 26, no. 4 (Fall 2012) and posted in 2009 by **http://www.roswila-dreamspoetry.blogspot.ca/**.

"It is the law," *Baba* always used to say. She could not add to his illness by telling him how much she hated it there—all that teasing, loneliness, and, worst of all, hearing about a bad disease the teachers called HIV/AIDS. Every word out of their mouths was like a stone hitting her, because every word described her father's condition.

Requiem for Alice

Alice passes away in May 2007. Jenny's only solace is somehow to make sure that her children, little Issa and Willy, are well taken care of. She walks to the Fox NGO. As it happens, an outreach visit is scheduled. "It may as well be Alice's village this time, Jenny," Kate tells her. "Why not come with us? Our social advisor, Hillary Lwanja [also a manager at Foxes' Highland Lodge], will join us. Hillary has deep roots around here and invaluable insights into how things are done."

They find Alice's grandmother, broken and bent, aged somewhere between eighty and ninety years. Alice was right. This frail old lady cannot possibly care for her great-grandchildren. Willy and Issa are both emaciated, covered in the ragged remains of clothes Jenny once gave Alice. Jenny bends down to hug them. Then gasps. "Look at Willy's mouth! It's completely covered in white. So is her tongue."

"Thrush," Kate says. "A fungal infection. Very uncomfortable. No wonder she's so thin. They clearly cannot stay here. We will try and have them admitted as the first occupants of the orphanage . . . even though it has not officially opened for permanent residents yet."

The village chairman agrees. And so it is that Alice's son and daughter, the first little occupants of the Children's Village, are scooped up into the loving arms of house mother Mama Lina Kyando.

"To Alice." Geoff K has bused in from where he is now teaching at a private school in Mafinga town. He raises his beer bottle, "to Alice."

"What a wonderful woman," Jenny murmurs, between sobs. "Poor as she was, she always wanted to help out—a born leader. Someone people could trust. And fun-loving. No wonder she had so many friends. In a way, she made it all happen. She broke the barrier of silence."

"Alice," Geoff K echoes, his arm around Jenny. "It will get better." They sit quietly for a while. Then Jenny adds, "Before Alice, no one around here was willing to talk about HIV. It only took one woman's courage to start a movement. She influenced a whole community ravaged by AIDS to take treatment and start living again."[67]

A NOSE AND TWO FRONT HOOVES

"Look at you, Foxey," Vicky says one day, "brimming over with enthusiasm. I would love to be more involved in the NGO myself. But there simply aren't enough hours in the day." With that, just as she does each morning and evening, she steps into her gumboots for her round of the farm with Julius.

A rather distraught herdsman informs them that a cow is having problems giving birth to her calf. Vicky runs with him back to where the cattle are grazing and after a quick assessment decides that the lesser of two evils is to take the whole herd back to the farm.

"We made an entertaining procession," she later tells Geoff. "As we crossed the bottom of the valley, we passed two visiting clergymen fishing from the dam wall. They were so intrigued that they packed away their fishing rods and followed along behind us. The calf by this time was showing a nose and two front hooves as its mother walked over a mile back to the paddock, where the two visitors watched us give her a helping hand to produce an enormous, very healthy bull calf immediately named Aidan after one of the clergymen."

OF ORPHANS, OUTREACH, HEALTH, AND EDUCATION

"How was the NGO meeting?" Vicky asks Geoff, who has just come in for lunch.

"The usual mix of good and bad news."

"Good news first, please."

"The government has agreed to take over Ibwanzi Clinic once we've upgraded it to a twenty-bed health centre. That's a first for the sixteen villages linked to our NGO!"

"Wonderful."

"And our outreach program has found homes for 124 orphans with surrogate families,"

"That's also wonderful, but can they afford it?"

---

67   Adapted from Georgia Bagnall, *Alice's Story,* **http://vimeo.com/61104860**

"The NGO will help out on a case-by-case basis, for example, if they can grow enough food for an extra mouth, but don't have the cash for house repairs, school uniforms, or buses to HIV and AIDS treatment.

"Now for the reality check. Our *HIV/AIDS Orphans Census* is confirming our worst fears." Geoff rubs his forehead distractedly as though somehow to erase the numbers. "Almost two-thirds of eighteen- to forty-year-olds have already contracted the disease in Igoda and three nearby villages."

"Two-thirds?"

"Actually, more like 60 percent. It's a bit lower for the general population (one in five) but shoots up again to every third person in areas adjacent to tea. Even worse, three clinics have unofficially, but independently, also found prenatal infection to be as high as two out of three births. This means that Mufindi is now Tanzania's most affected area, and confirms that seasonal tea workers are spreading the disease elsewhere."

"Oh, dear. Just as we thought. No luck yet, I suppose, with getting the tea companies to support our NGO?"

Geoff's expression says it all.

"You're right. Silly question . . . So what next?"

"We've decided to make youth education an outreach priority, including how to avoid infection. And, speaking of education, some more positive news: the last two classrooms are now almost complete at Igoda Primary School."

"God bless Ruth and Anne and their annual corn roast fundraiser in British Columbia."[68]

"God bless Alice, too. She really does seem to have opened a floodgate! The numbers of people now travelling to Mafinga town for treatment are so overwhelming that the government has agreed on a more practical approach. Instead of all the Mufindi patients going there, Mafinga Health Care staff will bring a mobile clinic to test blood and dispense medicines at the Mdabulo dispensary, twice a month."

"Right here? For the first time ever!"

"Indeed. It's going to take time to set up, but soon even more people will be able to access treatment relatively close by."

---

68   More details about the corn roast fundraiser can be found at **http://vimeo.com/61104860**.

Alice's daughter Willy and son Issa thriving
in the Children's Village.
(Fox NGO)

《·》《·》《·》《·》

As though to underscore the urgency, HIV/AIDS suddenly strikes Kate's and Patrick's own household. "Mama Ivan cooks for us," Kate writes to fundraisers abroad. "She is also my friend. She went to get tested for HIV last week, along with her daughter and Willy, Alice's orphaned daughter. The children came back negative. We were all thrilled." She pauses to hug one of her children, even more closely than usual, then continues: "But Mama Ivan came back positive. She was devastated. There are so many people here affected by HIV that I tend to think that people get a positive result and just say, 'Oh well!' But this was certainly not the case with Mama Ivan.

"All I could do was sit beside her, as my pathetic Swahili isn't up to the task of offering comfort to someone who has just been told they have an incurable disease that will eventually kill them. She asked me to come to her house, to be there when she told her husband . . . I gave them money to start on the long road of monthly trips, getting blood work done, and coming home with a packet of pills that hopefully will help them live long enough that their four children don't grow up as orphans."

LITTLE FELISITA COPES

Felisita walks to school just often enough to make sure Mama is not blamed for keeping her at home, although by now she is probably too sick to care. Felisita and *Bibi,* her old step-grandmother, take care of everything. Sometimes Felisita is sorry to be away from learning—but always glad to be away from the bullying. For some reason, the other children will not play with her. Instead, they say terrible things about her family. She pretends not to hear, so they laugh loudly behind her back. But she does miss learning how to read and write. The little girl stops digging in the garden for a moment, grabs a twig, and tries to etch a word into the ground.

One day she will learn all the letters of the alphabet, she vows. Then she can name the trees and the sky and maybe even name her Mama healthy.

"Felisita." Mama's call is hardly above a whisper. She now spends almost every day wrapped in her *kilago* mat on the floor in the dark or, on good days, she may ask to be helped into the sun. Today is a good day. Felisita struggles but at last Mama is comfortable. Now it is time to fetch water. With their precious plastic container balanced on her head, she starts down the hill.

OF THORNS AND BUFFALO HORNS

Meanwhile, Vicky takes advantage of a welcome breather during another insanely busy week in Ruaha. It is early afternoon. Dinners have been organized. Tourists are resting before going on their evening game-viewing drives. About to start a letter to Libby, Vicky first allows herself to take it all in, as the unrelenting sun leaches colour from the day, the sand, the shrubs. She makes a mental note to have someone renew the long, slippery carpets of dry grass tapered around camp *bandas* (sleeping huts) to hinder easy access by snakes. A stork lands close by. Wings still outspread, it pauses, gradually finds its balance, folds both wings, contemplates the water, and ignores a crested crane in graceful flight above. Farther down, an ungainly maribou stork cocks its head, eyeing with anticipation some carrion beyond Vicky's sight. So peaceful . . .

"Mama Fox! There's been an accident!" Vicky drops everything and rushes off. A buffalo on the other side of a thorn tree has charged and tossed a visitor into the prickles. As Big Sal later jokes, he isn't sure which hurt most: the horns of the buffalo or the thorns of the tree.

FOX NGO COMINGS AND GOINGS

"I'm sorry, Geoff," Patrick announces one day. "I've had a job offer in Canada that's too good to turn down."

"Of course you must take it, Patrick," Geoff says. "But we'll miss you and Kate. A lot has been achieved."

"Still a long way to go, I'm afraid. We've had to tear down most of Mdabulo hospital."

"But at least we will soon have a functioning maternity unit and doctors' consultancy rooms. Not to forget the new outpatients' treatment block, the small pharmacy, and temporary laboratory (stocked, courtesy of Marion Gough and her UK fundraising team). And the Tanzanian government has already taken on some salaries there!"

"However, many patients are still turned away for lack of staff, medicines, and room."

"No question. There's lots more to do, Patrick. Speaking of which, any ideas on who might take over from you and Kate?"

"We think Jenny Peck would be perfect."

"Of course! Jenny is doing great work in the village. I have never seen a Peace Corps volunteer achieve so much. Not just as a teacher, but through all her projects."

"Then there's her familiarity with HIV/AIDS and its impact in the community."

"Experience with income-generating initiatives for women," Kate throws in.

"And fluency in Swahili." This time it's Patrick again. He laughs ruefully. "Not knowing the language well was a huge drawback for us."

"The first we heard of the job offer," Geoff K tells friends, "was when Jenny and I were running in the Kilimanjaro half-marathon in Moshi. Kate called us and said, 'What would you think about replacing us? If anyone is going to take our place we think it should be Jenny. And Mr. Fox is really excited.'"

"What about you?" Geoff K's friends want to know.

"Oh, I'm sure at some point Kate must have said to Mr. Fox, 'Geoff Knight has to come too. It's a package deal.' Having Kate contact us alleviated a little awkwardness in the switchover. If we had heard from Mr. Fox first, it would have been sort of like talking behind someone's back."

The next weekend, March 8, 2008, Geoff K and Jenny visit the Fox farm. By now, there are thirty-nine orphans living in the Children's Village permanently—including, of course, Alice's two: Issa and Willy.

"Come to think of it, isn't it going to be a bit confusing with two Geoffs around here?" Patrick asks, looking at Geoff Fox and Geoff Knight.

"Call me Geoff K," Geoff Knight offers.

With that, the briefing begins. "Both community outreach and orphanage management would fall under Jenny's umbrella," Kate begins. "The key is to keep in close contact with village leaders. They are the ones who identify those children most in need and how best to support them—ideally, right in their own communities, with the orphanage as a home of last resort for those with nowhere else to go. We have to earn the leaders' trust, and through them, that of the villagers, so we can effectively bridge donor funding with what communities consider most important."

"For you, Geoff K, there are two options," Geoff Fox adds. "One is as teacher at the brand-new Luhunga Secondary School; the other as administrative manager for the Fox NGO. That would include taking over Patrick's role as building supervisor, not just for the hospital upgrading, but also for the school and whatever else comes up."

Back at Jenny's tiny Peace Corps house, they mull over their options with Geoff K's sister, Emily, who is visiting for three months.

"I still remember Kate telling me in a very nice way, 'If it were me, Geoff, I'd be a teacher, because Mr. Fox has a vision in mind. And often his vision is bigger than the funds available. From time to time, you're going to have to figure out how to say no. That might be difficult.'"

"The thing is," Emily says, smiling up at her brother, "Kate is obviously worried about you potentially butting heads with Mr. Fox. Now don't take offence, brother, but you don't butt heads with anyone." Jenny agrees, hugging Geoff K. And the balance tips in favour of both of them joining the Foxes.

GEOFF'S GROWING OBSESSION

"For a man not given to paperwork, Foxey, you are amazingly active around the NGO," Vicky laughs. Geoff agrees ruefully, as he prepares for the first staff meeting with his new team.

"I can't help it," he says. "How could one not become obsessed! Still, thank goodness Geoff K can relieve me of my least favourite part—the administrivia!"

"So it's official, then?"

"Yes. Geoff K will be the administrative manager, Jenny the Orphans' Centre and outreach supervisor, and Paulina Visulo will be head nurse and midwife in the Mdabulo Hospital."

"Well deserved," Vicky says. "Wasn't she a find!"

"Indeed. How lucky we are to have somebody with her years of experience in Tanzanian hospitals around the country."

"What about you?"

"I'll stay on as chairman of the board, or CEO, or whatever, for the NGO. Then, of course, there's Dr. Leena."

"An amazing woman, as some of you already know," Geoff tells new members of the Fox NGO team at their introductory meeting the next day. "For those who don't, Dr. Leena Pasanen is a pediatric missionary doctor, originally from Finland. She has practised near Mufindi for decades, is fluent in Swahili, and, in pre-retirement from her permanent work as mission doctor, has decided to volunteer with the Fox NGO. For ten days each month, she will give home-based care to villagers, administer antiretroviral (ARV) medications, and support all the medical facilities for the 40,000 people served by our

Dr. Leena and patient.
(Sasja Van Vechgel)

NGO. She will also train people in the care of HIV/AIDS victims, whether orphans, other children, or adults." Geoff then introduces Sauda Sebastian, the new head librarian and part-time English teacher at the Igoda Primary School; Geoff K; and Jenny.

"Now for our all-important house mamas," he says. "Lina Kyando needs no introduction." Lina, who became the first children's house mother on July 7, 2007, will remain as a senior member of the orphanage staff. "Eva Mahali has just joined us."

This is the same Eva who was orphaned early in life, lived in

Lina Kyando Jenny Peck, and Eva Mahali.
(Marion Golding)

various foster homes after her grandmother's death, and vowed one day to care for others like her. Today, her dream has come true. She is finally a house mother for children orphaned by HIV/AIDS. "Because I shared their fate, I understand the children I will now tend," she says shyly. "The Children's Village is one big family for me and my children."

LITTLE FELISITA CONFRONTS HIV/AIDS

The day has come when Felisita's mother no longer moves. "Mama!" cries Felisita. "Mama, please. Please answer. Mama!" *Bibi* is over-whelmed and too weak to help.

"In the old days," she weeps, "before this terrible disease, children outlived their parents. They were there to care for their elders. What am I to do?" So the little girl calls out to some neighbours, hoping they can assist with burying her mother. They shrink from her.

But how can they be frightened of a little girl? she thinks as she tackles everything that needs to be done. The time for the cows to come home is gone before she has finished fetching wood and water, roasting a few precious potatoes in the embers and rubbing *Bibi's* legs. The time when stories are told passes silently. Who is left to tell stories? Who to listen? She wraps herself in the rush mat on the floor and goes to sleep, but not before she puzzles again, *Why would they be frightened of a little girl?* And then she remembers what the teachers said about the disease called HIV/AIDS.

Baba Mkubwa, Big Father, arrives. Felisita is happy to see her father's brother. Especially when he takes her home with him to Mama Mkubwa. Although Felisita is often sick, the water she carries seems lighter now that she is once more part of a family; the firewood less heavy.

Then Mama Mkubwa dies, and *Baba* Mkubwa remarries. The new Mama Mkubwa has young children of her own and doesn't like Felisita. Felisita notices this especially at mealtimes, when very little of it comes her way. Big Father is not unkind, but often absent. And anyway, anything to do with children is more of the new Big Mother's business. Gradually Felisita is shunted aside. *Alone again*, she thinks. *Now even in the middle of my new family.*

THE SECOND HIGHLAND LODGE WEDDING

Several hills away, the second Highland Lodge wedding is under way. "Incidentally, Sarah Edwards [the bride] and our son Bruce were both born in Ilembula mission at about the same time," Geoff informs guests. "She went on to become a PhD forester, and I understand Chris Flowers' romantic proposal to her went something like this: 'How about I give you my name and you give me your doctorate? Then we can be known as Doctor and Mrs. Flowers!' She accepted."

The marquee occupies almost the total area of the tennis court, adorned with roses and decorative thistles grown in Uwemba and Kisolanza (for export to Amsterdam). Guests from all over the world—Mexico, Australia, Kenya, the UK—are housed in the Highland Lodge cabins. Festivities at the lodge extend over many days, starting with a stag night, after which Chris is carried unconscious to his car, and a driver takes him back home. (He made the mistake of appointing two best men from Mombasa, who filled a little teapot with *Konyagi*—East African gin—and juice. Every time Chris uttered a swear word, he had to drink this poison. And the more drunk he got, the more he swore.)

The ladies, left behind at his home in Stone Valley, are very concerned. Fortunately, the wedding is not the following day, although there will be a huge dinner party at the lodge for more than sixty guests.

"Vicky, as usual, performs at the piano in church and still manages to organize an amazing wedding feast for everyone," Geoff proudly relates to those who couldn't attend, "with excellent speeches and champagne on the croquet lawn after church—a lovely setting, especially bathed in evening light—followed by dinner in the marquee, including dancing on a big stage. Not to mention a huge curry lunch in the Secret Garden [croquet lawn] the next day—exhausting, but also great fun."

"The farm makes a splendid wedding venue," Vicky will later conclude. "But with just us two oldies, we've decided no more. They are hard work."

EASTER EGGS IN SECRET GARDENS

Vicky, in the meantime, has her hands full keeping the farm ticking, as well as supplying the growing number of Fox camps with her produce: ham, bacon, sausages, smoked beef, pork, lamb, and an enticing variety of vegetables. The main problem, especially in the rainy season, remains transport. Easter is particularly complicated. Because of school holidays, all the camps are full. However, Easter also falls in the rainy off-season, when their own planes are not flying regularly.

"Is anyone flying in this week?" she asks Geoff. "I can manage Ruaha, of course. Its lorry will be here soon and can collect larger quantities. But I'm worrying about the other camps. There is a full supply of meat and vegetables frozen and ready for Easter. They would like more, but we cannot get it there."

"I'll check if by chance any other chartered flight is coming into Ngwazi."

"Thanks, Geoff. With luck, it may be continuing to Ruaha and have enough space for the food, which Ruaha can then possibly send directly to the other camps."

"Or perhaps to our freezers in Dar es Salaam for later dispatch to the Selous or Lazy Lagoon."

"As a last resort, if we're really desperate, I can perhaps try to persuade our Mikumi Camps to send their lorry up to shop in Iringa, instead of Morogoro, so we can meet them there with our supplies."

Easters at the Highland Lodge are tremendous fun, with the lodge frequently fully booked a year in advance, usually by repeat family visitors from Dar es Salaam. The day begins with an Easter egg hunt involving visiting children together with those from the Children's Village. They hunt eggs in twos. Older orphaned children take the hand of little Lodge visitors, and vice-versa, to find sweets hidden in the Secret Garden and together they fill a central bucket whose contents are later divided evenly among all the kids.

An aggressive water balloon battle follows, with visiting fathers acting as targets, to the delight of screaming kids lined up on both sides.

"It's always a raging success," Geoff says. "You have no idea of the noise generated as several hundred water balloons fly through the air. And of course the fathers join in, even though — as targets — they are not supposed to grab balloons and throw them.

"A committee of mothers stands on a nearby rock to make sure that the fathers do not cheat by standing out of range. The punishment for cheating is to roll down the steep bank off the croquet lawn. Everyone gets wet."

1,000+ PATIENTS REGISTER FOR TREATMENT

"Would you believe that just a few months after the Mdabulo Dispensary had its first Mobile Care and Treatment Clinic on April 21, 2008, we now have more than 1,000 patients registered?"

"One thousand people, Foxey? Brilliant! It wasn't that long ago when nobody would even admit to having a problem, let alone seek treatment. Kudos again for Alice's courage in first coming forward. If only she could see it. Wait a minute, Foxey, why the long face?"

"The Mobile Clinic staff is completely overwhelmed. They have to carry files back and forth for all those people. Some files are being forgotten and even lost in the shuffle. Not only that, but they don't have enough health-care providers to treat everyone. There are only nine people, counting both Mafinga and Mdabulo dispensary staff, trying to treat more than 300 patients in one day. Mdabulo clearly needs its own permanent, stand-alone, full-time, Community-based Care and Treatment Clinic (CTC).

"What is that in English?"

"A place where qualified personnel can deliver antiretroviral medication continuously and matching HIV/AIDS patient need. Even more critical, Mdabulo needs its own CD–4 machine."

"And that is?"

"A machine that counts white blood cells. Each patient's CD–4 count is a measure of how badly HIV has affected him or her. Once the patient's CD–4 count is known, an exact dosage of antiretroviral drugs may be determined and administered. Without a CD–4 machine, treatments have to be based on guesswork."

《•》《•》《•》《•》

Any chance of publicity is a bonus—not just for the Foxes' business, but also to raise funds for their NGO. So the Foxes happily welcome a television team from Dar es Salaam looking for highland footage. The TV crew in question starts by filming people riding horses. "Too sedate," they say. "Boring. Could somebody please gallop?"

Daudi and eight-year-old Fox grandson Kiasile volunteer. Daudi is the Highland Farm Lodge's head horse guide, beloved by all the children.

Because the horses are so close to the cameras, it has to be a standing gallop, which involves some really severe digging into ribs. Kiasile's horse responds with an extraordinary buck. All on film, the little boy flies off in a graceful, somersaulting arc, disappears into the grass, reappears, stands up—indignant, hands on hips—and, to the astonishment of the gathered crowd, gets back on the horse for another round.

《•》《•》《•》《•》

Another little grandson, meanwhile, can barely remember his father. And now his mother is gone as well. But at least his *Bibi* and *Babu*, his grandparents, are still here. Or, wonders six-year-old Reuben, will they leave him, too?

Fox Orphanage Meets Best Practices

"Congratulations, Geoff," a visiting specialist on Tanzanian orphanages says one day. "Your NGO is getting a lot right in terms of incorporating best orphanage practices."

He is referring to common-sense guidelines set in place at the start by the Foxes. Such as employing house parents who consider this a commitment for life and not just a job ("who will work from the heart to mother the children," in Geoff's words); such as integrating the orphan's village into the community, beginning with making the orphanage look like a village, not an institution, and, crucially, raising the children as would be customary in any other village home.

For example, when people die in the village, orphans move in with relatives. In the case of the Children's Village, they are welcomed by the closest equivalent to a relative, their own house guardian. (Who, at the Foxes' insistence, are drawn from the surrounding area. Not only does this mean they are likely to stay for a long time—crucial for the orphans for whom they become the parental figure—but also that they remain part of the community fabric, easily mixing with leaders, widows, patients, heads of household, and *bibis*.)

《·》《·》《·》《·》

A few villages away, little Reuben watches his brothers heading to the field with Grandpa, *Babu*. These days *Babu* helps Grandma with the crops, while she still fetches water and wood and cooks. Little Reuben follows them, as fast as he can, but his head hurts, and somehow he cannot keep up anymore. *Babu* watches the child struggling. His eyes are feverish. He is losing weight.

Not Reuben, the old man thinks. *Dear God, not Reuben. Please. Not Reuben as well.*

"Tomorrow I will take Reuben to the hospital," he tells his wife when they get home.

"That is good," she says.

HAPPINESS IS . . .

"'Happiness' describes the children." Geoff is reading a draft NGO report for 2008. "Above all, they are looked after by caring house mothers in a 'home' environment." He pauses for a moment to watch the kids, who are screaming with laughter as they chase each other in and out of their houses.

"No kids can respond to simple pleasures like our orphans. They have seen the worst side of life and anything pleasant is great fun," the draft continues. "More and more families who are struggling to keep their orphaned relatives in the villages qualify for our help with school uniforms and general clothing, income-generating projects, limited food (such as formula milk to prevent HIV-positive mothers from transferring the disease to their babies) . . . Also exciting is the installation of a solar electricity system by Solaraid, including for the new secondary school—crucial for proposed computer studies, once some promised laptops arrive next year . . ."

Geoff stops reading. It is so hard to capture on paper the impact of working among these amazing people. How, for instance, does one convey a young mother's expression when she is finally reunited with her children? Not six weeks ago, one such single parent, Maria, was close to death. The Fox NGO took in her children while she underwent treatment and transitioned onto antiretroviral medicines. Now Maria is back at home and able to care for herself and her children.[69]

And how to put into words the inner world of each new child? Today they welcomed the latest member of the Children's Village family. Elkana (fourteen) has just lost both of her parents, is an only child, and her grandmother can no longer care for her at home. The older girls, happy to have another sister for their group, immediately surrounded her, and Elkana seemed to fit right in. Like them, she will carry her deeper pain privately.

HIPPO-PROOFING THE PROPOSED POOL

"And then there was Katavi!" Geoff and Vicky have joined Alexander on a rare short holiday at their latest lodge, this time in the third-largest and, in their view, possibly the best park in Tanzania. "Well

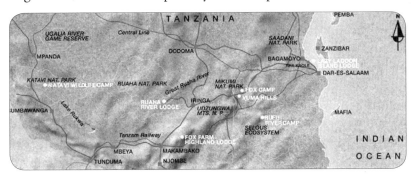

Map of Tanzania showing the Foxes' tourist lodges.
(Foxtreks, Foxes African Safaris, **http://www.tanzaniasafaris.info/foxfamily.htm**)

69   Based on Knight, *Annual Report, 2008*, **http://www.mufindiorphans.org**

From the Katavi lodge.
(Foxtreks)

done, Alexander!" The proud parents toast their youngest son, who has been instrumental in getting the lodge up and running.

They now employ about 450 people per year in eight tourist camps and lodges, including two luxury camps in Ruaha, (counting Christopher's Mwagussi safari camp), Katavi, Stanley's and Vuma Hills (in Mikumi), Rufiji (in the Selous), Lazy Lagoon (on the "island"), and the Mufindi Highland Lodge—all staffed from their corner of Mufindi. These many years later, despite political pressure to the contrary, they are still keeping their pact with Igoda and other host villages to hire locally—benefiting several times that number of family members.

"Great Herds without the Hordes" is how Foxtreks advertises Katavi National Park (gazetted in 1974 and covering about 2,735 square miles). "This park is for the connoisseur of Africa, for the traveller who likes to visit the most remote places, away from crowds. For every thousand tourists that visit Serengeti, one person might reach Katavi; so you will feel privileged . . . Katavi's three flood-plains—Lake Katavi, Katisunga (the main plain in between), and Lake Chada—are strung together by the Katuma River and boast one of the largest populations of hippopotami and crocodiles, while providing a habitat for an abundance of waterfowl. Katavi's vast size, infinite grassland plains, isolation, and inaccessibility have meant that herd sizes are huge, and it is not uncommon to see several thousand buffalo in a herd as they congregate on the plains during the dry season. Everything has to be kept in balance; so lions and other predators wait along fringed woodlands to ambush the game as it returns for shelter at sundown . . . There's nowhere else like it!"[70]

"Katavi can only be described by one word: Paradise," Geoff beams at son Alexander. "No other word will do. Imagine sitting here comfortably, drink in hand, overlooking the only watering hole available to the wildlife during the dry season and, in relative isolation, watching a constant stream of animals wander back and forth to drink."

The luxury Foxtreks camp is situated under fairly dense shady forest, looking out onto a massive *mbuga* plain that resembles Serengeti. There are literally thousands of animals on this huge *mbuga* and, during the dry season when the river dries, all the animals have to walk in front of their camp to access the only water just around the corner—similar to a fashion catwalk ("but more attractive," Geoff jokes; "the animals look healthier!").

The camp has tents, secluded from each other by forest vegetation in which elephant, hippo, buffalo, giraffe, and bushbuck roam freely without fear of humans (more the other way around, especially at night when one is walking back to the tent by torchlight!). The dining/bar lodge has a splendid upstairs lounge with a view over the plain. Although Vicky and Geoff don't want it, there will be a swimming pool one day, as that "sells" holidays when people are comparing brochures. "So we will need to make the pool elephant- and hippo-proof!"

LITTLE FELISITA MEETS DR. LEENA

Back in Mufindi and, as yet, still unbeknownst to the Foxes, there are now sores on Felisita's legs. She examines her arms. *Just skin and bones,* she thinks, *like Mama; like Baba. No wonder people are frightened of me.* She starts to cry, lies down, and decides she will never move again. *Just lie here. Lie here and . . . and what?* Her mind keeps jumping around like grasshoppers. Then she makes her big decision. Tomorrow she will walk all day to find a doctor at the mission. She will ask for medicine. She will ask to live.

---

70   http://www.tanzaniasafaris.info/Katavi/background.htm

"Mama Mkubwa (Big Mother)," she says the next morning, "I need to go to the hospital. I am not well."

"Who do you think will help me with firewood and water?"

"Please, Mama Mkubwa. Please come with me. I do not want to die like Mama and *Baba*."

"Perhaps I can take her." Felisita looks gratefully at *Baba* Mkubwa. Then back at Mama Mkubwa.

"You know you need to go to work. Impossible," Big Mother says. "If she must go, she's old enough to manage on her own." And so it is that little Felisita sets off alone in search of treatment at Mdabulo Mission Hospital—about twelve rural miles away.

《•》《•》《•》《•》

At Mdabulo Hospital, Dr. Leena is tired in the best sort of way. She is at the tail-end of her ten days per month as volunteer for the Fox NGO. Today she will support Dr. Ndenga, as she does when possible on "CTC" or "clinic" days. These happen every two weeks when Mafinga's Mobile AIDS Clinic manoeuvres the bone-jarring road to Mufindi.

Yesterday, she herself spent over eight hours on foot visiting more than twenty houses with Jenny, on a typical outreach and home-based care visit for the Fox NGO to an isolated village.

"Even after having lived in Tanzania for more than twenty years, I have never before visited such poor houses!" she reported to Finnish supporters last night. "Only a few households have proper beds or mattresses, and some have only one blanket for the entire family. Mufindi is very cold during the dry season. Jenny has been recording details on families and their urgent needs, and by good luck it has been possible to provide them with some clothing, shoes, and blankets. I am very thankful to some friends who have donated funds for buying more blankets.

"I have carried my stethoscope and otoscope with me on these visits, plus some basic medications. It is good to be able to help people in their homes, as sometimes distances to the nearest health-care facility can be extremely long. The hospitality of these people is so touching. Despite their poverty, nobody has hesitated to invite us into their homes and offer us treats such as tea and boiled potatoes."

Every month, Dr. Leena also spends two days accompanying

volunteer Susan Vinton, who, in the course of collecting data on more than 1,100 HIV-positive people living in the nearby villages, connects with many chronically ill children suffering from other diseases.

First they drive to distant villages. Then a guide leads them on foot. "Sometimes it takes more than an hour to reach people in deep valleys, and I get excellent exercise while climbing up long, steep hills," Dr. Leena jokes. Then, more seriously, "We have met so many malnourished children. Yet it is quite difficult to teach about "*chakula bora*" (nutritious food), when people do not have cows, milk, hens, eggs, peanuts, meat, and sometimes not even beans."

At Ibwanzi Dispensary, where there is no doctor, she managed in one day to examine about sixty of ninety waiting children as part of a "clinic" day. More children awaited her at Luhunga Dispensary, and of course here she is at Mdabulo.[71]

《•》《•》《•》《•》

"*Karibu*, welcome, child," Dr. Leena says with a smile as her next little patient enters. "What is your name?"

"My name is Felisita."

"Is your guardian outside, Felisita? Please ask her to come in."

"I came alone."

Dr. Leena is shocked. Children are always accompanied by adults at Care and Treatment Clinics for HIV-positive people. That's where she is today, helping out with the mobile CTC visit to Mdabulo arranged by the Fox NGO.

"How did you get here, Felisita?"

"I walked."

"How old are you, child?"

"Twelve?"

Dr. Leena hides her surprise. *Twelve years old and in such a tiny, tiny frame*, she thinks; then says: "How can I help you, Felisita?"

"My parents are both dead. From what my school has taught me about AIDS, I think that that is what they had. I, too, am often sick and I do not want to die like them. I am here to get tested and treated."

---

71   This and other reporting references are adapted from: Dr. Leena Pasanan, *Habari Ya Mufindi, Quarterly Newsletter* 4, no. 1 (March 2009), http://www.mufindiorphans.org.

LADDIE AND OTHER SHEEPDOGS

"See you in two weeks, Dr. Leena." All too soon, Geoff and Vicky are waving farewell again. "Unless you are having second thoughts about your decision to volunteer with us," Geoff quickly adds.

"Not at all," Dr. Leena replies. "Yes. The work in Mufindi is very challenging. And I am very, very happy to be able to spend some days each month among such lovely people!"

As the bus disappears, Geoff and Vicky head back to the farm. "I really do seem to have the dog cancer under control," Vicky says.

"Well done, Granny Fox!"

Working sheepdogs can run up to ninety miles a day, usually with their tongues hanging out. Sadly, the high altitude of Mufindi facilitates sunburn and makes them susceptible to cancer of the tongue, especially in the unrelenting suns of Africa. First Breeze and then Storm succumb to it. Heartbroken, Vicky looks for solutions. The only answer: breed enough dogs to allow for shift work, with regular periods of rest during the day.

New litters of border collie sheepdog puppies are slowly being trained. Laddie is the most intelligent of all. He even helps with clearing land for new pastures (to replace rough original pastures, which are virtually devoid of nutritional value to cattle, consisting as they do of deforested areas, depleted by overuse, and now reverting largely to scrub interspersed with thickets of very poor bushes).

After the thickets are cleared (except for any interesting trees), old tree roots and cuttings need to be pulled off the land. That is where Laddie comes in. He quickly realizes what people are doing and insists on taking one end of a heavy log in his mouth as Vicky carries the other. On occasion, Laddie even picks up large sticks and carries them off on his own—to accompanying incredulous laughter from the workforce.

The cleared land, dug over (manually and by tractor), is then interplanted with maize (which will end up in two huge pits for silage) and hardy Kikuyu grass (gradually to cover the whole pasture once the corn and a world of weeds are removed). Armed with slashers, herdsmen and shepherds then keep bracken at bay on what will ultimately yield about 200 acres of established pasture. This includes about forty acres of banner grass, which grows to a height of up to ten feet and remains green throughout the dry season, providing fodder for the cows.

Foxtreks' Flying Wing

After twenty years of managing the Ruaha River Lodge, son Peter and daughter-in-law Sarah Fox relocate close to the airport in Dar es Salaam. Sarah continues to manage Foxtreks' finances, while Peter nurtures its flying "wing," which began with a single six-seater Cessna 206, and now includes several Cessna 208s (caravans) and an executive jet.

"They keep him busy, as do the additional pilots he now employs," beams proud Papa Fox when friends ask where Peter is these days. "That reminds me," he continues. "While still in Ruaha, Peter voluntarily flew the Friends of Ruaha Society Cessna 182 on anti-poaching and other park purposes. One day, shortly after leaving Dar es Salaam with American clients in a Cessna 206, he hit a vulture that took a massive bite out of the leading edge of the wing. Petrol poured out and he had little control of the ailerons (flaps). Without alarming his passengers, he managed to turn the plane around, warn air traffic control, and make a forced landing at speed. Only when the passengers observed airport fire engines lining the runway did they remark: 'Is that for us?'

Some Fox light aircraft, Safari AIRlinks.
(http://www.safariaviation.info/contactus.htm)

"Other aircraft accidents are usually caused by animals, such as zebra and impala. They sometimes dart onto the runway just as planes are landing, causing no injury, but considerable expense. Such are some of the hazards and adventures of bush flying in Tanzania."

Tanzania's Global Contribution

"Speaking of the bush," Geoff continues, his expression unusually solemn. "This is probably as good a time as any to get something off my chest—a subject that has been so worrying over recent years: the future of wildlife in Tanzania. But before I get into the problems, let me first salute Tanzania's contribution to our global wildlife heritage. Because of its extraordinary concentration of biodiversity, this tiny nation—slightly smaller than the American state of Montana—has set aside a larger percentage of land for wildlife protection than any other country on earth. Some figures put it as high as 28 percent."

"Twenty-eight percent of Tanzania under protection? That is huge," one friend exclaims.

"And since much of it is as a global heritage, there should surely be an international responsibility to ante up," another adds. "In the meantime, one of the poorest countries in the world is left holding the bag."

With a Little Help from a Friend

Ana has three children. Her husband is sick and her house is in terrible shape. Her grass roof is falling apart with gaping holes, and the walls are beginning to cave in where the rains will certainly knock them down. A plan has been put in place for her to have some work at Igoda Children's Village while her children stay temporarily at the centre. During these rainy months, she'll save money for window and door frames, corrugated iron roofing, and a bit of cement so she may build her own home. Her husband can help with building the house if he gets well, and they will both make the bricks starting in June 2013. When the rains come next year, Ana will be able to move into her new house with her family, and the Fox NGO will hopefully have another success story similar to the earlier family from Mwefu village, whose children stayed at the Children's Village for a short time until their house was rebuilt, and are now living happily back in their home.

WILDLIFE—TANZANIA'S CHALLENGE

"Back to my wildlife concerns," Geoff says. "Man's interference with nature is seriously affecting both wildlife and tourism in Tanzania. And yet, with a little give and take and co-operation, this could so easily be avoided.

"Wildlife areas throughout the country were originally demarcated into 'Open Hunting Areas,' 'Game-Controlled Areas,' 'Game Reserves,' and 'National Parks,'" Geoff continues. "'Open Hunting Areas' for resident hunters (Tanzanians or expatriates living in Tanzania); 'Game-Controlled Areas' mainly for tourist hunting; 'Game Reserves' for exactly what it says—to preserve game; and 'National Parks' for tourist photographic safaris.

"'Open Hunting Areas' have gradually been wiped out, as have, largely, 'Game-Controlled Areas'—so much so that tourist hunting has moved into 'Game Reserves.' I remember the days when, driving to Ruaha Park, we would encounter giraffe, kudu, and elephant almost immediately after the Greek-owned tobacco farms not far from Iringa. This was a so-called 'Open Hunting Area,' available for resident hunting.

"Where does this leave resident hunting? Legally nowhere; so residents currently hunt illegally in 'Game Reserves,' and now, worryingly, also in 'National Parks.' The government seems either unaware or unconcerned about it, despite many warnings from knowledgeable witnesses. The Fox family has been operating in Tanzania's tourist sector for longer than any other present operator. We know what overseas clients want. Put simply, 95 percent of our clients come to Tanzania under one word: *safari*—*safari* to Tanzania. To them, *safari* conjures up animals. The problem: no animals = no *safari* = no tourist industry—as simple as that!"

LIKE THE PIED PIPER

The Social Welfare Officer of Mufindi District pays a surprise visit to the Fox NGO. Not only that, but today Elisha Nyamara brings with him a whole truck full of unexpected goods!

"That is amazing, Mr. Nyamara," Jenny exclaims. And, turning to the children who have gathered around him, she asks: "What do you say?"

"THANK YOU, SIR!" they scream and collapse laughing. Mr. Nyamara beams. He has become a very close friend of the Children's Village, as well as helping them with some serious, child-related issues.

"You are most welcome," he says.

"But one thousand dollars' worth of food and household goods!"

"It is a token of thanks from the district government for the help the Children's Village is offering to the community here in Mufindi."

With children hanging off him, and greeting everyone along the way, Mr. Nyamara then takes a tour of the Village. Suddenly he stops. Looks serious.

"Now for some really important work," he says grimly . . . "Who wants to learn a new song and dance?" With that, like the Pied Piper of Hamelin, he leads the younger children into the courtyard for a small and impromptu celebration.

TANZANIAN WILDLIFE — THE SOLUTIONS

Some three years ago, Geoff had the privilege of hosting Tanzania's current prime minister, Mr. Mizengo Pinda, for four nights in Katavi National Park. In Geoff's words, "The poor man had to suffer listening to Fox, there being no one else in the camp at the time. He showed considerable concern and understanding about risks to Tanzania's tourism sector, at that time the top foreign exchange earner in the country (now superseded only by mining).

"When asked my opinion for a solution, I told him that as a matter of urgency, resident hunting must be suspended, thereby making anyone carrying a gun a suspect and anyone with a game animal a poacher. Suspension would need to last until Tanzania's wildlife was less threatened. Tourist hunting blocks would also need to be very closely controlled, with quotas for maintaining sustainability, whereby the number of animals shot per year, per block, would be no greater than the replacement number needed by each species. Right now, it is a free-for-all. The government has even split up blocks and increased quotas to be shot, thereby earning more revenue—for the short term.

"No one is reliably preventing hunters from shooting a second animal with a larger trophy head than one already shot under licence—and this on land that was once classified as 'Game Reserve.' Unless checked, these, too, will follow the fate of 'Controlled Game Areas.' That would leave only 'National Parks,' which, as we speak, are already being penetrated by motorized hunting parties as well as illicit hunters for bush meat and ivory.

"We have learned from experience that building a road through Mikumi National Park led not only to easier access by hunters from Morogoro and elsewhere but also a demand for "*nyama choma*" (roasted game meat) by ever-increasing numbers of heavy transport crews stopping at Mikumi town.

"The Mikumi Park warden told me a couple of years ago that his rangers dismantle more than 1,000 snares each year; and, indeed, our own tourists have voiced their distress at seeing wild animals with snares around their necks or legs, some still alive. This doesn't help Mikumi tourism. Word gets back to overseas agents, who may decide to book elsewhere in future.

"A couple of years ago, Vicky and I conducted a ground survey of wildlife in Mikumi. Results showed critical levels with only just enough game to satisfy tourists. Any further reduction in wildlife would certainly lead to a shutdown of tourism in Mikumi as agents look elsewhere for tourist satisfaction.

"So, with that lesson behind us, why are we facing the danger of repeating the mistake in both Serengeti and Katavi national parks? And risking a total tourism shutdown? Even though the danger could be averted for both Serengeti and Katavi by realigning the trunk routes around southern and western park boundaries? And yet, as mentioned earlier, with a little give and take and co-operation, this could so easily be avoided.

"In the case of Katavi, for example, realigning the road would not involve any extra distance and could, in fact, stimulate cross-lake trade from the Congo to the railhead at Mpanda. Detouring proposed roads around the Serengeti and Katavi could be funded by overseas support to protect the world heritage wildlife. Unfortunately, the future seems to be of less consequence than the present, stemming from a combination of favouring today and self.

"Rice paddies upstream of Ruaha are another case in point — not the many smallholder, rain-fed paddies, but rather a few, huge, commercial enterprises requiring dry-season irrigation, which completely drain the four perennial Ruaha River tributaries. This, in turn, renders the Great Ruaha River totally dry for at least four months in the year, devastating precious wildlife, and not just threatening tourism but also, farther downstream, the vast and vital storage reservoir for both Mtera and Kidatu hydroelectric power.

"Then there is the major dam and hydroelectric construction planned for the Rufiji River. Without revisions, it will have devastating repercussions for wildlife and its accompanying tourism in the mighty Selous Game Reserve. Photographic tourism depends considerably on oxbow lakes currently replenished by natural flooding. Instead, proposed designs will artificially flood a huge area of Ruaha and Rufiji River valleys, by turns drowning and choking natural cycles. Not only that, but major access roads, to be constructed through pristine wilderness, will also give easy access to increased poaching. (Already, poachers have started coming up by river. This begs the need for a boat patrol.)

"Whereas Mufindi's long-term resident and founding member of the Friends of Ruaha Society, Shanna Sheridan–Johnson, has stoically remained active in the Society to this day, we have diverted our attention to our new NGO, which does include wildlife conservation — the purpose being to encourage clients at any of our camps to contribute to projects that the National Parks or the Wildlife Division need in those particular areas. In fact, our wildlife activity is mainly focused on lobbying governments, embassies, and conservation organizations, one priority being forest protection in Saadani and Mufindi, as well as on Lazy Lagoon."

SAIDI MASONDA AND AMON KALINGA

Geoff's comments linger as he and his friends walk past virgin forest later that day . . . especially when they run into Saidi. "This," says Geoff, after many greetings, placing his hand on the free shoulder of a gaunt but straight old man with a gun slung over his other shoulder. "This is Saidi Masonda. He patrols nearby forests, dismantling snares and discouraging hunters."

They chat for a while, some of it social, some of it business between Geoff and Saidi about his recent findings. "Until recently, Saidi worked for Christopher at Mwagusi camp in Ruaha," Geoff tells them as they eventually go their separate ways, "where Saidi, together with Amon Kalinga, were given the responsibility of naming Christopher's son, our youngest grandson. They chose '*Kiasile*' (Kihehe for 'The lost one shall return').

"Amon worked for us, together with his brother Amos Kalinga, as tracker/porters on our

Saidi and Geoff.
(Gord Breedyk)

walking safaris. Amos went on to become chairman of Iyegeya Village for twenty years, a position he still retains. His daughter, Sylvia, is one of our waitresses at the Highland lodge. For forty years, until his recent death, Amon first worked with us and then with Christopher in Ruaha, where for years he and Saidi used to take our grandson Kiasile for his early morning game walks before breakfast. Those two *wazee* were his guardians.

"Kiasile became expert at identifying animal tracks, all in Swahili, from the age of two. His parents were not allowed to go with him, but we grandparents were once privileged to tag along. On that occasion, he never made a mistake on any track, easily differentiating between leopard and hyena tracks of the same size (but one without visible claws, since hyenas cannot retract their claws but leopards can).

"When Amon died, Christopher and Kiasile took him to be buried in his village near here. There, among 300 village mourners, Kiasile took his turn with the spade, to honour the man who had named him and, together with Saidi, taught him so much, especially about the wilderness, on his daily walking safaris.

"Diagnosed with prostate cancer, Saidi has now opted to stay at home in Mufindi as our forest guard. He protects forests around the

Highland Farm, Lupeme Estate, and the Mufindi Tea Company, an area rife with snaring activity. Sadly, hunting with dogs and muzzle-loaders has depleted this rich heritage, leaving very little game to be seen in Mufindi these days. In the forest around our farm, we do have a few red duiker, more suni antelope, no bush pig, and probably no leopard. But monkeys abound, and there are many other smaller things—mongooses, civets, otters, etcetera. We even have our forest cobras on the farm that are quite aggressive and don't seem to occur in the higher and colder dense forests around the tea estates.

"With his condition, Saidi is unlikely to return to Ruaha. We sought treatment for him, but the Italian surgeon, who will later stitch up the person scalped by a lion in Ruaha, said he needed a specialist. Saidi is now seventy-four—a lovely guy."

Ever the Farmer

Once a year, the Foxes return to their family home in Tavistock for a few months—usually coinciding with the down season in Mufindi tourism. Their "holiday" includes, as ever, a mad round of Foxtreks purchases and arrangements. "Hot and hectic here," Geoff emails friends prior to their return. "Vicky will forever be the farmer and has purchased a complete sheep shearing machine, two poultry incuba-tors, fertile 'dual purpose' chicken eggs, trout hatchery feed, and a lot else—all to pack into our baggage allowance! If the plane hits a bump, her 'smalls' will be smelling of rotten egg!"

Tanzanian Wildlife—Lingering Concerns

"Now, back to the prime minister." Geoff has again been asked his views on the future of wildlife—read "tourism"—in Tanzania. "To his considerable credit, he called a Parliamentary debate in Dodoma on suspending resident hunting. Sadly, the vote was narrowly lost, perhaps due to the strong hunting lobby. If this problem cannot be urgently addressed, I see no future for wildlife and tourism in Tanzania.

"I should say here that Tanzanian National Parks (TANAPA) is a well-funded body and its rangers well paid, but, compared to TANAPA, those working in the Wildlife Division are significantly underpaid and consequently unmotivated. A restructuring and training, in conjunction with improving the value of their employment, would raise their status and efforts. Retraining would ideally include how to protect wildlife, combat poachers, and help others to appreciate the value of keeping animals alive. Right now, I believe that in the minds of most folk, a wild animal is there to be shot. Why else would the only Swahili name for game be '*nyama*' (meat) and for wildlife be '*wanyama pori*' (bush meat)? Motivation and training are imperative—and urgently so—for the protection of wildlife.

"Although national parks fare better, authorities seem to be devoting more time to extracting maximum revenue from tourists than to game preservation. Rangers are now tasked with stopping viewing vehicles and demanding to see tourists' game drive and park entry permits, whereas their core purpose should be that of protecting wildlife from increased poaching, not policing tourists and making them feel unwelcome.

"A recent directive has confined expatriate managers to their camps. It stipulates that any time an expatriate camp manager leaves the camp boundary within the park, for example, to guide clients, he/she is to be charged tourist park fees. Not only is this a grave management hindrance but also detrimental to wildlife. Managers help to monitor and report poaching activities, which is in the interest of park authorities, as well as tourist camps and lodges.

"So different to earlier attitudes," he adds as an aside, "whereby the private sector is again treated with hostility and obstruction. Nowadays, expatriates are being openly discouraged from investing and are often hounded by Immigration. TANAPA in the national parks and the Wildlife Division in the Selous seem to spend more time 'policing' tourists and camp operators than combatting and preventing poaching. I don't know why. There was a time when we were partners in facilitating and encouraging tourism to Tanzania.

"I remember the words of the Iringa regional commissioner when we were about to start in Ruaha. He had come down on an official visit to the park and, in a speech, urged the authorities to give all the help they could to the Foxes, declaring that we were showing confidence and investing in Tanzania at a time when no one else would. In those days, Vicky had to drive to Dar very frequently to get permits from the appropriate Ministry every time she needed building materials and, later, kitchen ingredients and other requirements (cooking oil, flour, soap, etc.). Tanzania in those days just had nothing that could be sold in shops. But, wherever Vicky went, she received all the assistance that was possible at that time; government officials were kind and encouraging."

"What worries me is that no one seems to recognize how serious the situation is. Perhaps we ourselves are more aware of trends because, after fifty-three years in Tanzania, we have witnessed the past, while others are now just observing the present. But, again, none of this should detract from Tanzania's salutary dedication of 28 percent of its territory to parks, reserves, and conservation areas."

Fox NGO Celebrities and Celebrants

"We have our very own NGO celebrities," Geoff announces after visiting the Children's Village one day.

"This must have something to do with Dr. Leena," Vicky guesses.

"That's right. Finland has just named her 'The Most Outstanding Finn Living outside Finland.'"

"Why don't we have a little celebration? Not only to mark this honour, but also in appreciation of her part-time work with the NGO. How many doctors (let alone with twenty-seven years' experience in Tanzania) would donate ten days a month to work in a place as isolated as ours?"

"Great idea, Vicky. But it will have to be a double one!"

"Why's that?"

"Luhunga Ward has asked Jenny to be the celebrated guest in its commemoration of Africa Day on June 16. Now there's a true sign of community acceptance of our work!"

Also in Luhunga, a teenager is beside herself with excitement. Sifa Chumi has just received word of a scholarship. *Imagine*, she thinks, *I can study!* For years now, this remarkable student has helped out at Luhunga Secondary School, where HIV/AIDS has created a massive shortage of teachers, even with healthy staff covering as best they can for their sick and dying colleagues. They do this partly because they don't know if they might be the next to fall ill and need shielding in turn, and partly to provide for their own families for as long as possible.

Geoff and students as Luhunga Secondary school receives library books and equipment.
(African Book Box Society)

A new agreement between the Fox NGO and Luhunga will help to stem the growing shortage of teachers by providing students with scholarships to earn a teaching degree, on condition they return to teach in Luhunga—an easy commitment for the first recipient, Sifa, since her whole family lives in neighbouring Igoda Village. "Imagine," she tells her family. "Imagine!"

Conquering Kilimanjaro—or Not

A little while later, Geoff and Vicky are relishing a few quiet moments over drinks and popcorn in front of their fireplace, despite the whirl-wind demands of their filled-to-capacity Highland Lodge, peak farm production, mushrooming NGO activities, and expanding Foxtreks enterprises. Geoff hands Vicky the latest report. "Great photo of the MOMs," he says.

"Who are the MOMs again?"

"The Mufindi Orphans Mountaineers.[72] The ones who conquered Kilimanjaro to raise funds for our NGO."

"Wonderful," Vicky agrees. "Say, Geoff. It's strange, isn't it: Our family has been here for decades, and only one of us has ever climbed Kili."

"Two, actually—Bruce and Jane."

"True. I wonder why more Mufindi folk didn't do it."

"Vertigo is my excuse," says Geoff. "Remember—"

---

72   David Still, Rod Nuss, Gerald Meyr, Gary Drobnack, Ronda and Brad Miller.

Before he can say another word, Vicky jumps in. "You did propose to me on top of Vixen Tor!" They laugh. "Seriously," Vicky continues, "Why didn't more of us climb Kili?"

"Too much to see at this end of the country," Geoff jokes. "But those who did climb it showed Mufindi's true mettle." He is referring to Jack Devlin, a Brooke Bond company engineer who, as Geoff likes to put it when reminiscing with friends, "succeeded in impressing his Norwegian wife-to-be, Barbo, by reaching the summit at the age of fifty-something, with only one functioning lung. Earlier, he had been told that he had a malignant growth in the other. We all said our goodbyes when he left for treatment in England, more or less not expecting to see him again. There, they drained out about a litre of black guck, established that it was not cancerous, and back he came to climb Kili and win the hand of Barbo, then working at the Norwegian Saw Mill project in Sao Hill.

"Not to be trumped by Jack, some of the fittest and most macho Norwegian men working with Barbo were determined to conquer Kilimanjaro as well. To this end, they went on a serious, two-week training schedule, which included a daily run around the Mufindi golf course. One of them even stopped smoking. Another had once been Norway's 5,000-metre champion.

"Fit and confident, they headed for Kilimanjaro, leaving their wives at home ('because this is a man's thing'). On their return, they all filed into Mufindi club one Saturday evening sporting Kilimanjaro T-shirts, which had originally read: 'I have climbed Kilimanjaro,' and now sported a beautifully embroidered 'nearly,' courtesy of their wives' needlework. Not one of them made it to the top.

"This of course spurred on said wives," Geoff continues. "'Right,' they decided. 'Let us girls try.' Every one of them reached the summit. (They sensibly took the climb slowly, while their husbands, competitive as they were, tried to race up and consequently succumbed to mountain sickness.)

"Then there was Pat Mathers (once Helga and Werner's neighbour and now living in Australia), who tried his luck many years later, at sixty, with a stent near his heart and only one leg, plus a pegleg. He also made it. (Incidentally, during the same visit to Tanzania, Pat and Jane came to Mufindi with their daughter Anita and her husband in a six-seater Cessna flown by our son Peter. On arrival at the Sao Hill airstrip, owned by the National Service Army, the doors of the plane opened and out flew a human leg. There were gasps of astonishment from assembled soldiers. It turned out that this was Pat's dress leg. He much prefers his peg leg.)"

WHAT CHICKENS, HOSPITALS, AND COMPUTERS HAVE IN COMMON

Vicky has just glanced again at Marion Gough's latest report to fundraisers. "Not bad, Foxey," she says after a while, tipping her glass and reading out loud: 'NGO initiatives completed in 2009 include the Ibwanzi Health Centre (which was officially opened on 14th September). A small hospital, with thirty beds in ten wards, it will provide important in-patient treatment facilities for some 20,000 people in eight villages.'

"It did look splendid when we handed it over to the government," says Geoff, "with all the equipment donated by the UK and Canada. The best part, of course, is that the government has provided a clinical officer, one step down from a doctor, assisted by nurses. In other words, it is now a fully functioning medical facility, officially reclassified and run by the Ministry of Health."

Vicky pauses to raise her glass, then continues: "I.T. Schools Africa has donated twenty laptops to Igoda and Luhunga Schools. A library has been set up at Luhunga Secondary School. Each member of a Luhunga village community group called '*Tumaini*' (Hope) is raising their own chickens to create some supplementary income, as well as feed their families—protein being in short supply. The list goes on and on, Geoff. Well done!"

"Thanks, Mrs. Fox. We do sometimes lose track, when all we face is day-to-day hurdles." Geoff raises his glass. "To everyone who helps to make it happen: Geoff K and Jenny, the house mothers, house fathers, volunteers, and of course the pioneers like Alice."

"The villagers and fundraisers," Vicky adds, then continues reading out loud, "'The school improvements themselves were made possible through donations and on-site supervision by the African Children's Book Box Society of Canada.' On-site supervision? Does that refer to Ruth and Anne?"

"Yes, it does. By the way, their house is almost ready." (Because the two retired Canadian teachers now regularly spend months at a time in Mufindi, they have paid for the construction of a home large enough for themselves and other short-term volunteers.)

"I've obviously been too busy with the farm to keep up with the NGO, Geoff. For example, I didn't know that the orphanage now has lighting and running water. That should save a bit of time—"

"And money—no more water carriers or kerosene lamps."

"Or that you're already reducing food bills with the orphanage farm. And I love that the younger children will each rear a chicken to help pay for Secondary School education!"

Vicky reads on silently for a while. Then, "What a great way for Marion to end her report, Geoff, and how true: 'A long way to go; but there is no doubt that the people of Mufindi will recapture the self-sufficiency they enjoyed before AIDS devastated their communities.'[73]

Geoff nods then suddenly leaps out of his chair. "No more dilly-dallying, Mrs. Fox. Time to go." With that, they grab a flashlight each and head out through the Mufindi night to mingle with guests over dinner at their Highland Lodge.

GRANDMA FOX TO THE RESCUE

"Well done, Grandma!" Geoff is about to boast about Vicky's latest stunt. "Christopher's is the best-built dam in Mufindi," he tells guests over supper. "I have created many, and not one as well as his. Christopher supervised it to the point of blocking. [As soon as you think you have enough soil, you block the river, with the soil only on one side, and then fill it quickly before the water has a chance to rise.]

"Vicky took over supervising the final block only to find the water level rising too fast because of unusually high rains the previous year. Around seven p.m., there were only a few inches to go. Had she left it at that, the dam would have burst overnight, taking the whole thing down, including two lower dams. So she asked the workers to help her build a small ridge near the water's edge, by dragging soil over in sacks to keep the water at bay.

"Our employees, who had worked hard all day, wanted to go home," says Geoff. "So Mama Fox continued hauling in the soil by

73   Adapted from: Marion Gough, *Habari Ya Mufindi, Quarterly Newsletter,* 4, no. 3 (September 2009), **http://www.mufindiorphans.org.**

herself. One by one, they joined her, and in the end, not a single worker gave up—until nine p.m. They couldn't let Granny Fox do all the hard work on her own. It was pretty terrifying because she could see the water level rising up and up. Again, well done, Grandma!"

Vicky smiles, thinking back over all the years she and Geoff have been together. Certainly they've had their challenges, some amazing ones. But as she has confided in friends, "Young people these days give up much too easily. The secret is to decide what's important in the relationship, face the issues, and then move on." She's glad that that is what they have managed to do.

WILL ANYONE SHOW UP?

In November, it's full steam ahead with officially inaugurating the new community hall. It all started with Igoda Primary School's needing an assembly hall and has ended up with Igoda Village receiving a full-blown community hall, complete with meeting rooms, a huge central space large enough to seat several hundred villagers, and a kitchen. There, among others, grannies and HIV-positive single mums will earn some pocket money by preparing a nutritious "meal in a mug" for more than 500 primary schoolchildren. Four days a week, they will blend cereals and nuts, ground into flour, and serve the resulting *uji* (liquid porridge) warm with sugar to students who otherwise are away from home (and food) for twelve hours each day![74]

"Why don't we have the formal opening on December first?" The Fox NGO staff are brainstorming on how best to use the grand opening for deepening NGO links with the communities it serves, and spreading the word about HIV/AIDS treatment.

"Why December first?" someone asks.

"That's World AIDS Day," another answers.

"Perfect! Our invitations to dignitaries could stress how community hall activities will support World AIDS Day, by focusing on prevention education and letting countless people know that there is hope with treatment."

"Not to mention, through performances and seminars on the day, to highlight how the hall can become a village focal point for community awareness about HIV/AIDS (the disease, its prevention,

---

74   Based on Knight, *Annual Report, 2008,* **http://www.mufindiorphans.org**.

and, most important, the need to break down various stigmas associated with it) . . ."

"Also, how it will be a perfect meeting place for grandmothers . . ."

"A venue for hosting regular tribal traditions—like oral history."

"Adult education."

"Other community celebrations!"

"How many guests shall we plan for?"

"Let's be optimistic and assume several hundred."

"Fingers crossed that the rains hold off and lots of people show up."

《·》《·》《·》《·》

Geoff and Vicky have no idea what to expect on the day. Neither do Geoff K and Jenny, rushing to dress themselves and their own new baby girl, Twilumba (Kihehe for "let us rejoice"), before manoeuvring bumpy dirt roads to get to the grand opening.

As early as they are, they can hardly move through the crowds already gathered. In fact, more than 1,000 people attend! They include several dignitaries, representing 1.7 million Iringa residents.

Speeches follow, laughter, tears, dancing, singing, more tears, more laughter, more speeches, interspersed with acknowledgement of the biggest meeting hall in the Iringa region, its many purposes, and its sponsor—the Canada-based African Children's Book Box Society—for funding the community hall in its entirety.

SCALPED BY A LION

Packed community hall.
(Fox NGO)

Not long after, Geoff returns home elated from mingling with the orphans at the Children's Village. He finds Vicky uncharacteristically pale. "Dreadful news from Ruaha, Geoff. I just had a call from Christopher."

"Is he all right?"

"Yes, he's fine. It's Bryson (their River Lodge barman). He was washing his pots and pans, when a lioness grabbed him by his head. Josafat (Julius's son) heard him, picked up a charcoal stove and smashed it against the offending lion's shoulder. All the lions then ran off. The barman was unconscious and scalped. Christopher and his head cook (the invalid's brother) took him to the nearest hospital at the Tosamaganga mission, several hours' drive away. There, at Christopher's insistence, two doctors agreed to operate. They soon discovered that, not only had his skull been punctured, but a dessert spoon of his brain had also been released."

However, a few days later, Bryson is sitting up in bed and talking on his phone. The Foxes promise to find him a job in Mufindi.

"Why?" he asks.

"Surely you don't want to go back to Ruaha?"

"Why ever not? That's where I always work."

"What about the lions?"

"Oh, they won't be back."

LITTLE FELISITA DEFIES HIV/AIDS

Determined to stay alive, Felisita dutifully journeys alone for testing and treatment every month. Big Mother is not happy about it, although Felisita does fit in all her chores, even if it means missing school. Sometimes the treatment makes Felisita feel a little better, other times not. Perhaps, she tells herself, it's because there is not always enough food at home. Ever more the outsider — not just at school but now also at home — Felisita eats last, and least.

INCREASED SCHOOL ATTENDANCE IN A MUG

Meanwhile, teachers at Igoda School are crediting the Foxes' "Meal in a Mug" program for raising school attendance there by 10 percent and improving classroom behaviour.[75]

"Which will likely translate into better results," Vicky says, stifling a momentary longing to be teaching again.

"And is hardly surprising," Geoff adds. "Imagine trying to concentrate at school on an empty stomach." He pauses then laughs. "You should see the grannies and single mothers joking as they cook up gallons of *uji*. You would never know how HIV/AIDS has affected them all."

《•》《•》《•》《•》

AIDING GRANDMOTHERS

"My back is breaking, Oh, mother of my mother.
My tears are dry, dry as the earth;
dry as my mind which hungers for the days when I sang of learning
with my brothers and my sisters;
for the days, when we danced with tomorrow, together, in school."

"Enough of pain, oh daughter of my daughter!
Instead, let my toothless mouth still smile and sing!
Let my ancient hands find strength to cradle you
and all my other children of my children in your sleep.
Let my toothless mouth still find a smile
to ease your laughter and your games;
to keep your tiny hands warm against my sagging breast.
Together let us feast on leaves! And drink the rains!"

"The rains; the rains, oh mother of my mother?
Where are the rains? Where are the strong ones?
Where are the strong ones now?
Where have they gone, the fathers all,
with their juices of virile manhood
their thrusting shovels that once brought food, and thatch, and school

75　Geoff Knight, project administration manager, Foxes' Community and Wildlife Conservation Trust (Tanzania), *Habari Ya Mufindi, Quarterly Newsletter*, 6, no. 3 (September 2011). A quarterly newsletter designed to inform donors about progress made in the implementation of the Mufindi Highlands Orphans Project in the Mufindi District of Tanzania, East Africa, a project supported by Mufindi Orphans, Inc, **http://www.mufindiorphans.org**.

before they drank of poisoned honey?
Where have they gone: the mothers all, the mothers,
who knew the ways of water, and of wood, of plantains and of manioc;
the mothers who should be here with me to feed their children's dreams
and rub your swelling joints? Where are they now?"

"And still you make me smile, oh daughter of my daughter
when with your little hands you caress the world around me.
And still you make me smile, oh children of my children,
when you reach and bend and carry, one tiny, earnest,
handful of earth in turn
to patch the gaping holes that let in sky through broken walls."

"And still you smile, oh mother of my mother,
even as you fade . . . fade . . . fade . . ."
"Fade? Me? (laughter) Oh daughter of my daughter,
No! Not yet! Not yet! Not yet!"

IGODA SCHOOL
NOW RANKED SEVENTH IN THE DISTRICT!

"The 2009 National Exam results are in!" Geoff hands Vicky the paper. She cannot believe her eyes.

"Ranked seventh in the district! And twenty-fifth in the region! Are we really talking about Igoda Primary School?"

"Brilliant, isn't it!"

"Out of how many, again?"

"District schools, 149, and more than 837 regional schools," Geoff exults. "Previous rankings were much nearer the bottom in both. Hurrah for our '*uji*' porridge program!"

"And classroom upgrades! Not to forget the all-important toilets."

"Ruth and Anne will be over the moon about this. That Igoda has the only primary school teaching library in Tanzania has surely also played a role in its overall school ratings."

"Do you think the jury is still out on the pros and cons of introducing something that most schools cannot afford?"

"Not if we look at it from the NGO's perspective. How did you put it, Geoff? 'What we are introducing here is above all the concept of a child-friendly learning library—a model that other schools can adapt to their own needs and within their own means.' It also gives the children crucial exposure to English before entering secondary school, where they suddenly switch from being taught everything in Swahili to everything in English. Imagine trying to cope with that, when fellow students are already fluent!"[76]

THE GROWING FOX TROOP

The Foxes now have nine grandchildren. "Like their fathers, it seems that they are all growing up to be very independent," in Geoff's view. "This pleases me greatly and should be encouraged because it could hopefully lead to a more lucrative and creative life. A nine-to-five employee's existence must be so dull. When you are working for yourself, you don't mind the extra days and hours, but when you work for others, you resent it. All my life I have worked on Saturdays and very often on Sundays, too, without regret. With their hardworking and talented wives, I reckon our independent boys have done very well.

"Now, back to our grandchildren. Having had no daughters of my own, I wanted lots of girls to spoil Grandpa, but they are all boys except for one, so Rachel is going to have a busy time."

"When Rachel was born," Vicky adds, "Grandpa was over the moon, telling everyone that he had a granddaughter—the only girl in two generations."

Geoff glares at her—partly because she has interrupted the flow of his story and partly in jest. "In Africa," he continues, "some say it's a woman's fault if she does not obey her husband by granting his wishes." (This in relation to the daughters he never had. Vicky ignores him.) "Our eldest grandson, Mathew, just turning twenty, is now a qualified commercial pilot working in the family business. His sister, Rachel, still at school, is learning to be a pilot. On her next holiday in Dar es Salaam, she'll have enough hours for a private licence. It will be fun to have the pilot give Grandpa a hug whenever she lands in Mufindi.

"Young Felix will certainly follow suit; he dreams of being a pilot. Jenny Coxell, our efficient young Ruaha manager, used to complain about having to use the computer in the dark, because five-year-old

---

76 Adapted from Gary Drobnack, *Habari Ya Mufindi, Quarterly Newsletter*, 5, no. 2 (March 2010).

Felix was practising night landings with his little toy plane! (In many ways, Jenny brought him up. From when he was born, she was his constant companion and even now looks after Felix and Rachel when they have weekends off from school in South Africa.)

"Bruce and Jane's boys, Oliver and Jeremy, are certainly well on their way to success in whatever they choose to do. Both are excelling at school in England and, to Grandma Vicky's delight, are showing interest in playing the piano. Jeremy is very keen on games, excelling at rugby and hockey. They still love their holidays here in Mufindi.

"Alexander and Jeanie's three, rather out of control in Dar es Salaam, had to be transferred to a fantastic school in Nairobi where, to everyone's surprise, they were awarded the Headmaster's Certificate for good behaviour. I told this to their nanny, Upendu, and she just shook her head in disbelief with a smile on her face. They are very spirited young boys who will certainly flourish. Michael, the oldest, has a hard time with his two identical twin brothers, David and James. I imagine later on the girls will, too!

"Michael stayed with me whilst Jeanie was in hospital having the twins," Vicky interjects. She was in England at the time and acted as Jeanie's birthing partner. "He was so upset about his mum being away that he would go to bed with his gumboots and all his clothes on in case he would miss going to see Mum in hospital. Once he was asleep, I managed to take them off."

"Meanwhile," Geoff adds, "I agreed to do a 'caretaker' shift on the 'island' for Alex and Jeanie (still building up Lazy Lagoon at the time). Before they left, much to their mirth, I descended noisily into their badly made long-drop loo. It wasn't built for my weight! And before they returned, I built them a splendid long-drop that is still in use to this day! All three of their children simply love the Highland farm.

"Finally, the youngest, Kiasile, only son of Christopher and Sylvia, is fluently trilingual in English, Kiswahili, and Italian. As mentioned earlier, not only did two of Christopher's old trackers, Amon Kalinga and Saidi Masonda, name him, they also trained him, from the age of two, on their daily game walks before breakfast in the Ruaha Park.

"President Kikwete of Tanzania was invited to lunch at Christopher's Mwagusi Safari Camp one day and insisted that Kiasile sit next to him. 'Who is your teacher?' the president asked the six-year-old.

"Who will finish first?" Geoff, grandchild, and stiff drink. (This brings to mind Geoff's October 17, 1973 letter to his parents, about visiting children not even being "house trained, and don't tell you until you have trodden on it on the floor! One doesn't even dare sit on a chair without examining it carefully first …")

Kiasile replied with a name and then asked the same question of the president. 'Mwalimu Julius Nyerere,' came the reply.

"'You are our boss,' little Kiasile told the president and then wanted to know, 'who is your boss?'

"'God, I suppose,' President Kikwete answered. Then, relaxing in the lounge after lunch, he spent the afternoon helping Kiasile with his homework.

"Nothing would make us happier than to see our grandchildren building up further a company that started with Vicky's building a little camp in Ruaha, but they must be free to make their own decisions," Geoff concludes, comfortably the paterfamilias.

《•》《•》《•》《•》

Little Reuben's grandmother, meanwhile, lies down. This is unusual, so early in the afternoon. "Come," she says to the youngest child; "come and keep *Bibi* warm." Reuben curls up against his grandmother. The older ones tempt her with *uji*. But she just smiles and shakes her head. Grandfather looks worried.

Later that evening, he takes Reuben by the hand. "Come, children," he says. "Let *Bibi* rest. It's storytelling time (eight to ten p.m., according to Hehe custom). *Babu* sits on his three-legged stool near the open fire. The children arrange themselves in a circle on the ground around him ("Careful. Not too close to the fire!") and settle down to listen.

Dr. Leena on duty.
(Fox NGO)

Fox NGO Outreach and Home-Based Care

Akida Mdalingwa, a highly motivated young volunteer at the Fox NGO, already has the confidence of many village committees on orphans and the vulnerable children. So much so that his information on families most in need and key community priorities has fed into a community outreach plan that the NGO will use as a guide for managing their outreach activities, including prioritizing family visits by the home-based care team.

Today he is accompanying Dr. Leena, Jenny, and others on community visits. A very sick mother is begging them please to take her baby with them. They agree to do so on a temporary basis, knowing full well the child will never return. With the baby strapped on Jenny's back, Tanzanian style, they continue to the next homestead.

The NGO now works with over 1,000 vulnerable orphans, and about 2,000 adults, in some cases by providing shelter and sustenance, in other cases by temporarily caring for orphans, conducting self-improvement programs such as English language classes, and community-based income-generating projects, including basket-making by HIV-positive mothers too sick to work in the fields.

("Twenty women sit in a circle on the ground," a visitor recently wrote home. "The hot sun shines down on their faces as they laugh and tell stories. Babies cling to their backs, wrapped in colourful cloths, as these women work. Their hands move in an intentional and flowing rhythm as the yellow reed slides through their fingers. The rounded sides start to form as the baskets take shape. Each woman contours her basket differently, some short and fat, others long and slim, but either way all are being created with dedication and hard work. Coloured fabrics are woven in for extra flair and visual appeal and the baskets are almost ready. These women aren't just weaving baskets, they're weaving their life."[77])

A few miles farther on, the outreach and homecare team reaches Felisita's village. Dr. Leena first brought her to Jenny's attention.

"I know that Felisita is keeping all her appointments for treatment at Mdabulo," she said. "Such a determined little girl, she should be doing much better. We need to find out why she is ailing."

Geoff K's and Jenny's initial thought was, *Who is Felisita?* But they know and trust Dr. Leena, so here they now are at her school. Not only is Felisita HIV positive, they are told, she is also being stigmatized by fellow students, has no friends to play with, and hates school because of it. Next they consult village leaders, and the head of the children's committee, whose job it is to identify those in the most dangerous living environment. Finally they need to know whether Felisita is living with relatives. She is. Her uncle has taken her in, but his second wife favours her own children. Despite all of this, Felisita has gamely continued her monthly visits to the hospital, alone, for treatment.

Exceptionally, the village executive officer agrees that Felisita should come to the Children's Village because only children without relatives to care for them are to be admitted.

FELISITA MAKES FRIENDS

Although Felisita has great faith in Dr. Leena, she is nervous because she has no idea what is awaiting her. Children . . . lots of children, that's what . . . all laughing and chasing each other. Felisita cringes. *Just like school*, she thinks. *I won't be able to keep up, and everyone will make fun of me.*

To her surprise, warm arms sweep her up into a long hug. "*Karibu*, Felisita. I will be your house mama, Ene." Children gather round her.

---

77   Rebeccah Kuntz, "Mufindi Orphans, Inc: Empowering Women in Tanzania—Inspiring Changemakers," *Stirring the Fire* (March 7, 2012), **http://stirringthefire.org/blog/author/admin/**.

"*Karibu*, Felisita," they echo. One takes her by the hand and shows her a bed, her very own, real bed. And soon a second child holds her other hand. Imagine that!

Time passes, and Jenny marvels at Felisita's transformation since her arrival at the Igoda Children's Village. *What a difference friends can make!* she thinks. *And schooling without bullying, and a guardian who cares for her, listens to her, hugs her . . .*

Felisita Mpangile.
(Fox NGO)

Then one day, "Come on, Felisita. Let's play." Her friends are waiting. Felisita tries to join them, but her head hurts too much. And her tummy is also sore. "I can't," she says. "I don't feel very well."

"Perhaps you should tell Mama Ene?"

"I'll be all right."

But Felisita is not all right. She finally goes to her house mama. Mama Ene, in turn, confides her concerns to Jenny. "I don't understand it," she says, echoing Dr. Leena. "Felisita has gone to her HIV/AIDS check ups regularly. She should be doing better."

"She has certainly put on weight since she's been here. And until recently she was very energetic."

"We'll all keep a close eye on her."

ANOTHER ACCIDENT

Meanwhile, son Bruce Fox and Jane are on their annual visit to Mufindi from the UK. As soon as their car stops, their boys leap out and rush off to see Daudi, the head horse guide, just as they did every day when they lived here permanently.

"Do you remember, Bruce? Daudi always fed them *ugali*, maize-meal porridge," Geoff says. "They loved it. So much so that Jane actually had to send them there with maize flour to supplement his supplies. Then there was the time, as you were leaving to fly back to the UK. Most of the farm staff came to wave goodbye. Suddenly your car door opened and young Jeremy (then aged four) got out, ran and took Daudi's hand, dragging him back to the car and — to everyone's delight — said: 'You're coming to England with us.'"

Many years have passed since then, and here they all are again. A bittersweet homecoming, as ever, given their forced relocation to England since the accident. Not that Bruce would ever let that get in the way of a good time.

"He is very strong," proud father Geoff comments. "Although he is wheelchair bound and for medical reasons needs to live in Britain, Bruce really runs the company. Whatever comes up, it's 'Bruce . . . Bruce . . . Bruce' — whether we're hiring expatriates, training Tanzanians, designing new camps, figuring out logistics, or right down to 'how many timbers of this size and that size' we need; everything! No wonder Alexander calls him 'the Professor.'"

Bruce's next accident doesn't happen during one of his madcap inspection tours, racing around the farm on the all-terrain vehicle (known as "Bruce's Legs"), to inspect every project and store each detail for future reference. It doesn't happen as he is careening over bumpy tracks. Instead, it happens as he puts weight on his leg at home. Weakened by osteoporosis, it collapses, bending and crumpling the calipers.

Peter immediately pilots a plane to Mufindi and flies Bruce and Jane to Dar es Salaam. During the flight, he keeps taking photos of Bruce's "S"-shaped leg. An orthopaedic surgeon greets them at the Aga Khan hospital. "Come with me," he says to Jane. "Since no other staff is available right now, you are my assistant. Please push the trolley."

During the procedure, Jane's mobile rings. Bruce retrieves it from her pocket. "Hello. It's Sarah. Peter wants to know when you're coming back." Bruce and Sarah chat for a while, with Bruce still on the operating table, Jane still trying to hold Bruce's broken bones straight, and the surgeon still working. Then, "Hold on, Bruce," Sarah says. "Here's Peter."

"Tell the doctor to set your leg at an angle, so I can fit you into the plane more easily." They fly back to Mufindi the next day.

In Mourning

The Children's Village is in mourning. Felisita died yesterday, June 26, 2010. Today, sounds of voices raised in song drift over the countryside as the Fox lorry transports most of the children and their house-mamas from the Village to her funeral. It takes close to an hour on rough dirt roads. Throughout that journey they sing her farewell.

"My husband, daughter Lauren, and I were in Mufindi when Felisita's health took a turn for the worst," Anne Pearson writes to Canadian friends. "I was teaching Jenny's adult English class while they were in Dar. Felisita would wait in the *ukumbi* (porch) until the class was over and would sit on my lap in the car while Terry drove us home. She didn't have the strength to walk back to the Children's Village at the end of her long days but somehow summoned the courage to walk that distance to school in the early mornings. Elsewhere, a child as determined as Felisita would have flourished; instead, in rural Mufindi, she painfully withered and died. I believe her story has acted as a catalyst inspiring so many to work harder to help improve people's lives."

Anne confers with Ruth. Together, they vow to raise enough funds to fully equip the Mdabulo HIV/AIDS clinic.

《•》《•》《•》《•》

After *Bibi's* death, Reuben's *Babu*/grandfather is determined to care for his seven grandchildren. "I can still manage to grow food," he tells the Fox outreach and homecare staff. "My oldest granddaughter, a fourteen-year-old girl, will cook. The others can all help around the house. Together, we will manage, with a bit of support for school uniforms and (touching the shoulder of the youngest boy at his side) AIDS medicine for Reuben."

"Since you are doing so well, Mzee, of course."

Babu and seven grandchildren later wave goodbye. From their huge smiles, you would think that they had won a million dollars. On the other hand, what would a million dollars be, compared to keeping a family together?

《•》《•》《•》《•》

For every Felisita, there is a Reuben, Geoff thinks. *How could one not be affected by such a maelstrom of hope, and desperation, and triumph . . . little triumphs . . . the child who now stays awake in class, the teacher who now has the energy to teach, the parent who can lift the hoe again, the child who can wear the school uniform. Then there are the smiles, the eyes . . . the eyes . . .*

JENNY'S STORIES

"We were at fifty-five children," Jenny writes home in a haunting email to Canadian fundraisers, "but in the last four months, we have lost two children, Felisita (twelve years old) and Joshua (one) to HIV/ AIDS-related complications. I feel now is an appropriate time to tell their stories, as neither of the deaths were in vain, but instead have brought around change — NEEDED change — that will help save lives in our community here forever.

"Joshua, a little one-year-old man, met me at the Care and Treatment Centre day with his father. Joshua's mother had died just two days before, and his dad was worried he couldn't take care of the baby and work.

"Could we take in the child, he asked, just until he was three? This is a common request at our Children's Village, one that we take very seriously. The father / family member makes a monthly contribution to show that they actually DO care about the child, and don't get the child back until they do "pay in full" (10,000 Tanzanian shillings or about $7 or £4.50 a month). This will buy about three-fourths of a tin of milk and is obviously not enough to cover the care of a baby, but we just want the family to do SOMETHING!

"This father proved himself a TREASURE! When he brought Joshua, he brought payment for two months in a row, and came every other day to make sure his son was adjusting. He called every day to see if his baby was doing okay at night, because after the mother died, the baby didn't want to drink the tinned milk he was given, cried continuously, and had diarrhea. About one week after Joshua was in our care, the house mamas knocked at my door at nine p.m. He wasn't doing well. Diarrhea. Vomiting. Lack of appetite . . . [while] I was with all the house mamas overnight, I found out the TRUE story about Joshua and his biological mother.

"During her pregnancy, Joshua's mom had tested HIV positive but because of lack of education and embarrassment about her status, she changed her result slip on her paper to say she was negative. So, when the time came to give birth, she wasn't given the pill to protect the mother to child transmission that may occur during childbirth. The nurses that did know her tried to convince her to join the CTC program. Her husband had been tested and was receiving treatment—why not her? They also advised her to stop breastfeeding the baby after six months . . . even suggesting that she could come and talk with me about our milk powder program . . . which helps to prevent HIV-positive mothers from transmitting HIV/AIDS to their babies."

《・》《・》《・》《・》

Here in Tanzania, and, according to World Health Organization guidelines, HIV-positive women are advised to breastfeed for six months, during which time the intestinal tracts of infants can resist HIV infection from mothers' milk [unless there are open lesions]. After that, mothers are advised to stop cold turkey, because the introduction of new foods usually causes small lacerations in the lining of the baby's gut through which the AIDS virus can enter.

Instead, they should start using milk powder, cow's milk, and/or nutritional supplements. This is not easy. Cow's milk can be scarce in the villages, and milk powder very expensive. One tin to feed an infant for three to five days costs about ten U.S. dollars, almost half of the twenty-three dollars farmers around here generally earn per month! An average family can't stop long-term breastfeeding without help.

The Milk Powder Program also addresses potentially fatal protein and caloric deficiencies. These show up as soon as impoverished mothers, who cannot afford eggs, milk, meat, or fish, stop breastfeeding. Instead, the program helps them obtain clean milk powder, along with a nutritious blend of maize, peanuts, soybeans, millet, and other locally grown items. This helps our community stave off severe malnutrition and the high child mortality rates it has endured.

At the same time, many mothers don't live in extremely

sanitary conditions, so bottle-feeding may introduce dirty water, which can cause diarrhea—life-threatening in a child. Very dangerous! So breastfeeding for six months it is, and then milk powder, the lesser of two evils. We have women knocking on our doors daily, anxious to save their children.[78]

《•》《•》《•》《•》

"But Joshua's mother still refused," Jenny's 2010 email continues. "She breastfed Joshua until he was more than a year old; until she passed away. Part of me is FURIOUS with this woman. How selfish can a person truly be, to do this to his or her own child? Any sane mother does anything in her power to protect her children from harm, to do her best by them . . . which does not include giving them a FATAL DISEASE! But the other part of me just feels sad. Are we still at the point in time where people feel alone? Embarrassed by a disease well near half the community has? Keeping it a secret from their family and neighbours, because of SHAME?! Risking the health of their child, to protect their own name? It breaks my heart; she must have felt so alone.

"Joshua made it just one more week. His condition never changed. We took him to the hospital a total of five times . . . in three weeks. The day he passed away, he had woken up with the house mother to take some milk. He took one sip, turned his head, and just went. This poor little guy just didn't have the fight in him anymore. He just looked like he was sleeping and when I was called shortly after, it was the first time I had ever had to feel a corpse, and check for a pulse, or a look for a heartbeat. On a one-year-old baby.

"At Joshua's funeral, I talked with the village leaders about the WHOLE story. About what the mother did, and what was beautiful about such a tragedy was that the village leaders started talking. 'It is time to start getting back into the village,' they said. 'Time to start educating our youth and women, not only on HOW someone can get AIDS, but also that you aren't alone if you DO have AIDS, and how to help someone living with AIDS, and how you can get treatment if you do have AIDS.'

---

78 Adapted from Jenny Peck, *Habari Ya Mufindi, Quarterly Newsletter* 5, no. 3 (September 2010). **http://www.mufindiorphans.org**.

"They went so far as to start talking about how they could talk to church congregations (as here we're having a serious problem with a group of women who believe that if they are HIV positive, 'Faith will heal me,' which is fine, but you also need medicine. Why have the people chosen to stigmatize those with AIDS? If you break your leg, do you just pray that God will heal you? No! You go to the doctor. You get a cast. AND you pray that God will give you a quick recovery.

"Joshua's death is bringing about social change. It's making people talk. And think. And realize what they can do for their community. As I have a ten-month-old baby, and another one on the way, Joshua's death has been very tough for me. Losing a child is not something our culture is used to. Here, child mortality is something more common than I would like to admit. It will happen, but avoidable deaths need to stop. And by sharing stories like Joshua's, hopefully they will.

"Felisita was brought to our attention by Dr. Leena Pasanen, the Finnish Expatriate of the Year 2009 and pediatrician from Ilembula Hospital (in Tanzania) who has lived more than thirty years in Tanzania, and who we are fortunate enough to have volunteering precious time with us: ten to fourteen days every month! To see Dr. Leena, Felisita had taken her tiny-framed self twelve miles from her village of Ibwanzi to Mdabulo on a bus, alone, as her stepmother didn't want to go, and her uncle couldn't go, and her parents had passed away from HIV/AIDS . . .

"She was welcomed into the Children's Village with open arms and learned that there ARE kids, just like her, living with the same disease that CAN play with other children with no problems, and CAN go to school without being made fun of for something she could not control . . . She started living again. The smile came back to her face. She had friends! A home! A guardian that cared about her well-being and went with her to her clinic days!

"Unfortunately, the system in Tanzania is a broken one. (Although the Fox NGO is now in the process of building an HIV/AIDS Care and Treatment Clinic here in Mufindi.) For now, the clinic still consists of the hospital about thirty-five miles away, sending a car to Mufindi twice a month, carrying all the patient files and medicine along with the doctors and staff. Files are forgotten. Not enough medicine is brought. After all, these doctors are just guests in this village. How should they know who is actually going to show up or how many people might need medication? It's a matter of good guessing SOMETIMES, but other times, these overworked and underpaid doctors just FORGET things. Such as Felisita's file . . . THREE MONTHS IN A ROW.

"The file that has all her medical history: her previous weights to see if she is gaining, losing, or staying the same; the medication she has used and is currently using, or any other interesting things of note for the doctor seeing her to know how she is progressing. Felisita started feeling unwell, complaining of stomach aches or headaches. She was given Tylenol. She lost a bit of weight, but because no file was there, no one knew.

"They kept giving her the same medication, as, without the files, they didn't know it was now time to check her CD–4 count (the level of protection the body has against infection: the higher the number, the healthier you are; the lower the number, the worse you are. By World Health Organization standards, if you have less than a count of 300, you should be on antiretrovirals.)

"Usually, if there is any sign of weight loss in an HIV-positive patient, a CD–4 count is taken to see if the medication needs to be changed . . . That didn't happen. Why? Felisita's file was thirty-five miles away. The same story the next month and the month after. My Geoff and I went away to a wedding, and when we got back, Felisita was a pile of bones. She couldn't sit up in bed, couldn't walk around . . . and, despite it all, was still trying to joke around with her friends. We rushed her to the hospital, where she was admitted, and her CD–4 count was checked. It was TWO.

"At zero, she would not be able to fight off a sneeze. She was immediately given antiretrovirals and, amazingly, recovered! Slowly she started walking around the children's village, gaining energy day by day . . . but one month later, she fell ill again and just didn't have enough strength to fight the infection. Her last minutes in the ward of the hospital had everyone in tears... "WHY, GOD? Why are you punishing me? Take me! I am not the one who made the mistake. My parents caused this. They made the mistake. Stop punishing me!" This from the mouth of a twelve-year-old girl.

HIV/AIDS Clinic Day in Mdabulo at the clinic built and equipped through the Fox NGO.
(Fox NGO)

FELISITA'S LIFE-GIVING HERITAGE

Felisita's death was the final catalyst toward a major fundraising drive in Canada by Anne and Ruth to raise funds for a life-saving CD–4 machine. It arrives at last; too late for Felisita, but, thanks to her, the Fox-sponsored Care and Treatment Centre at Mdabulo is now a permanent and full-treatment facility for diagnosis as well as routine treatment of HIV/AIDS right here in Mufindi.

"Felisita's death has touched many hearts," writes Jenny, "from all who knew her and lived with her at the Children's Village, to those volunteering, to those just hearing her story. The trials of Felisita are NOT hers alone. Files are forgotten EVERY time the visiting doctors come. What could prevent this? Keeping the files in the village! But we couldn't do that without a testing and treatment centre (CTC). And with the help of donors, that CTC has now been built by the Fox NGO and registered just recently by the government of Tanzania!"

News of it spreads from one to another in Mufindi, from staff to volunteer, from caregiver to patient, and on through the communities.

Villagers prepare an extra-warm welcome for their beloved Canadian sponsors, Ruth and Anne, whose tireless fundraising has made so many things possible. For their part, the retired teachers are just happy, on their next field visit, to sing and dance and read and laugh and sometimes weep together in the interactive Igoda School library.

Felisita's playground.
(Fox NGO)

"When it's not a rare sighting to see women carrying back-breaking loads, cooking on open fires, badly burned toddlers, raggedy waifs toiling in fields beside their families, idle young men, people of all ages diminished by HIV, it causes one to wonder. But I am an eternal optimist," Anne writes home to Canadian friends, "and have the privilege of seeing first-hand on the ground the positive influence of the Foxes' NGO. The changes are staggering and uplifting."

Jenny adds to her letter, "Because of Felisita's story, and her warm and addicting personality, some wonderful people from Canada (you all know who you are!) came together and found funding ($50,000/£32,000) to buy a CD–4 machine to go into our new CTC. This means that we now have a treatment facility for a catchment of 40,000 people, a facility that is equipped with one of the MOST precious machines to anyone who is HIV positive, which in our area is 35 percent.

"This is the BEST and MOST exciting news our community has had—and it was due to Felisita's story being told. THANK YOU!

"And, not only did we receive news of a CD–4 machine, but, more child-related, and in Felisita's memory: a playground will be constructed . . . teaching kids that EVERYONE can play together . . . no matter what. These people I live with are wonderful and beautiful and carry an inner strength that amazes me. The impact of AIDS does not have to be negative."[79]

79   Closely based on an email from Jenny Peck.

THE WORLD NEEDS LAUGHTER

Geoff and Vicky have just returned from a cousin's wedding in Devon. "It was at a church largely full of farmers, family, and friends," Geoff tells Mufindi friends. "The young pastor with a cheeky twinkle behind his glasses asks if anyone has heard the story of St. Peter and the pearly gates. Stunned silence for a moment until from the back of the house a voice (remarkably like Geoff's) says: 'No.' Whereupon the pastor is given licence to relate his story. 'The time had come for three old men to apply to enter the pearly gates, but St. Peter stood in their way. Telling them that he would only let them through if they could each produce a symbol of the church.

"'The first put a hand in his pocket and produced his car keys; clanging them, he asked, "Church bells?"

"'"Oh, all right," said St. Peter and let him through.

"'The second put his hand in his pocket and brought out a cigarette lighter. "Church candles?" he enquired.

"'"Oh, okay," replied St. Peter, and he, too, was admitted.

"'The third put his hand in his pocket and drew out a pair of red lady's knickers.

"'"What are those?" demanded St. Peter.

"'"Carol's."'

"The church explodes in general hysterics (but for the bride's mother and a few traditional churchgoers). Encouraged, the pastor goes on to another. 'We are today marrying two farmers,' he announced, 'and as we know, all Devon farmers have no money. [Murmurs of assent all around.] So one day, when a farmer's wife died, he could only afford to put three words in the paper: "Muriel died Thursday." The newspaper felt sorry for him and offered him another three words for free. The old Devon farmer thought for a moment and came up with "Hay for sale."' The rest of the service was a joyous affair," Geoff concludes, "for most."

《•》《•》《•》《•》

President Kikwete is re-elected in October 2010, this time on a platform to maintain fiscal policies and keep Tanzania's economy growing. His broad economic policies have worked, if measured in gross domestic production. Unfortunately, he has neither managed to redistribute wealth internally, nor reduce corruption, as is most evident in ineffective prosecution (if at all) of high-profile graft cases.

CORRUPTION

"Corruption is perhaps the most worrying trend afflicting Africa these days, and is getting ever worse in Tanzania." Geoff is uncharacteristically solemn. "The joys and happiness of living in this wonderful country are being threatened by those in a position to intimidate for personal gain. No government has been able to control this ever-deepening cancer on the economy, development, and reputation of this country. Seemingly, no one of significance has been successfully prosecuted, making it open season for opportunists.

"Many years ago, I found myself at the receiving end after accidentally driving into an elderly man emerging from a roadside drain. He was 100 percent stone deaf and didn't hear the vehicle. I was dawdling along, but when you get someone suddenly coming out, you can't stop in time. He's on the road in one step. His leg broke. I quickly took him to hospital and reported the accident. When I took the policeman to the spot of the mishap, he made a sketch map and brazenly demanded a bribe. Of course I refused. Whereupon he forwarded the case to the public prosecutor and I found myself up in court.

"Albert Mwanjessa, the personnel director of Brooke Bond, was asked by the magistrate's clerk of the court no less than three times to pay a bribe. He, too, declined. The next thing I knew I had been convicted for dangerous driving. And grievous bodily harm. And sentenced to two years' imprisonment. At my appeal hearing, the judge and state prosecutor agreed that they could find no reason at all for the conviction, so, without a word from my lawyer, the case was dismissed.

"Our Farm Lodge bookings have sharply declined, largely because of traffic police harassment (one recent group took fifteen hours to make the 400-mile journey up from Dar es Salaam). Then there is the District health and hygiene official who makes his money seeking out items past their sell-by date and charging over $1,800 per item. And so it goes on—'rampant corruption' threatening to destroy our adopted homeland."

VICKY'S COWS ON STRIKE

The day Vicky's Highland Farm cows go on strike starts like any other. At 6:30 a.m., Vicky and Julius (farm overseer and Vicky's right-hand man) begin their daily rounds. First stop: the pigpen, to make sure that all the leftover vegetables and skimmed milk have reached their destination in the troughs; that the pigs are getting the right mixture of maize bran germ and sunflower cake; and, when they reach a certain weight and are ready for slaughter, that they are taken to the butchery to be processed.

Vicky's two butchers are now very adept at butchering carcasses into very neat joints. Legs of pork are put into refrigerated brine tanks, together with hams (for three days) and deboned bacon joints (for two). The bacon is then rolled and frozen. Ham joints are deboned and put into ham nets. Everything is weighed, packeted, frozen, and eventually sent off to the camps.

After visiting the pigs, Vicky and Julius walk the length of the golf course to the cows, this time to make sure that all the calves are healthy and to watch the cows being milked — completely milked!

Then they join a procession of people with plastic buckets and churns on their heads to climb up the golf course again, across the secret garden, and into the dairy, where the milk is tallied, mixed with the previous evening's milk, and then separated. The cream is frozen in plastic bags for later transport to Fox camps. Some separated milk ends up as cottage cheese, some is sold off to the staff (very cheaply) and to the lodge. A portion of cream is then churned into butter, frozen, and ready for dispatch. This part of the tour ends with Vicky arriving home for breakfast. Later, she and Julius, with Johanna, who now helps there, visit the vegetable garden — a source of vegetables for all the camps and lodges, especially when unavailable at the market.

One day, the farm runs out of the sunflower cake and *pumba* (maize bran) mix usually enjoyed by Vicky's cows during milking. As if to say, "no *pumba*, no milk," the cows all solidly refuse to give any. Not one litre. Even though they are clearly in distress and bursting. Those with calves are fine because their udders can be relieved, but the others are about to explode. And still they refuse to give up even a drop. It turns out that the *pumba* delivery lorry is firmly stuck in rainy season mud. Emergency is declared! The Fox car scours surrounding villages for at least some *pumba*.

The next day, the main food supply arrives at last, unfortunately with much too high a proportion of sunflower cake to *pumba* (greater than one part in four is considered unpalatable). So more time passes in manually extricating the excess. When the cows are given the right mix at last, they immediately and willingly give up their milk—but in reduced amounts.

"They have forgiven us, at last!" Vicky announces triumphantly two days later. "We are back to normal quantities."

MAMA REHEMA'S PREGNANCY

"Something is bothering you, Mama Rehema," Jenny observes one day. "What is it?" Mama Rehema hesitates. Then almost whispers, "I'm pregnant."

"I understand, Mama, an HIV-positive pregnancy is clearly challenging. But you know that you can do a lot to prevent passing the AIDS virus on to your baby, don't you?"

"Strange, isn't it? Telling others how to prevent mother-to-child transmission is one thing. Going through it yourself is very different. I need to go over everything again. That way I know nothing will be neglected." Her eyes are suspiciously moist.

"Of course. First things first: It's really important to take care of yourself during pregnancy. The healthier you are, the healthier the baby will be. That includes nourishing food, like adding peanuts to your *uji* in the morning. And rest when possible. I know you'll find that difficult, but it's very important. Later, you'll need to take a pill to protect your child during childbirth. Then either go straight to powdered milk (only if you're sure that you can keep the bottle and the water sterile) or breastfeed for six months—definitely no longer. After that, switch immediately to milk powder dissolved in boiled water. Whatever you do, don't mix breast and bottle. Solids with milk powder can cause very small abrasions in the baby's insides, which could allow the virus to enter your baby's bloodstream from your own milk. Just using powdered milk is safest, but, again, only if the water and bottle can be sterilized."

"Thank you, Jenny."

"Welcome. And, Mama Rehema, you will both do just fine!"

Fox NGO Celebrates Fifth Anniversary

"Five years already!"

"Already? Actually, five years from the official registration of the Fox NGO, seven years since Ruth and Anne injected life-saving capital and energy."

"Still, it sometimes feels like twenty-five!"

"I just wish I could find that young boy who was trying to help his grandmother by looking for work the day everything changed for us," Geoff says wistfully. "But to all of you," he turns to those helping to celebrate the occasion, "thank you so very much."

Viewed as a whole, the Fox NGO has all but reached the goals set in late 2004. In early 2005, the most obvious problem was caring for large numbers of children orphaned by HIV/AIDS, hence its focus on building the Igoda Children's Village. Then came the Outreach Program, providing school space for orphans, renovating existing medical facilities for the care of orphans and other HIV/AIDS victims, and creating a local social environment geared to dissemination of HIV/AIDS awareness education, village income generation projects, and improved morale by reinforcing community hope and togetherness.

"We now even have a permanent Care and Treatment Centre (CTC) at Mdabulo Hospital," Geoff says, raising his glass. "It is already saving and extending the lives of hundreds of villagers. Fewer people are afraid to discuss HIV/AIDS openly these days, and willingly talk with CTC medical staff about their fears and misunderstandings. More and more people volunteer for testing after assurances that they will not be ostracized should they be found HIV positive. And increasing numbers are willing to practise preventative measures to stop the spread of HIV/AIDS.

"Today we celebrate all this." He pauses for effect.

"Tomorrow we start again. Thanks to Ruth and Anne, the NGO now has housing for volunteers, so Dr. Leena and Marion are already putting their feelers out for medical specialists from abroad who might volunteer a few weeks a year to treat folk in the Mdabulo hospital, given the shortage of medical specialists in Tanzania. Without Swahili, general practitioners are limited in what they can offer.

"Speaking of Dr. Leena, some of you may not know that the World Medical Association has named her one of the world's most compassionate doctors (this on top of her earlier honour as Finland's Most Outstanding Finn Living Outside Finland in 2009)? And have you heard about Dr. Leena's latest medical miracle?

ANOTHER DR. LEENA MIRACLE

"The parents of a ten-year-old boy from the village of Ikaningombe, brought him to one of Dr. Leena's clinics saying that the boy was blind, had been taken out of school, and now had to stay at home with nothing to do. The parents were worried about the boy's future in a community that had no facilities for helping the blind.

"Dr. Leena examined him and noted the cloudiness in his pupils. She then made arrangements for the boy and a guardian to visit the Ilembula Hospital's optometrist, Dr. Eric Msigomba. Dr. Msigomba assessed the situation and determined that the boy had blinding cataracts. The doctor then performed the necessary operation and sent the boy home to recover. Almost immediately, the boy regained his ability to see. He is now back at school and doing well according to his teachers.

"One could easily deny that the boy's recovery was a miracle, calling it simply the result of a couple of competent doctors working together to apply common medical treatment for a common ailment. The miracle is that Dr. Leena was there to initiate the series of events, which gave the boy back his life."[80]

《•》《•》《•》《•》

STILL DREAMING OF RETIREMENT

"Here in Mufindi, Vicky and I still dream of retirement," Geoff writes to friends in the UK, "but, after fifty-two years, we shall never leave—apart from our annual (May to July) search in England for chocolates, cheese, and more socks. Our boys (actually, Bruce!) are taking advantage of a 'cheap option' by dragging the old folks out to stand in for managers who need a long break! Recently we both went to the Selous during quite a difficult time with a full camp, and then to Katavi for a protracted spell.

---

80 Based on Geoff Knight, Project Administration Manager, Foxes' Community and Wildlife Conservation Trust (Tanzania), *Habari Ya Mufindi, Quarterly Newsletter* 6, no. 3 (Sept 2011). **http://www.mufindiorphans.org**.

In between, we stopped over in Dar to attend an evening Garden Party for Charles and Camilla, where I nearly spilled Camilla's red wine all over her white dress (I usually talk with my arms flailing around!). They had asked me to chat with her about our NGO.

"Selous was HOT. But our Rufiji River Camp is amazing. Having totally replaced the old (Karl Jaehn's) camp with very large luxury tents and lodge buildings, I am convinced it is the best out of the many camps in Selous. The very big dining/bar lodge, with upstairs lounge and smoking bar areas, is made of treated Mufindi eucalyptus (from our farm), Kilombero teak flooring, and Makuti thatch, while the spacious tents (with fabulous bathrooms) are raised onto large platforms with plenty of verandah space—also under tall makuti thatch. All this is mainly Bruce and Jane's design. With the heat at this time of year, the attractive shaded swimming pool is always popular.

"Rufiji provides riverboat safaris that differentiate it from Ruaha, but I prefer Ruaha. However, the boys are now planning an upmarket 'posh' camp on a beautiful lake close to the Rufiji River and largely surrounded by an attractive forest of trees—only about two miles upriver and full of game (this is why the Foxes are always short of cash!). More later!"

THAT GIRL WAS TOUGH

"It's confirmed, Foxey. Jenny is leaving Ruaha." Young Jenny Coxell has now been Ruaha River Camp manager for seven years.

"We'll miss her," Geoff answers. "But at least she'll be close to our grandchildren in South Africa."

Like others, Geoff and Vicky have marvelled at Jenny's constitution over the years.

At the end of one season, after she hosted Foxtreks' final group of the season in Katavi, there was no room for her on the last plane out. Undaunted, she managed to get a lift on the back of a lorry to Sumbawanga, a long day's journey away. (Just as buses load and disgorge people along the route, so these trucks take on and drop off provisions.) At Sumbawanga, Jenny decided to spend the night on the station's cement floor, since her onward bus was leaving early the next morning. Someone took her reserved seat up front. So Jenny shrugged and chose another one behind him. Only a short distance out of Sumbawanga, heading toward the Zambian border, the bus crashed headlong into another.

Among those killed were the driver and the man who had taken Jenny's reserved seat. She herself got away with a bit of a neck whiplash. Since all the rescue vehicles were returning to Sumbawanga with bodies and marooned passengers, and Jenny wanted to go the other way, she stopped a passing low-loader carrying a grader and jumped on—all the way to Mbeya. From there, she took a bus to Makambako, then another to Mafinga, where she met the Foxes with a grin. "That girl is tough!" Geoff laughs.

《•》《•》《•》《•》

"A donation from Hong Kong? How on earth did Hong Kong find out about the Fox NGO?"

"An interesting coincidence, that." Geoff is chatting with the Fox NGO team. "Remember Helga and Werner Voigt, our German settler friends who used to have a tea and coffee farm in Mufindi West? In April 1937, an itinerant minister passing through the area christened their first-born son.

"With respect, Mr. Fox—the link with the Foxes' project at Mdabulo hospital?"

"Patience. I'm getting there. Fast-forward to Christmas 2008 when Helga, by then retired in Canada, received a letter from Hong Kong. It read something like, 'Dear Mrs. Voigt, Do you recognize my name? If not, please turn to page 141 of your book (*Letters from Helga*[81]). I am the son of Erich Boost, the "all-around nice guy" you chose as your son's godfather.'

"Joern Boost and his wife Maureen later visited Helga's daughter, Evelyn, and her husband, Gordon—unfortunately, after Helga's death. Just as the Boosts were heading out the door for their onward journey, Joern saw a pamphlet advertising Gord and Evelyn's upcoming Ottawa fundraiser for Mufindi Orphans.[82] It turns out that the Boosts are very active in the Hong Kong Rotary movement. So, they are supplementing what Ottawa raised toward our "united nations" wing at Mdabulo's surgery.

---

81 Helga Voigt, *Letters from Helga: A Teen Bride Writes Home from East Africa* (Renfrew, ON: General Store Publishing House, 2008).

82 **http://mufindiorphans.ca** (held every August)

Timeline construction (2011–13) of Mdabulo's "united nations" surgery wing, so called because it is being built, staffed, and equipped with money donated, coin by coin, in the US, UK, Canada, Hong Kong, and, of course, Tanzania. Not only that, but also through a three-way co-operation in Tanzania of private sector, voluntary, and (for sustainability) government efforts. Mwalimu might well have smiled on yet another Tanzanian manifestation of his dream: *Ujamaa*. Communality.
(Justin Dominges, Geoff Knight)

《 • 》《 • 》《 • 》《 • 》

"Back in Mufindi everything is green." Geoff finally makes some time for letter writing. "The rains started on December 7th. The farm looks fantastic with the two-kilometre driveway Jacaranda Avenue still in full, purple bloom. Everything has greatly reforested since the days we took over the village land (twenty-four years ago) and looks amazing. Dams on the farm are stocked with trout, and one has black bass to provide variety. Up to now, the trout ova have had to be imported from South Africa, but I have now completed the hatchery and trout farm series of holding tanks, so we hope always to have our own brood fish for future ova supplies. Although we have only a little and poor-looking coffee on this farm, our Kimbwe and Ibwanzi estates have about 150 acres of better coffee, plus a further 50 acres of macadamia trees, some pecan trees, and over 2,000 hectares (5,000 acres) of pine plantations. There are also areas of scenic pastures, forest plantations, striking gardens, and a wide variety of recreation facilities (tennis, badminton, croquet, golf, lawn bowls, trout fishing, and horseback riding) to satisfy visitors to our lodge and its many cabins. In short, plenty to do (I always tease guests that this is the Fox Health Farm, where it is illegal to read books and have an afternoon siesta—unless you're over seventy!).

"The Igoda Children's Village—yes, back to our project. I'm obsessed!—now houses some seventy-five orphaned and foster children in six houses. Accompanying these are a number of volunteer and other administrative buildings. The policy remains that only orphaned kids without any surviving relative can be admitted. However, if the relatives (and often it's just an old grandmother/*bibi*) are struggling, outreach support kicks in.

"Among Mufindi *bibis* caring for grandchildren are a couple with only one leg. Yesterday, Marion and I gave the oldest one a pair of crutches. I wish you could have seen her face. This grandmother is just learning to use her new crutches. Recently, her children died of AIDS and left her with several grandchildren. She did her best, but had little to do it on. The Project has moved her from the tiny hut she lived in to a newly built house and welcomed her younger grandchildren into the Children's Village. Thanks to small Project subsidies, she says she can now cope with life.[83]

"More than 1,000 orphaned children have been helped directly in the surrounding sixteen villages, and many others indirectly through guardians. So the total number is huge. Our outreach program also assists particularly AIDS-sick, single mothers and single grandparents.

"Vicky is in charge of 'her' farm, which gives her great joy, and she continues to do an evening round with our old headman (Julius), discussing this cow, that sheep—pig, horse, vegetable supply, etcetera. The sheep are so numerous that all our border collies are essential, and she has twenty-four horses (with several pregnant), which I am now threatening to put on the menu! She butchers six pigs per week

---

83 Adapted from Marion Gough, *Habari Ya Mufindi, Quarterly Newsletter* 3, no. 3 (March 2008). **http://www.mufindiorphans.org**.

on average around the year to supply all our camps with meat and vegetables from this farm."

DIVING FOR COVER

"It is the honest truth," Geoff complains to visitors when the subject of butchering comes up, "that Vicky, on emerging from the butcher's where the freezers are kept, will frequently walk around muttering, 'I need to kill something,' as the freezers run low. That's when I dive for cover."

MAMA REHEMA'S BABY, RAHABU

Mama Rehema's due date is fast approaching. She has followed all the rules. "God grant us a healthy child," she prays as the labour pains start. She prays through the birthing. In 2011, her third child, Rahabu, is born. More prayers as they face the interminable wait for HIV/AIDS test results. Oblivious to their fears, Rahabu suckles hungrily at the bottle. Mama Rehema wonders what possible poisons might be in the water. But at least they can't be worse than the actual poisons in her milk. Then she chides herself. Is she not a peer counsellor? Aren't she and her husband going door to door in the village, giving group counselling? Showing people how if they test themselves, they can prevent the AIDS disease itself? How they can protect themselves in childbirth? Enough of this weakness! Her determined laughter rings out, momentarily breaking Rahabu's single-minded concentration.

Today is the day. Baby Rahabu's results are in. Mama Rehema and her husband await their turn at the clinic, sitting up straight. Tense. Silent. Only Baby Rahabu, the picture of health, gurgles contentedly. Finally, the doctor calls them. With a smile he pronounces Rahabu both HIV negative and thriving.

Mama Rehema gives thanks — not just in words but also in actions. She shares her experience openly. "With vigilance, HIV-positive living can be normal living," she tells villagers on regular outreach visits. "See here, Sisters," she comforts expectant mothers, lifting her fat little daughter, "Just because you are sick, it does not mean your children cannot be healthy."

DEAD MOTHERS CANNOT CRY

Another mother passes the mound of earth now covering her husband. Even though she is still angry with him, she also remembers how once she loved this man. *That was long before he passed his sickness to me*, she thinks. *And could he not have spared me this last child?* She knows she does not have the strength for another pregnancy. But what can she do? She looks down at the cloth covering her stomach. *Not too far gone yet*, she thinks. *I can still get rid of it, but how to do so safely? I need to stay alive as long as possible for my other children.*

She bends and whispers to the new life within her. "Forgive me. Even now, I barely have the energy to move. How will it be later? Would I even live to see you?" Finally, she makes up her mind. To carry both the sickness and the child is impossible. She will find a way.

"Dead Mothers Cannot Cry"[84]

She speaks to her womb
Empty of child
And filled with acid
Magic potions
Leaves
Rusting metal

She whispers to her womb
Empty of another desperate mouth to feed

In the night, her children
Gather round her,
She strains to see their smiles
Beyond her tears

At least, she thinks,
Dead mothers cannot cry.[85]

---

84   The title is adapted from BBC's *Dead Mums Don't Cry*, the text inspired by the Anna Project.
85   Also published in *Bout de Papier* 26, no.4 (Fall 2012).

Hers is not an isolated story, which is why the Foxes' Home-Based Care Team hosts a family planning seminar at the Children's Village. Subsequent demand for such education and services has brought the seminar into the wider community, now in Mkonge village, now at the NGO's Mdabulo Care and Treatment Centre, often hosted by Dr. Onyango and drawing an average of fifty women.

CHRISTMAS IN MUFINDI

At Christmas and New Year's, all the Highland Lodge tables are put together to form a single, massive seating arrangement, with very traditional English fare, including turkey, Christmas pudding, crackers, and so on.

"Everyone has to wear a silly paper hat," says Geoff. "I remember the Danish ambassador putting his Christmas hat to one side on the table after pulling the cracker and I sternly reminded this very nice guy that even ambassadors have to look silly. New Year's is much the same, with fun and frivolity. The lodge really is a family destination rather than just a tourist hotel. And the best part is that most of the people are repeat visitors, so they know what to expect and what to do to create the atmosphere. Our other lodges are still more of a wildlife experience, regardless of the day, and can never quite achieve the same ambience.

"Peter and Rob Glenn [the sculptor who camps and works in Ruaha with his partner, fellow artist Susan Stolberger, author of the fabulous *Ruaha Sketchbook*], were sitting around the fire one New Year's Eve, in the Ruaha River bed—there being no flow at the time. Having consumed far too much, they complained loudly about the dreadful wine that the Ruaha River Lodge supplied. A guest confided to Sarah (Peter's wife) that some lodge visitors were being awfully rude, not knowing that it was Peter (the owner) himself."

I AM STRONG AND I AM WORKING

Meanwhile, the Igoda Community Hall is hopping. It has already hosted nearly sixty major events so far, counting seminars, education, and entertainment. And, by offering dignitaries a large platform, it is beginning to put this often-forgotten community, and its need for public services, on the map. Even more significant, its activities are reducing the stigma of HIV/AIDS. Witness the number of people coming forward to tell their stories and sign up for treatment.

But World AIDS Day remains the most important in Igoda Community Hall's calendar. That's when the centre welcomes everyone. They sing, they dance, they act, and they play — each group telling in its own way their stories about AIDS and how it has affected them.

This year, one of the speakers is Mama Rehema. In front of 500 people, with healthy baby Rahabu in her arms, she tells her story. How she lost a baby because she did not know she was infected. How she became infected. She talks about prevention. She talks about avoiding full-blown AIDS. She talks about living a normal life. And — raising chubby little Rahabu — she talks about how you can have a healthy child, even if you are HIV positive.

"I am continuing the HIV treatment," she concludes. "Since I started taking the medication until today I am no longer sad. I am strong and I am working. I hope I will live my life as long as anyone else who does not have HIV/AIDS." The Foxes are there, of course. As are Geoff and Jenny, close to tears, not just from listening to their friend, Mama Rehema, but also because it is so amazing to see this many people openly discussing AIDS!

"Hard to imagine that not so long ago, it was completely taboo to even talk about it," they remind each other. "When I arrived in 2006 not one person was open about it," Jenny says. "Because of Alice, because of her looking the stigma in the face and saying, 'I'm not ready to die yet,' over 2,000 people in our part of the valley have now received treatment."[86]

《•》《•》《•》《•》

It's another stunning day at the Fox Highland Farm, all blue skies and brilliant red flame lilies burning beside cool, green ferns in the undergrowth. The music of conversation in Kihehe drifts over the fields, and the smell of woodsmoke blends with evaporating morning mist. Geoff is beaming.

"I just came back from the Children's Village, Vicky," this, as he settles into his favourite armchair for a few minutes before lunch.

---

86   Adapted from: *Alice's Story*, Georgia Bagnall, **http://vimeo.com/61104860**.

Evangeline Twilumba, Ethan Tukelye, Jenny Peck, Geoff Knight.
(Geoff K and Jenny Peck)

"At the pre-school, there they were, all the little kids sitting on the mat, having their lunch. '*Shikamoo, Babu* [I clasp your feet, Grandfather],' they all said, with *posho* (maize meal) and beans all over their faces as they grinned at me. You should see the young ones sitting on their potties, 'reading' their books, with little red-headed Evangeline *Twilumba* ['we are grateful'] among them." (Geoff and Jenny's daughter, now three, attends the Igoda Village kindergarten. Their equally red-headed infant son, Ethan *Tukelye* [Kihehe for 'we are happy'], can be seen crawling with other babes in the next room.) They joke that if they have a third, they will name him or her *Tusinzile* "we are finished," and if they have a fourth, *Tusotzile*, "we are tired." Finally (the joke continues), if they have twins: the first of the two born could be named *Kamwene* ("hallo"), and the second *Weoli* ("we meet again"), as they'll be seeing the "same person" for the second time in the same day!

"When's Dr. Leena starting full time, Foxey?"

"Probably early 2013."

Dr. Leena has chosen to move to Mufindi permanently on her tiny Lutheran pension and practise full-time — *pro bono!* — as part of the Igoda Children's Village. Her friends and family in Finland are fundraising for medication and have bought her an old car, her first car ever, to use for medical visits. "Extraordinary! The community's very own, permanent, volunteer doctor — with almost thirty years of experience, and fluent in Swahili to boot!"

"Will her house be ready by then?"

"Definitely, thanks to a generous anonymous donor. And the Ottawa folks are generating funds for her clinic [through their annual fundraiser in the beautiful Peter and Janet van Zyl garden, where Gord Breedyk's brother, Nick, one year literally auctioned the shirt off his back!]."

GIVING BACK— IGODA CHILDREN'S VILLAGE STYLE

Other children from the Igoda Children's Village have volunteered at the clinic before her. This month, it is Datai Masonda's turn. The fifteen-year-old hopes to be a doctor when she grows up. So, during her school break, she has helped at each and every "CTC" day and today she is again heading for the Mdabulo Care and Treatment Clinic.

As usual, Jenny will be there with the home-based care team of volunteers to support the staff as they manage hundreds of patients coming for HIV/AIDS treatment. Not only does Datai help patients, but she also witnesses how HIV is affecting her own community, and she learns more about the disease itself. For their part, the patients at the CTC have clearly appreciated that a child orphaned by AIDS is helping her community as she herself has been helped in her own life.

Meanwhile, more children from the Children's Village (also on school leave at the moment) are accompanying home-based care volunteers on home visits to the most sick and vulnerable. They, too, are learning to give back. Already elders have expressed their appreciation. ("We thought of them as having nothing. But here they are, helping us!") In Geoff's words, "In this way, the NGO hopes the community will see that everyone is in this struggle together, that everyone must help, and that even vulnerable children from difficult backgrounds can do their part!"

JUST KEEPING MUM ALIVE IS A HUGE THING

Exciting news, and early days yet, but already it seems that the new CD–4 machine in the Foxes' HIV Care and Treatment Centre is having a measurable social impact in the communities it serves. Only a little data is available at this point, but it is all pointing in the right direction. Igoda primary school records show that there are now only eighteen children who have lost both parents, as compared to fifty-five just a few years ago.

Fewer people are taking time off from work to attend funerals, and of course many more are attending the Care and Treatment Centre clinic. In a single year, we have seen the amazing impact on people being kept alive. Just keeping Mum alive is a huge thing for her children. And it's not the structural Care and Treatment Centre alone that helps but also (and most important) a steady supply of reagents.[87]

HIGHEST PRAISE FROM ELDERS

"A wildly successful meeting was held with almost fifty leaders from all over the sixteen villages served by the NGO," Geoff K jubilantly reports in 2012.

"Many leaders went so far as to compare the house parents to parents in the village caring for these children as their own. What greater compliment can there be than the positive comparison between orphanage guardians and village parents? It means the Fox NGO truly is achieving what it set out to do — mirroring village homes for orphaned children."

THREE MUFINDI FORESTS NOW PROTECTED

Elsewhere in Mufindi, three unique forests are now officially protected as Village Forest Reserves, thanks to two years of hard work by the Tanzania Forest Conservation Group and, more recently, to funding from the Critical Ecosystem Partnership Fund.

Colin Congdon and Geoff Fox can both take some credit. Over the years, Geoff observed massive destruction of forest trees in the government Udzungwa (Kigogo) Forest Reserve. Sawyers would buy a licence for one tree and then carry on, illegally felling many others under the same licence over a big area above the Mufindi escarpment.

Then, in 1976, came the planning of Mwalimu's prestigious pulp and paper mill below the escarpment — the biggest development project since Independence and the pride of President Nyerere. Such mills need a ready source of water, threatened in this case by the disappearing forest.

---

87   Geoff Knight, in conversation.

Geoff brought the issue to Colin Congdon, then a director of the Brooke Bond Liebig Tea Company. He, in turn, wrote a company letter to the Ministry concerned, expressing alarm that the vital catchment area for the paper mill was under great threat. Timber licences were immediately stopped (a situation that stands to this day).

Now, thirty-six years later, Christopher is also actively engaged in protecting the rainforest and wildlife in the area on and surrounding the Foxes' Highland holdings. Brooke Bond has long since sold its tea holdings to Unilever Tea Company, which still has some 25,000 acres of dense rainforest that adjoins the government Udzungwa Forest Reserve, probably amounting to about another 25,000 acres.

"Dad," Christopher said one day in 2009, calling from his camp in the Ruaha Park. ("God bless cell phones. How they have revolutionized doing business in Africa," to quote Geoff.) "Two top Dutch executives, retired from Unilever, are staying with me in Mwagusi. They are close friends of the present chairman of Unilever in Amsterdam. Why don't we arrange to have them fly into Mufindi for the day so you can put a bee in their bonnet about the need to protect their forest reserves?"

"Great idea! I'll contact Peter and see if he can fly them up in the Cessna [our first-ever plane, a six-seater].

Peter agreed, and Geoff took the executives on a tour of the Unilever forests, around Luisenga and Luiga.

"Our fear," he explained to them, "is what would happen, should Unilever ever sell the tea company [as big multinationals are wont to do]. We believe the only buyers would almost certainly be from India or China, where concern for the protection of the rainforest would be secondary to their business needs. The Chinese, in particular, have a huge demand for hardwood timber, and would clear the forest land for crops."

The two Dutch executives subsequently contacted the incumbent Dutch chairman of Unilever, whom they knew. He in turn flew out to Mufindi to see the situation for himself and, just before retirement, set up a Forest Protection Fund as his outgoing legacy. Geoff asked for the Mufindi forest to be made into a reserve.

"Unfortunately, the forest areas are too scattered to be gazetted as a single block," Geoff notes years later. "So, instead, Unilever had to set up the Forest Protection Fund to protect their 25,000 acres of dense rainforest. It covers fourteen forest patches, each under protection from one of eight villages, and collectively covering 1,700 acres of land. Unilever also makes one of their unused company houses available to visiting researchers, who are studying everything from frogs and chameleons to snakes and trees.

"It turns out that the forest does indeed have endemic species, both fauna and flora, unique to Mufindi. These could focus worldwide attention on the forest and would hopefully protect it even under any future new management.

"Besides," Geoff half-jokes, "I have already told them, 'Don't forget that this old man is here ready to blow the whistle! It wouldn't be difficult to publicize: "Don't buy Unilever soap, etcetera, because they fell rainforest trees in Tanzania."'

"Actually," he adds, more seriously, "long may Unilever remain in Mufindi. As early as the first Rio Conference on the environment, Unilever pledged not to destroy forests in any of their plantations around the world. Yet with tea profitability continuing to be very low, not to mention the percentage yields on the asset value of all the tea fields, houses, and factories, it could be deemed madness for a multinational company to keep going. This is the worry."

HOW PROUD ALICE WOULD BE

"Vicky," Geoff yells one day. "The 2012 school results are in, and look at this!" Vicky takes the paper from him. There, leaping out at her, are the names of students from their Children's Village:

Standard 1: 1st Naila, 2nd Evalina; Standard 2: 1st Ashim, 2nd Abigail, 3rd Willy (Alice's daughter!); Standard 4: 2nd Sipiriana, 3rd Kandida; Standard 5: 1st Mark, 3rd Dasna; Standard 6: 3rd Florian; Standard 7: Boniface received the first position in *Utaaluma*, which means he was the best student according to all of the teachers. He is graduating and one of the few lucky ones to move on to high school.

"If only Alice were here," Jenny later says of the brave woman who, for the sake of her children, dared to admit to her sickness and indirectly influenced hundreds of others to do the same. Alice's son, Issa, now ten, is in Standard 5. Her daughter, Willy, is in the top three of her class.

AND NOW IN CLOSING . . .

"Our boys all had an adventurous childhood." Geoff smiles. "And I suppose they can say they were dragged up instead of being brought up. We weren't the best of parents. Twice we left Christopher behind in Kibao and had to be reminded by a Brooke Bond head office messenger on a bicycle. The first time was at Walji Sachedina's *duka* (shop); the second time in the post office. On both occasions, his devoted mother didn't even notice his absence ten miles away!

"Aside from falling out of the car on the South Africa trip, Bruce was left behind at Luisenga Fishing Lodge. And Alexander [the Foxes' fourth son], on his own, was allowed to wander upriver from the Ruaha River Camp for regular, all-day fishing outings when he was only six. He would take his rod, put a Coke in his pocket, walk up the riverbank, and fish in a place crawling with animals. With four boys, I suppose we had a few spares.

"Actually, my sons were probably no better. Alexander took his eldest boy, Michael, aged four, to the Vuma Hills camp in Mikumi, leaving Jeanie and the twins behind at Lazy Lagoon. One day, he was so busy working on the generators that he didn't notice Michael's absence. A subsequent search of the whole camp revealed nothing. He was gone. Consternation.

"Then they received a radio call from the main gate to report that a passing Indian family had seen this little boy almost four miles away. Michael had walked off down the camp road and just carried on, holding a dining room knife, which he declared was to fend off lions.

"Over the radio call [the 'Fox Family Chat Show,' initiated to keep the Foxes in regular contact in a telephone-challenged environment as their business grew], Jeanie declared Alexander a disastrous father and immediately made plans to fetch Michael. Whereupon Sarah (listening in at the Ruaha River Camp) couldn't resist suggesting that Michael would probably be able to walk back to Lazy Lagoon [roughly 150 miles]. Silence from Jeanie.

"Each of our boys having developed a strong measure of independence, they have more than contributed their fair share toward developing the family business in Africa. And each one has his individual talents. It is not a Fox thing to tell them how proud we are of them, but nevertheless that is the case.

"I always wanted adoring daughters who would fuss over Father, and in Africa, I am told, it is the fault of the woman if she doesn't produce what her husband demands, so I gave up and looked forward to having adoring granddaughters instead. After nine grandchildren we now have eight boys. And of course a perfect granddaughter! But our grandsons are great, too.

"Finally, as mentioned earlier, my friend Julius Mdegela and I have planned for our burial, when the time comes. Together we have planted many *mitanga* trees (Albizia) all around the site — that indigenous tree so lovely in all seasons (with stark red leaves in spring and a canopy of white blossoms in the dry season), which appears to have no commercial value, so it will not likely be chopped down.

"My original plan is to be the first occupant, followed by Julius, who to date (2012) has worked with us for forty-five years. Now the farm headman, he started out as our gardener. However, worryingly, Julius is not looking so strong these days and may precede me.

"Even now, as we speak, Vicky will be walking around with Julius, talking about this sick sheep here and what to do about that lamb there. He has been so loyal. We employ nine of his family. Wiston is his fifteenth child, with 2.5 wives (the first mother was a girlfriend, not a wife). When he presented baby Wiston to us, he rather embarrassedly said, 'This is another Fox employee — and the last.'"

Julius and Geoff.
(*Gord Breedyk*)

MY RIGHT-HAND "MAN"—VICKY!

"Whatever I have wanted to do, Vicky has joined in, and enthusiastically so. Although she has had the odd lapse in memory and judgment, going way back to Dartmoor. Our favourite of the tors is Vixen Tor, set in a wild, natural landscape, and privately owned (we tried many times to buy it). Now, for those who don't know, Vixen Tor presents a challenging climb to the top, where Vicky claims I proposed to her when we were seventeen and eighteen, respectively. However, I know this to be untrue as I suffer severely from vertigo and would most certainly have been speechless with fright. And then, as I told you earlier, she also got her own engagement ring and presented me with a bill that set me back a month's salary, which then was £50 (about $160). But £50 was £50!

"That said, not many wives would have enjoyed camping on the ground. Our old friend Werner had dreams. I always have dreams. And Vicky is consistently right there beside me, like Helga was with Werner . . . In fact, Vicky is not just beside me, she's doing most of the work. Indeed, Vicky has always been my right-hand man. So, when we are buried, Julius will have to be on the other side."

Vicky and Geoff looking out over the hills below the Lulanda escarpment, through which most of their walking safaris passed.

LIST OF CHARACTERS

For ease of reference, people are listed alphabetically by given name, surname, or both, depending on their appellation in the text. Excluded are those mentioned once, or in one self-contained context. Some names have been changed to protect privacy. All references to "Fox NGO" and "Project" denote the Mufindi Orphaned Children's Project, registered under Foxes Community & Wildlife Conservation Trust [FCWCT].

Akida Mdalingwa	Outreach assistant, Mufindi Orphaned Children's Project
Albert Mwanjessa	Brooke Bond personnel manager
Alex Boswell	Brooke Bond employee, then married to Liz (now Baker)
Alex Wilson, Dr.	Director of Zimbabwe Veterinary Services, Coopers Animal Products representative
Alexander Fox	Foxtreks Tanzania, son of Geoff and Vicky Fox
Ali Hassan Mwinyi	Tanzania's second president
Alice	Pioneering HIV/AIDS mother in Mufindi
Amon Kalinga	Long-term Fox employee and Mwagusi Camp overseer
Anne Pearson	One of the beloved Canadian volunteers affectionately referred to as "Teenage Grannies"; also a highly experienced teacher, Canadian fundraiser for the Mufindi Orphans project, and executive of the African Children's Book Box Society
Bob Ellis	Family friend, see Ellises, Bob and Mary
Brooke, Charles Vyner	(1874–1963) Last White Rajah of Sarawak, in Malaysia
Brooke, Sir James	(1803–68) First White Rajah of Sarawak, in Malaysia
Bruce Fox	Son of Geoff and Vicky; Married to Jane, Foxtreks director, Marketing and Strategic Planning

Chris Flowers	Groom at the second Highland Lodge wedding, to Sarah Flowers
Chris McIntyre	Brooke Bond employee and childhood friend of Geoff Fox
Christina Mvinge	Also known as Mama Rehema, HIV-positive ambassador, guardian in Mufindi Orphans Village
Christopher Fox	Entrepreneur, including Mwagusi camp; son of Geoff and Vicky Fox
Colin Congdon	Brooke Bond employee, later internationally recognized lepidopterist
Cranford Pratt	Emeritus professor of political science, University of Toronto
Crippen, Dr.	The first murderer apprehended by use of radio
Cyril Dye	Early manager at Ngwazi, created Ngwazi dam
Daudi	Highland Farm's head horse guide, long-term employee, and loved by all children
David Babu	Director general of Tanzania National Parks
David Gordon	Son of Vicky's godmother, who buried the hatchet with the descendant of his great uncle's executioner in Khartoum, "The Mahdi," as given under Mahdi, below
David MacDonald	Brooke Bond employee
De Jong, Dr.	Brooke Bond/Liebig Company doctor, Mufindi
Derrick Hester	Geoff's first manager, later chairman of Brooke Bond Liebig Tea Company
Dunstan Manzi Ndamugoba	First officer-in-charge of the government tea research station, formerly the Voigts' Kifyulilo estate in Mufindi
Elias	Youngest child in orphanage
Ellises	Bob and Mary; US fundraisers, family friends, founders, and voting members of Mufindi Orphans Inc.
Ene	Among others, also Felisita's house mama, mother
Eva Mahali	HIV/AIDS-affected child, later house mother at Children's Village
Evelyn Voigt	Daughter of Werner and Helga Voigt, author of this book and of poetry

Everisto	Young Fox employee
Felisita	HIV/AIDS-affected child
Foxes	Vicky and Geoff; Foxtreks, Fox family matriarch and patriarch; children: Alexander, Bruce, Peter, and Christopher
Foxey	Vicky's nickname for Geoff
Gelly	Geoff Fox's mother
General Gordon	See Gordon of Khartoum
Geoff Fox	Fox family patriarch in Tanzania, see Foxey
Geoff K/ Geoff Knight	Fox NGO manager, married to Jenny Peck
Goebels	See Juergen Goebel
Gordon Breedyk	Evelyn Voigt's husband; Canadian fundraiser
Gordon of Khartoum	Last British governor of the Sudan
Helga Voigt (Stein)	Wife of Werner Voigt, German settlers in Mufindi, friends of the Foxes; children: Werner, Peter, Evelyn, Veronika
Hesters	June and Derrick; Brooke Bond manager, later chairman
Hezeroni	Charismatic HIV/AIDS-affected orphan, "miracle child"
Hillary Lwanja	Senior manager, Fox Highland Lodge, advisor to Fox NGO
Ian Summerville	Brooke Bond employee, married to Pat
James Frederick Elton	British colonial officer
Jane Fox	Married to Bruce Fox
Jane Tamé	British settler caring for WWI German and African soldiers
Jeanie Fox	Married to Alexander Fox
Jenny Coxell	Assistant manager at Fox Ruaha River Lodge
Jenny Peck	Community outreach manager for Fox NGO; married to Geoff Knight; children: Evangeline *Twilumba* (we give thanks) and Ethan *Tukelye* (rejoice)
John Gray	British settler in Mufindi

John Savidge	Ruaha Park Warden
Jonny Niblett	Brooke Bond employee
Juergen Goebel	General manager of Amboni
Julius Kambarage Nyerere	Tanzania's first president, also called *Mwalimu* (The Teacher)
Julius Mdegela	Fox Highland Farm overseer, long-term Fox employee and friend, to be buried with Geoff and Vicky
Kate Ney	Early Fox NGO volunteer, married to Patrick
Leena Pasanen, Dr.	Pediatric missionary doctor, full-time volunteer in Mufindi, responsible for the Fox NGO health component
Libby White	Vicky's best friend and correspondent in the UK
Lina Kyando	First house mother at Igoda Children's Village
Lota Melamari	Director general, Tanzania National Parks
Lucy Finch	Married to Sao Hill forestry officer Tony Finch; family friend
Mahdi Muhamad Ahmad	("Redeemer of the Muslim faith") Self-proclaimed Sudanese leader, fought General Gordon
Mama Gideon	House mother at Igoda Children's Village
Mama Rehema	Also Christina Mvinge
Manfred Brandt	European Union employee, family friend
Marion Gough	UK fundraiser with Orphans in the Wild
Marjory Beaver	Vicky's godmother, first married to General Gordon's nephew
Mary Ellis	See Ellises
Mary Schaeffer	Married to Wolfgang, German diplomat, EU employee, later Tanzanian country director for GTZ; friends of the Foxes
Merere	Chief of the Wasangu
Micky Shaw	Vicky Fox's mother
Mike Ghaui	Married to Debbie, son of Phyl and Albert Ghaui, wildlife painter and sculptor
Mkapa, Benjamin William	Tanzania's third president
Mkwawa	Paramount chief of the Wahehe; also "Black Napoleon"

Mzee Ruben Mpilka	Respected Lwanga Chairman, Voigt family friend
Mwalimu ("The Teacher")	Honorific title for Tanzania's first president
Nallos Kihega	Brooke Bond employee and Geoff Fox's tea mentor
Nick Ginner	Brooke Bond employee, close Fox friend, drowned at Ngwazi
Nyaganyilwa, Mr.	Luhunga *Diwani* (Ward Councillor)
Nyamara, Elisha	Social Welfare Officer, Mufindi District
Old Mac	Custodian of Enemy Property, WWII; Voigt family friend
Pat and Jane Mathers	Neighbours of Werner and Helga
Pat Summerville (now Dale)	Wife of Brooke Bond employee
Patrick Ney	First long-term Fox NGO volunteer; married to Kate
Paul Emil von Lettow–Vorbeck	Charismatic German general in East Africa during WWI
Paulina Visulo	Volunteer head nurse and midwife at Mdabulo hospital
Peter Fox	Director of Foxtreks and Safari Air Link; a Fox son; married to Sarah Fox
Peter Schachenmann	Vet in Mufindi, later general manager of Amboni Ltd.; Geoff's boss at Mkwaja Ranch
Phyl Ghaui	Married to Albert Ghaui, settler, friend of Foxes and Voigts, also market gardener
Ruben Mpilka, Mzee	Respected Lwanga Chairman, Voigt family friend
Reuben	HIV/AIDS-affected boy
Rune Skarstein	Economist, Norwegian University of Science and Technology
Ruth James	One of the "Teenage Grannies"
Saidi Masonda	Tracker par excellence, long-term Fox employee
Samuel Mbando, Dr.	Veterinary surgeon at Mkwaja Ranch
Sarah Fox	Foxtreks TZ, Fox daughter-in-law, married to son Peter Fox
Sauda Sebastian	Head Librarian at interactive library at Igoda School
Schaeffers	Mary and Wolfgang; see Mary Schaeffer

Sifa Chumi	Student volunteer, first recipient of a FCWCT scholarship
Ulrich Albers, Dr.	Chairman of the Swiss Schoeller group and owner of Amboni and Mkwaja, among others
Voigts	Werner and Helga, children: Werner, Peter, Evelyn, and Veronika (now Hart, the artist)
Werner Voigt	Early German settler in Mufindi, Foxes' friend, married to Helga; children: Werner, Peter, Evelyn, Veronika
White Rajahs of Sarawak	Three generations of Englishmen descended from Sir James Brooke, who ruled over Sarawak in Malaysia

Fox Family, Tanzania

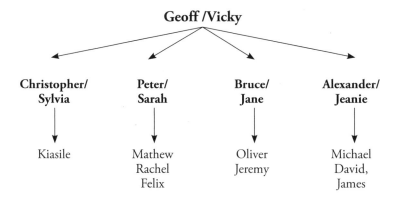

Geoff /Vicky

Christopher/ Sylvia	Peter/ Sarah	Bruce/ Jane	Alexander/ Jeanie
Kiasile	Mathew Rachel Felix	Oliver Jeremy	Michael David, James

Appendix

Organizations Linked to the Fox Safari Enterprise and Fox Project for AIDS-affected Orphans and Their Communities

ORGANIZATION	MANDATE
African Children's Book Box Society (ACBBS) **http://www.africanbookbox. org** Major fundraising event: annual corn roast in British Columbia, Canada (August) **http://www. cornroast@africanbookbox.org**	Canada-based. General: Since 1991: to support and increase literacy in Africa by providing children with their own stories and literature written by African authors. Since 2007, ACBBS additionally collaborates with FCWT to support the welfare of needy African children and their caregivers.
Foxes Community and Wildlife Trust (FCWT)/ Orphans in the Wild **http://www.wildorphans.org** Fundraising: In Canada, USA, and UK, see sister organizations listed in this appendix. In Tanzania, by cash at Fox camps and lodges, **http:// tanzaniasafaris.info**. By bank transfer: see bank details at **http://www.wildorphans.org**.	FCWT is an umbrella trust fund for Fox environmental and community support. Orphans in the Wild, registered as an NGO in 2005, operates under the FCWT umbrella. Initiatives include educational support, establishing a Children's Village for AIDS orphans, building dispensaries in the remoter regions of Mufindi District, establishing a counselling and treatment clinic (CTC) in the local hospital for administering antiretroviral drugs and — key — an outreach program to support orphans and families in extreme poverty to remain in their communities with relatives or foster families.
Foxtreks / Foxes Safari Camps **http://www.tanzaniasafaris.info**	The Foxes' website offers detailed information on safaris to the Fox family camps and lodges in Tanzania.

Mufindi Orphans Canada

Major fundraising event: annual garden party in Ottawa (August)

http://www.mufindiorphans.ca

Ottawa/Canada-based fundraiser for Mufindi Highlands Orphans Project. The aim is, through FCWT, to provide shelter, sustenance, education, and medical care for orphans and foster families in the Mufindi District of Tanzania. Donations are made through the African Children's Book Box Society in Victoria, BC.

Mufindi Orphans Inc.

http://www.mufindiorphans. com

US-based fundraising charity.

USA-based fundraiser for Mufindi Highlands Orphans Project.

Orphans in the Wild, UK

http://www.wildorphans.org

(also, donate while shopping at **http://www.easyfundraising. org.uk**)

UK and Europe-based fundraiser for Mufindi Highlands Orphans Project.

GLOSSARY

Achtung (German)	Attention
Askari	African soldier
Babu	Grandfather; also honorific for elderly male
Banda	Small huts, used as single dwelling bedrooms in tourist lodges
Bati	Corrugated iron
Betsaal (German)	Prayer hall
Bibi	Grandmother, also honorific for elderly female, and wife
Biltong (Afrikaans)	Cured meat
Bui-Bui	Black cloth worn as a shawl by Muslim women in East Africa
Chama cha Mapinduzi	CCM Revolutionary Party
Choo	Toilet
Dalla dalla	Minibus, often charging a dollar
Debes	Four-gallon tins
Dhow	Traditional Arab trading vessel
Diwani	Ward councillor
Duka	Shop
Fanusi	Tall glass chimneys for Aladdin lamps
Haba na haba hujaza kibaba	Grain by grain to fill the vessel
Hapana	No
Hehe	*Hehe* people, an ethnic group in Tanzania. Also *Wahehe* (plural) and *Mhehe* (singular), members of the Hehe people. Refer also to Mkwawa, their chief, in the "List of Characters," above.

Hodi	"Hello. Anyone home?" Often spoken instead of knocking.
Hongo	Toll charge
Hyrax (Greek)	A small, herbivorous mammal.
Idara ya Kichaa Cha Unilever	Department of Unilever Health and Safety
Kachelofen (German)	German tiled stove
Kali	Strict, angry, fierce
Kambarage	The spirit that gives rain
Kanzu	Traditional cream or white robe worn by men
Khanga	Traditional piece of sarong-like cloth worn by women
Kiasile (Kihehe)	The lost one shall return
Kilago	Reed mat
Kitenge	East African sarong-like cloth
Klipspringer (Afrikaans)	A small, lithe antelope
Kopje (Dutch/ Afrikaans)	Small, lone-standing hillock
Kopo	Tin can
Kumbi kumbi	Flying ants
Kuni	Wood
Loh!	Wow!
Mashua	Sailing boats, like small *dhows*
Mbuga	Wide-open plain
Mchicha	Wild, spinach-like plant
Mgambo	Militia unit of government-trained, auxiliary police
Mhehe	Mhehe (singular) and Wahehe (plural), members of the Hehe people
Miombo	Temperate and tropical grasslands mixed with shrub
Mitanga	*Albizia*, a lovely, indigenous, umbrella-shaped tree
Mninga	A tree, now protected, known for its lumber
Mzee	Elder, old one, also honorific
Mzungu	White person

Ngalawa	Dugout, outrigger sailboat
Nyumba kumi kumi	Ten ten household principle (whereby every ten households elect a spokesman to represent them at monthly meetings or on village councils)
Paka	Cat
Papaya	Tropical fruit; sometimes referred to as pawpaw
Piki piki	Motorbike
Pole	An all-encompassing Swahili word of empathy that is impossible to translate
Posho	Maize meal
Pumba	Maize bran
Rondavel (Afrikaans)	A round or oval African-style hut, initially adapted by Boers in South Africa
Saba saba Day	Literally seven seven day, a Tanzanian holiday akin to Labour Day in the US and Canada
Sabuni	Soap
Sana	Very, very much, extremely, a great deal
Shamba	Field
Shikamoo	Respectful greeting, literally "I clasp your feet"
Simba amefika Lugoda	The lion has reached Lugoda
Simba yuko karibu	The lion is near
Tonga (Hindi)	Horse-drawn cart
Tukelye (Kihehe)	Rejoice
Twilumba (Kihehe)	We give thanks
"Uhuru na Kazi"	Freedom and Work
"Uhuru na Umoja"	Freedom and Unity
Uji	Runny maize meal porridge
Ukimwi	AIDS
Ukumbi	Porch
Ulanzi	Bamboo wine
Wahehe	Wahehe (plural) and Mhehe (singular), members of Hehe people
Wazee	Old ones, the elderly; also an honorific title

ABOUT THE AUTHOR

Evelyn Voigt (with Geoff and Vicky Fox at a pub in Devon, 2013, plus Gord's beer).
(Gord Breedyk)

Evelyn Voigt was born in Africa, raised in Mufindi, Tanzania, and worked for many years on the East Africa desk of Canada's International Development Program. She lives in Ottawa with her husband and anchor, Gordon Breedyk, returning frequently to Tanzania. Her spoken word / song CDs celebrate diversity, peace, and healing; Evelyn has performed them in Canada, Europe, and Africa. She currently volunteers with Gordon toward the profession-wide accreditation of peace professionals through the Civilian Peace Service Canada (**http://civilianpeaceservice.ca**) and helps to raise funds for the Fox NGO through **http://mufindiorphans.ca**.

TO ORDER MORE COPIES:

GENERAL STORE PUBLISHING HOUSE INC.

499 O'Brien Road, Renfrew, Ontario, Canada K7V 3Z3
Tel 1.613.599.2064 • Fax 1.613.432.3634
www.gsph.com